Marine Protected Areas

A Multidisciplinary Approach

Human-induced environmental disturbance – through fishery activities, coastal development, tourism, and pollution – is a major challenge to the restoration and conservation of marine biodiversity. Synthesizing the latest research into marine biodiversity conservation and fisheries management, this book provides regional and global perspectives on the role of marine protected areas (MPAs) in confronting this challenge.

The approach is multidisciplinary, covering all the fields involved in designating and assessing MPAs: ecology, fisheries science, statistics, economics, sociology, and genetics. The book is structured around key topics, including threats to marine ecosystems and resources, the effects and effectiveness of MPAs, and the scaling-up of MPA systems. Both theoretical and empirical approaches are considered.

Recognizing the diversity of MPA sciences, the book also includes one part designed specifically as a practical guide to implementing scientific assessment studies of MPAs and monitoring programs.

JOACHIM CLAUDET is a Researcher at the National Center for Scientific Research (CNRS) in Perpignan, France. An ecologist, he specializes in MPAs, environmental impact assessment studies, and coastal management. He also teaches international workshops on MPAs.

ECOLOGY, BIODIVERSITY AND CONSERVATION

The world's biological diversity faces unprecedented threats. The urgent challenge facing the concerned biologist is to understand ecological processes well enough to maintain their functioning in the face of the pressures resulting from human population growth. Those concerned with the conservation of biodiversity and with restoration also need to be acquainted with the political, social, historical, economic, and legal frameworks within which ecological and conservation practice must be developed. The new Ecology, Biodiversity, and Conservation series will present balanced, comprehensive, up-to-date, and critical reviews of selected topics within the sciences of ecology and conservation biology, both botanical and zoological, and both "pure" and "applied." It is aimed at advanced final-year undergraduates, graduate students, researchers, and university teachers, as well as ecologists and conservationists in industry, government, and the voluntary sectors. The series encompasses a wide range of approaches and scales (spatial, temporal, and taxonomic), including quantitative, theoretical, population, community, ecosystem, landscape, historical, experimental, behavioral, and evolutionary studies. The emphasis is on science related to the real world of plants and animals rather than on purely theoretical abstractions and mathematical models. Books in this series will, wherever possible, consider issues from a broad perspective. Some books will challenge existing paradigms and present new ecological concepts, empirical or theoretical models, and testable hypotheses. Other books will explore new approaches and present syntheses on topics of ecological importance.

Ecology and Control of Introduced Plants
Judith H. Myers and Dawn Bazely

Invertebrate Conservation and Agricultural Ecosystems
T. R. New

Risks and Decisions for Conservation and Environmental Management
Mark Burgman

Marine Protected Areas

A Multidisciplinary Approach

Edited by

JOACHIM CLAUDET

National Center for Scientific Research, Laboratoire d'Excellence "CORAIL", USR 3278 CNRS-EPHE CRIOBE, Perpignan, France

CAMBRIDGE UNIVERSITY PRESS
Cambridge, New York, Melbourne, Madrid, Cape Town,
Singapore, São Paulo, Delhi, Tokyo, Mexico City

Cambridge University Press
The Edinburgh Building, Cambridge CB2 8RU, UK

Published in the United States of America by Cambridge University Press, New York

www.cambridge.org
Information on this title: www.cambridge.org/9780521766050

First published 2011

Printed in the United Kingdom at the University Press, Cambridge

A catalog record for this publication is available from the British Library

Library of Congress Cataloging in Publication data
Marine protected areas : a multidisciplinary approach / [edited by] Joachim Claudet.
  p.   cm. – (Ecology, biodiversity and conservation)
Includes index.
ISBN 978-0-521-76605-0 (hardback)
1. Marine parks and reserves.   I. Claudet, Joachim, 1979–
QH91.75.A1M265   2011
333.95′6 – dc23   2011023019

ISBN 978-0-521-76605-0 Hardback
ISBN 978-0-521-14108-6 Paperback

Contents

Contributors

FRÉDÉRIQUE ALBAN
UMR AMURE, Université de Brest, France

FABIO BADALAMENTI
Laboratorio di Ecologia Marina, Istituto per l'Ambiente Marino Costiero, Consiglio Nazionale delle Ricerche, Mazara del Vallo, Italy

JEAN BONCOEUR
UMR AMURE, Université de Brest, France

MARK CARR
Department of Ecology and Evolutionary Biology, and Institute of Marine Sciences, University of California, Santa Cruz, USA

JENNIFER CASELLE
Marine Science Institute, University of California, Santa Barbara, USA

PATRICK CHRISTIE
School of Marine and Environmental Affairs and Jackson School of International Studies, University of Washington, Seattle, USA

JOACHIM CLAUDET
National Center for Scientific Research, Laboratoire d'Excellence "CORAIL," USR 3278 CNRS-EPHE CRIOBE, Perpignan, France

JON DAY
Great Barrier Reef Marine Park Authority, Townsville, QLD, Australia

SIMONETTA FRASCHETTI
Laboratory of Zoology and Marine Biology, Department of Biological and Environmental Science and Technologies, University of Salento, Lecce, Italy

ALAN FRIEDLANDER
US Geological Survey – Hawaii Cooperative Fishery Research Unit, University of Hawaii, Honolulu, USA

EDWARD T. GAME
The Nature Conservancy, West End, QLD, Australia

RAQUEL GOÑI
Centro Oceanográfico de Baleares, Instituto Español de Oceanografía, Palma de Mallorca, Spain

HEDLEY S. GRANTHAM
The Ecology Centre, University of Queensland, St Lucia, QLD, Australia

KIRSTEN GRORUD–COLVERT
PISCO/COMPASS, Department of Zoology, Oregon State University, Corvallis, USA

PAOLO GUIDETTI
Laboratory of Zoology and Marine Biology, Department of Biological and Environmental Science and Technologies, University of Salento, Lecce, Italy

ALISTAIR HOBDAY
CSIRO Marine and Atmospheric Research, Hobart, Tasmania, Australia

SARAH E. LESTER
Marine Science Institute, University of California, Santa Barbara, USA

THIERRY LISON DE LOMA
Centre de recherches insulaires et observatoire de l'environnement (CRIOBE), Moorea, French Polynesia and Centre de Biologie et d'Ecologie Tropicale et Méditerranéenne, Université de Perpignan, France

DAN MALONE
Santa Cruz Long Marine Laboratory, University of California, Santa Cruz, USA

FIORENZA MICHELI
Hopkins Marine Station, Stanford University, Pacific Grove, USA

SONJA L. MILLER
School of Biological Sciences, Victoria University of Wellington, New Zealand

CAMILO MORA
Department of Biology, Dalhousie University, Halifax, NS, Canada

DAVID MOUILLOT
Ecosystèmes Lagunaires, Université de Montpellier 2, Montpellier, France

CRAIG W. OSENBERG
Department of Biology, University of Florida, Gainesville, USA

DOMINIQUE PELLETIER
Laboratoire de Biologie Halieutique (LBH), IFREMER Centre de Brest, Plouzané, France

JOHN K. PINNEGAR
Centre for Environment, Fisheries and Aquaculture Science (Cefas), Lowestoft, UK

SERGE PLANES
Laboratoire d'Excellence "CORAIL," and USR 3278 CNRS-EPHE, Moorea, French Polynesia

RICHARD POLLNAC
Department of Marine Affairs, University of Rhode Island, Kingston, USA

ANTHONY J. RICHARDSON
CSIRO Marine and Atmospheric Research, Cleveland, QLD, Australia

NICOLAS RONCIN
UMR AMURE, Université de Brest, France

JAMES N. SANCHIRICO
Department of Environmental Science and Policy, University of California, Davis, USA

NICK T. SHEARS
Marine Science Institute, University of California, Santa Barbara, USA

JEFFREY S. SHIMA
School of Biological Sciences, Victoria University of Wellington, New Zealand

VANESSA STELZENMÜLLER
Johann Heinrich von Thünen Institute (VTI), Federal Research Institute for Rural Areas, Forestry and Fisheries, Institute of Sea Fisheries, Hamburg, Germany

ADRIAN C. STIER
Department of Biology, University of Florida, Gainesville, USA

OLIVIER THÉBAUD
UMR AMURE, IFREMER Centre de Brest, France; CSIRO Marine and Atmospheric Research, Brisbane, QLD, Australia

BRIAN TISSOT
Washington State University, Vancouver, USA

MARK H. TUPPER
The WorldFish Center, Penang, Malaysia

Introduction

JOACHIM CLAUDET

Early in their history, humans were just a new species, *Homo sapiens sapiens*, evolving within a broader history, natural history. As they continually struggled for survival, the world around them seemed probably hostile and inhospitable. Death from predation, starvation, and disease was rife. At the same time, like all other species, humans used their environment to meet their needs for food and habitat, and, over time, for some cultural artefacts. With the evolution of their customs and the invention of agriculture, humans settled and created the first civilizations. Their relationship with nature changed. Humans then shaped their environment, the use of nature turned into exploitation. Rationalization was not far off.

Changes wrought by humans on terrestrial realms were clearly visible. The awareness that these changes were impacting the natural environments led to the creation of the first nature reserves. Freud (1916) found in these creations a perfect parallel with the creation of the mental realm of phantasy, "withdrawn from the reality principle." For him, "a nation whose wealth rests on the exploitation of the produce of its soil will yet set aside certain areas for reservation in their original state and for protection from the changes brought about by civilization" (Freud, 1911). "The requirements of agriculture, communication and industry threaten to bring about changes in the original face of the earth which will quickly make it unrecognizable. A nature reserve preserves its original state which everywhere else has to our regret been sacrificed to necessity. Everything, including what is useless and even what is noxious, can grow and proliferate there as it pleases" (Freud, 1916). Now, a trend in conservation practice is no longer to use reserves only as conservation fortresses outside of human "necessity" but rather to use them as management tools

Marine Protected Areas: A Multidisciplinary Approach, ed. Joachim Claudet. Published by Cambridge University Press. © Cambridge University Press 2011.

to improve the sustainability of human uses, creating trade-offs between conservation and use.

The marine environment was not exempt from early human pressure. The exploitation of marine resources, primarily as a source of food through fishing activities, is as old as the establishment of the first civilizations (Braudel, 2001). It has continuously increased during human history. The industrial revolution dramatically modernized fishing practices, leading to fishing efforts without any comparison with previous periods. However, given the amount of catch, marine resources seemed inexhaustible. It brought Huxley to declare, 10 years after the establishment of the Yellowstone Park, that "any attempt to regulate [all the great sea] fisheries seems consequently, from the nature of the case, to be useless" (Huxley, 1883). Today, thanks to the reconstitution of archeological (Erlandson and Rick, 2010) and historical (Jackson et al., 2001) data, we know that it was not the case for almost all world fisheries. Human-induced changes had already occurred and created shifting baselines (Pauly, 1995). However, as everything was taking place under water, out of sight, it was almost impossible to perceive.

At sea, the awareness of the need to manage resources and create reserves occurred later than in terrestrial environments. These ideas were supported by the observed restoration of fishery stocks in the North Sea after fishing had been interrupted during World War II (Gulland, 1974). The first evidence of the potential benefits of areas closed to fishing came from there. Since then, the protection of parts of the ocean has been recommended as a tool to manage part of the numerous anthropogenic threats on the world's coastal and offshore marine areas. Today, 0.65% of the world's oceans and 1.6% of the total marine area within Exclusive Economic Zones are currently within marine protected areas (MPAs); 0.08% and 0.2%, respectively, are fully protected by marine reserves (Wood et al., 2008) (see Box).

Types of marine protection

MARINE PROTECTED AREA (MPA): A Marine Protected Area is defined as a discrete geographic area of the sea established by international, national, territorial, tribal, or local laws designated to enhance the long-term conservation of natural resources therein. This objective is rarely exclusive and is often related to the sustainable use and management of marine resources and to socio-economic development. MPAs can have multiple uses and allow some restricted uses such as traditional fisheries and scuba-diving, or combine a set of uses within a spatial zoning. Partially protected areas, fishery reserves, fishery closures, gear restriction zones, and buffer zones are all specific cases of MPAs where one or more extractive uses are forbidden (but the others allowed). Multiple objectives can lead to the creation of an MPA; the most common ones can be summarized as follows (Claudet and Pelletier, 2004):

(1) conservation and protection of natural resources in areas that are recognized as particularly important in terms of ecological diversity to ensure their long-term viability and to maintain their genetic diversity or to allow populations to recover to more pristine levels

(2) restoration of damaged or overexploited areas considered as critical to the survival of such species, or of significant importance for the life cycles of economically important species

(3) improvement of the relationship between humans, their environment, and economic activities, by maintaining traditional uses and the sustainable exploitation of resources, by preventing outside activities from detrimentally affecting the MPA, and by protecting and managing historical, cultural, and esthetic sites

(4) improvement of fishing yields, by protecting spawning stock biomass, by acting as a source of recruited and post-recruited stages for surrounding areas, by restoring the age structure of natural populations, and by acting as an insurance against mismanagement in fishing areas

(5) resolution of present or anticipated conflicts between coastal area users

(6) improvement of knowledge about the marine environment by dealing with research and educational aspects

(7) valuation of heritage for the local administration through tourism and economic profitability for the residents.

MARINE RESERVE: A marine reserve is defined as a specific type of MPA where all extractive uses are forbidden. No-take zones and fully protected areas are synonymous with marine reserves. In some marine reserves, some or all non–extractive uses (e.g. swimming, boating) can also be excluded. Those marine reserves can be called no-take/no-go or no-take/no-use zones. Many marine reserves worldwide are embedded within MPAs, therefore being a no-take zone of a multiple use MPA.

This book is motivated by several converging reasons. First, there is worldwide an increasing interest in MPAs, from scientists, managers, and policy-makers. Almost all marine ecosystems have been transformed by human activities. The need to protect and/or restore marine biodiversity has led to increasing calls for the establishment of MPAs. International commitments were made to protect 10% of the world's coastal and marine Exclusive Economic Zones (EEZ) by 2010 (Convention on Biological Diversity: http://www.cbd.int). This deadline is already behind us and thus the target is far from being met. However, this means also that efforts are being made at establishing MPAs worldwide. This book can prove to be a useful tool for MPA practitioners, managers, and policy-makers in this respect.

Second, MPAs have linked social, economic, and ecological dynamics. They are a complex tool for conservation and management, involving effects both inside and outside their boundaries, with goals extending beyond conservation and fisheries (see Box). The assessment and design of MPAs thus involve, among other fields: ecology to study how marine assemblages respond to protection and can spill over the MPA boundaries; genetic and otolith analyses to study the connectivity among MPAs or among MPAs and adjacent areas; statistics to design impact assessment studies; mathematical modeling to predict expected effects of protection or of some MPA design features; economy and fisheries science to analyze how the MPAs may fulfill their fisheries management goals; sociology and economy to assess how MPAs can befit local communities. Moreover, the economic and socio-cultural context of each MPA can have strong feedbacks, both positive and negative, on MPA effects. This volume is innovative as it takes a multidisciplinary standpoint throughout its structure that anchors it to the diverse reality of MPA sciences.

Third, MPAs are a tool that can be used within broader frameworks of integrated management and spatialization of marine systems. It is therefore important to show, as does this book, how MPAs are useful for ecosystem-based management and marine spatial planning.

Following the growing interest in MPAs by the scientific community, much new information and knowledge has emerged worldwide since the most recent books on MPAs. It is therefore appropriate to present and summarize the recent advances made in each field of the sciences related to MPAs.

This new knowledge does not focus solely on studying the effects of MPAs, but also on how to measure their effectiveness and monitor their effects. This book thus presents the latest advances in each disciplinary field on monitoring and assessment of MPAs.

In addition, new areas of investigation on the study of MPAs have recently emerged, especially on the networks of MPAs and establishment of offshore MPAs (the overwhelming majority of current MPAs are located in coastal areas). These innovations are presented in this volume.

Finally, MPAs are not the sole solution to all the threats incurred by the coupled human–environment marine systems. It is therefore important to leave room for some critical views on the use of MPAs. This is done in this book.

The book is structured to address these issues in the most comprehensive way. The book is organized into four distinct but sequentially logical parts; each with individual chapters that can be read sequentially or independently of each other, entering the book from any field or topic of interest. A multidisciplinary standpoint is taken within each part. Part I deals with the threats encountered by marine ecosystems and with their management. It is the sole part with only one chapter (Chapter 1, Fraschetti *et al.*), addressing how MPAs can be used within ecosystem-based management and marine spatial planning frameworks. Part II covers all major advances of sciences linked with MPAs, and is built as a synthesis of current knowledge on MPA effects. Since MPA effects are by essence multidisciplinary, this synthesis is tackled by four chapters, each of them focusing on a given field of investigation. Ecological (Chapter 2, Claudet *et al.*), fisheries (Chapter 3, Goñi *et al.*), bioeconomic (Chapter 4, Sanchirico), and socio-economic (Chapter 5, Christie and Pollnac) aspects are addressed. Both modeling and experimental approaches are considered to take full advantage of the complementarities between theoretical and empirical approaches. Part III keeps the same structure as Part II, with one chapter for each field of investigation, but focuses on assessment and monitoring methodologies of MPA effects (Chapter 6, Osenberg *et al.*; Chapter 7, Stelzenmüller and Pinnegar; Chapter 8, Boncoeur *et al.*; Chapter 9, Alban *et al.*). One additional transdisciplinary chapter focuses on the creation and use of indicators (Chapter 10, Pelletier). Part IV deals with the last innovations regarding MPA sciences in scaling-up MPA systems. It also presents a critical view. Chapter 11 (Grorud-Colvert *et al.*) presents innovative views on MPA networks and on their assessments. Chapter 12 (Planes) presents how recent advances in population and community connectivity can be incorporated in the design of MPA networks. Chapter 13 (Mora) assesses and discusses the representativeness of the MPAs worldwide and criticizes the use of MPAs for managing the global threats on marine biodiversity. Finally, Chapter 14 (Hobday *et al.*) presents the importance of protecting the largest habitat on Earth: the pelagic ocean.

A core question of MPA sciences is the design of the protected areas. However, on purpose, no chapter will be specifically dedicated to this issue since it is highly dependent on the objectives of the MPA (e.g. too small MPAs should be avoided for strict conservation objectives, whereas they might be needed for socio-economic objectives). The theory of MPA design is tackled within the various chapters of Part II, and Chapters 11 and 12 address how MPA size can be optimized to benefit both conservation and fisheries objectives of MPAs.

The chapters of this multidisciplinary book are written by recognized experts in MPA sciences, most of them being used to work at the interface between one or more scientific fields. A strength of this book is that it gives an international view of the sate of MPA sciences. The 38 authors are from 30 institutes, representing 10 countries in America, Europe, Asia, and Oceania.

This volume is aimed at three audiences. The first group includes academic and research scientists, as well as PhD students, in all communities of sciences working on MPAs (i.e., ecology, fisheries science, economy, sociology). In particular, researchers in a given field wanting to have a complete and practical synthesis of their field or wanting to know more about other aspects of MPAs should find what they are looking for in this book. Besides, this scientific audience will also find in this volume directions towards technical and conceptual issues that require further research.

In that MPAs are a management tool of coastal and marine areas, the second audience consists of managers, regulators, and policy-makers involved in the management of human use of marine resources. They will find in this volume the state of the art of MPA sciences and the synthesis of the MPA ecological, fisheries, economic, and social benefits. Further, Part III is designed as a practical handbook for implementing scientific assessment studies of MPAs and monitoring programs.

The third audience to which this book is aimed at is made up of graduate students and upper-division undergraduates in the environmental, conservation, and fisheries sciences (including all their ecological, economic, and social aspects). It is critically important that the next generation of environmental, conservation and fisheries scientists, managers and policy-makers understand well the ins and outs of MPA sciences. Part of the future of the oceans is in their hands.

References

Braudel, F. (2001). *Memory and the Mediterranean*. New York: Knopf.

Claudet, J. and Pelletier, D. (2004). Marine protected areas and artificial reefs: a review of the interactions between management and scientific studies. *Aquatic Living Resources*, **17**, 129–38.

Erlandson, J. M. and Rick, T. C. (2010). Archaeology meets marine ecology: the antiquity of maritime cultures and human impacts on marine fisheries and ecosystems. *Annual Review of Marine Science*, **2**, 231–51.

Freud, S. (1911). Formulations on the Two Principles of Mental Functioning. In *Standard Edition*, vol. 12. London: Hogarth Press and The Institute of Psychoanalysis.

Freud, S. (1916). A General Introduction to Psychoanalysis. In *Standard Edition*, vol. 16. London: Hogarth Press and The Institute of Psychoanalysis.

Gulland, J. A. (1974). *The Management of Marine Fisheries*. Seattle, WA: University of Washington Press.

Huxley, T. H. (1883). Address by Professor Huxley. In *Inaugural Meeting of the Fishery Congress*. London: William Clowes.

Jackson, J. B. C., Kirby, M. X., Berger, W. H., *et al.* (2001). Historical overfishing and the recent collapse of coastal ecosystems. *Science*, **293**, 629–38.

Pauly, D. (1995). Anecdotes and the shifting baseline syndrome of fisheries. *Trends in Ecology and Evolution*, **10**, 430–30.

Wood, L. J., Fish, L., Laughren, J., and Pauly, D. (2008). Assessing progress towards global marine protection targets: shortfalls in information and action. *Oryx*, **42**, 340–51.

Part I

Threats to marine ecosystems and resources

1 · MANAGEMENT – Transitioning from single-sector management to ecosystem-based management: what can marine protected areas offer?

SIMONETTA FRASCHETTI, JOACHIM CLAUDET, AND KIRSTEN GRORUD-COLVERT

1.1 Introduction

Over the past 30 years, as coastal areas have been severely affected by a wide variety of human activities, traditional resource management has failed to prevent overexploitation and habitat degradation (Lauck *et al.*, 1998; Claudet *et al.*, 2006; Crowder *et al.*, 2008). Ecosystem-based management (EBM) is a relatively new approach, and it is considered a promising solution to maintain ecosystem structure and function (Ruckelshaus *et al.*, 2008). It represents an evolution from traditional management of single threats along single portions of ecosystems to large-scale management strategies within complex natural and socio-economic systems (Tallis *et al.*, 2010). The aim of EBM is to sustain the long-term capacity of marine ecosystems to deliver the goods and services that society enjoys (e.g., seafood, clean water, protection from coastal erosion) while at the same time addressing the inherent trade-offs required to meet multiple management goals (Halpern *et al.*, 2010). The consideration of human uses of and interactions with natural resources in EBM approaches improves the likelihood of achieving desired ecosystem outcomes (Gallagher *et al.*, 2004). In 2005, McLeod *et al.* made a large contribution to defining EBM, but such efforts can still be considered as only the early stages of implementation and evaluation. The scientific

Marine Protected Areas: A Multidisciplinary Approach, ed. Joachim Claudet. Published by Cambridge University Press. © Cambridge University Press 2011.

community does not always agree about the principles that should inspire the management, conservation, and monitoring of marine environments (Worm *et al.*, 2006; Bulleri *et al.*, 2007; Hilborn, 2007; Stewart-Oaten, 2008; Lindenmayer and Likens, 2009). Although the importance of an ecosystem approach is widely accepted, its implementation is challenging in part due to perceptions that it is too complicated and has prohibitive information requirements (Tallis *et al.*, 2010) and in part because it is ill-defined (Lotze, 2004). Scientific advice on the status of biodiversity and fish stocks, the effects of fishing and the role of marine protected areas (MPAs) are only small components in a complex management and decision-making process, in which scientific information often carries little weight in relation to immediate social and economic considerations (Jennings, 2004). Given the current worldwide biodiversity decline, there is an urgent need for immediate reassessment of present conservation strategies to develop initiatives aimed at reversing present trajectories of ecological degradation in the ocean.

Only recently have there been attempts to build a management framework for all the activities carried out along the coast and in the open sea in order to overcome the intrinsic difficulties in addressing the complexity of marine systems. Since every piece of land belongs to a governing body, jurisdictional responsibility for terrestrial management is less complex than management of the sea, and terrestrial regulations are comparatively easier to issue and enforce. There are typically no property rights in the ocean other than the recently established Exclusive Economic Zones (EEZ). Within the EEZ, modifications to ineffective fisheries management are extremely rare (Mora *et al.*, 2009). International waters beyond this narrow coastal belt are not owned and thus are even more difficult to manage. The difficulty in enforcing regulations across the coastal and further offshore environments may make many conservation and management attempts ineffective (but see Chapter 14). As a consequence, notwithstanding the growing consensus for EBM as a promising approach, we are still deliberating about how to deal with the ailing marine environment while human pressure is continuously increasing.

Marine protected areas are considered to be a key management tool to achieve some of the goals of an EBM approach. Implementing MPAs as a tool for the protection of marine biodiversity and the local management of marine resources is considered effective worldwide (Lubchenco *et al.*, 2003; Lester *et al.*, 2009). Protection from fishing/harvesting may directly restore populations of target species and indirectly drive whole communities towards a non-exploited condition (Gell and Roberts, 2003; Guidetti and Sala, 2007; Claudet *et al.*, 2008). Fishing tends to remove whole functional groups from marine ecosystems, and the recovery of fish species richness and diversity within MPAs coincides with an increased functional richness (Micheli and Halpern, 2005). There is also evidence that recovery of marine assemblages from uncontrollable disturbances may be faster in MPAs than in unprotected locations (Bevilacqua *et al.*, 2006). A continuous refinement of conservation management plans is vital for ensuring that protection is maintained under different ecological settings. Instances of no apparent biological response to protection are presently ascribed either to lack of effective enforcement (Guidetti *et al.*, 2008) or to insufficient power and inadequate design of empirical studies (Fraschetti *et al.*, 2009). However, the tendency to use MPAs as the preferred management tool may preclude consideration of other management options (Christie *et al.*, 2009).

Here, we provide an overview of the importance of and limitations to implementing EBM in the ocean and the role, potential drawbacks, and challenges of MPAs in contributing towards the objectives of EBM. We end by stressing the urgent need for baseline information in order to understand and predict consequences of increasing human pressure on marine systems, for quantitative long-term data sets addressing natural and human-driven changes in the sea, and for integration across different disciplines to untangle the substantial complexity of managing the marine environment at the proper scale. These are critical elements for successfully applying an EBM approach and reversing the present trajectory of changes to the structure and function of marine ecosystems.

1.2 Human impacts and the loss of goods and services

Humans have caused dramatic changes both in terrestrial and in marine ecosystems. However, a clear literature bias towards terrestrial systems characterizes baseline information about present state and historical use of ecosystems (Menge *et al.*, 2009) with the consequence that how human pressures have changed over time is better known in terrestrial than in marine environments. For example, we have a good understanding of land transformation resulting in loss and fragmentation of habitat in many different ecosystem types (Vitousek *et al.*, 1997). In Europe, terrestrial ecologists mapped land cover changes between 2000 and 2006 (http://terrestrial.eionet.europa.eu/CLC2006) and showed that the development of artificial land cover for urban fabric and industry, trade, and transport infrastructure is one of the main concerns. Cultivated systems (areas where at least 30% of the landscape is in croplands, shifting cultivation, confined livestock production, or freshwater aquaculture) now cover one-quarter of Earth's terrestrial surface (Millennium Ecosystem Assessment, 2005). At the current margin, ecosystems provide at least US$33 trillion worth of services annually. About 38% of the estimated value comes from terrestrial systems, mainly from forests (US$4.7 trillion per year) and wetlands (US$4.9 trillion per year) (Costanza *et al.*, 1999). Alteration of terrestrial ecosystems via species invasions and extinctions caused by human activities has negatively impacted ecosystem goods and services in many well-documented cases (Vandermeer *et al.*, 2002). Most of these changes are difficult, expensive, or impossible to reverse or fix with technological solutions (Hooper *et al.*, 2005). Thus, in the last century, terrestrial systems characterized by a strong background in ecological research and a more evolved legislation framework have received a greater conservation priority than marine systems (Roberts *et al.*, 2003).

Processes shaping marine ecosystems are still clouded by uncertainty due to a lack of basic knowledge about specific aspects such as life cycles and functional traits of most taxa, distribution of species and habitat types, long-term changes at species and assemblage levels, and outcomes of interactions under different ecological settings. In the marine environment, we can produce a global map of human impacts on marine systems (Halpern *et al.*, 2008), and global and regional analyses of some of these drivers exist (e.g., Myers and Worm, 2003; Hoegh-Guldberg *et al.*, 2007; Mora, 2008). However, in many cases we can only infer their effects on biodiversity, since both the distribution and the state of habitat diversity are scarcely known (Fraschetti *et al.*, 2008).

In 1883, while the American bison and the homing pigeon were nearing extinction, fish seemed to still be so abundant that Huxley (1883) declared: "I believe that the cod fishery, the herring fishery, the pilchard fishery, the mackerel fishery, and probably all the great sea fisheries, are inexhaustible; that is to say, that nothing we do seriously affects the number of the fish. And any attempt to regulate these fisheries seems consequently, from the nature of the case, to be useless." After more than a century, the perception of marine ecosystems' vulnerability to human threats has greatly changed, even though projections into the future of marine biodiversity are sometimes contradictory. In a much discussed paper, for instance, Worm *et al.* (2006) depicted the global collapse of fisheries by the mid twenty-first century, reaching 100% exploitation by the year 2048. However, some members of the scientific community do not agree about the severity of both ocean exploitation and habitat degradation (Hilborn, 2007). This is likely because the extent of the ocean and the difficulty in accessing its environs make our quantification and forecast of human impacts incredibly cumbersome (Halpern *et al.*, 2007; Halpern *et al.*, 2008). Some results of effective management may not yet be evident as increasing efforts to restore marine ecosystems and rebuild fisheries are still under way (Worm *et al.*, 2009).

Large-scale evaluations of marine biodiversity loss have shown that intensification of human activities at sea has depleted >90% of formerly important species, destroyed >65% of seagrass and wetland habitat, degraded water quality, and accelerated species invasions (Lotze *et al.*, 2006). In Europe, shellfish beds and biogenic reefs have been nearly eliminated (Airoldi and Beck, 2007; Beck *et al.*, 2009). Mangroves are disappearing worldwide by 1–2% per year, a rate greater than or equal to declines in adjacent coral reefs or tropical rainforests (Duke *et al.*, 2007). Global assessments of stock biomass recently showed that 90% of the world's large predatory fish is overexploited (Myers and Worm, 2003). Overfishing nearly extirpated the larger fish fauna of coastal ecosystems, ranging from sharks and rays on Caribbean reefs to cod in coastal Maine (Jackson *et al.*, 2001). Declines in top predators may cascade down food webs, and the implications of these cascading processes on system functioning and resilience can be dramatic (Pauly *et al.*, 1998), for instance changing a fish-dominated ocean to one dominated by jellyfish (Boero *et al.*, 2008b). In addition, Pinsky *et al.* (2011) showed the collapse of small, low trophic-level species, suggesting that large-bodied species and top predators are not the only groups at risk in the oceans and stressing fundamental differences in the ways that industrial fisheries and land conversion affect natural communities. No oceanic area is totally unaffected by humans, and about 41% of the oceans is strongly affected by multiple threats (Halpern *et al.*, 2008).

Valuing marine biodiversity in terms of ecosystem services provided to humans suffers the added complication that marine environments are extremely diverse (Beaumont *et al.*, 2008). Several efforts have been made by Whitehead (1993), King (1995), and Costanza *et al.* (1997) to identify and evaluate the goods and services that marine ecosystems provide. Recently, it has been estimated that seagrass meadows provide a suite of ecosystem services at the global scale, including an estimated US$1.9 trillion per year in the form of nutrient cycling (Waycott *et al.*, 2009). At a minimum for the UK, the value of food provision in terms of plants and animals taken from the sea for human consumption has been estimated at £513 million (Beaumont *et al.*, 2008). These valuations should facilitate biodiversity management by enabling optimal allocation of limited management resources. It is also true that a systematic economic valuation of the benefits deriving from healthy ecosystems can be controversial as, in some cases, we might reach the risky conclusion that destroying a marine landscape is economically more effective than protecting it (Gatto and De Leo, 2000). Economical valuations can also lead to the idea that the marine environment should be protected for economic reasons rather than for ethical ones (CIESM, 2008). However, all efforts towards raising awareness of the importance of marine biodiversity should be a priority.

Ecosystem-based management represents a means of achieving the long-term delivery of a suite of ecosystem services, rather than single services. The analysis of the spatial distribution of the different ecosystem services, rather than a rough global estimate of each ecosystem service, represents an issue that deserves more attention in order to strengthen the connection between ecological and social systems within EBM. At a regional scale, once key services have been identified, assessing the biophysical quantities and the spatial distribution of services can be crucial for translating their economic and social value to people, which will in turn influence management decisions. Also, maps of ecosystem services have the potential to suggest areas where multiple services are delivered, and thus can help to identify where conflicts in management are likely to arise and where addressing multiple objectives is most critical (Lester *et al.*, in press).

Beyond the differences between terrestrial and marine environments, and the need for more investment in the marine realm, cross-system threats are now pervasive in most coastal ecosystems, making their consideration essential for successful management. Conservation planning that ignores multiple interacting stressors may identify strategies to remove threats that leave protected communities at high risk from external impacts (Tallis *et al.*, 2010).

1.3 A complex scenario driven by multiple stressors

In the marine realm, besides the lack of reliable historical records about what pristine systems may have looked like (Bulleri *et al.*, 2007), assessment and interpretation of ecological impacts is compromised by the tendency of current scientific and management practices to consider the effects of individual threats in isolation. Attempts to address the increasing diversity and intensity of anthropogenic stressors should first recognize that human activities are acting at multiple temporal and spatial scales (Figure 1.1, B1), making it particularly difficult to quantify past historical changes and present human effects and to predict future changes in biodiversity (McLeod *et al.*, 2005).

Effects of multiple stressors can lead to the loss of resilience and an increased risk of regime shifts, which are often long-lasting and difficult to reverse (Hughes, 1994; Hughes *et al.*, 2003; Hughes *et al.*, 2005; Boero *et al.*, 2008a; Casini *et al.*, 2009). Regime shifts are also currently difficult to predict (de Young *et al.*, 2008), but implications in highly impacted ecosystems are clear: they result in homogenization of communities and ecosystems due to reductions in food-web complexity, diversity within functional groups and biogenic habitat structure, as well as decreases in the size of organisms. Localized human perturbations combined with new threats such as climate change, invasive species, and ocean acidification all contribute to generating new regimes of disturbances that are expected to greatly affect the stability and productivity of marine coastal ecosystems (Figure 1.1, C1) (Easterling *et al.*, 2000; Loreau *et al.*, 2002; Hooper *et al.*, 2005; Halpern *et al.*, 2008). Moreover, global warming and variations of extreme weather conditions result in shifts in mean intensity and temporal variance of climatic variables, thus affecting biological systems at different hierarchies of organization (Benedetti-Cecchi *et al.*, 2006). Changes in physiological response to environmental stress, fragmentation of populations, modification of distributional patterns of key species, and direct or indirect alteration of interactions among populations are only a few examples of the likely impact of climate change on marine ecosystems (Hughes *et al.*, 2003; De'ath *et al.*, 2009). This significant erosion of ecosystem resistance and resilience has dramatic consequences for social systems that depend on ecosystems services (Figure 1.1, A2–A5) (Adger *et al.*, 2005).

By focusing on the combined effects of multiple disturbances on marine coastal biodiversity, it should be possible to forecast the ecological consequences associated with different scenarios of environmental management with greater accuracy and precision than allowed by current ecological models based on single drivers. These forecasts based on our understanding of cumulative impacts will be critical to future management seeking to reduce the threat of human pressures on the functioning of marine ecosystems (Crain *et al.*, 2009). Such a shift in management will require ecological, fishery, and socio-economic

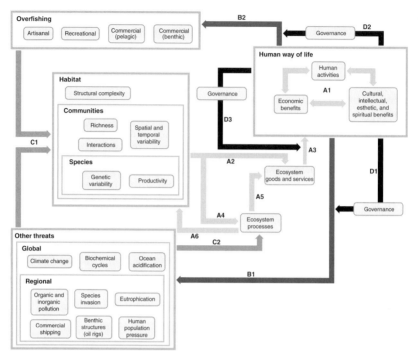

Figure 1.1 The role of humans as agents of change in ecosystem functioning. Marine systems are adapted to natural levels of disturbance, but they are presently exposed to increasing, cumulative, and synergistic effects of both natural and anthropogenic factors that threaten their resilience (e.g., Halpern *et al.*, 2008). Human activities that are motivated by economic, cultural, intellectual, esthetic, and spiritual goals (A1) are causing ecological changes of regional to global significance (B1), in particular through fishing activities (B2). By a variety of mechanisms, these changes contribute to changing biodiversity at the habitat (*sensu* Airoldi and Beck, 2007), community, and/or species levels (C1). For instance, fishing activities can impact habitats through destructive or ghost fishing gears and impact species and assemblages through harvest, catch-and-release, or bycatch. Changes in biodiversity can have direct consequences for ecosystem services (A2) and, as a result, human economic and social activities (A3). In addition, changes in biodiversity can directly influence ecosystem processes (A4). Altered ecosystem processes can thereby influence ecosystem services that benefit humanity (A5) and cycle back to further alter biodiversity (A6). Global and regional changes may also directly affect ecosystem processes (C2). Effective governance can regulate anthropogenic influence and decrease human-induced regional and global changes (D1). The use of marine protected areas within an ecosystem-based framework can specifically mitigate the effects of fishing (D2). Governance that focuses on the resilience of the socio-ecosystem in the face of regional and global changes can also influence the way humans are adapting their uses of ecosystem goods and services (D3). Modified from Chapin *et al.* (2000) and Crowder *et al.* (2008).

disciplines to develop into an integrated and sufficiently predictive science to inform managing, conserving, and restoring damaged ecosystems at local, regional, and global scales.

1.4 The failure of many traditional fisheries management approaches

Overfishing is one of the most important threats to marine ecosystems (Figure 1.1) (Halpern *et al.*, 2008). The general objective of fisheries management is to maintain the sustainability of fisheries (i.e., to provide food and to maintain related economic activities) by protecting fish populations (i.e., to provide conditions guaranteeing marine resources renewal). Various regulatory measures are usually implemented to achieve the desired goals of productivity and sustainability, but traditional, open-access fisheries management has generally failed to prevent massive over-fishing at a global level (Jackson *et al.*, 2001; Worm *et al.*, 2006; Costello *et al.*, 2008; Mora *et al.*, 2009).

Coastal resources are generally managed through business sector regulation or institutional arrangements. These strategies cover a broad range of rules, laws, economic instruments (i.e., voluntary agreements, taxes and subsidies, rights allocation), and community-based management (Abdullah *et al.*, 1998; Wiber *et al.*, 2004) to ensure efficient exploitation and equity among stakeholders. Management regulations may include spatial and temporal controls on either catch or nominal effort, commonly supplemented with technical measures such as gear restrictions or size limits (Holland and Brazee, 1996; Holland, 2003). These management measures attempt to protect resources by allowing a sufficient fraction of the population to reach maturity and to reproduce. Traditional fisheries management, however, still primarily relies on single-species stock assessments, even though more holistic approaches such as multispecies and EBM approaches have been recognized as necessary to appraise consequences of fishing on resources and ecosystems (Crowder *et al.*, 2008). Most countries continue to follow these traditional approaches and manage inshore areas and marine resources on a species-by-species regulatory basis (Ehler, 2003).

Besides direct effects on fished species, there are numerous indirect effects of fisheries on ecosystem health (Figure 1.1, C1). The use of some fishing gears, such as trawls, can cause severe habitat degradation. While managing fisheries, protecting habitats may also provide a significant value, either by increasing fishery productivity through higher growth or lower natural mortality of commercial stocks, or by protecting non-commercial species (Holland, 2003). Bringing these considerations into fisheries management could thus ensure fishery sustainability and, at the same time, maintain non-fisheries benefits of marine ecosystems to society, such as non-extractive uses including tourism and scuba-diving.

Success stories of traditional fisheries management exist in localized areas (Costello *et al.*, 2008; Worm *et al.*, 2009). Most successful examples come from areas with relatively low human densities, which can facilitate governance and fisheries management, and where property-rights-based management has been implemented. Correctly aligning incentives can make fishermen good stewards of the resources. In Alaska, Iceland, New Zealand, and Australia, management systems are effective in achieving fishery sustainability (Cunningham and Bostock, 2005; Grafton *et al.*, 2006; Hilborn, 2007) and in many cases have resulted in highly productive and valuable fisheries. Castilla *et al.* (2009) illustrated that, in Chile, a mix of conservation and management tools implemented along a spatial network showed evidence of coastal inshore biodiversity enhancement. In areas such as the Mediterranean Sea, high human density, intense coastal development, a long history of human uses, and numerous bordering states combine to generate a complex ecological and socio-economic matrix, making the development of strategies for conservation, management, and restoration very difficult.

It is also true that while the importance of overfishing has been largely recognized, there are numerous arguments about the potential to reverse its causes and impacts and to provide solutions. Lotze (2004) remarks that current perceptions of the status of marine species and ecosystems tends to be alarmist and that many scientific papers prefer to exaggerate the severity and apparent hopelessness of the situation. Success stories have largely been ignored and simplistic "solutions" (e.g., MPAs by themselves) or complex, non-operational "solutions" (e.g., convoluted systems of ecosystem indicators) have frequently been proposed. However, a new tendency in the scientific community is to highlight conservation efforts that are making the difference around the world, allowing conservation professionals to learn from the success of others, and demonstrating to colleagues, the public, and policy-makers that the situation is not hopeless. Examples of relative successes can be found, for instance, in a recent synthesis by Worm *et al.* (2009), who analyzed global data sets from both a fisheries and conservation perspective and showed that, while 63% of fish stocks still require rebuilding, the average exploitation rate has recently declined in five out of ten ecosystems. Costello *et al.* (2008), who analyzed a global database of fisheries institutions and catch statistics in 11 135 fisheries from 1950 to 2003, showed that implementation of catch shares can halt, and even reverse, the global trend toward widespread collapse of fisheries. Therefore, institutional change has the potential for greatly altering the future of global fisheries.

1.5 Ecosystem-based management as a change of perspective

With the increasing evidence that traditional, single-sector forms of marine resource management are failing to meet their goals for sustainability and conservation there is a growing recognition of the need for management practices that address marine ecosystems as a whole. For example, integrated coastal zone management (ICZM) was promoted in the past decade as a means for achieving sustainable regional development in coastal areas. Integrated coastal zone management recognizes that ignoring land-sea connections may be inefficient and inappropriate. However, even though this approach has been continuously advocated, fully integrated practical applications are still rare; for instance, few nations in the European Union are seriously concerned with systematic ICZM implementation (Shipman and Stojanovic, 2007). As peer-reviewed research on marine EBM has increased rapidly in the past 15 years (Halpern et al., 2010), EBM has simultaneously risen to the fore of many management discussions as a means to manage an ecosystem holistically and to preserve the goods and services they provide (e.g., Guerry, 2005; McLeod and Leslie, 2009; Pollnac and Christie, 2009 and references therein). The basic tenet of EBM is an integrated and interdisciplinary approach that considers all ocean sectors and aspects of an ecosystem, including humans (McLeod et al., 2005). Not only are humans incorporated into EBM as decision-makers, stakeholders, and managers of resources, but people are viewed as a key component of the ecosystem, relying on the goods and services they provide and altering ecosystems through their use, and sometimes abuse (Figure 1.1) (Shackeroff et al., 2009).

Ecosystem services can be diverse and generally fall under the categories of provisioning (e.g., fisheries and pharmaceuticals from marine algae), regulating (e.g., maintenance of water quality through filters provided by coastal mangroves and seagrass meadows), cultural (e.g., coastal tourism and traditional marine resource uses), and supporting (e.g., coastal mangroves that serve as nurseries for young fish) (Millennium Ecosystem Assessment, 2005). Provisioning services are the services most likely to be addressed by management due to their tangible nature and relatively easier valuation (Howarth and Farber, 2002). However, in order to have productive fisheries and algae harvests, the services supporting these resources, such as habitat structure and food availability, must also be accounted for. As multiple interacting stressors threaten marine systems and provide another dimension of complexity (Halpern *et al.*, 2008), an understanding of the interconnectedness within a system is vital to ensure that management choices do not have unintended effects on interacting services. Trade-off analysis uses data about ecosystem functions, social factors, and the possible interactions among them to identify the services that are most difficult to manage jointly, identifying management outcomes that may produce similar or better results with the least conflict (Lester *et al.*, in press).

Ecosystem-based management is place-based, therefore the spatial scale of EBM is determined by the management goals pertaining to a specific place. Moreover, because there are complex linkages both among and within ecosystems, the scales at which processes are operating (both spatial and temporal) should inform the management goals and therefore determine the scales at which management must occur. Determining temporal scales of management requires knowledge about the temporal characteristics of a specific area: What were the historical levels of biodiversity? Has the system remained resilient over time? If not, how has it changed in the face of natural and human-induced disturbances? These are not simple questions to answer, particularly because it can be incredibly difficult to reconstruct what pristine ecosystems may have looked like. They underscore the need for baseline information about the structure of assemblages and habitats, and associated temporal and spatial scales of variation as well as the ability to evaluate how a system, threatened by multiple stressors, responds when one or more stressors are removed in different order (Bulleri *et al.*, 2007).

While this need for ever more data can seem daunting, marine EBM can move forward in a variety of contexts despite the potential pitfalls of complex governance, short timeframe to implementation, and remaining data gaps, as evidenced by experiences in the Bering Sea–Aleutian Islands ecosystem, the Great Barrier Reef Marine Park in Australia, or the Californian coast (Ruckelshaus *et al.*, 2008). Other EBM initiatives include areas such as Puget Sound, Washington, USA and Raja Ampat, Indonesia (Tallis *et al.*, 2010). Frameworks for EBM implementation such as the Integrated Ecosystem Assessment developed by the USA's National Oceanic and Atmospheric Administration (NOAA) (Levin *et al.*, 2009) are beginning to provide concrete and systematic ways to approach EBM from a range of starting points, including both data-poor and data-rich regions. Assessments of EBM feasibility and success all tend to underscore the need to involve stakeholders as active participants in the process, from the beginning scoping stages through to monitoring and evaluation of EBM applications (Christie *et al.*, 2005; Leslie and McLeod, 2007; Tallis *et al.*, 2010).

1.6 Managing marine biodiversity and human uses with marine protected areas

Marine protected areas are a specific type of management zone and one component of the larger suite of ocean zoning possibilities encompassed by marine spatial planning (MSP: e.g., Douvere, 2008). Marine protected areas may be strictly no-take, such as marine reserves, or they may be complete no-access zones, where neither extractive nor non-extractive uses are allowed. Other MPAs may receive partial protection, allowing restricted uses such as traditional/artisanal fisheries or scuba-diving. Most MPAs include another layer of complexity by combining different levels of protection within a spatially zoned management scheme. Zones may be dedicated to strict conservation, act as a buffer zone that can be used for research, education or traditional uses, and/or allow non-consumptive uses and limited consumptive uses, providing space-related incentives to users (Agardy *et al.*, 2003). Zoning the MPA can allow coexistence of different resource users and must be established according to the management goals of the MPA (Claudet and Pelletier, 2004). All of these regulatory means must be combined with the establishment of conspicuous borders (with or without access fees) to reduce possible impacts of incidental intrusions, public information about uses permitted in different zones, and voluntary and participatory involvement of local communities and diverse users who contribute to the process (Christie, 2004). Compliance with spatial zoning regulations such as within an MPA depends on whether the users understand the regulations designed to ensure the orderly and sustainable use of marine resources (Bohnsack, 1996). If compliance is good, additional management costs to ensure the zoning enforcement will be reduced.

While traditional fisheries management approaches provide a refuge based on population numbers, MPAs provide a refuge in space and are implemented over smaller spatial scales than traditional fisheries management measures. Marine protected areas are also ecosystem-oriented: they aim to manage and protect the resources, the associated habitat, and other components of the ecosystem, including humans. Ideally, MPAs should be adaptively managed, their design and planning should consider multiple external influences, and they should strive to balance diverse ecological, economic, and societal objectives. In areas where fishing and fishing-related impacts (e.g., habitat damage from destructive fishing practices and bycatch of non-target species) are responsible for more than 50% of the overall impact, Halpern *et al.* (2010) showed that well-designed and enforced no-take reserves could significantly improve overall ocean health and enhance the delivery of a suite of ecosystem services by decreasing cumulative impacts within their boundaries.

In these respects, MPAs could be considered a potentially effective component of EBM (Halpern *et al.*, 2010) even though the quantity and quality of conservation efforts should be deeply refined to make MPAs more effective on a global scale (see Mora *et al.*, 2006 and Chapter 13). Firstly, MPAs are place-based, which is the starting point for EBM at the initial scale. In addition, MPAs protect a range of resources and can address both conservation and fisheries goals if properly designed (Roberts *et al.*, 2001; Claudet *et al.*, 2008), moving beyond a single-sector focus to address a suite of ecosystem characteristics, as EBM does. Ideally, MPA planning should incorporate from the outset key EBM concepts, such as cross-system management actions and explicit recognition of the link between social and ecological system (Christie *et al.*, 2009). Properly implemented MPAs can protect connections within a system if they are established to include multiple species and connected habitats. Further, MPAs can protect many ecosystem services within their borders, including services from each of the four categories discussed in the previous section. Finally, MPAs protected for substantial time periods of multiple decades or longer can provide a source of information about temporal variability and directional change which can be useful within an EBM approach. For example, data from the oldest marine reserves in the world show that indirect effects of protection were evident only after an average of 14 years, lagging behind direct effects, which were evident within 5 years (Babcock *et al.*, 2010). Acknowledging that certain impacts may not be immediately evident, EBM must account for temporal change and incorporate adapting management strategies to address future, potentially unplanned-for, effects of protection.

However, MPAs can only manage what is inside their borders and thus cannot address land- and air-based connections to protect the full suite of ecosystem services. These areas can offer only limited protection from large-scale disturbances such as climate change (McLeod *et al.*, 2009) or invasive species (Riegl *et al.*, 2009), even though increased biodiversity within MPAs and appropriately designed MPA networks may increase resilience through community stability and resistance to and recovery from perturbations (Bevilacqua *et al.*, 2006; McLeod *et al.*, 2009). Although MPAs are an important component of many EBM approaches, they alone cannot address all aspects of EBM; MPAs are not EBM even though marine EBM and MPA planning have been used interchangeably and are often assumed to be synonymous (Halpern *et al.*, 2010). Additional joint management tools are needed, including those addressing the terrestrial and offshore areas of a given system. One of the main EBM principles is spatial integration, bringing together the management of resources from the land side of the coastal zone (including up-river issues related to watersheds and river basins) as well as protection of the marine area (Cicin-Sain and Belfiore, 2005; Tallis *et al.*, 2010).

The small number of MPAs worldwide is another limitation of efficiently incorporating this tool into a larger EBM framework (Spalding *et al.*, 2008; Wood *et al.*, 2008). For example, Mora (Chapter 13) showed that the global distribution of MPAs is still insufficient to ensure population viability. A recent global evaluation of the potential of marine reserves (i.e., no-take zones) to achieve EBM goals found that while there are large stretches of coastline that can benefit from the use of MPAs as an EBM tool, it is unlikely that the small number of marine reserves globally are playing a significant role in advancing EBM (Halpern *et al.*, 2010). Management costs of implementing a global network of MPAs are expensive, although it remains difficult to assign economic value to their social benefits (e.g., direct benefits such as tourism and indirect benefits such as securing vital ecosystem services) (Balmford *et al.*, 2004). Finally, escalating human population sizes can in turn increase resource consumption, undermining the goals of MPAs as pressures increase (Mora, 2008). These limitations combined with extreme poverty in some parts of the world make it increasingly harder to appropriately enforce MPAs, thus reducing their overall effectiveness.

To date, there are few fully implemented EBM initiatives that have resulted from a deliberate and well-thought-out management strategy. The great majority of marine EBM initiatives build upon pre-existing management landscapes with their own inherent challenges, such as disparate governance, limited institutional capacity, and local controversy (Christie *et al.*, 2009). However, EBM can provide a strategic framework for coalescing and leveraging pre-existing management. Existing MPAs are often the starting point for scaling-up to larger, more integrated marine EBM. For example, in the Philippines, an ongoing and not yet fully realized process to implement EBM began with two no-take MPAs protected and managed by local communities at Apo and Sumilon Islands. These marine reserves provided compelling evidence for the positive ecological effects of full protection, not only to the species and habitats they protected but also to the adjacent fisheries that were enhanced (Alcala *et al.*, 2005; Abesamis *et al.*, 2006). As a result, a national shift in policy occurred, leading to co-management of marine resources within 15 km of the coast by the local communities and national government (Alcala and Russ, 2006). From this original proof of concept, MPAs flourished as a management tool throughout the Philippines; they now form the starting point for region-wide conversations about how to implement EBM by scaling-up from the regional collection of MPAs (Eisma-Osorio *et al.*, 2009; Lowry *et al.*, 2009). One critical aspect at this stage is trying to assess whether the inclusion of MPAs within an EBM context is key for meeting EBM goals since empirical data are largely lacking in this field.

1.7 Are we ready to implement EBM? Moving forward in the face of present limitations

An evaluation of progress towards implementing ecosystem-based fisheries management (Pitcher *et al.*, 2009) showed that out of 33 countries, only four countries were ranked as "adequate," while over half received "fail" grades, with some developing countries performing better than many developed nations. No country rated overall as "good." Another attempt to assess the current effectiveness of fisheries management regimes worldwide conducted by Mora *et al.* (2009) shows that only 7% of all coastal states worldwide employ rigorous scientific assessment when generating management policies, 1.4% also have participatory and transparent processes to convert scientific recommendations into policy, and only 0.95% also provide for robust mechanisms to ensure compliance with regulations. None of the coastal states enacting these management measures are free from the effects of excess fishing capacity, subsidies, or access to foreign fishing. In the context of fisheries EBM, Bundy *et al.* (2009) consider the holistic objectives of EBM currently unattainable due to the persistent lack of acceptance that humans are components of ecosystems and must be included in ecosystem management. However, social science to inform EBM lags behind progress made in compiling natural science data to inform of EBM (Lester *et al.*, in press).

To enable effective ecosystem management approaches, the authors advocate three linked and supporting concepts: corporate responsibility, social justice, and ethics (Bundy *et al.*, 2009). Corporate responsibility takes into account the total costs of fishing (including externalities such as damage to ecosystems and local communities as well as the distribution of costs and benefits among social groups and generations) (Sumaila and Walters, 2005). Social justice refers to fairness in the distribution of benefits from, and access to, ocean resources (Loomis and Ditton, 1993), and ethics concern principles that guide common people and scientists in their day-to-day behavior (Bearzi, 2008; Bundy *et al.*, 2009).

The lack of successful progress towards EBM can also be attributed to the absence of systematic guidelines for EBM in different ecological, social, and cultural contexts, the chronic jurisdictional dissociation between the land and sea in coastal zones, and the lack of baseline knowledge about processes shaping natural coastal communities. There is an urgent need to encourage multidisciplinary research in this direction, with the goal of untangling the complex processes operating at different scales and, in the same framework, to explore the impact of global changes in time and space. Ecosystem-based management still means different things to different individuals, leading to all-too-slow progress towards multidisciplinary collaborations, involving both scientists and managers. One other component of the ecosystem approach that should play an increasing role in shaping the future of marine environmental management is the use of environmental impact assessments as a means for moving above and beyond the precautionary approach. This represents an implicit recognition that we do not have enough knowledge about the target systems to quantify the effects of human activities and plan adequate mitigation strategies.

Most importantly, current EBM approaches will still fail where there is a lack of political and social commitment to sustainable management of marine resources and cohesive governance (Figure 1.1, D1–3). Thus, in order to effectively move forward with EBM, it is critical to view marine resources holistically since they are tied to terrestrial systems and span political and jurisdictional boundaries. Multidisciplinary consortia, involving both social and natural scientists, can prioritize and collect the necessary data for science-based EBM, the planning of which is ideally governed by robust scientific guidelines and undertaken by a diverse group of decision-makers, managers, stakeholders, and the general public. Where they exist, MPAs should be viewed as a starting point for EBM. Although MPAs such as marine reserves can provide a refuge from fishing and other extractive activities, they cannot solely be used to manage marine resources and therefore must be used in connection with other forms of cross-sector, multi-use management.

References

Abdullah, N. M. R., Kuperan, K., and Pommeroy, R. S. (1998). Transaction costs and fisheries co-management. *Marine Resource Economics*, **13**, 103–14.

Abesamis, R. A., Alcala, A. C., and Russ, G. R. (2006). How much does the fishery at Apo Island benefit from spillover of adult fish from the adjacent marine reserve? *Fishery Bulletin*, **104**, 360–75.

Adger, W. N., Hughes, T. P., Folke, C., Carpenter, S. R., and Rockstrom, J. (2005). Social–ecological resilience to coastal disasters. *Science*, **309**, 1036–9.

Agardy, T., Bridgewater, P., Crosby, M. P., *et al.* (2003). Dangerous targets? Unresolved issues and ideological clashes around marine protected areas. *Aquatic Conservation – Marine and Freshwater Ecosystems*, **13**, 353–67.

Airoldi, L. and Beck, M. W. (2007). Loss, status and trends for coastal marine habitats of Europe. *Oceanography and Marine Biology*, **45**, 345–405.

Alcala, A. C. and Russ, G. R. (2006). No-take marine reserves and reef fisheries management in the Philippines: a new people power revolution. *Ambio*, **35**, 245–54.

Alcala, A. C., Russ, G. R., Maypa, A. P., and Calumpong, H. P. (2005). A long-term, spatially replicated experimental test of the effect of marine reserves on local fish yields. *Canadian Journal of Fisheries and Aquatic Sciences*, **62**, 98–108.

Babcock, R. C., Shears, N. T., Alcala, A. C., *et al.* (2010). Decadal trends in marine reserves reveal differential rates of change in direct and indirect effects. *Proceedings of the National Academy of Sciences of the United States of America*, **107**, 18 256–61.

Balmford, A., Gravestock, P., Hockley, N., McClean, C. J., and Roberts, C. M. (2004). The worldwide costs of marine protected areas. *Proceedings of the National Academy of Sciences of the United States of America*, **101**, 9694–7.

Bearzi, G. (2008). When swordfish conservation biologists eat swordfish. *Conservation Biology*, **23**, 1–2.

Beaumont, N. J., Austen, M. C., Mangi, S. C., and Townsend, M. (2008). Economic valuation for the conservation of marine biodiversity. *Marine Pollution Bulletin*, **56**, 386–96.

Beck, M. B., Brumbaugh, R. D., Airoldi, L., *et al.* (2009). *Shellfish Reefs at Risk: A Global Analysis of Problems and Solutions*. Arlington, VA: The Nature Conservancy.

Benedetti-Cecchi, L., Bertocci, I., Vaselli, S., and Maggi, E. (2006). Temporal variance reverses the impact of high mean intensity of stress in climate change experiments. *Ecology*, **87**, 2489–99.

Bevilacqua, S., Terlizzi, A., Fraschetti, S., Russo, G. F., and Boero, F. (2006). Mitigating human disturbance: can protection influence trajectories of recovery in benthic assemblages? *Journal of Animal Ecology*, **75**, 908–20.

Boero, F., Bouillon, J., Gravili, C., *et al.* (2008a). Gelatinous plankton: irregularities rule the world (sometimes). *Marine Ecology Progress Series*, **356**, 299–310.

Boero, F., Féral, J. P., Azzuro, E., *et al.* (2008b). Climate warming and related changes in Mediterranean marine biota. In *CIESM Workshop Monograph 35*, ed. F. Briand. Monaco: CIESM, pp. 5–21.

Bohnsack, J. A. (1996). Marine reserves, zoning, and the future of fishery management. *Fisheries*, **21**, 14–16.

Bulleri, F., Underwood, A. J., and Benedetti-Cecchi, L. (2007). The assessment and interpretation of ecological impacts in human-dominated environments. *Environmental Conservation*, **34**, 181–2.

Bundy, A., Chuenpagdee, R., Jentoft, S., and Mahon, R. (2009). If science is not the answer, what is? An alternative governance model for the world's fisheries. *Frontiers in Ecology and the Environment*, **6**, 152–5.

Casini, M., Hjelm, J., Molinero, J. C., *et al.* (2009). Trophic cascades promote threshold-like shifts in pelagic marine ecosystems. *Proceedings of the National Academy of Sciences of the United States of America*, **106**, 197–202.

Castilla, J. C., Gelcich, S., and Fernández, M. (2009). Add-on inshore marine biodiversity enhancement via territorial user rights for fisheries allocations. In *World Conference on Marine Biodiversity*, Valencia, Spain, eds. C. Heip and C. Duarte, p. 8.

Chapin, F. S. III, Zavaleta, E. S., Eviner, V. T., *et al.* (2000). Consequences of changing biodiversity. *Nature*, **405**, 234–42.

Christie, P. (2004). Marine protected areas as biological successes and social failures in southeast Asia. *Aquatic Protected Areas as Fisheries Management Tools*, **42**, 155–64.

Christie, P., Lowry, K., White, A. T., *et al.* (2005). Key findings from a multidisciplinary examination of integrated coastal management process sustainability. *Ocean and Coastal Management*, **48**, 468–83.

Christie, P., Pollnac, R. B., Oracion, E. G., *et al.* (2009). Back to basics: an empirical study demonstrating the importance of local-level dynamics for the success of tropical marine ecosystem-based management. *Coastal Management*, **37**, 349–73.

Cicin-Sain, B. and Belfiore, S. (2005). Linking marine protected areas to integrated coastal and ocean management: a review of theory and practice. *Ocean and Coastal Management*, **48**, 847–68.

CIESM (2008). *Economic Valuation of Natural Coastal and Marine Ecosystems*. CIESM Conference, 22–5 October 2008, Bodrum, Turkey.

Claudet, J. and Pelletier, D. (2004). Marine protected areas and artificial reefs: a review of the interactions between management and scientific studies. *Aquatic Living Resources*, **17**, 129–38.

Claudet, J., Roussel, S., Pelletier, D., and Rey-Valette, H. (2006). Spatial management of inshore areas: theory and practice. *Vie et Milieu – Life and Environment*, **56**, 301–5.

Claudet, J., Osenberg, C. W., Benedetti-Cecchi, L., *et al.* (2008). Marine reserves: size and age do matter. *Ecology Letters*, **11**, 481–9.

Costanza, R., Andrade, F., Antunes, P., *et al.* (1999). Ecological economics and sustainable governance of the oceans. *Ecological Economics*, **31**, 171–87.

Costanza, R., dArge, R., deGroot, R., *et al.* (1997). The value of the world's ecosystem services and natural capital. *Nature*, **387**, 253–60.

Costello, C., Gaines, S. D., and Lynham, J. (2008). Can catch shares prevent fisheries collapse? *Science*, **321**, 1678–81.

Crain, C. M., Halpern, B. S., Beck, M. W., and Kappel, C. V. (2009). Understanding and managing human threats to the coastal marine environment. *Annals of the New York Academy of Sciences*, **1162**, 39–62.

Crowder, L. B., Hazen, E. L., Avissar, N., *et al.* (2008). The impacts of fisheries on marine ecosystems and the transition to ecosystem-based management. *Annual Review of Ecology, Evolution and Systematics*, **39**, 259–78.

Cunningham, S. and Bostock, T. (2005). *Successful Fisheries Management: Issues, Case Studies and Perspectives.* Delft, the Netherlands: Eburon.

De'ath, G., Lough, J. M., and Fabricius, K. E. (2009). Declining coral calcification on the Great Barrier Reef. *Science*, **323**, 116–19.

de Young, B., Barange, M., Beaugrand, G., *et al.* (2008). Regime shifts in marine ecosystems: detection, prediction and management. *Trends in Ecology and Evolution*, **23**, 402–9.

Douvere, F. (2008). The importance of marine spatial planning in advancing ecosystem-based sea use management. *Marine Policy*, **32**, 762–71.

Duke, N. C., Meynecke, J. O., Dittmann, S., *et al.* (2007). A world without mangroves? *Science*, **317**, 41–2.

Easterling, D. R., Meehl, G. A., Parmesan, C., *et al.* (2000). Climate extremes: observations, modeling, and impacts. *Science*, **289**, 2068–74.

Ehler, C. N. (2003). Indicators to measure governance performance in integrated coastal management. *Ocean and Coastal Management*, **46**, 335–45.

Eisma-Osorio, R. L., Amolo, R. C., Maypa, A. P., White, A. T., and Christie, P. (2009). Scaling up local government initiatives toward ecosystem-based fisheries management in Southeast Cebu Island, Philippines. *Coastal Management*, **37**, 291–307.

Fraschetti, S., Terlizzi, A., and Boero, F. (2008). How many habitats are there in the sea (and where)? *Journal of Experimental Marine Biology and Ecology*, **366**, 109–15.

Fraschetti, S., D'Ambrosio, P., Micheli, F., *et al.* (2009). Planning Marine Protected Areas in a human-dominated seascape. *Marine Ecology Progress Series*, **375**, 13–24.

Gallagher, A., Johnson, D., Glegg, G., and Trier, C. (2004). Constructs of sustainability in coastal management. *Marine Policy*, **28**, 249–55.

Gatto, M. and De Leo, G. A. (2000). Pricing biodiversity and ecosystem services: the never-ending story. *BioScience*, **50**, 347–55.

Gell, F. R. and Roberts, C. M. (2003). Benefits beyond boundaries: the fishery effects of marine reserves. *Trends in Ecology and Evolution*, **18**, 448–55.

Grafton, R. Q., Arnason, R., Bjorndal, T., *et al.* (2006). Incentive-based approaches to sustainable fisheries. *Canadian Journal of Fisheries and Aquatic Sciences*, **63**, 699–710.

Guerry, A. D. (2005). Icarus and Daedalus: conceptual and tactical lessons for marine ecosystem-based management. *Frontiers in Ecology and the Environment*, **3**, 202–11.

Guidetti, P. and Sala, E. (2007). Community-wide effects of marine reserves in the Mediterranean Sea. *Marine Ecology Progress Series*, **335**, 43–56.

Guidetti, P., Milazzo, M., Bussotti, S., *et al.* (2008). Italian marine reserve effectiveness: does enforcement matter? *Biological Conservation*, **141**, 699–709.

Halpern, B. S., Selkoe, K. A., Micheli, F., and Kappel, C. V. (2007). Evaluating and ranking the vulnerability of global marine ecosystems to anthropogenic threats. *Conservation Biology*, **21**, 1301–15.

Halpern, B. S., Walbridge, S., Selkoe, K. A., *et al.* (2008). A global map of human impact on marine ecosystems. *Science*, **319**, 948–52.

Halpern, B. S., Lester, S. E., and McLeod, E. (2010). Placing marine protected areas onto the ecosystem-based management seascape. *Proceedings of the National Academy of Sciences of the United States of America*, **107**, 18 312–17.

Hilborn, R. (2007). Reinterpreting the state of fisheries and their management. *Ecosystems*, **10**, 1362–9.

Hoegh-Guldberg, O., Mumby, P. J., Hooten, A. J., *et al.* (2007). Coral reefs under rapid climate change and ocean acidification. *Science*, **318**, 1737–42.

Holland, D. S. (2003). Integrating spatial management measures into traditional fishery management systems: the case of the Georges Bank multispecies groundfish fishery. *ICES Journal of Marine Science*, **60**, 915–29.

Holland, D. S. and Brazee, R. J. (1996). Marine reserves for fisheries management. *Marine Resource Economics*, **11**, 157–71.

Hooper, D. U., Chapin, F. S. III, Ewel, J. J., *et al.* (2005). Effects of biodiversity on ecosystem functioning: a consensus of current knowledge. *Ecological Monographs*, **75**, 3–35.

Howarth, R. B. and Farber, S. (2002). Accounting for the value of ecosystem services. *Ecological Economics*, **41**, 421–9.

Hughes, T. P. (1994). Catastrophes, phase-shifts, and large-scale degradation of a Caribbean coral reef. *Science*, **265**, 1547–51.

Hughes, T. P., Baird, A. H., Bellwood, D. R., *et al.* (2003). Climate change, human impacts, and the resilience of coral reefs. *Science*, **301**, 929–33.

Hughes, T. P., Bellwood, D. R., Folke, C., Steneck, R. S., and Wilson, J. (2005). New paradigms for supporting the resilience of marine ecosystems. *Trends in Ecology and Evolution*, **20**, 380–6.

Huxley, T. H. (1883). Address by Professor Huxley. In *Inaugural Meeting of the Fishery Congress*. London: William Clowes.

Jackson, J. B. C., Kirby, M. X., Berger, W. H., *et al.* (2001). Historical overfishing and the recent collapse of coastal ecosystems. *Science*, **293**, 629–38.

Jennings, S. (2004). The ecosystem approach to fishery management: a significant step towards sustainable use of the marine environment? *Marine Ecology Progress Series*, **274**, 279–82.

King, O. H. (1995). Estimating the value of marine resources: a marine recreation case. *Ocean and Coastal Management*, **27**, 129–41.

Lauck, T., Clark, C. W., Mangel, M., and Munro, G. R. (1998). Implementing the precautionary principle in fisheries management through marine reserves. *Ecological Applications*, **8**, S72–S78.

Leslie, H. M. and McLeod, K. L. (2007). Confronting the challenges of implementing marine ecosystem-based management. *Frontiers in Ecology and the Environment*, **5**, 540–8.

Lester, S. E., Halpern, B. S., Grorud-Colvert, K., *et al.* (2009). Biological effects within no-take marine reserves: a global synthesis. *Marine Ecology Progress Series*, **384**, 33–46.

Lester, S. E., Costello, C., Barth, J. A., *et al.* (in press). Ecosystem service trade-off analysis. *Frontiers in Ecology and the Environment*.

Levin, P. S., Fogarty, M. J., Murawski, S. A., and Fluharty, D. (2009). Integrated ecosystem assessments: developing the scientific basis for ecosystem-based management of the ocean. *PLoS Biology*, **7**.

Lindenmayer, D. B. and Likens, G. E. (2009). Adaptive monitoring: a new paradigm for long-term research and monitoring. *Trends in Ecology and Evolution*, **24**, 482–6.

Loomis, D. K. and Ditton, R. B. (1993). Distributive justice in fisheries management. *Fisheries*, **18**, 14–18.

Loreau, M., Downing, A., Emmerson, M., *et al.* (2002). A new look at the relationship between diversity and stability. In *Biodiversity and Ecosystem Functioning: Synthesis and Perspectives*, eds. M. Loreau, S. Naheem, and P. Inchausti. Oxford, UK: Oxford University Press, pp. 79–91.

Lotze, H. K. (2004). Repetitive history of resource depletion and mismanagement: the need for a shift in perspective. *Marine Ecology Progress Series*, **274**, 282–5.

Lotze, H. K., Lenihan, H. S., Bourque, B. J., *et al.* (2006). Depletion, degradation, and recovery potential of estuaries and coastal seas. *Science*, **312**, 1806–9.

Lowry, G. K., White, A. T., and Christie, P. (2009). Scaling up to networks of marine protected areas in the Philippines: biophysical, legal, institutional, and social considerations. *Coastal Management*, **37**, 274–90.

Lubchenco, J., Palumbi, S. R., Gaines, S. D., and Andelman, S. (2003). Plugging a hole in the ocean: the emerging science of marine reserves. *Ecological Applications*, **13**, S3–S7.

McLeod, E., Salm, R., Green, A., and Almany, J. (2009). Designing marine protected area networks to address the impacts of climate change. *Frontiers in Ecology and the Environment*, **7**, 362–70.

McLeod, K. L. and Leslie, H. (eds.) (2009). *Ecosystem-Based Management for the Oceans*. Washington, DC: Island Press.

McLeod, K., Lubchenco, J., Palumbi, S., and Rosenberg, A. (2005). *Scientific Consensus Statement on Marine Ecosystem-Based Management*. Portland, OR: COMPASS (Communication Partnership for Science and the Sea).

Menge, B. A., Chan, F., Dudas, S., *et al.* (2009). Terrestrial ecologists ignore aquatic literature: asymmetry in citation breadth in ecological publications and implications for generality and progress in ecology. *Journal of Experimental Marine Biology and Ecology*, **377**, 93–100.

Micheli, F. and Halpern, B. S. (2005). Low functional redundancy in coastal marine assemblages. *Ecology Letters*, **8**, 391–400.

Millennium Ecosystem Assessment (2005). *Ecosystems and Human Well-Being: Current State and Trends*. Washington, DC: Island Press.

Mora, C. (2008). A clear human footprint in the coral reefs of the Caribbean. *Proceedings of the Royal Society Series B*, **275**, 767–73.

Mora, C., Andrèfouët, S., Costello, M. J., *et al.* (2006). Coral reefs and the global network of marine protected areas. *Science*, **312**, 1750–1.

Mora, C., Myers, R. A., Coll, M., *et al.* (2009). Management effectiveness of the world's marine fisheries. *PLoS Biology*, **7**.

Myers, R. A. and Worm, B. (2003). Rapid worldwide depletion of predatory fish communities. *Nature*, **423**, 280–3.

Pauly, D., Christensen, V., Dalsgaard, J., Froese, R., and Torres, F. (1998). Fishing down marine food webs. *Science*, **279**, 860–3.

Pinsky, M. L., Jensen, O. P., Richard, D., and Palumbi, S. R. (2011). Unexpected patterns of fisheries collapse in the world's oceans. *Proceedings of the National Academy of Sciences of the United States of America*, **108**, 8317–22.

Pitcher, T. J., Kalikoski, D., Short, K., Varkey, D., and Pramod, G. (2009). An evaluation of progress in implementing ecosystem-based management of fisheries in 33 countries. *Marine Policy*, **33**, 223–32.

Pollnac, R. B. and Christie, P. (2009). Introduction: scaling up to ecosystem-based management – case studies and comparative analysis. *Coastal Management*, **37**, 215–18.

Riegl, B., Bruckner, A., Coles, S. L., Renaud, P., and Dodge, R. E. (2009). Coral reefs: threats and conservation in a era of global change. *Annals of the New York Academy of Sciences*, **1162**, 136–86.

Roberts, C. M., Bohnsack, J. A., Gell, F. R., Hawkins, J. P., and Goodridge, R. (2001). Effects of marine reserves on adjacent fisheries. *Science*, **294**, 1920–3.

Roberts, C. M., Andelman, S., Branch, G., *et al.* (2003). Ecological criteria for evaluating candidate sites for marine reserves. *Ecological Applications*, **13**, S199–S214.

Ruckelshaus, M., Klinger, T., Knowlton, N., and Demaster, D. P. (2008). Marine ecosystem-based management in practice: scientific and governance challenges. *BioScience*, **58**, 53–63.

Shackeroff, J. M., Hazen, E. L., and Crowder, L. B. (2009). The oceans as peopled seascapes. In *Ecosystem-Based Management for the Oceans*, eds. K. L. McLeod and H. Leslie. Washington, DC: Island Press, pp. 33–54.

Shipman, B. and Stojanovic, T. (2007). Facts, fictions, and failures of integrated coastal zone management in Europe. *Coastal Management*, **35**, 375–98.

Spalding, M. D., Fish, L., and Wood, L. J. (2008). Toward representative protection of the world's coasts and oceans: progress, gaps, and opportunities. *Conservation Letters*, **1**, 217–26.

Stewart-Oaten, A. (2008). Chance and randomness in design versus model-based approaches to impact assessment: comments on Bulleri *et al.*, (2007). *Environmental Conservation*, **35**, 8–10.

Sumaila, U. R. and Walters, C. (2005). Intergenerational discounting: a new intuitive approach. *Ecological Economics*, **52**, 135–42.

Tallis, H., Levin, P. S., Ruckelshaus, M., *et al.* (2010). The many faces of ecosystem-based management: making the process work today in real places. *Marine Policy*, **34**, 340–8.

Vandermeer, J., Lawrence, D., Symstad, A., and Hobbie, S. (2002). Effect of bio-diversity on ecosystems functioning in managed ecosystems. In *Biodiversity and Ecosystem Functioning: Synthesis and Perspective*, eds. M. Loreau, S. Naeem, and P. Inchausti. Oxford, UK: Oxford University Press, pp. 209–20.

Vitousek, P. M., Aber, J. D., Howarth, R. W., *et al.* (1997). Human alteration of the global nitrogen cycle: sources and consequences. *Ecological Applications*, **7**, 737–50.

Waycott, M., Duarte, C. M., Carruthers, T. J. B., *et al.* (2009). Accelerating loss of seagrasses across the globe threatens coastal ecosystems. *Proceedings of the National Academy of Sciences of the United States of America*, **106**, 12 377–81.

Whitehead, J. C. (1993). Total economic values for coastal and marine wildlife: specification, validity, and valuation Issues. *Marine Resource Economics*, **8**, 119–32.

Wiber, M., Berkes, F., Charles, A., and Kearney, J. (2004). Participatory research supporting community-based fishery management. *Marine Policy*, **28**, 459–68.

Wood, L. J., Fish, L., Laughren, J., and Pauly, D. (2008). Assessing progress towards global marine protection targets: shortfalls in information and action. *Oryx*, **42**, 340–51.

Worm, B., Barbier, E. B., Beaumont, N., *et al.* (2006). Impacts of biodiversity loss on ocean ecosystem services. *Science*, **314**, 787–90.

Worm, B., Hilborn, R., Baum, J. K., *et al.* (2009). Rebuilding global fisheries. *Science*, **325**, 578–85.

Part II
Effects of marine protected areas

2 · ECOLOGY – *Ecological effects of marine protected areas: conservation, restoration, and functioning*

JOACHIM CLAUDET, PAOLO GUIDETTI,
DAVID MOUILLOT, NICK T. SHEARS, AND
FIORENZA MICHELI

2.1 Introduction

Human-induced disturbance, e.g., through unsustainable fishery activities, can affect the ecology of coastal areas (Jackson *et al.*, 2001; Lotze *et al.*, 2006) and reduce the associated goods and services required for human welfare (Worm *et al.*, 2006). Major concerns are rising over observed declines in the abundance of particular species as well as reductions in functional diversity and changes in food web structure (Pauly *et al.*, 1998; Micheli and Halpern, 2005; Villéger *et al.*, 2010). As a result, the conservation and restoration of marine biodiversity and functions is a major concern (Balmford *et al.*, 2005). Marine protected areas (MPAs) are recommended to promote the recovery of exploited populations and conserve or restore habitats, ecosystems, and biodiversity (Lubchenco *et al.*, 2003). Marine protected areas have also been recommended as tools for ecosystem-based management (EBM) of marine resources (Pauly *et al.*, 2002; Halpern *et al.*, 2010) and for restoration of ecosystem function (Mumby *et al.*, 2007; Mouillot *et al.*, 2008). However, some studies have failed to detect significant differences in ecological response variables between no-take and reference areas, or have criticized the design of existing studies, fuelling the view that the importance of MPAs as a management tool may have been overstated (Hilborn *et al.*, 2004; Murawski *et al.*, 2005; Osenberg *et al.*, 2006).

Marine Protected Areas: A Multidisciplinary Approach, ed. Joachim Claudet. Published by Cambridge University Press. © Cambridge University Press 2011.

Some attempts have been made recently to generalize the ecological effects of MPAs (Mosquera *et al.*, 2000; Côté *et al.*, 2001; Halpern, 2003; Micheli *et al.*, 2004; Guidetti and Sala, 2007; Claudet *et al.*, 2008; García-Charton *et al.*, 2008; Harmelin-Vivien *et al.*, 2008; Lester and Halpern, 2008; Lester *et al.*, 2009; Molloy *et al.*, 2009; Claudet *et al.*, 2010). However, ecological effects can vary both in direction and magnitude (Micheli *et al.*, 2004; Claudet *et al.*, 2008; Guidetti *et al.*, 2008; Lester *et al.*, 2009; Molloy *et al.*, 2009; Claudet *et al.*, 2010). This heterogeneity in response to protection may stem from differences in the design or age of MPAs, life histories of focal taxa, the socio-cultural context within which MPAs are established, or a combination of these effects.

The recovery of exploited species in marine reserves also can have a wide variety of indirect effects, which in some cases can lead to declines in other species (Micheli *et al.*, 2004). These declines occur via indirect effects that are typically mediated through trophic or competitive interactions between harvested species and other species that they interact with. Understanding the variety and complexity of such indirect effects is necessary to predict how populations of non-target species will be affected by protection, to understand how ecological processes change, and to evaluate whether marine reserves are achieving their conservation or restoration goals.

Here, we first summarize the direct ecological effects of MPAs on populations and present the factors affecting the direction and magnitude of MPAs' effectiveness. Then we review indirect effects of MPAs on assemblages, and show how MPAs can restore communities and degraded habitats. Finally, we illustrate that MPAs can enhance biological originality and functional diversity using data from a Mediterranean MPA. In each of the three sections, implications for management are discussed and recommendations are provided to guide future research. Throughout, we focus on MPA effects occurring within their boundaries. Ecological effects extending outside the MPA boundaries (e.g., spillover) are discussed in Chapter 3.

2.2 Populations conservation and restoration: direct effects of protection

2.2.1 Direct effects: theoretical insights

The anticipated direct ecological effects of MPAs on populations and habitats have been synthesized by Ward *et al.* (2001) (see Figure 7.1).

Following the cessation of fishing activities, fishing mortality is immediately eliminated and targeted individuals can live longer. In the short term, habitat quality is improved and fish densities and sizes are increased, leading in turn to increases in individual and spawning biomasses. In the medium to long term, the pre-harvested population structure in age and size should be re-established and the spawning activities increased, leading to several indirect ecological or fisheries-related effects (see Section 2.3 and Chapters 3 and 4).

Although some modeling studies have focused on all of these expected effects (e.g., see review in Gerber *et al.*, 2003), empirical studies have provided evidence for a subset of these anticipated effects (Hilborn *et al.*, 2004; Pelletier *et al.*, 2005; Sale *et al.*, 2005; Pelletier *et al.*, 2008).

2.2.2 Direct effects: empirical findings

2.2.2.1 Direct effects related to full protection

The observed direct ecological effects of marine reserves have been synthesized in several reviews and meta-analyses (Mosquera *et al.*, 2000; Côté *et al.*, 2001; Halpern, 2003; Micheli *et al.*, 2004; Guidetti and Sala, 2007; Claudet *et al.*, 2008; García-Charton *et al.*, 2008; Harmelin-Vivien *et al.*, 2008; Lester *et al.*, 2009; Molloy *et al.*, 2009). From these studies, it has been shown that reserves often lead to significant increases of fish density, size, biomass, and richness, mainly of commercial species.

Using a global database built from 124 marine reserves, Lester *et al.* (2009) showed average density and size increases of 166% and 28%, respectively, in reserves in comparison to surrounding fishing grounds. Biomass, being an aggregate of responses in density and size, showed the largest increase (446%). Such responses to full protection can be illustrated through individual size-specific changes over time in abundance of the Mediterranean rainbow wrasse, *Coris julis*, between a French Mediterranean reserve and the surrounding fishing grounds (Figure 2.1). In this area, this species is targeted by professional and recreational fisheries and for the aquarium trade.

Species richness was also found to respond positively to marine reserve establishments (Côté *et al.*, 2001; Halpern, 2003; Harmelin-Vivien *et al.*, 2008). In their global synthesis, Lester *et al.* (2009) showed an average species richness increase of 21% in reserves. However, in other meta-analyses, this positive response was statistically non-significant (e.g., Claudet *et al.*, 2008). Because of rarity, true species richness is often underestimated in studies with lower sample size. In ecological

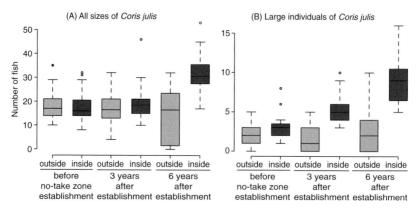

Figure 2.1 Fish individual size-specific increase in abundance across time after a no-take zone establishment. Boxplots ($n = 24$) of the abundances inside and outside a no-take zone and across time of (A) all sizes of *Coris julis* and (B) large individuals of *Coris julis* (i.e., individuals of size greater than 2/3 of species maximum size). In both cases, no inside/outside differences were found before the no-take zone establishment. Three years after protection, significant differences appeared only for large individuals (pair-wise comparisons; $p < 0.001$). Six years after protection, inside/outside differences increased for large individuals and were significant when considering all sizes combined of the populations ($p < 0.001$). Modified from Claudet et al. (2006).

assessments of MPAs, sample sizes outside the marine reserve are often greater than (and seldom less than) inside the reserve, therefore leading to possible underestimation of the effect of MPAs on species richness, unless rarefaction analyses are conducted. On the other hand, because densities often increase within reserves, a given sampling unit (e.g., transect) often represents more individuals within a reserve (all else being equal this will lead to an increased estimate of richness relative to outside). Studies of species richness need to better incorporate sampling considerations (e.g., rarefaction) in their analyses.

2.2.2.2 Direct effects related to partial protection

Partial protection provided by multiple use MPAs or by buffer zones surrounding no-take zones may, in some cases, confer the same benefits as full protection provided by no-take zones. Most of the time, however, such effects are much lower than in no-take zones (Lester and Halpern, 2008), if not non-existent (Di Franco *et al.*, 2009). Besides, big partially protected buffer zones, which may attract fishermen with a subsequent significant increase in fishing effort (Stelzenmüller *et al.*,

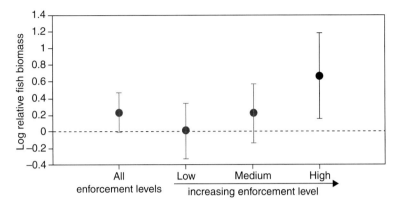

Figure 2.2 Role of enforcement levels on the ecological effectiveness of marine protected areas. Response ratios (and 95% confidence intervals) of fish biomass from inside to outside Italian MPAs. At the Italian regional level, no overall positive response in terms of biomass increase is detected in the system of MPAs ($n = 15$). The positive response existing in some well-enforced MPAs ($n = 3$) is masked by the poor effectiveness of MPAs with medium ($n = 6$) or low ($n = 6$) levels of enforcement. Modified from Guidetti *et al.* (2008).

2007), can have negative impacts on the overall ecological effectiveness of the MPA (Claudet *et al.*, 2008).

2.2.3 Heterogeneity and complexities: trajectories and correlates

The average magnitudes of ecological direct effects of MPAs reported above may be poor predictors for any single MPA as the response to protection may vary greatly, from local to regional and global scales. At a local scale, the biggest source of variation in the response to protection is driven by multi-scale differences in habitat (García-Charton and Pérez-Ruzafa, 1999; García-Charton *et al.*, 2004), leading to different pools of species assemblages within and/or outside the MPAs.

At a regional scale, the heterogeneity in the direct ecological response to protection between MPAs can be attributed, in part, to socio-cultural factors (Lundquist and Granek, 2005). It has clearly been demonstrated, both theoretically (Byers and Noonburg, 2007) and empirically (Guidetti *et al.*, 2008) that enforcement and compliance are fundamental aspects of effective MPAs (Figure 2.2). The social acceptance of the MPA by local human communities is a key factor for enforcement and ecological success of the MPAs (Christie, 2004).

(A) (B)

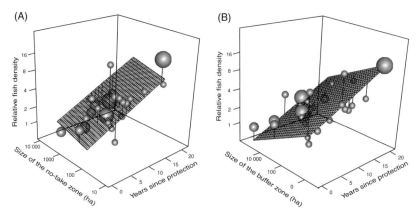

Figure 2.3. Role of age and design of marine protected areas on their ecological effectiveness. Relative commercial fish density in 12 European marine reserves as a function of years since protection and (A) the size of the no-take zone or (B) the size of the partially protected buffer zone. Planes give the fitted effect, the size of the spheres is proportional to the weight of each study, and the stems indicate the distance between the calculated weighted effect size and the fitted effect. For each year since protection, the mean relative density of commercial fishes increased by 8.3%. For every tenfold increase in the size of a no-take zone, there was a 35% increase in the density of commercial fishes. For every tenfold increase in the size of the partially protected buffer zone, there was a 31% decrease in density. Taken from Claudet *et al.* (2008).

Direct effects of marine reserves, especially those that increase with commercial fish density, typically require time to accrue (Micheli *et al.*, 2004; Claudet *et al.*, 2008; Molloy *et al.*, 2009). In some cases, those changes can be rapid (± 3 yr: e.g., Claudet *et al.*, 2006), but in many cases (e.g., for long-lived, slow-growing fishes, like groupers) the effects may take many years to accumulate (Russ and Alcala, 2004). Indirect effects on densities (e.g., trophic cascades from top predators) or changes in species composition may require even greater times to accrue (see Section 2.3).

The effectiveness of marine reserves is also linked to their design (Claudet *et al.*, 2008). Although small reserves can be effective (Halpern, 2003), increasing the size of a reserve increases the ratio of commercial fish density within the reserve relative to outside, whereas the size of the partially protected buffer zone has the opposite effect (Figure 2.3). Theoretical studies suggest that large reserves should be more effective for conservation than small reserves (Botsford *et al.*, 2001; Botsford *et al.*, 2003; Hastings and Botsford, 2003; Roberts *et al.*, 2003). However, syntheses and meta-analyses other than the one presented in Figure 2.3 have failed to find support for this hypothesis of reserve size dependency (Côté *et al.*, 2001; Halpern, 2003; Guidetti and Sala, 2007; Molloy *et al.*, 2009). This failure could arise because many syntheses of data combine studies across both temperate and tropical ecosystems, and heterogeneity among regions could obscure the reserve size effects (Claudet *et al.* [2008], but see Guidetti and Sala [2007]). Similarly, analytic schemes might also use inappropriate weighting schemes (Claudet *et al.*, 2008). A potential third explanation involves the interaction between two correlates of marine reserves effectiveness: size of the reserve and enforcement level. It is harder to maintain high levels of enforcement in big reserves than in small ones and, for a given socio-cultural context, poaching may therefore more likely occur in big marine reserves, thus reducing their effectiveness.

The life history and ecological traits of the protected species can also influence the effectiveness of MPAs (Mosquera *et al.*, 2000; Micheli *et al.*, 2004; Blyth-Skyrme *et al.*, 2006; Molloy *et al.*, 2009; Claudet *et al.*, 2010). For example, Claudet *et al.* (2010) showed that the effectiveness of reserves increased as the maximum body size of the targeted species increased and that it was greater for species that were not necessarily in schools (Figure 2.4). Non-commercial bycatch and unexploited species rarely responded to protection, and when they did (in the case of unexploited bentho-pelagic species), they exhibited the opposite response: their densities were lower inside reserves (Figure 2.4), suggesting an indirect response due to the increased density of their predators. In addition, contrary to previous theoretical findings, mobile species with wide home ranges benefited from protection. The effect of protection was at least as strong for mobile species as it was for sedentary ones (Figure 2.4). This was indirectly illustrated by Lester *et al.* (2009), who showed that temperate marine reserves, where most bentho-pelagic species tend to be more mobile than in tropical environments, performed as well as or better than marine reserves in the tropics.

Finally, the ecological effectiveness of MPAs can depend on human activities that occur outside the MPA, even when they are prohibited within the MPA. For example, overfishing of the spawning stock biomass in the surrounding fishing grounds may limit adult immigration or larval dispersal into the MPA, leading to smaller effects when stocks are more severely overfished (e.g., Lloret *et al.*, 2008). Stressors occurring outside the MPAs also can introduce a bias in the assessment of MPAs' effectiveness, as many conclusions drawn about the effectiveness of an

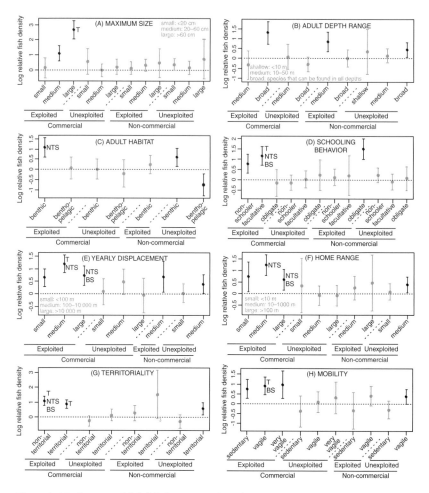

Figure 2.4 Influence of fish life history and ecological traits on the effectiveness of MPAs. Log relative fish density in 12 European MPAs (and 95% confidence intervals) for different ecological and commercial categories (commercial fishes were considered as: exploited [individuals with body size ≥33% of the maximum size of that species for that study locale] or unexploited [body size <33%]; non-commercial species were considered as: exploited [individuals of bycatch species with body size ≥33% of the maximum size of that species] or unexploited [all individuals of non-bycatch species and individuals of bycatch species with body size <33%]). Fishes differed in their response to protection depending on their maximum size, habitat preferences (i.e., habitat type and depth range), or schooling behavior. Not all the trait characteristics of the fish species responded positively to the time since enforcement (T) and the size of the no-take zones (NTS), or negatively to the size of the partially protected buffer zones (BS). Time of protection more strongly affected large species. The size of the no-take zone had strong positive effects especially on species that are non-territorial or have large home ranges. Increased sizes of partially protected buffer zones have negative effects on species with the highest level of displacements (i.e., non-territorial species with large home ranges). Modified from Claudet *et al.* (2010).

MPA depend on the state of the populations in these control locations. When looking only at relative differences between control and protected locations, one MPA could appear more effective than an other simply because its surrounding fishing grounds are more intensively fished. Quantifying the actual fishing pressure occurring outside an MPA, the potential spillover across MPA boundaries, as well as human behavior in control areas (e.g., displacement effects: Mascia *et al.*, 2003; Stelzenmüller *et al.*, 2008) is therefore essential for an appropriate assessment of MPA effectiveness (Claudet and Guidetti, 2010).

2.2.4 Implications for management

In light of the direct ecological effects of MPAs summarized above, we can say that MPAs are an effective tool to conserve marine resources, but that the effectiveness of MPAs varies considerably. This variability in effectiveness has several management implications.

First, enforcement and compliance are the most essential attributes of an effective MPA. Communities' involvement in the planning phases can increase the support for the reserve and therefore increase compliance (Lundquist and Granek, 2005). In addition, information activities and education could raise the recognition by stakeholders that MPAs benefit also to them and therefore also increase compliance (Pietri *et al.*, 2009). In this respect, success stories are important.

Second, although some MPAs may be effective quickly, most MPAs may initially appear ineffective. Therefore their effectiveness and its perception by local human communities should be framed in a temporal context.

Third, even if larger MPAs are more effective than smaller ones, it is not clear that larger MPAs are more desirable. Larger reserves require greater enforcement, and may impose higher displacement costs for fishers and greater hardship for other local stakeholders (Mascia and Claus, 2009).

Fourth, large partially protected buffer zones can have negative impacts on the overall MPA effectiveness but they are multiple-use areas designed for non-ecological purposes such as conflicts mediation or local incomes increase through the development of coastal uses (Chapter 9). The choice of their size is a complex problem involving ecology as well as economics and politics. However, if partially protected buffer zones are correctly managed and appropriate allocation and regulation of activities around MPAs are enforced, overall MPA effectiveness can be improved (Hilborn *et al.*, 2006; Guidetti and Claudet, 2010).

Fifth, the use of marine reserves as an EBM tool for marine conservation might lead to the perception that they should ensure protection for a wide range of species with different life history and ecological traits. This is not always the case, and instead effects vary with economic value, body size, habitat, depth range, and schooling behavior. These changes – or absence of changes – may reflect the restoration of assemblages towards more pristine communities (see Section 2.3).

Finally, because the effectiveness of an MPA depends on potential stressors acting outside its perimeter, MPA management should not focus only on the MPA but also should include activities outside the MPA. Fishing pressure outside reserves appears to be a particularly important factor affecting the effectiveness of reserves (Hilborn *et al.*, 2006; Baskett *et al.*, 2007). Similarly, it is critical to address other external factors affecting reserves, such as coastal development, invasive species, and climate change. These factors should be addressed when selecting the reserve location and through regulation of activities outside reserves once the reserve is established (e.g., Game *et al.*, 2008).

2.3 Communities and habitat restoration: indirect effects of protection

2.3.1 Predator–prey interactions and trophic cascades

2.3.1.1 Theoretical insights

Because fishing has historically targeted the higher trophic levels of marine food webs and many marine ecosystems are now dominated by lower-trophic-level species (Pauly *et al.*, 1998), many of the species that show the greatest increases within marine reserves are upper-trophic-level predators (see Section 2.2.3). This increase in predator abundance and size can have indirect effects that propagate through entire food webs and can influence the structure and dynamics of whole communities within marine reserves (Figure 2.5). Consequently, the simplest and most commonly described indirect effect of marine reserves involves a trophic cascade: i.e., the removal of human fishing leads to an increase in harvested predators and a decrease in their prey. As a result of these direct effects on prey, predators may indirectly influence entire communities through trophic cascades (Paine, 1980; Polis *et al.*, 2000; Witman and Dayton, 2001). Trophic cascades are classically defined as the indirect effects of apical species in the food web (e.g., carnivores) on basal species (e.g., primary producers) mediated by intermediate consumers

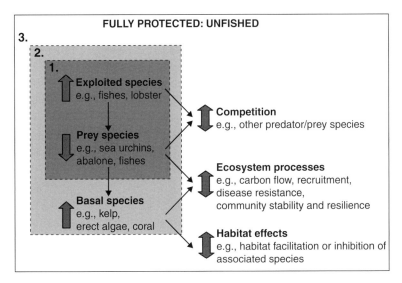

Figure 2.5 Indirect effects of marine reserve protection. Indirect effects of protection can be driven by different interaction types: predator–prey interactions (1); trophic cascades (2); or other population-, community- and ecosystem-level indirect effects (3).

(e.g., herbivores). A trophic cascade, therefore, is a top–down process capable of shaping the structure of entire communities (Babcock *et al.*, 1999), whenever changes in predator density, size, and behavior trigger a sequence of indirect effects throughout the food web, spanning at least three trophic levels. These indirect effects potentially explain a portion of the heterogeneity in species responses to protection.

Theoretical studies have explored how fishing pressure, species life history traits, and reserve design influence responses of individual species to marine reserves (reviewed by Guénette *et al.*, 1998; Gerber *et al.*, 2003). In contrast, relatively fewer models to date have focused on the possible indirect consequences of protection through species interactions (e.g., Gerber *et al.*, 2003). A review of recent models addressing species interactions in the context of marine reserves, combined with new extensions of these existing models, produced some general insights on the expected indirect effects of protection (Baskett *et al.*, 2007). Specifically: (1) larger reserves are needed to protect multispecies communities with strong interactions; (2) models including species interactions identify specialists, top predators, inferior competitors, and long-distance dispersers as most vulnerable to fishing impacts; (3) fishing pressure outside reserves is a key factor influencing multispecies interactions and responses; (4) species interactions, including positive interactions, tend to increase the temporal dynamics and time lags in responses.

2.3.1.2 Empirical findings

Several studies have showed that increased abundance and size of predators within marine reserves can reduce the density of prey species. For example, in New Zealand, small cryptobenthic fishes density was lower within marine reserves (Willis and Anderson, 2003), potentially due to increased predation by piscivorous fishes. In many temperate and tropical regions, predation rates on benthic invertebrates (especially sea urchins) are higher within marine reserves hosting more abundant and larger predators (fish or large invertebrates such as lobsters) than in fished areas. These great predation rates often lead to lower prey density within reserves (McClanahan and Muthiga, 1989; Shears and Babcock, 2003; Guidetti, 2006).

Some studies have illustrated that predator–prey interactions often cross ecosystem boundaries, connecting among habitats and ecosystems (Knight *et al.*, 2005). In New Zealand, protected sites with a significantly higher density of snappers and lobsters in reef habitats also had lower biomass of bivalves in adjacent soft-sediment habitats (Langlois *et al.*, 2005). This pattern was caused by foraging forays of predators from the reef onto the adjacent non-reef habitat (Langlois *et al.*, 2006).

Marine benthic systems seem to be more susceptible than other systems to trophic cascades (Polis *et al.*, 2000; Shurin *et al.*, 2002). In many regions of the world, trophic cascades induced by fishing have caused dramatic community changes and ecosystem shifts between alternate states. Such changes have been seen in the form of shifts from macroalgal forests to coralline barrens in temperate regions (Figure 2.6) (Sala *et al.*, 1998; Babcock *et al.*, 1999; Tegner and Dayton, 2000; Shears and Babcock, 2002; Behrens and Lafferty, 2004; Guidetti, 2006). In coral reef ecosystems, on the contrary, macroalgae tend to outcompete corals if grazing pressure is low (Bellwood *et al.*, 2004). The re-establishment of lost predatory interactions (Guidetti, 2006; Guidetti and Sala, 2007) or the maintenance of interactions unaffected by fisheries (Mumby *et al.*, 2006; Mumby *et al.*, 2007) within marine reserves can respectively help to reverse or avoid those shifts in the reserves.

Figure 2.6 Contrasting community states and habitat recovery following marine reserve protection and the recovery of sea urchin predators. In Mediterranean subtidal rocky reefs (A), after effective protection, erect macroalgal beds (left panel) succeeded coralline barren (right panel) (photos: P. Guidetti). In the Leigh marine reserve (B), New Zealand, subtidal rocky reefs dominated by brown macroalgae with abundant predatory snapper (*Pagrus auratus*) (left panel) (photo: N. Shears, 2006) succeeded large areas heavily grazed by sea urchins (*Evechinus chloroticus*) (right panel) (photo: R. Babcock, 1993).

2.3.2 Other interactions at the population, community, and ecosystem level

2.3.2.1 Theoretical insights

More recently, theoretical and empirical studies have started to address other types of interactions that are likely influenced by reserve establishment and may affect community structure and dynamics, including competitive, mutualistic, and host–parasite interactions, highlighting the potential for all these interaction types to affect the outcomes of protection for marine communities.

Regarding the potential of marine reserves to facilitate or hinder the establishment and spread of invasive species, it is hypothesized that maintenance of high species diversity may increase the resistance of local communities to invasions (e.g., Stachowicz *et al.*, 1999). Similarly, high abundance of potential predators or competitors of invasives may prevent their establishment in reserves (e.g., Whitfield *et al.*, 2007). Conversely, if reserves protect invasives from harvesting impacts, their abundances may increase in reserves, with possible negative indirect effects on natives through competitive or predatory interactions. Moreover, local reduction of native species abundance resulting from the concentration of displaced fishing effort, following reserve establishment, may facilitate regional spread of invasives even when these are inferior competitors (Kellner and Hastings, 2009).

Another type of indirect effect of reserves that has received relatively little attention until recently is the consequences of protection on host–parasite and host–pathogen interactions and host population and community dynamics. Fishing may reduce the density of hosts, especially large individuals (which tend to carry more parasites than small individuals), thereby negatively affecting parasite transmission rates and abundances. A review of the literature supports this hypothesis and indicates that fishing may be reducing the diversity and abundances of parasites in marine communities (Wood *et al.*, 2010). The consequences of such effects are unknown, though some authors have suggested that parasites may play important ecological roles in regulating natural populations and communities, transferring energy through food webs (Lafferty *et al.*, 2006; Kuris *et al.*, 2008), and indicating ecosystem health (Hudson *et al.*, 2006).

Review of the theory also highlights some important gaps. First, little is known on the implications of positive interactions for reserve effects. Second, the effects of habitat heterogeneity also need further study. Third, predictions from theoretical models are still largely untested and more work needs to relate theoretical hypotheses to empirical case studies (Baskett *et al.*, 2007; Kellner *et al.*, 2010).

2.3.2.2 Empirical findings

Few empirical studies have tested whether reserves facilitate or hinder the establishment and spread of invasive species (Simberloff, 2000; Byers, 2005; Klinger *et al.*, 2006; Kellner and Hastings, 2009). The scant empirical research addressing these hypotheses suggests that local facilitation of invasives can indeed occur, though no assessment exists of whether these local effects result in enhanced regional invasion. Abundances of non-native oysters (*Crassostrea gigas*) and algae (*Sargassum muticum*) were significantly greater in multiple marine reserves of the San Juan Archipelago (Washington, USA) compared to control locations, though the mechanisms underlying this pattern are unclear (Klinger *et al.*, 2006). Abundances of the non-native clam *Venerupis philippinarum* were also greater in reserves of the same region, whereas the native clam *Protothaca staminea* showed no significant benefit of the reserves (Byers, 2005). Experimental analyses indicated that shallower burial of *V. philippinarum* compared to *P. staminea* makes it more susceptible to crab predation and human harvesting, partially protecting *P. staminea* from these sources of mortality and maintaining high *P. staminea* abundances outside reserves. Although marine reserves strongly enhance the non-native clam, its increase did not affect native populations of its competitors. Negative impacts on *P. staminea* resulting from the increase of *V. philippinarum* are small and indirect, with crabs that track *V. philippinarum* abundance slightly affecting *P. staminea*'s growth and size-dependent fecundity. Thus, the few empirical studies available highlight that the effect of reserves on invasive species and their competitive interactions with native species are likely highly variable and dependent on harvesting patterns and the biological characteristics of species.

Studies of marine reserves support the generalization that fishing may indirectly affect parasites through effects on their hosts. A parasitic trematode was more abundant in intermediate hosts (intertidal mussels and the keyhole limpet *Fissurella crassa*) and a definitive host (the clingfish *Sicyases sanguineus*) in Chilean MPAs, containing greater host densities, than in fished areas (Loot *et al.*, 2005). Parasite species richness in the gobiid fish *Gobius bucchichii* was higher within the Cerbère–Banyuls French MPA, than at adjacent, unprotected sites (Sasal *et al.*, 1996). This effect was attributed to the greater size and older age of fishes in the MPA. Similarly, Bartoli *et al.* (2005) found a greater mean number of trematode parasite species per fish species within the Scandola Nature Reserve, in Corsica, France, than in unprotected areas with similar habitat characteristics. They attributed this difference to the greater diversity of potential hosts in the reserve.

However, effects of reserves on pathogens and parasites can be more complex. For example, Lafferty (2004) found that protecting lobsters (one of the main predators of sea urchins) in reserves caused urchin populations to decrease and released algae from overgrazing. This trophic cascade, while interesting in its own right, also led to changes in the dynamics of urchin disease. Outside reserves, urchin densities sometimes exceeded the density threshold for outbreaks of urchin-specific pathogens. As a result, dense urchin populations outside the reserves were more likely to experience epidemics that urchin populations inside the reserves. As a result, the pathogen acted as an important density-dependent mortality source at fished sites but not within reserves.

Changes in communities and biogenic habitats in marine reserves due to trophic cascades can have effects on other species that utilize these habitats (Figure 2.6). Due to strong associations between species and their habitats, large-scale changes in habitat can have major consequences for the communities that inhabit them (Graham, 2004). The large-scale changes in habitats observed in New Zealand's oldest marine reserve have been shown to have indirect effects on other species that were not directly involved in the trophic cascade (Shears and Babcock, 2003). In this case, one species of gastropod (*Cookia sulcata*) responded positively to habitat change (habitat facilitation), while another (*Cellana stellifera*) declined (habitat inhibition).

Trophic cascades can also lead to changes in overall benthic productivity and secondary production in marine reserves (Babcock *et al.*, 1999). Kelp is an important source of carbon in fueling benthic food webs on temperate reefs (Duggins *et al.*, 1989) and increases in kelp habitats in marine reserves has been shown to alter important ecosystem functions such as carbon flux. Salomon *et al.* (2008) found that kelp production was increased at reserve sites, and as a result filter feeders assimilated a higher proportion of kelp-derived organic carbon compared to adjacent fished sites.

2.3.3 Heterogeneity and complexities: trajectories and correlates

Although MPAs can induce community/ecosystem-wide changes within or around their boundaries, patterns and trajectories are not always consistent. The occurrence and strength of cascading effects is determined by several factors, acting in synergies or in isolation: the intensity and patterns of fishing outside reserves (e.g., whether and how fishing targets species at different trophic levels), the presence of size or habitat refuges for prey species, prey preferences of predators, predatory efficiency, the availability of alternative prey and size-mediated predator–prey relationship, species diversity, physical disturbances, and oceanographic features affecting recruitment of species (Shears *et al.*, 2008).

Indirect effects present some time lags with respect to direct effects. These time lags arise for two reasons: (1) indirect effects can take many years to occur (because they involve the response of intermediate species); and (2) they involve non-linearities (e.g., hysteresis and thresholds), which can lead to situations where large changes in one variable are needed before demonstrable changes in another can be seen. Therefore, reserves need to have been in place for sufficient periods to allow predators to reach these critical densities or size to mediate indirect effects. For example, in Tasmania the indirect effect of lobsters on urchins was not evident in the first 7 years during which *Heliocidaris erythrogramma* abundance was stable, but over the following 4 years urchin abundance declined by approximately 30% (Barrett *et al.*, 2009). This lag in response is most likely related to the time taken for lobster to increase in abundance in the reserve and to reach a size that is sufficient to consume adult urchins (120 mm C.L.: Pederson and Johnson, 2006). Similarly, in the Mediterranean, the relationship between predatory fish and sea urchins is non-linear and densities of fish need to reach a critical threshold in order to reduce urchins and drive a transition between urchin barrens and erect macroalgal assemblages (Guidetti and Sala, 2007).

Critical densities between lower trophic levels and behavioral modifications of prey species can further delay cascading indirect effects. In New Zealand, low numbers of urchins are required to maintain urchin barrens habitats and it took ~15 years to reduce urchins below a threshold density to allow macroalgal habitats to recover (Shears and Babcock, 2003). Furthermore, a switch in behavior where urchins became more cryptic in the presence of predators meant that urchins were able to persist at relatively high densities for an extended period despite high predator densities. Consequently, understanding how trophic interactions between species or trophic levels depends on density, size, and behavior is key to predicting the magnitude and timing of the indirect effects of marine reserves.

2.3.4 Implications for management

Indirect effects of protection lead to long-lived transient dynamics often occurring decades after reserve establishment (e.g., Shears and Babcock, 2003; Micheli *et al.*, 2004; Babcock *et al.*, 2010). In particular, a recent analysis of 16 years of monitoring data from Tasmanian marine reserves, complemented by additional data from 14 Australian reserves, indicated that cascading trophic interactions and subsequent feedbacks of habitat changes on communities continued to occur for two decades (Edgar *et al.*, 2009). These results highlight how most studies are inadequate for assessing the long-term consequences of reserves. It is important that monitoring and research programs be carried out for sufficient periods of time to detect indirect effects. This requires a long-term commitment from funding agencies, governing bodies, and researchers. Moreover, it is also important to recognize that old well-enforced marine reserves contain

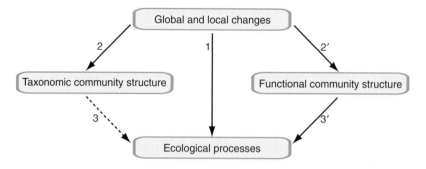

Figure 2.7 Relationships between global and local changes, ecological processes, and community structure. Some paths are widely known (1, 2, 3), with a strong (1, 2) or weak (3) relationship, while others have been overlooked (2′ and 3′).

communities and habitat features not represented within younger reserves (e.g., Stevenson *et al.*, 2007; Edgar *et al.*, 2009). Thus, a commitment to maintaining and managing reserves in the long term (several decades) is also necessary to better understand how natural marine ecosystems function, and how they are affected by human activities. Understanding how marine communities will respond to the recovery of exploited species inside marine reserves is also necessary to ensure that stakeholders have realistic expectations as to the ecological effects of marine reserves and that managers set appropriate goals for marine reserves.

As underlined here, much uncertainty remains as to the magnitudes and trajectories of indirect effects. It is critical that this uncertainty is acknowledged and possibly reduced through monitoring and research, particularly regarding possible indirect effects of protection on habitat, invasions, and parasites or pathogens.

2.4 Ecosystem functioning: do we protect species or function in marine protected areas?

2.4.1 Function restoration: theoretical insights

The relationships between local and global changes and between the structure of communities and ecological processes have attracted most of the attention of ecological and environmental scientists during the last two decades (Figure 2.7). In a world increasingly transformed by human activities (Chapter 1), there is a large body of evidence that ecological communities are deeply modified, sometimes irreversibly, and that ecological processes are disrupted (Figure 2.7, path 1) (e.g., Ludwig *et al.*, 2009). Global climatic shifts or local pressures on populations, such as fisheries, may erode the taxonomic biodiversity of communities (Figure 2.7, path 2) (e.g., Worm *et al.*, 2006). This loss of biodiversity is a critical issue for ecosystem services sustainability (Chapter 1).

Local species richness influences many ecological processes (Hooper *et al.*, 2005). Species richness also increases many beneficial properties of ecosystems such as productivity, resistance to invasion, stability, and resilience (e.g., Loreau *et al.*, 2001). However, species richness does not take into account abundance distribution and biological differences among species while these two facets of biodiversity are fundamental to explaining most ecological processes (Solan *et al.*, 2004; Hillebrand *et al.*, 2008). There is a growing consensus that the taxonomic composition of a community is less important than its functional structure (Figure 2.7, paths 3 and 3′) (e.g., Petchey *et al.*, 2004; Danovaro *et al.*, 2008; Reiss *et al.*, 2009). Hence, the effects of disturbance or restoration at the level of functional diversity – defined as the diversity of functions performed by organisms in a community – is of primary interest but still largely overlooked.

Recently, studies have suggested that increasing habitat degradations may decrease functional diversity (Figure 2.7, path 2′) (Ernst *et al.*, 2006; Flynn *et al.*, 2009; Villéger *et al.*, 2010), and remarkably few studies have evaluated functional recovery after habitat restoration (Figure 2.7, path 2′) (e.g., Micheli and Halpern, 2005). If functional diversity matters more than taxonomic diversity, then species that play relatively unique roles in communities should be of primary importance: i.e., they are not functionally redundant with other species and their loss should therefore have disproportionate effects on ecosystem properties (Figure 2.8). This question is critical because losing the most original species (*sensu* Pavoine *et al.*, 2005) results in losing some unique biological features such as life history traits, morphological attributes, or behaviors and the loss of a high amount of functional diversity (Figure 2.8). For instance only a few species of parrotfish, with particularly long and strong jaws, can substantially erode reef carbonate of dead corals (Bellwood and Choat, 1990). When these species are reduced by overfishing, the bioerosion of dead corals by fish decreases, which, in turn, may prevent new coral settlement on fragile or unstable foundations (Bellwood *et al.*, 2004). The absence of other species able to play the same role as bioeroding parrotfish (i.e., lack of redundancy) thus makes the preservation of these functionally original traits essential to the resilience of coral reef ecosystems. The

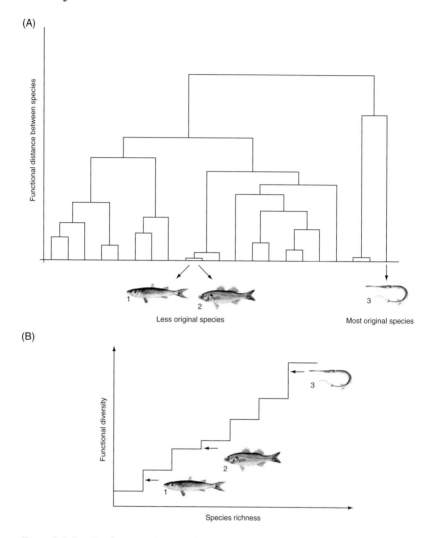

Figure 2.8 Species functional originality. (A) Location of the most original species (3) and the less original species (1 and 2) on a dendrogram based on functional distances between species. (B) Species 1, 2, and 3 contribute in different ways to the relationship between functional diversity and species richness. Each species contributes equally to species richness, but their contributions to functional diversity depend on their originality relative to the species already in the assemblages. As an illustration, the loss of the most original species (3) would substantially decrease functional diversity whereas the loss of species 2 would have a much smaller effect because a redundant species (1) is present in the assemblage.

crucial question is no longer whether MPAs protect and restore species richness but whether MPAs are able to protect and restore original species performing particular functions.

2.4.2 Function restoration: empirical findings

To test the effect of MPAs on the protection of biological originality and functional diversity, we used data from traditional artisanal fisheries in the Lavezzi Islands Reserve (LIR; 5050 ha; France, Mediterranean Sea). The LIR, predominantly characterized by rocky substrates and *Posidonia oceanica* beds at shallow depths, was created in 1982, and is now encompassed within the Bonifacio Strait Natural Reserve (80 000 ha), which was created in 1999 (Mouillot *et al.*, 1999; Mouillot *et al.*, 2002). Since its creation, the LIR has been fully protected from spearfishing and partially protected from other recreational fishing activities, although traditional trammel net fisheries are allowed. In 1999, protection was strengthened in the LIR with the full prohibition of longlines for tourists and with the creation of a 90-ha no-take zone embedded within its perimeter. All zones are well enforced by the MPA staff.

Data were collected from an artisanal fleet between April and September for two distinct periods of time, before and after the no-take zone establishment (1992–1993 and 2000–2003, respectively). For each species, 14 traits were measured on adult specimens, providing information on three niche dimensions: diet, prey capture mode, and position in the water column (Table 2.1) (Dumay *et al.*, 2004; Mouillot *et al.*, 2007). For each functional trait and for each species, we estimated a mean trait value from eight individuals on average. We then estimated the originality value for each species according to Pavoine *et al.* (2005) (Table 2.2).

We used a new conservation of biological originality (CBO) index to test the hypothesis whether biological originality was significantly protected in the LIR (see Mouillot *et al.* [2008] for more details). This index tends to be positive when the most original species increase in biomass over time, while it tends to be negative when biomass of the most original species decreases over time. In addition we calculated functional diversity using the Rao's quadratic entropy (Rao, 1982), proposed by Botta-Dukát (2005), which measures the mean functional distance between two randomly chosen individuals.

Although an increase of 25% in total fish biomass was observed after the reinforcement in the LIR, it was not evenly distributed among fish

Table 2.1 *Morphological parameters measured and their relevance for functional considerations*

Parameter	Functional interest
Biomass	The biomass of the fish indicates the size of the body, the energy content, and the impact on the food web
Caudal ratio	The length/height ratio of the caudal fin indicates fish propulsion (ambush or pursuit catching mode)
Eye diameter[a]	This parameter is linked to visual acuity
Eye position	Ratio of the distance between the bottom of the head to the eye's center to the head depth in line with the eye's center. Related to vertical habitat preferences (Mahon, 1984; Watson and Balon, 1984)
Oral gape height	The oral gape gives information on maximum prey size
Mouth protrusion length[a]	This parameter is related to prey catching mode (aspiration, ambush, or gulping)
Height of gill raker[a]	This reflects the capacity of fish species to filter plankton
Ratio of maximal body depth to standard length	Related to swimming ability through hydrodynamics (Gatz, 1979; Sibbing and Nagelkerke, 2001) and turning ability (Nikolski, 1933)
Ratio of maximal body depth to body width	Related to swimming ability through hydrodynamics (Gatz, 1979; Sibbing and Nagelkerke, 2001)
Caudal peduncle length[b]	Swimming speed and endurance (Holcik *et al.*, 1989)
Position of the mouth	Ratio of the distance between the extremity of the mouth and the bottom of the head to the head depth in line with the eye's center. Related to the prey catching mode
Orientation of the mouth	Method of food acquisition (Sibbing and Nagelkerke, 2001; Dumay *et al.*, 2004); this parameter is semi-quantitative: $-90°$ to $-45°$ (-3); $-45°$ to $-30°$ (-2); $-30°$ to $-10°$ (-1); $-10°$ to $10°$ (0); $10°$ to $30°$ (1); $30°$ to $45°$ (2); and $45°$ to $90°$ (3)
Teeth	Teeth were coded from 0 to 5 along a gradient of their utility in prey capture mode: (0) nothing, (1) cardiform, (2) viliform, (3) vomerine, (4) incisiform, and (5) caniniform
Gut length[b]	The gut length is directly linked to fish diet

[a] Parameters standardized by the biomass after using $\log(x+1)$ transformation.
[b] Parameters standardized by the standard length.

Table 2.2 *Originality values of the species observed in the samples. Species status can be winner (i.e., species with biomass increase over time; W; with a weight equal to 1) or loser (i.e., species with biomass decrease over time; L; with a weight equal to −1). The rank is given according to originality values which are provided on a continuous scale (no tied ranks needed)*

Species name	Species code	Originality (o_i)	Status	Weight (w_i)	Rank (r_i)
Seriola dumerili	Sdu	0.130		0.00	37
Raja miraletus	Rmi	0.121	W★★★	1.00	36
Zeus faber	Zfa	0.114	W★★★	1.00	35
Solea vulgaris	Svu	0.082	W★★	1.00	34
Scyliorhinus canicula	Sca	0.075	W★	1.00	33
Sphyraena sphyraena	Ssp	0.072		0.00	32
Uranoscopus scaber	Usc	0.069		0.00	31
Sarpa salpa	Ssa	0.047		0.00	30
Conger conger	Cco	0.031		0.00	29
Muraena helena	Mhe	0.031	W★★★	1.00	28
Mullus surmuletus	Msu	0.028	W★	1.00	27
Trigla lucerna	Tlu	0.028		0.00	26
Merluccius merluccius	Mme	0.024		0.00	25
Scorpaena scrofa	Ssco	0.022	W★	1.00	24
Phycis phycis	Pph	0.022	W★	1.00	23
Dentex dentex	Dde	0.012		0.00	22
Sparus aurata	Sau	0.012		0.00	21
Boops boops	Bbo	0.008		0.00	20
Oblada melanura	Ome	0.008		0.00	19
Epinephelus marginatus	Ema	0.007	W★	1.00	18
Sciaena umbra	Sum	0.007		0.00	17
Scorpaena porcus	Spo	0.006		0.00	16
Trachinus draco	Tdr	0.004	W★	1.00	15
Pagellus erythrinus	Per	0.004	W★★★	1.00	14
Pagellus acarne	Pac	0.004	W★★★	1.00	13
Spondyliosoma cantharus	Sca	0.004	W★★★	1.00	12
Spicara maena	Sma	0.004	L★★	−1.00	11
Serranus scriba	Ssi	0.004		0.00	10
Serranus cabrilla	Sca	0.004		0.00	9
Pagrus pagrus	Ppa	0.003		0.00	8
Diplodus vulgaris	Dvu	0.003		0.00	7
Diplodus annularis	Dan	0.003		0.00	6
Labrus merula	Lme	0.002	L★	−1.00	5
Diplodus puntazzo	Dpu	0.002		0.00	4
Diplodus sargus	Dsa	0.002		0.00	3
Symphodus tinca	Sti	0.002		0.00	2
Labrus viridis	Lvi	0.002	L★★★	−1.00	1

★ $p < 0.05$; ★★ $p < 0.01$; ★★★ $p < 0.001$.

species. Amongst the 37 species, 13 and 3 species were significantly identified as increasing versus decreasing, respectively, while biomasses of the 21 remaining species were statistically stable between the two periods (Table 2.2). The most original species were the greater amberjack *Seriola dumerili*, the brown ray *Raja miraletus*, and the John Dory *Zeus faber* (Table 2.2). Among the five most functionally original species, four increased significantly in abundance and presence within the reserve (the brown ray, the small-spotted catshark *Scyliorhinus canicula*, the common sole *Solea vulgaris*, and the John Dory). The three species that did not benefit from the reserve (the blotched picarel *Spicara maena* and the green and brown wrasses *Labrus viridis* and *Labrus merula*) were among the more functionally redundant species (i.e., they shared many traits with other coexisting species). The CBO index increased significantly between the two periods (Mouillot *et al.*, 2008). The functional diversity also increased after the LIR reinforcement. Some species were functionally redundant while others had a very uncommon combination of functional traits (Figure 2.9). Most species located on the boundaries of the functional space filled by the fish assemblages (i.e., the most functionally original species) benefited from the protection with an increase in both abundance and presence.

Thus, MPAs are able to increase other facets of biodiversity beyond species richness: they can significantly protect functional originality and diversity, by protecting functions performed by some functionally rare and irreplaceable species. Our example suggests that protecting the most original species is an insurance against functional diversity erosion and that MPAs can be used to sustain coastal goods and services derived from ecosystem functioning.

We propose two hypotheses to explain why most original species would benefit more from protection in MPAs than less original species. First, the number of species is limited by the number of niches available and a large spectrum of niches is needed to maintain or increase species richness. Indeed, according to niche theory, coexisting species are the best competitors in their own ecological niche and compete for alternative resources and different habitats. Thus, human impacts on coastal marine habitats may reduce fish species richness by removing niches (e.g., Guidetti *et al.*, 2002; Pihl *et al.*, 2006). At the opposite end, MPAs may protect or restore particular habitats which may offer more resources to the most functionally original species that have particular requirements to survive. For instance, the salema *Sarpa salpa* is strictly herbivorous and feeds mainly on *P. oceanica*. Its high degree of originality and

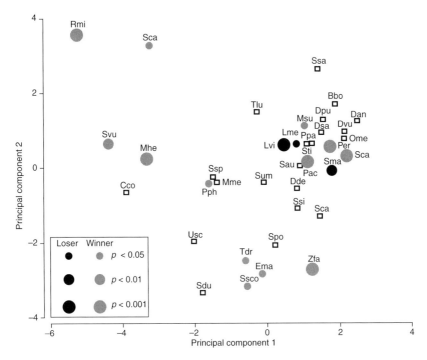

Figure 2.9 Functional relatedness among species with increases in biomass (winner) and species with decreases in biomass (loser) after establishment of a no-take marine reserve. Two-dimension functional plot of the 37 species collected in the case study, obtained through a principal component analysis of the species–functional traits matrix. The two first axes explain 48.9% of the total variation. See Table 2.2 for species code.

specialization (both are often linked since rarity of traits begets specialization: Devictor *et al.*, 2010) makes this species more sensitive to destruction or loss of this habitat. Hence, the occurrence and abundance of biologically original species would benefit from the protection or the restoration of habitats in MPAs.

Second, interspecific competition may be more intense among species with similar traits as they have the same resource and habitat requirements (MacArthur and Levins, 1967). If MPAs increase population densities then competition should increase after the establishment of a reserve (Gardmark *et al.*, 2006) and resource limitation (McClanahan and Kaunda-Arara, 1996). Because functionally original species have more unique niches (i.e., low overlap with other species) (Mouillot *et al.*, 2005), they may not incur the same increase in interspecific competition.

We rejected the first hypothesis on specialization to explain our findings because no major habitat alterations were reported before the no-take zone establishment and changes of regulations in the partially protected buffer zone. It is therefore more plausible that differences in competitive intensity explain why the most original species benefited from protection. The process of limiting similarity has been demonstrated for freshwater fish communities (Werner *et al.*, 1977) but is still debated (Grossman *et al.*, 1998; Peres-Neto, 2004; Mouillot *et al.*, 2007). Conversely, competitive interactions in open-sea waters, potentially leading to abundance compensation among the most similar species, are still lacking but our findings suggest that the most functionally original species can benefit from protection by avoiding increasing competition due to increased densities and biomasses.

2.4.3 Implications for management

Our approach has important application to the wider context of resilience-based management of ecosystems and restoration ecology. A challenging issue is to determine the ability of ecosystems to durably provide goods and services upon which human welfare depends. It is feared that pressures on ecosystems will become more intense and that alterations will be more frequent as a result of increasing human population density and associated unregulated human uses of natural resources. Thus, the question is no longer whether ecosystems will face more disturbances but whether they will be able to cope with these disturbances, i.e., whether they will be resilient. With this aim, developing new metrics that account for ecological processes underlying ecosystem dynamics is a priority for ecosystem management (Hughes *et al.*, 2005).

We therefore suggest relying on indices that include species traits to assess the effects of restoration management measures such as MPAs. Indeed, an emerging approach to conservation management highlights the need to take into account ecological roles and key processes undertaken by particular species (Bellwood *et al.*, 2006). The underlying idea is that the focus of conservation must shift from species with patrimonial or commercial values to species that support unique and essential processes and thus sustain ecosystem services. For instance, Bellwood *et al.* (2006) demonstrated that the reversal from a macroalgal-dominated to a coral- and epilithic algal-dominated ecosystem was surprisingly driven by a single batfish species (*Platax pinnatus*), while the 43 herbivorous fishes in the local fauna played only a minor role. This batfish has the ability to remove and ingest large amounts of macroalgae and no other herbivorous fish was able to provide the same function. Thus, the protection of batfish should be a conservation priority to prevent a reversal shift from a coral- to macroalgal-dominated state.

More generally, within the context of process-oriented management of ecosystems, functional originality and functional diversity certainly deserves more attention. Solan *et al.* (2004) demonstrated that the impact of species loss on ecosystem functioning is closely related to the covariation between species functional traits and their extinction risks. When species with particular traits go extinct first, we may expect greater ecosystem-level consequences following biodiversity loss. Again, this calls for a shift of perspective from conservation of targeted, emblematic, and patrimonial species to conservation of functional entities that support essential ecosystem services (although, in some cases, they might be the same).

2.5 Acknowledgments

We thank Craig W. Osenberg for useful comments on an earlier draft of the manuscript. DM was supported by a LITEAU III (PAMPA) and two ANR (GAIUS and AMPHORE) projects. FM thanks support from The Pew Charitable Trust and EPA STAR grant R832223.

References

Babcock, R. C., Kelly, S., Shears, N. T., Walker, J. W., and Willis, T. J. (1999). Changes in community structure in temperate marine reserves. *Marine Ecology Progress Series*, **189**, 125–34.

Babcock, R. C., Shears, N. T., Alcala, A. C., *et al.* (2010). Decadal trends in marine reserves reveal differential rates of change in direct and indirect effects. *Proceedings of the National Academy of Sciences of the United States of America*, **107**, 18 256–61.

Balmford, A., Bennun, L., ten Brink, B., *et al.* (2005). The Convention on Biological Diversity's 2010 target. *Science*, **307**, 212–13.

Barrett, N. S., Buxton, C. D., and Edgar, G. J. (2009). Changes in invertebrate and macroalgal populations in Tasmanian marine reserves in the decade following protection. *Journal of Experimental Marine Biology and Ecology*, **370**, 104–19.

Bartoli, P., Gibson, D. I., and Bray, R. A. (2005). Digenean species diversity in teleost fish from a nature reserve off Corsica, France (Western Mediterranean), and a comparison with other Mediterranean regions. *Journal of Natural History*, **39**, 47–70.

Baskett, M. L., Micheli, F., and Levin, S. A. (2007). Designing marine reserves for interacting species: insights from theory. *Biological Conservation*, **137**, 163–79.

Behrens, M. D. and Lafferty, K. D. (2004). Effects of marine reserves and urchin disease on southern Californian rocky reef communities. *Marine Ecology Progress Series*, **279**, 129–39.

Bellwood, D. R. and Choat, J. H. (1990). A functional-analysis of grazing in parrotfishes (family Scaridae): the ecological implications. *Environmental Biology of Fishes*, **28**, 189–214.

Bellwood, D. R., Hughes, T. P., Folke, C., and Nystrom, M. (2004). Confronting the coral reef crisis. *Nature*, **429**, 827–33.

Bellwood, D. R., Hughes, T. P., and Hoey, A. S. (2006). Sleeping functional group drives coral-reef recovery. *Current Biology*, **16**, 2434–9.

Blyth-Skyrme, R. E., Kaiser, M. J., Hiddink, J. G., Edwards-Jones, G., and Hart, P. J. B. (2006). Conservation benefits of temperate marine protected areas: variation among fish species. *Conservation Biology*, **20**, 811–20.

Botsford, L. W., Hastings, A., and Gaines, S. D. (2001). Dependence of sustainability on the configuration of marine reserves and larval dispersal distance. *Ecology Letters*, **4**, 144–50.

Botsford, L. W., Micheli, F., and Hastings, A. (2003). Principles for the design of marine reserves. *Ecological Applications*, **13**, S25–S31.

Bottá-Dukat, Z. (2005). Rao's quadratic entropy as a measure of functional diversity based on multiple traits. *Journal of Vegetation Science*, **16**, 533–40.

Byers, J. E. (2005). Marine reserves enhance abundance but not competitive impacts of a harvested nonindigenous species. *Ecology*, **86**, 487–500.

Byers, J. E. and Noonburg, E. G. (2007). Poaching, enforcement, and the efficacy of marine reserves. *Ecological Applications*, **17**, 1851–6.

Christie, P. (2004). Marine protected areas as biological successes and social failures in Southeast Asia. *American Fisheries Society Symposium*, **42**, 155–64.

Claudet, J. and Guidetti, P. (2010). Improving assessments of marine protected areas. *Aquatic Conservation: Marine and Freshwater Ecosystems*, **20**, 239–42.

Claudet, J., Pelletier, D., Jouvenel, J. Y., Bachet, F., and Galzin, R. (2006). Assessing the effects of marine protected area (MPA) on a reef fish assemblage in a northwestern Mediterranean marine reserve: identifying community-based indicators. *Biological Conservation*, **130**, 349–69.

Claudet, J., Osenberg, C. W., Benedetti-Cecchi, L., et al. (2008). Marine reserves: size and age do matter. *Ecology Letters*, **11**, 481–9.

Claudet, J., Osenberg, C. W., Domenici, P., et al. (2010). Marine reserves: fish life history and ecological traits matter. *Ecological Applications*, **20**, 830–9.

Côté, I. M., Mosqueira, I., and Reynolds, J. D. (2001). Effects of marine reserve characteristics on the protection of fish populations: a meta-analysis. *Journal of Fish Biology*, **59**, 178–89.

Danovaro, R., Gambi, C., Dell'Anno, A., et al. (2008). Exponential decline of deep-sea ecosystem functioning linked to benthic biodiversity loss. *Current Biology*, **18**, 1–8.

Devictor, V., Clavel, J., Juillard, R., et al. (2010). Towards a general framework for defining and measuring ecological specialization. *Journal of Applied Ecology*, **47**, 15–25.

Di Franco, A., Bussotti, S., Navone, A., Panzalis, P., and Guidetti, P. (2009). Evaluating effects of total and partial restrictions to fishing on Mediterranean rocky-reef fish assemblages. *Marine Ecology Progress Series*, **387**, 275–85.

Duggins, D. O., Simenstad, C. A., and Estes, J. A. (1989). Magnification of secondary production by kelp detritus in coastal marine ecosystems. *Science*, **245**, 170–3.

Dumay, O., Tari, P. S., Tomasini, J. A., and Mouillot, D. (2004). Functional groups of lagoon fish species in Languedoc Roussillon, southern France. *Journal of Fish Biology*, **64**, 970–83.

Edgar, G. J., Barrett, N. S., and Stuart-Smith, R. D. (2009). Exploited reefs protected from fishing transform over decades into conservation features otherwise absent from seascapes. *Ecological Applications*, **19**, 1967–74.

Ernst, R., Linsenmair, K. E., and Rodel, M. O. (2006). Diversity erosion beyond the species level: dramatic loss of functional diversity after selective logging in two tropical amphibian communities. *Biological Conservation*, **133**, 143–55.

Flynn, D. F. B., Gogol-Prokurat, M., Nogeire, T., *et al.* (2009). Loss of functional diversity under land use intensification across multiple taxa. *Ecology Letters*, **12**, 22–33.

Game, E. T., Watts, M. E., Wooldridge, S., and Possingham, H. P. (2008). Planning for persistence in marine reserves: a question of catastrophic importance. *Ecological Applications*, **18**, 670–80.

García-Charton, J.-A. and Pérez-Ruzafa, Á. (1999). Ecological heterogeneity and the evaluation of the effects of marine reserves. *Fisheries Research*, **42**, 1–20.

García-Charton, J.-A., Pérez-Ruzafa, Á., Sánchez-Jerez, P., *et al.* (2004). Multi-scale spatial heterogeneity, habitat structure, and the effect of marine reserves on Western Mediterranean rocky reef fish assemblages. *Marine Biology*, **144**, 161–82.

García-Charton, J. A., Pérez-Ruzafa, Á., Marcos, C., *et al* (2008). Effectiveness of European Atlanto-Mediterranean MPAs: do they accomplish the expected effects on populations, communities and ecosystems? *Journal for Nature Conservation*, **16**, 193–221.

Gardmark, A., Jonzen, N., and Mangel, M. (2006). Density-dependent body growth reduces the potential of marine reserves to enhance yields. *Journal of Applied Ecology*, **43**, 61–9.

Gatz, A. J. J. (1979). Ecological morphology of freshwater stream fishes. *Tulane Studies in Zoology and Botany*, **21**, 91–124.

Gerber, L. R., Botsford, L. W., Hastings, A., *et al.* (2003). Population models for marine reserve design: a retrospective and prospective synthesis. *Ecological Applications*, **13**, S47–S64.

Graham, M. H. (2004). Effects of local deforestation on the diversity and structure of Southern California giant kelp forest food webs. *Ecosystems*, **7**, 341–57.

Grossman, G. D., Ratajczak, R. E., Crawford, M., and Freeman, M. C. (1998). Assemblage organization in stream fishes: effects of environmental variation and interspecific interactions. *Ecological Monographs*, **68**, 395–420.

Guénette, S., Lauck, T., and Clark, C. (1998). Marine reserves: from Beverton and Holt to the present. *Reviews in Fish Biology and Fisheries*, **8**, 251–72.

Guidetti, P. (2006). Marine reserves reestablish lost predatory interactions and cause community changes in rocky reefs. *Ecological Applications*, **16**, 963–76.

Guidetti, P. and Claudet, J. (2010). Co-management practices enhance fisheries in marine protected areas. *Conservation Biology*, **24**, 312–18.

Guidetti, P. and Sala, E. (2007). Community-wide effects of marine reserves in the Mediterranean Sea. *Marine Ecology Progress Series*, **335**, 43–56.

Guidetti, P., Fanelli, G., Fraschetti, S., Terlizzi, A., and Boero, F. (2002). Coastal fish indicate human-induced changes in the Mediterranean littoral. *Marine Environmental Research*, **53**, 77–94.

Guidetti, P., Milazzo, M., Bussotti, S., *et al.* (2008). Italian marine reserve effectiveness: does enforcement matter? *Biological Conservation*, **141**, 699–709.

Halpern, B. S. (2003). The impact of marine reserves: do reserves work and does reserve size matter? *Ecological Applications*, **13**, S17–S37.

Halpern, B. S., Lester, S. E., and McLeod, E. (2010). Placing marine protected areas onto the ecosystem-based management seascape. *Proceedings of the National Academy of Sciences of the United States of America*, **107**, 18 312–17.

Harmelin-Vivien, M., Le Diréach, L., Bayle-Sempere, J., *et al.* (2008). Gradients of abundance and biomass across reserve boundaries in six Mediterranean marine protected areas: evidence of fish spillover? *Biological Conservation*, **141**, 1829–39.

Hastings, A. and Botsford, L. W. (2003). Comparing designs of marine reserves for fisheries and for biodiversity. *Ecological Applications*, **13**, S65–S70.

Hilborn, R., Stokes, K., Maguire, J.-J., *et al.* (2004). When can marine reserve improve fisheries management? *Ocean and Coastal Management*, **47**, 197–205.

Hilborn, R., Micheli, F., and De Leo, G. A. (2006). Integrating marine protected areas with catch regulation. *Canadian Journal of Fisheries and Aquatic Sciences*, **63**, 642–9.

Hillebrand, H., Bennett, D. M., and Cadotte, M. W. (2008). Consequences of dominance: a review of evenness effects on local and regional ecosystem processes. *Ecology*, **89**, 1510–20.

Holcik, J., Banarescu, P., and Diana, E. (1989). General introduction to fishes. In *The Freshwater Fishes of Europe: General Introduction to Fishes – Acipenseriformes*, vol. 1/2, ed. J. Holcik. Wiesbaden, Germany: Aula Verlag, pp. 19–59.

Hooper, D. U., Chapin, F. S. III, Ewel, J. J., *et al.* (2005). Effects of biodiversity on ecosystem functioning: a consensus of current knowledge. *Ecological Monographs*, **75**, 3–35.

Hudson, P. J., Dobson, A. P., and Lafferty, K. D. (2006). Is a healthy ecosystem one that is rich in parasites? *Trends in Ecology and Evolution*, **21**, 381–5.

Hughes, T. P., Bellwood, D. R., Folke, C., Steneck, R. S., and Wilson, J. (2005). New paradigms for supporting the resilience of marine ecosystems. *Trends in Ecology and Evolution*, **20**, 380–6.

Jackson, J. B. C., Kirby, M. X., Berger, W. H., (2001). Historical overfishing and the recent collapse of coastal ecosystems. *Science*, **293**, 629–37.

Kellner, J. B. and Hastings, A. (2009). A reserve paradox: introduced heterogeneity may increase regional invisibility. *Conservation Letters*, **2**, 115–22.

Kellner, J. B., Litvin, S. Y., Hastings, A., Micheli, F., and Mumby, P. J. (2010). Disentangling trophic interactions inside a Caribbean marine reserve. *Ecological Applications*, **20**, 1979–92.

Klinger, T., Padilla, D. K., and Britton-Simmons, K. (2006). Two invaders achieve higher densities in reserves. *Aquatic Conservation: Marine and Freshwater Ecosystems*, **16**, 301–11.

Knight, T. M., McCoy, M. W., Chase, J. M., McCoy, K. A., and Holt, R. D. (2005). Trophic cascades across ecosystems. *Nature*, **437**, 880–3.

Kuris, A. M., Hechinger, R. F., Shaw, J. C., *et al.* (2008). Ecosystem energetic implications of parasite and free-living biomass in three estuaries. *Nature*, **454**, 515–18.

Lafferty, K. D. (2004). Fishing for lobsters indirectly increases epidemics in sea urchins. *Ecological Applications*, **14**, 1566–73.

Lafferty, K. D., Dobson, A. P., and Kuris, A. M. (2006). Parasites dominate food web links. *Proceedings of the National Academy of Sciences of the United States of America*, **103**, 11211–16.

Langlois, T. J., Anderson, M. J., and Babcock, R. C., (2005). Reef-associated predators influence adjacent soft-sediment communities. *Ecology*, **86**, 1508–19.

Langlois, T. J., Anderson, M. J., Babcock, R. C., and Kato, S. (2006). Marine reserves demonstrate trophic interactions across habitats. *Oecologia*, **147**, 134–40.

Lester, S. E. and Halpern, B. S. (2008). Biological responses in marine no-take reserves versus partially protected areas. *Marine Ecology Progress Series*, **367**, 49–56.

Lester, S. E., Halpern, B. S., Grorud-Colvert, K., *et al.* (2009). Biological effects within no-take marine reserves: a global synthesis. *Marine Ecology Progress Series*, **384**, 33–46.

Lloret, J., Zaragoza, N. R., Caballero, D., *et al.* (2008). Spearfishing pressure on fish communities in rocky coastal habitats in a Mediterranean marine protected area. *Fisheries Research*, **94**, 84–91.

Loot, G., Aldana, M., and Navarrete, S. A. (2005). Effects of human exclusion on parasitism in intertidal food webs of central Chile. *Conservation Biology*, **19**, 203–12.

Loreau, M., Naeem, S., Inchausti, P., *et al.* (2001). Biodiversity and ecosystem functioning: current knowledge and future challenges. *Science*, **294**, 804–8.

Lotze, H. K., Lenihan, H. S., Bourque, B. J., *et al.* (2006). Depletion, degradation, and recovery potential of estuaries and coastal seas. *Science*, **312**, 1806–9.

Lubchenco, J., Palumbi, S. R., Gaines, S. D., and Andelman, S. (2003). Plugging a hole in the ocean: the emerging science of marine reserves. *Ecological Applications*, **13**, S3–S7.

Ludwig, W., Dumont, E., Meybeck, M., and Heussner, S. (2009). River discharges of water and nutrients to the Mediterranean and Black Sea: major drivers for ecosystem changes during past and future decades? *Progress in Oceanography*, **80**, 199–217.

Lundquist, C. J. and Granek, E. F. (2005). Strategies for successful marine conservation: integrating socioeconomic, political, and scientific factors. *Conservation Biology*, **19**, 1771–8.

MacArthur, R. and Levins, R. (1967). Limiting similarity convergence and divergence of coexisting species. *American Naturalist*, **101**, 377–87.

Mahon, R. (1984). Divergent structure in fish taxocenes of north temperate streams. *Canadian Journal of Fisheries and Aquatic Sciences*, **41**, 330–50.

Mascia, M. B. and Claus, C. A. (2009). A property rights approach to understanding human displacement from protected areas: the case of marine protected areas. *Conservation Biology*, **23**, 16–23.

Mascia, M. B., Brosius, J. P., Dobson, T. A., *et al.* (2003). Conservation and the social sciences. *Conservation Biology*, **17**, 649–50.

McClanahan, T. R. and Kaunda-Arara, B. (1996). Fishery recovery in a coral-reef marine park and its effect on the adjacent fishery. *Conservation Biology*, **10**, 1187–99.

McClanahan, T. R. and Muthiga, N. A. (1989). Patterns of predation on a sea-urchin, *Echinometra mathaei* (Deblainville), on Kenyan coral reefs. *Journal of Experimental Marine Biology and Ecology*, **126**, 77–94.

Micheli, F. and Halpern, B. S. (2005). Low functional redundancy in coastal marine assemblages. *Ecology Letters*, **8**, 391–400.

Micheli, F., Halpern, B. S., Botsford, L. W., and Warner, R. R. (2004). Trajectories and correlates of community change in no-take marine reserves. *Ecological Applications*, **14**, 1709–23.

Molloy, P. P., McLean, I. B., and Côté, I. M. (2009). Effects of marine reserve age on fish populations: a global meta-analysis. *Journal of Applied Ecology*, **46**, 743–51.

Mosquera, I., Côté, I. M., Jennings, S., and Reynolds, J. (2000). Conservation benefits of marine reserves for fish populations. *Animal Conservation*, **4**, 321–32.

Mouillot, D., Culioli, J.-M., LeprÃtre, A., and Tomasini, J.-A. (1999). Dispersion statistics and sample size estimates for three fish species (*Symphodus ocellatus*, *Serranus scriba* and *Diplodus annularis*) in the Lavezzi Islands Marine Reserve (South Corsica, Mediterranean Sea). *Marine Ecology*, **20**, 19–34.

Mouillot, D., Culioli, J.-M., and Do Chi, T. (2002). Indicator species analysis as a test of non-random distribution of species in the context of marine protected areas. *Environmental Conservation*, **29**, 385–90.

Mouillot, D., Stubbs, W., Faure, M., *et al.* (2005). Niche overlap estimates based on quantitative functional traits: a new family of non-parametric indices. *Oecologia*, **145**, 345–53.

Mouillot, D., Dumay, O., and Tomasini, J. A. (2007). Limiting similarity, niche filtering and functional diversity in coastal lagoon fish communities. *Estuarine, Coastal and Shelf Science*, **71**, 443–56.

Mouillot, D., Culioli, J. M., Pelletier, D., and Tomasini, J. A. (2008). Do we protect biological originality in protected areas? A new index and an application to the Bonifacio Strait Natural Reserve. *Biological Conservation*, **141**, 1569–80.

Mumby, P. J., Dahlgren, C. P., Harborne, A. R., *et al.* (2006). Fishing, trophic cascades, and the process of grazing on coral reefs. *Science*, **311**, 98–101.

Mumby, P. J., Harborne, A. R., Williams, J., *et al.* (2007). Trophic cascade facilitates coral recruitment in a marine reserve. *Proceedings of the National Academy of Sciences of the United States of America*, **104**, 8362–7.

Murawski, S. A., Wigley, S. E., Fogarty, M. J., Rago, P. J., and Mountain, D. G. (2005). Effort distribution and catch patterns adjacent to temperate MPAs. *ICES Journal of Marine Science*, **62**, 1150–67.

Nikolski, G. V. (1933). On the influence of the rate of flow on the fish fauna of the rivers of central Asia. *Journal of Animal Ecology*, **2**, 266–81.

Osenberg, C. W., Bolker, B. M., White, J. S. S., St. Mary, C. M., and Shima, J. S. (2006). Statistical issues and study design in ecological restorations: lessons learned from marine reserves. In *Foundations of Restoration Ecology*, eds. D. Falk, N. Palmer, and J. Zedler. Washington, DC: Island Press for Ecological Restoration International, pp. 280–302.

Paine, R. T. (1980). Food webs, linkage, interaction strength, and community infrastructure. *Journal of Animal Ecology*, **49**, 667–85.

Pauly, D., Christensen, V., Dalsgaard, J., Froese, R., and Torres, F. (1998). Fishing down marine food webs. *Science*, **279**, 860–3.

Pauly, D., Christensen, V., Guénette, S., *et al.* (2002). Towards sustainability in world fisheries. *Nature*, **418**, 689–95.

Pavoine, S., Ollier, S., and Dufour, A. B. (2005). Is the originality of a species measurable? *Ecology Letters*, **8**, 579–86.

Pederson, H. G. and Johnson, C. R. (2006). Predation of the sea urchin *Heliocidaris erythrogramma* by rock lobsters (*Jasus edwardsii*) in no-take marine reserves. *Journal of Experimental Marine Biology and Ecology*, **336**, 120–34.

Pelletier, D., García-Charton, J. A., Ferraris, J., *et al.* (2005). Designing indicators for assessing the effects of marine protected areas on coral reef ecosystems: a multidisciplinary standpoint. *Aquatic Living Resources*, **18**, 15–33.

Pelletier, D., Claudet, J., Ferraris, J., Benedetti-Cecchi, L., and GarcÃ-a-Charton, J. A. (2008). Models and indicators for assessing conservation and fisheries-related effects of Marine Protected Areas. *Canadian Journal of Fisheries and Aquatic Sciences*, **65**, 765–79.

Peres-Neto, P. R. (2004). Patterns in the co-occurrence of fish species in streams: the role of site suitability, morphology and phylogeny versus species interactions. *Oecologia*, **140**, 352–60.

Petchey, O. L., Hector, A., and Gaston, K. J. (2004). How do different measures of functional diversity perform? *Ecology*, **85**, 847–57.

Pietri, D., Christie, P., Pollnac, R. B., Diaz, R., and Sabonsolin, A. (2009). Information diffusion in two marine protected area networks in the Central Visayas region, Philippines. *Coastal Management*, **37**, 331–48.

Pihl, L., Baden, S., Kautsky, N., *et al.* (2006). Shift in fish assemblage structure due to loss of seagrass *Zostera marina* habitats in Sweden. *Estuarine, Coastal and Shelf Science*, **67**, 123–32.

Polis, G. A., Sears, A. L. W., Huxel, G. R., Strong, D. R., and Maron, J. (2000). When is a trophic cascade a trophic cascade? *Trends in Ecology and Evolution*, **15**, 473–5.

Rao, C. R. (1982). Diversity and dissimilarity coefficients: a unified approach. *Theoretical Population Biology*, **21**, 24–43.

Reiss, J., Bridle, J. R., Montoya, J. M., and Woodward, G. (2009). Emerging horizons in biodiversity and ecosystem functioning research. *Trends in Ecology and Evolution*, **24**, 205–14.

Roberts, C. M., Branch, G., Bustamante, R. H., *et al.* (2003). Application of ecological criteria in selecting marine reserves and developing reserve networks. *Ecological Applications*, **13**, S21–S28.

Russ, G. R. and Alcala, A. C. (2004). Marine reserves: long-term protection is required for full recovery of predatory fish populations. *Oecologia*, **138**, 622–7.

Sala, E., Boudouresque, C. F., and Harmelin-Vivien, M. (1998). Fishing, trophic cascades, and the structure of algal assemblages: evaluation of an old but untested paradigm. *Oikos*, **82**, 425–39.

Sale, P., Cowen, R., Danilowicz, B., *et al.* (2005). Critical science gaps impede use of no-take fishery reserves. *Trends in Ecology and Evolution*, **20**, 74–80.

Salomon, A. K., Shears, N. T., Langlois, T. J., and Babcock, R. C. (2008). Cascading effects of fishing can alter carbon flow through a temperate coastal ecosystem. *Ecological Applications*, **18**, 1874–87.

Sasal, P., Faliex, E., and Morand, S. (1996). Parasitism of *Gobius bucchichii* Steindachner, 1870 (Teleostei, Gobiidae) in protected and unprotected marine environments. *Journal of Wildlife Diseases*, **32**, 607–13.

Shears, N. T. and Babcock, R. C. (2002). Marine reserves demonstrate top-down control of community structure on temperate reefs. *Oecologia*, **132**, 131–42.

Shears, N. T. and Babcock, R. C. (2003). Continuing trophic cascade effects after 25 years of no-take marine reserve protection. *Marine Ecology Progress Series*, **246**, 1–16.

Shears, N. T., Babcock, R. C., and Salomon, A. K. (2008). Context-dependent effects of fishing: variation in trophic cascades across environmental gradients. *Ecological Applications*, **18**, 1860–73.

Shurin, J. B., Borer, E. T., Seabloom, E. W., *et al.* (2002). A cross-ecosystem comparison of the strength of trophic cascades. *Ecology Letters*, **5**, 785–91.

Sibbing, F. A. and Nagelkerke, L. A. J. (2001). Resource partitioning by Lake Tana barbs predicted from fish morphometrics and prey characteristics. *Reviews in Fish Biology and Fisheries*, **10**, 393–437.

Simberloff, D. (2000). No reserve is an island: marine reserves and nonindigenous species. *Bulletin of Marine Science*, **66**, 567–80.

Solan, M., Cardinale, B. J., Downing, A. L., *et al.* (2004). Extinction and ecosystem function in the marine benthos. *Science*, **306**, 1177–80.

Stachowicz, J. J., Whitlatch, R. B., and Osman, R. W. (1999). Species diversity and invasion resistance in a marine ecosystem. *Science*, **286**, 1577–9.

Stelzenmüller, V., Maynou, F., and Martin, P. (2007). Spatial assessment of benefits of a coastal Mediterranean Marine Protected Area. *Biological Conservation*, **136**, 571–83.

Stelzenmüller, V., Maynou, F., Bernard, G., *et al.* (2008). Spatial assessment of fishing effort around European marine reserves: implications for successful fisheries management. *Marine Pollution Bulletin*, **56**, 2018–26.

Stevenson, C., Katz, L. S., Micheli, F., *et al.* (2007). High apex predator biomass on remote Pacific islands. *Coral Reefs*, **26**, 47–51.

Tegner, M. J. and Dayton, P. K. (2000). Ecosystem effects of fishing in kelp forest communities. *ICES Journal of Marine Science*, **57**, 579–89.

Villéger, S., Miranda, J. R., Hernández, D. F., and Mouillot, D. (2010). Contrasting changes in taxonomic vs. functional diversity of tropical fish communities after habitat degradation. *Ecological Applications*, **20**, 1512–22.

Ward, T. J., Heinemann, D., and Evans, N. (2001). *The Role of Marine Reserves as Fisheries Management Tools: A Review of Concepts, Evidence and International Experience*. Canberra, ACT: Bureau of Rural Sciences.

Watson, D. J. and Balon, E. K. (1984). Ecomorphological analysis of fish taxocenes in rainforest streams of northern Borneo. *Journal of Fish Biology*, **25**, 371–84.

Werner, E. E., Hall, D. J., Laughlin, D. R., *et al.* (1977). Habitat partitioning in a freshwater community. *Journal of the Fisheries Research Board of Canada*, **34**, 360–70.

Whitfield, P. E., Hare, J. A., David, A. W., *et al.* (2007). Abundance estimates of the Pacific lionfish *Pterois volitans/miles* complex in the Western North Atlantic. *Biological Invasions*, **9**, 53–64.

Willis, T. J. and Anderson, M. J. (2003). Structure of cryptic reef fish assemblages: relationships with habitat characteristics and predator density. *Marine Ecology Progress Series*, **257**, 209–21.

Witman, J. D. and Dayton, P. K. (2001). Rocky subtidal communities. In *Marine Community Ecology*, eds. M. D. Bertness, S. Gaines, and M. Hay. Sunderland, MA: Sinauer Associates, pp. 339–66.

Wood, C. L., Lafferty, K. D., and Micheli, F. (2010). Fishing out marine parasites? Impacts of fishing on rates of parasitism in the ocean. *Ecology Letters*, **13**, 761–75.

Worm, B., Barbier, E. B., Beaumont, N., *et al.* (2006). Impacts of biodiversity loss on ocean ecosystem services. *Science*, **314**, 787–90.

3 · FISHERIES – Effects of marine protected areas on local fisheries: evidence from empirical studies

RAQUEL GOÑI, FABIO BADALAMENTI, AND MARK H. TUPPER

3.1 Marine protected areas for fisheries

Marine fisheries throughout the world are in serious decline due to over-harvesting (National Research Council, 2001), and management for sustainable fisheries requires effective tactics for limiting exploitation rates. Limitations based on annual stock assessments and total allowable catches calculated from these assessments can be dangerous, and marine protected areas (MPAs) are one tool to limit exploitation rates directly even when total stock size is highly uncertain (Walters, 2000). Contrary to other management strategies usually involving a suite of regulations (e.g., gear and vessel restrictions, minimum sizes, catch and effort limits, prohibited species), MPAs are easier to enforce and can be more easily understood by the public and the fishing industry (Guidetti and Claudet, 2010). Within a fisheries management context the main expected outcome of MPAs is yield enhancement, but MPAs also hold the potential to reduce impacts of fishing on marine ecosystems and to establish undisturbed, reference locations for scientific studies (Fogarty *et al.*, 2000). However, creating an MPA reduces the area that can be fished, thus potentially reducing yield. The question is therefore whether the yield in the area remaining open will increase enough to offset losses from the closed area (Hilborn *et al.*, 2004; Jones, 2008; see also Chapter 4), and whether the displaced fishing effort reduces the sustainability of remaining fishing grounds (Hilborn *et al.*, 2004). These concerns would be lessened if total catch was reduced

Marine Protected Areas: A Multidisciplinary Approach, ed. Joachim Claudet. Published by Cambridge University Press. © Cambridge University Press 2011.

by a percentage equivalent to the habitat protected within MPAs (Parrish, 1999).

During recent years there has been a proliferation of studies assessing the efficacy of MPAs in rebuilding exploited populations within their boundaries. Most of them document increases in target species abundance, biomass, individual size, and egg production following the reduction or cessation of fishing (see reviews by Fogarty *et al.*, 2000; Sánchez-Lizaso *et al.*, 2000; National Research Council, 2001; Russ, 2002; Claudet *et al.*, 2008; Molloy *et al.*, 2009; Claudet *et al.*, 2010; see also Chapter 2). However, while there is general agreement about the potential of MPAs as conservation tools, attention to their effects on fisheries has grown particularly controversial (Hilborn *et al.*, 2004). Controversy is nurtured by the above-mentioned concerns of loss of fishing grounds and impacts of effort displacement, although the scarcity of empirical studies rigorously evaluating such effects is also slowing down progress in the research and implementation of MPAs with fishery management objectives (Russ, 2002; Willis *et al.*, 2003a; Hilborn, 2006; see also Chapter 7).

Contributions that may shed light on this issue come from empirical and theoretical studies. Empirical studies generally evaluate the potential fishery effects of spillover (i.e., net export of juveniles and adults: Russ, 2002) from MPAs to adjacent fished areas. Such studies usually collect data from onboard sampling of fisheries catch and effort or landings, experimental fishing, or tag–recapture experiments. Theoretical modeling studies simulate fishery effects of MPAs under different scenarios of MPA configuration, recruitment, connectivity, patterns of adult mobility, and exploitation rates (e.g. Polacheck, 1990; DeMartini, 1993; Acosta, 2002; Walters *et al.*, 2007; Moffitt *et al.*, 2009, to name some that account for movement dynamics; see also the review by Pelletier and Mahevas, 2005 and Chapter 4).

Many difficulties plague empirical studies. In particular, MPAs are commonly too small and too few to affect fisheries in ways that are detectable at the management scale (Russ, 2002). Hence, empirical studies focus on small-scale effects on local fisheries. Model-based studies do not have such constraints but rely on many assumptions and may lead to unrealistic or conflicting conclusions (e.g., Willis *et al.*, 2003a). Furthermore, most published models are neither fitted nor calibrated from real data and thus it is not possible to assess their relevance in real situations (Pelletier *et al.*, 2008). In contrast with the wealth of modeling studies and reviews about the potential applications of MPAs for fisheries, there is a paucity of empirical studies assessing those effects (Russ, 2002; Pelletier *et al.*, 2008). This has been aleviated in recent years by both growing research efforts and sufficient time for those effects to develop in MPAs.

This chapter reviews and assesses current empirical evidence of MPA effects on fisheries. First, we briefly describe the mechanisms by which MPAs may affect fisheries. Second, we synthesize empirical evidence of those effects, essentially transfer of exploitable biomass from MPAs to fished areas and ensuing changes in catch and effort patterns. Lastly, we discuss this evidence, highlighting the strengths and weaknesses of MPAs for fisheries management based on current empirical knowledge.

3.2 Mechanisms of effects of marine protected area on fisheries

MPAs may affect fisheries if: (1) fishing mortality has been eliminated (i.e., no-take areas) or substantially reduced (e.g. gear-exclusion MPAs); and (2) if fishery restrictions are effectively enforced, and are permanent or have lasted long enough to have developed observable recovery of the exploited species within their boundaries. Recovery in this context means increase in biomass and numbers of individuals when fishing mortality is reduced (Jennings, 2001). Although recovery should ideally be assessed from historical levels, most empirical studies lack baseline data. Well-protected MPAs can then contribute to enhance or sustain nearby fisheries through biomass and egg and larval export.

3.2.1 Biomass export

It is well established that biomass of exploited species is generally higher within well-protected MPAs than on adjacent fished areas (see references above). The ideal free distribution predicts that animals should prefer to move towards areas where density is low relative to available resources if this is beneficial to their fitness (Fretwell and Lucas, 1970). Hence, increases in density of exploited species within MPAs could result in enhancement of yields in neighboring fisheries through density-dependent emigration (Tupper and Juanes 1999; Sánchez-Lizaso *et al.*, 2000; Zeller *et al.*, 2003; Abesamis and Russ, 2005), provided species can move and habitats are continuous. Additionally, random movements (Dugan and Davis, 1993; Rakitin and Kramer, 1996), ontogenetic habitat shifts (Gitschlag, 1986; Tupper, 2007), or migration to foraging or spawning areas (Kelly *et al.*, 2002; Rhodes and Tupper, 2008) from MPAs could enhance yields in adjacent grounds. Although empirical support for yield enhancement at the stock or fisheries management scale is non-existent, evidence of enhancement at the local scale is growing, as shown below.

3.2.2 Egg and larvae export

Because MPAs can increase the reproductive output of target populations, increased recruitment from egg and larval export is anticipated to produce even larger benefits for fisheries than spillover of adults (Jennings, 2001; Russ, 2002; Moffitt et al., 2009). However, such a recruitment effect is hard to detect due to the high spatial and temporal variability of larval survival and settlement, as well as the large area over which it can occur (Botsford et al., 2009). This has hampered research, and few empirical studies have addressed the recruitment effects of MPAs. One example is Tilney et al. (1996) who combined ichthyoplankton sampling and current measurements to show that larvae of commercial Sparidae fishes protected in a South African MPA were exported to adjacent exploited areas. However, along with other similar studies, the location and contribution of those larvae to effective recruitment to fished populations was not determined. Recently, Pelc et al. (2009) observed that the density of recruits of an exploited sessile mollusk declined with distance to the boundaries of two MPAs in South Africa. Their results indicated for the first time that larval export can be detected above natural variability of recruitment and that it can enhance recruitment in fished areas up to several kilometers. New methods for individual identification techniques such as larval tagging or parentage analysis have provided new information on self-sustainability or connectivity among MPAs (Jones et al., 2009). Using DNA parentage analysis, Planes et al. (2009) demonstrated that within a MPA network, 10% of the recruitment in the peripheral MPAs originated from spawners within a small, centrally located MPA. However, the ability of different genetic techniques to identify natal origins in marine species depends critically upon the levels of genetic structure within and among focal populations and the degree of sampling of potential parents (Saenz-Agudelo et al., 2009). At present, and despite their intuitiveness, empirical evidence of such egg and larval export effects on fisheries remains non-existent and most research is currently focused on unraveling larval dispersal and population connectivity patterns (Jones et al., 2009; Chapter 12). For this reason, we do not cover larval export in this chapter and refer the reader to the reviews of recruitment effects of MPAs by Planes *et al.* (2000), and of the latest developments in the field of dispersal and connectivity in the context of MPA design by Jones *et al.* (2009), Bostford *et al.* (2009), and Almany *et al.* (2009).

3.3 Evidence of fisheries effects of marine protected areas

Direct evidence of spillover is given by any positive value of the net transfer of exploitable individuals from the MPA to the fished areas (Russ, 2002). Spillover effects may also be evidenced by spatial or temporal changes in catch and effort patterns in fisheries near MPAs. To evaluate the evidence of spillover on adjacent fisheries in this chapter we have selected studies for which there is evidence of recovery of biomass of the studied species within the MPA boundaries. Design factors – such as habitat type or heterogeneity – are considered only in reference to their potential effects on spillover (e.g., boundary permeability) but not on the overall effectiveness of MPAs to rebuild or sustain greater biomass within their boundaries. For MPAs explicitly created to rebuild the biomass of particular species or groups of species within their boundaries, the biomass rebuilding itself is the fisheries effect assessed. The search for empirical studies focused on the best-studied marine ecosystems and where most existing MPAs are sited: (1) tropical reefs; (2) temperate reefs; and (3) temperate soft-bottom areas.

The search yielded 41 studies, 10 in tropical reefs (Table 3.1), 17 in temperate reefs (Table 3.2), and 17 in temperate soft-bottom MPAs (Table 3.3), the latter being towed-gear-exclusion areas. Although not meant to be exhaustive, this review covers the majority of relevant studies and provides a comprehensive overview of the types of empirical evidence of fisheries effects of MPAs currently available (see Tables 3.1, 3.2, and 3.3). The reef MPAs reviewed are either no-take zones closed to all extractive activities or, more generally, MPAs that contain no-take and buffer zones; in buffer zones some artisanal or recreational fishing may be allowed. Hence, the fisheries studied were commercial or subsistence fisheries adjacent to no-take areas or to buffer areas that did not allow those fisheries. The effects of towed-gear-exclusion MPAs are generally evaluated by means of experimental fishing to assess biomass rebuilding, although in some cases effects of spillover have also been evidenced from commercial fishery data (see Section 3.1). The literature search on peer-reviewed studies in this category excluded those not fully protected against the impact of heavy fishing activities such as small trawlers

Table 3.1 *Coral reef ecosystems: observed effects of marine protected areas on fisheries from empirical studies*

Effect	Observation		Species/group (Reference)
Spillover effect	YES	Limited evidence (only 1 of 3 species) for spillover of tagged fish biomass from MPAs to open areas	Hogfish (Tupper and Rudd, 2002)
		Limited spillover of several exploited species	Exploited reef fish assemblage (Kaunda-Arara and Rose, 2004)
			Exploited reef fish assemblage (Francini-Filho and Moura, 2008)
		Net transfer from MPA to fished area due to ontogenetic migration	Lobster (Davis and Dodrill, 1989)
Increased CPUE near MPA	YES	Declining gradient of CPUE with increasing distance from MPA	Unicornfish (Abesamis and Russ, 2005)
			Exploited reef fish assemblage (Abesamis *et al.*, 2006)
			Exploited reef fish assemblage (McClanahan and Kaunda-Arara, 1996)
			Exploited reef fish assemblage (McClanahan and Mangi, 2000)
			Exploited reef fish assemblage (Rakitin and Kramer, 1996)
			Hogfish (Tupper and Rudd 2002)
	NO	No relationship between CPUE and distance from MPA	Nassau grouper and white margate (Tupper and Rudd, 2002)
Increased yields (total catch or catch per gear type) near MPA	YES	Higher trap, gillnet, and total catches near MPA	Exploited reef fish assemblage (Alcala *et al.*, 2005; Abesamis *et al.*, 2006)
		46% increase in total large trap catches and 90% increase in total small trap catches	Exploited reef fish assemblage (Roberts *et al.*, 2001)
	NO	Lower total catches since implementation of MPA	Exploited reef fish assemblage (McClanahan and Kaunda-Arara, 1996)
Increased seasonal variability of catch rates near MPA	YES	Greater variability of CPUE near MPA than farther away	Exploited reef fish assemblage (Abesamis *et al.*, 2006)

(cont.)

Table 3.1 (*cont.*)

Effect		Observation	Species/group (Reference)
Increased mean size of target species in adjacent exploited areas	YES	Declining gradient of mean size with increasing distance from MPA	Unicornfish (Abesamis and Russ, 2005)
	NO	Equal or smaller size of target commercial species	Exploited reef fish assemblage (Abesamis *et al.*, 2006)
		Steeper biomass size spectra in protected vs. unprotected areas	
Effort concentration near MPA boundaries	YES	Effort aggregates near MPA boundaries because of greater catch or value of catch	Exploited reef fish assemblage (McClanahan and Mangi, 2000)
	NO	Effort is dispersed to other areas because of high seasonal variability in fish availability	Exploited reef fish assemblage (Abesamis *et al.*, 2006)

CPUE, catch per unit effort.

(e.g., plaice box: Piet and Rijnsdorp, 1998). In reef MPAs, fishes and lobsters are the main focus of study, although a few examine effects on multispecies catches. Effects on mollusk and crab fisheries are addressed solely in soft-bottom towed-gear-exclusion MPAs.

3.3.1 Effects on adjacent fisheries

3.3.1.1 Direct evidence of spillover

Direct measures of fish movement across MPA boundaries are done by conventional tag-and-release studies, with recaptures coming either from the fishery or from experimental fishing (e.g., Rakitin and Kramer, 1996; Rowe, 2001; Kaunda-Arara and Rose, 2004), and by sonic tracking studies (e.g., Holland *et al.*, 1996; Zeller and Russ, 1998; Wetherbee *et al.*, 2004; Meyer and Holland, 2005; Rhodes and Tupper, 2008). However, net emigration of exploitable individuals from MPAs to fished areas has been demonstrated in only a handful of cases for lobsters and reef fish, or surmised from spatiotemporal patterns of fishery recaptures (Tables 3.1 and 3.2). Spillover studies from tag–recapture experiments in coral reef

Table 3.2 *Temperate reef ecosystems: observed effects of marine protected areas on fisheries from empirical studies*

Effect		Observation	Species/Group (Reference)
Spillover effect	YES	Mean annual emigration rates 4.2% and 0.8% in 2 MPAs (depending on density difference between MPAs and unfished areas)	Lobster (Rowe, 2001)
		Declining tags/unit effort and proportion tagged in fishery catches with distance from MPA (up to 1.5 km)	Lobster (Goñi et al., 2006)
		Mean annual emigration rate 6% (years 8–17); immigration assumed negligible	Lobster (Goñi et al., 2010)
		Emigration rate of 0.18–0.40/year depending on proportion of resident vs. nomadic morphs; immigration assumed negligible	Galjoen (Coracinidae fish) (Attwood and Bennett, 1994)
Contribution of spillover to catch	YES	Mean net contribution of spillover to annual commercial catch in weight = 11% (years 8–17 of protection)	Lobster (Goñi et al., 2010)
	NO	Effort does not aggregate around MPA because of high cost of traveling and low exploitation near ports	Multispecies reef fish (Wilcox and Pomeroy, 2003)
		Pattern of effort aggregation likley due to habitat distribution, rather than spillover	Multispecies reef fish (2 MPAs: Goñi et al., 2008)
Increased CPUE near MPA	YES	Declining gradient of CPUE with distance from MPA (up to 2 km)	Lobster (Goñi et al., 2006) Sparid fish (Millar and Willis, 1999)
		Highest daily CPUE near MPA. Mean CPUE near MPA similar to farther grounds despite effort concentration	Lobster (Kelly et al., 2002)
		CPUE near MPA increasing over the period of 8–16 years of protection	Multispecies reef fish (Stobart et al., 2009)
		Experimental CPUE in MPA increasing towards the MPA centre	Lobster (Davidson et al., 2002)
		Yields near MPA (0.5 km) higher than farther away (1 km)	Seagrass and reef fish (2 MPAs: Forcada et al., 2009)
	NO	CPUE near boundary not higher than farther away	Lobster (Forcada et al., 2009)

(cont.)

Table 3.2 (*cont.*)

Effect	Observation		Species/Group (Reference)
Increased catch (per unit area) near MPA	YES	Catch (number) per area linearly declining with distance away from MPA	Lobster (Goñi *et al.*, 2006) Multispecies reef fish (4 MPAs: Goñi *et al.*, 2008)
		Catch/km of coastline similar near and far from the MPA	Lobster (Kelly *et al.*, 2002)
	NO	Declining catch/area gradients around MPA attributed to habitat effects	Multispecies reef fish (3 MPAs: Goñi *et al.*, 2008)
Increased seasonal variability of catch rates near MPA	YES	Greater variability of CPUE near MPA than farther away	Lobster (Kelly *et al.*, 2002); Lobster (Goñi *et al.*, 2006)
	NO	Seasonal variability of catch rates near MPA similar to those farther away	Reef fishes (Forcada *et al.*, 2009)
Increased size of target species in adjacent fishery catch	YES	Greater (and increasing over time) mean size of target species near MPA than farther away (years 8–17)	Lobster (Goñi *et al.*, 2010)
		Greater proportion of large individuals near the MPA than farther away (mean of 8–16 years)	Multispecies reef fish (Stobart *et al.*, 2009)
Changes in species composition in adjacent fishery catch	YES	Taxonomic distinctness in catches near MPA intermediate between MPA and farther fished locations (years 8–16)	Multispecies reef fish (Stobart *et al.*, 2009)
		Multivariate dispersion of catch maximum near MPA border (lowest inside MPA)	Multispecies reef fish (Stobart *et al.*, 2009)
	NO	Mean species richness and diversity similar near MPA than farther away (lowest inside MPA) (years 8–16)	Multispecies reef fish (Stobart *et al.*, 2009)
Effort concentration near MPA boundaries	YES	Effort aggregates near MPA boundaries because of greater catch or value of catch	Lobster (Davis and Dodrill, 1989; Kelly *et al.*, 2002; Goñi *et al.*, 2006; Parnell *et al.*, 2007) Multispecies reef fish (6 MPAs: Goñi *et al.*, 2008) Sparid fish (Willis *et al.*, 2003b)

Table 3.3 *Temperate soft-bottom ecosystems: observed effects of towed-gear exclusion marine protected areas on fisheries from empirical studies*

Effect	Observation		Species/group (Reference)
Increased CPUE near MPA	YES	Declining gradient of CPUE with increasing distance from MPA	Multispecies fish, in particular haddock (Murawski *et al.*, 2004; Murawski *et al.*, 2005) Zuwai crab (Yamasaki and Kuwahara, 1989)
		Hypothesized because a reference area faced a parallel increase in abundance of finfish species but with a 1–3 years time lag	Herring, winter flounder, and red fish (Fisher and Frank, 2002)
Increased abundance or production inside the MPA	YES	Increased production (kcal/m^2 per year) inside vs. outside the MPA	Sea scallop and sea urchin (Hermsen *et al.*, 2003)
		Increased abundance (number/haul) inside vs. outside the trawl ban areas	Sea scallop (Murawski *et al.*, 2000) Several elasmobranch species (Rodrìguez-Cabello *et al.*, 2008)
		Heavier adductor muscle tissue and gonads	Great scallop (Kaiser *et al.*, 2007)
		Larger fish inside the protected area compared to controls for sport fishing	Trophy fish (Blyth-Skyrme *et al.*, 2006)
		Increased abundance (mean number/tow) in before after comparison within the protected area	Herring, winter flounder, and red fish (Fisher and Frank, 2002)
		Increased CPUE (number/pot)	Zuwai crab (Yamasaki and Kuwahara, 1989)
		Increased CPUE, eightfold (experimental trawl survey) comparing period before vs. after protection	Multispecies trawlable assemblage (Pipitone *et al.*, 2000; Badalamenti *et al.*, 2008)
Increased catch (per unit area) near MPA	YES	Relative abundance and biomass assessed by annual standardized dredge survey (catch, number/area)	Sea scallop (Murawski *et al.*, 2005)

(cont.)

Table 3.3 (*cont.*)

Effect	Observation		Species/group (Reference)
Increased seasonal variability of catch rates near MPA	YES	Greater variability near MPA than farther away	Groundfish from trawl data (Murawski *et al.*, 2005)
Increased mean size of target species inside the MPA	YES	Greater shell height within closed area than outside closed areas	Sea scallop (Murawski *et al.*, 2000)
		Increased mean size of two elasmobranch species inside the MPA	Small-spotted catshark and thornback ray (Rodriguez-Cabello *et al.*, 2008)
		Greater shell length and age within closed area than outside closed areas	Great scallop (Bradshaw *et al.*, 2001; Beukers-Stewart *et al.*, 2005)
		Greater size for mature female in protected area vs. control	Red mullet (Fiorentino *et al.*, 2008)
	NO	Equal or smaller size for target commercial species	Hake, monkfish, and red mullet (Badalamenti *et al.*, 2002)
		Steeper biomass size spectra in protected vs. unprotected areas	Fish trawlable assemblage (Sweeting *et al.*, 2009)
Effort concentration near MPA boundaries	YES	Effort aggregates near MPA boundaries because of greater catch or value of catch	Sea scallop (Murawski *et al.*, 2005) Multispecies fish (Murawski *et al.*, 2005)

MPAs show that most reef fishes, even highly vagile species such as carangids, have limited home ranges and low net movement across MPA boundaries (Holland *et al.*, 1996; Rakitin and Kramer, 1996; Abesamis and Russ, 2005; Meyer and Holland, 2005). Emigration rates from isolated reefs tend to be low (Cole *et al.*, 2000; Barrett *et al.*, 2009) but may be much greater where MPAs and fished areas are joined by contiguous reefs (Kaunda-Arara and Rose, 2004). Besides, spillover may be limited when the size of the MPA is large relative to fish mobility (e.g., 50 × 5 km MPA size and median mobility <2 km: Buxton and Allen, 1989). For species that are polymorphic with respect to movement, emigration rates depend on the proportion of nomadic and resident morphs in the protected population (Attwood and Bennet, 1994) and protection in MPAs could select for individuals with the highest tendency to exhibit residential behavior (Parsons *et al.*, 2003). The potential of net emigration to offset the loss of fishing grounds in MPAs was addressed by one study. Goñi *et al.* (2010) estimated that 7% of the lobster residing in the Columbretes MPA emigrated every year to the adjacent fishery, where 90% of them were harvested within 1 year. The resulting spillover contributed 31–43% of the annual local catch and, when compared to the proportion of fishing area closed in the MPA, provided a net gain of over 10% of the catch in weight. This benefit was derived primarily from the fact that lobsters grew larger in the MPA before they emigrated.

3.3.1.2 Indirect evidence of spillover
Patterns of catch per unit effort   The best evidence of spillover from catch per unit effort (CPUE) patterns is the increase in CPUE over time in fisheries near MPAs. This effect has now been documented for long periods (>1 decade) in the Apo (Alcala *et al.*, 2005) and Columbretes (Stobart *et al.*, 2009) MPAs (Tables 3.1 and 3.2). Declining gradients of CPUE with distance from the MPA boundaries (Figure 3.1) also evidence spillover in tropical and temperate MPAs for most, but not all, target species (Tables 3.1 and 3.2) (see Tupper and Rudd, 2002; Forcada *et al.*, 2009). Biomass spillover has also been observed around towed-gear-exclusion MPAs, as in Georges Bank where CPUE of multispecies, and haddock catch in particular, increased in fisheries adjacent to the MPAs (Murawski *et al.*, 2005), or as around the Kyoto Prefecture MPA for crab CPUE (Table 3.3) (Yamasaki and Kuwahara 1989). Also, maximum (Kelly *et al.*, 2002; Forcada *et al.*, 2009) or highly variable (Kelly *et al.*, 2002; Murawski *et al.*, 2005; Goñi *et al.*, 2006) CPUEs near MPA boundaries reveal environmentally or seasonally driven fluctuations of spillover.

Catch   Whether spillover causing these CPUE patterns translates into greater catches in fisheries adjoining MPAs is less documented. Again, the clearest evidence is the increase of fish catches over time in fisheries around tropical reef MPAs (Tables 3.1 and 3.2) (Roberts *et al.*, 2001; Alcala *et al.*, 2005; Abesamis *et al.*, 2006). Spillover has also been evidenced by declining gradients of catch/km^2 of lobster (Goñi *et al.*, 2006) and of multispecies fish (Goñi *et al.*, 2008) with distance from several Mediterranean MPAs. Similar catches close to and far from the MPA when effort concentrates and depletes CPUE near the MPA has been interpreted as a sign that spillover offsets the loss of fishing grounds (Kelly *et al.*, 2002). However, none of the above evidence assures that total catch

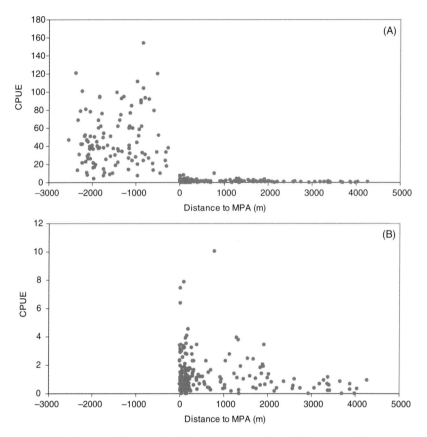

Figure 3.1 Lobster catch per unit effort (CPUE: number of lobsters caught per 600 m of net per day) versus distance from fishing set to the Columbretes Islands Marine Reserve boundary. (A) Commercial and experimental data combined; (B) Commercial fishery data on expanded *y*-axis scale. Adapted from Goñi *et al.* (2006).

will increase after MPA implementation. In one of the most complete appraisals of fishery changes associated with MPAs, McClanahan and Kaunda-Arara (1996) noted that following the creation of Mombasa Marine Park (Kenya), total catch decreased due to the closure of 65% of fishing grounds and subsequent relocation of fishing effort, whereas CPUE increased by 110%, catch per fisher by 25%, and catch per unit area by 83%.

Mean size in catch   As exploited species are allowed to grow larger inside MPAs, spillover may also be evidenced by greater mean sizes of species in catches of adjacent fisheries (Tables 3.1 and 3.2). Besides, since larger fishes generally have larger home ranges and therefore move greater distances (Chapman and Kramer, 1999), spillover may primarily involve the emigration of large individuals. This has been evidenced from gradients of decreasing target species size with distance from MPAs in the Philippines (Abesamis and Russ, 2005), Kenya (McClanahan and Mangi, 2000), and Spain, where mean size of fish near the boundary were intermediate between larger sizes within the MPA and smaller sizes in farther fishing grounds (Stobart *et al.*, 2009). However, and in apparent contradiction, larger individuals, which are generally more dominant, have been shown to exclude subordinate fish through interference competition in old Kenyan (McClanahan *et al.*, 2007) and Philippine MPAs (Abesamis and Russ 2005). This process has also been inferred for lobster by the mean size of migrants which, despite growing over time, always remained smaller than that of lobster residing within the MPA (Goñi *et al.*, 2010).

Species diversity in catch   Whether spillover can supply a more diverse catch has been poorly studied. As a consequence of spillover processes, Stobart *et al.* (2009) observed that mean taxonomic distinctness of the multispecies fish catch near the Columbretes MPA was lower than within the MPA but higher than in farther fished areas. The multivariate dispersion was highest in catches of the border fishery, indicating that the border was a transitional zone between the MPA and the fishery. Unexpectedly, species richness and diversity indices were lowest inside the MPA and similar among close and far fished areas, indicating the current lack of understanding of the responses of these indices to fishing in temperate areas.

Fishing effort distribution   If spillover occurs, fishing effort is expected to concentrate along the MPA boundaries – a phenomenon known as "fishing the line" (Kellner *et al.*, 2007). Concentration of displaced fishing effort as a response to improved fishing opportunities near MPAs has been well documented in temperate MPAs (Figure 3.2). Aggregation of effort is documented in most reviewed studies and is occurring in all studies on lobster fisheries (Table 3.2). Moreover, effort redistribution upon MPA creation and potential concentration near the boundaries has been observed in the large soft-bottom towed-gear-exclusion zones of Georges Bank, for both the scallop and mutispecies groundfish fisheries. Before protection roughly one-third of trawl effort was deployed in the closed areas and after closure 35% occurred within 5 km of the MPA (Table 3.3)

Figure 3.2 Spatial distribution of commercial effort in the regional lobster fishery around the Columbretes Islands Marine Reserve. Each dot represents a fishing set. Adapted from Goñi *et al.*, (2010).

(Murawski *et al.*, 2005). In contrast to temperate MPAs, fishing effort patterns around tropical MPAs have been documented in few studies and with contrasting results (Table 3.1). Effort either aggregated in response to CPUE increases (Mombasa Marine Park: McClanahan and Mangi, 2000), or was lower than in other grounds because of high variability of fish abundance due to seasonal changes in weather conditions (Apo Reserve: Abesamis *et al.*, 2006). Lack of effort aggregation around MPAs may also be due to high costs of traveling or availability of good fishing grounds close to harbor (e.g., Wilcox and Pomeroy, 2003).

Confounding factors   It is important to note that fishing effort distribution and the other variables reviewed above related to fishery effects of MPAs do not necessarily respond to the presence of spillover. In particular, habitat distribution may drive or confound observed fishery patterns (e.g., Goñi *et al.*, 2008; Forcada *et al.*, 2009).

3.3.2 Biomass rebuilding within towed-gear-exclusion MPAs

Two towed-gear-exclusion zones aimed at rebuilding the biomass of exploited assemblages have been intensively studied and their ability to attain their objectives evaluated: the Gulf of Castellammare, a bottom-trawl ban of about 200 km^2 (1990), and the Georges Bank and Southern New England areas (1994) covering over 22 000 km^2 closed to all mobile fishing gear (Table 3.3). In the Gulf of Castellammare CPUE from experimental trawl surveys carried out before and up to 10 years after the ban showed an overall and stable increase in abundance within the MPA of about eight-fold (Pipitone *et al.*, 2000; Pipitone *et al.*, 2004; Badalamenti *et al.*, 2008). Interestingly, biomass size spectra showed slopes significantly steeper in the MPA than in control unprotected gulfs (Sweeting *et al.*, 2009). This unpredictable result was attributed to the exclusion of trawlers, which lacked catch-size selectivity and to the continued, more size-selective fishing by artisanal gears within the MPA. Notably, the biomass increase in the Castellammare MPA was not accompanied by substantial size-related trophodynamic shifts (Badalamenti *et al.*, 2002) and the exclusion of trawling had limited effect on fish trophic level at size, discounting a large bottom–up influence on fish trophodynamics (Badalamenti *et al.*, 2008; Fanelli *et al.*, 2009; Fanelli *et al.*, 2010).

In the Georges Bank MPAs the spawning stock of groundfish species increased following the MPA establishement, in particular for the shallow-water sedentary fish assemblages. The biomass and mean size of the scallop *Placopecten magellanicus* grew dramatically (14-fold) during the period 1994–1998 (Murawski *et al.*, 2000).

Some MPAs closed to trawling have the explicit objective of rebuilding biomass of specific target species. Both the Devon Inshore Potting Agreement areas of about 500 km^2 (Kaiser *et al.*, 2007) and the much smaller 2 km^2 Isle of Man MPA (Bradshaw *et al.*, 2001; Beukers-Stewart *et al.*, 2005) succeeded in increasing biomass of the scallop *Pecten maximus* (Table 3.3). The Kyoto Prefecture towed gear closure aimed at protecting the crab *Chionectes opilio* accomplished its objective of rebuilding its biomass and mean size (Yamasaki and Kuwahara, 1989).

Other MPAs where towed gears were excluded with the objective of protecting particular fish species were also successful in increasing their biomass and that of other species. The Emerald/Western Bank closed area (established in 1987) on the Scotian Shelf (∼13700 km^2), designed to protect juvenile haddock, also benefited several other species with up to 39-fold increases in abundance (mean number per tow) comparing pre- and post-closure survey data (1970–2000) (Fisher and Frank, 2002). A similar trend was evident in a reference area (the Brown's Bank) but with a time lag of 1–3 years. The authors concluded that the dynamics of the Brown's Bank finfish community are coupled to the closed area through spillover. MPAs in the Cantabrian Sea closed to trawling for the conservation of elasmobranch species also experienced increases in biomass and mean size of several species, in particular of the small-spotted catshark and the thornback ray (Rodriguez-Cabello *et al.*, 2008).

3.4 Summary and discussion of empirical evidence of effects of marine protected areas on fisheries

Along with the impetus of the creation MPAs worldwide (Allison *et al.*, 1998), empirical research on their effects flourished in the 1980s. For two decades most research focused on assessing the responses of exploited species within their boundaries. By the 2000s it was well established that where properly enforced and where significant fishing restrictions had been in place for sufficient time, biomass of target species increased within MPAs. Subsequently studies investigated relationships between observed biomass responses and species life history traits and MPA characteristics, mainly size and age, combining data from several MPAs (e.g., Halpern, 2003; Russ *et al.*, 2005; McClanahan *et al.*, 2007; Claudet *et al.*, 2008; Claudet *et al.*, 2010). Positive relationships were generally found between the degree of biomass recovery and MPA size and age. Greater or faster biomass responses were associated with sedentary or moderately mobile species, although mobile species could also respond positively to protection within MPAs (Claudet *et al.*, 2010). Attention was then shifted towards investigating the effects of these recoveries within MPAs on fisheries surrounding MPAs. The aims of such empirical studies have so far been modest. Most focused on ascertaining changes in fishing effort and/or catches in commercial or subsistence fisheries near MPAs and only a few measured transfer rates from protected to fished populations.

Our review of MPAs of various types and histories and in various ecosystems indicates that in successful MPAs with permeable boundaries, spillover can induce increases in CPUE of target species in fisheries surrounding MPAs. These increases constitute a yield surplus and fishers' CPUE tends to be higher, although often more variable due to seasonal processes underlying spillover (MacClanahan and Kaunda-Arara, 1996; Kelly *et al.*, 2002; Goñi *et al.*, 2006). Nevertheless, spillover is species and habitat specific and when more than one exploited species was studied, not all target species CPUE increased near MPA boundaries (e.g., Tupper and Rudd 2002).

So far, few studies have explored the spatial patterns of total catch following MPA establishment. Because MPA effects on CPUE can be confounded by "leakage," i.e., overdepletion due to relocation of fishing pressure into a smaller area (Ewers and Rodrigues, 2008), changes in total catch or catch per unit area, rather than CPUE, provide the most unequivocal measure of spillover effects on local fisheries. However, estimating total catch is more data-demanding as both spatial effort and CPUE data are required. Where reported, catches per unit area were higher near the MPAs (but see McClanahan and Kaunda-Arara, 1996). Well-enforced MPAs also lead to increases in species mean size within their boundaries (but see Badalamenti et al., 2002). Consequently, mean size increases in catches outside MPAs can be observed when spillover occurs. Effects of MPAs on multispecies catch size spectra have been more difficult to ascertain, with reports of either a greater (Stobart et al., 2009) or smaller (Sweeting et al., 2009) proportion of large animals (as when a non-size-selective gear is excluded) in comparison to fished areas or to the same areas before protection, respectively. Nevertheless, species size in the catch can be affected by numerous factors, e.g., gear selectivity, catchability, habitat, or species behavior, and may therefore not be straightforward to obtain representative or unequivocal results.

In the medium term, most MPAs attract fishers to their boundaries. Although effort data prior to MPA establishment are usually not available (but see Murawski et al., 2005), at the time of MPA creation fishing effort relocated either homogeneously around available grounds or in preferred areas outside the Columbretes Islands Marine Reserve, coalescing gradually towards its boundaries as biomass in the MPA grew, expanding and contracting thereafter as a function of fishing success on the MPA edge. Once spillover occurs, fishers continue to occupy those desirable fishing spots throughout the season regardless of catch rates. In fishing grounds not associated with MPAs, fishermen are more likely to relocate when fishing depletes the area and catch rates drop. Nevertheless, due to high costs of traveling or catch variability, aggregation of effort near MPA boundaries does not always occur.

Optimal MPA benefits to fisheries are argued for species with intermediate dispersal characteristics. Lobsters and reef fish reviewed here exhibit these dispersal characteristics and most studies reported fisheries effects consistent with spillover. In spite of this, estimates of net transfer are scarce and range from 0.8% to 7% per year for lobsters (Rowe, 2001; Goñi *et al.*, 2010). Net benefits from spillover to local fishery catches (i.e., accounting for the loss of fishing area due to the MPA) have been estimated at over 10% per year for lobster (Goñi *et al.*, 2010).

Although only a few MPAs have been deliberately located on soft bottoms and generally consist of towed-gear-exclusion zones, they include most of the MPAs specifically designed for fisheries management objectives. The primary goal of existing soft-bottom gear-exclusion MPAs is rebuilding the biomass of exploited fish assemblages or of particular fish or shellfish species. Therefore studies evaluate their performance on those grounds rather than focusing on effects on fisheries outside their boundaries. Our synthesis indicates that all soft-bottom MPAs reviewed succeeded in doing so. Furthermore, since towed gears affect whole assemblages, positive responses on other exploited species have also been documented. With two exceptions reporting spillover, no studies assessed wider fisheries effects. Also, gear-exclusion MPAs may be expected to affect the fisheries allowed within the MPA if they harvest common species, but no study evaluating such effects was found.

Gear-exclusion MPAs have shown potential in replenishing fish and some commercial invertebrate stocks in a matter of years. They are also a useful tool for resolving conflicts among artisanal and industrial fisheries in coastal areas. When large enough with respect to the scale of fisheries and well enforced they offer a good solution for fisheries management of soft bottom areas.

The shortage of fishery data evaluating the effects of towed-gear-exclusion MPAs seems to be attributable mainly to the design features of MPAs on soft bottoms. They are fairly large compared to those on coastal reefs and tend to be located offshore. This implies higher costs to assess fishery effects of these MPAs than that needed for small coastal MPAs on reef areas. Hence, funding for large-scale projects should be encouraged.

3.5 Conclusions and future research directions

Our current empirical understanding of direct effects of MPAs on fisheries is limited by the scale of the process most amenable to study: biomass spillover. Although some studies document positive responses of highly mobile species inside MPAs (e.g., Claudet *et al.*, 2010), biomass increases are favored by the limited movement of organisms. As a result, the spatial extent of observable spillover is generally restricted to the extent of the movements of low to moderate mobility species, that is, few hundred to thousand meters from MPA boundaries, depending on species mobility, MPA size, and habitat characteristics.

Effects of MPAs on fisheries are difficult to demonstrate empirically. A first reason is that most MPAs are small and were not designed with fisheries management objectives, while MPA success is dependent upon the initial goals laid out (Palumbi, 2001). Except for gear-exclusion zones, which often have explicit fisheries management objectives, most MPAs have been established to meet unspecified conservation benefits, precluding the choice of their location, design, and protected habitats based on specific criteria. Thus, *ad hoc* evaluation of MPA effectiveness should not be used primarily as tests of their benefits, but rather to draw recommendations for the establishment of MPAs in the future. A second explanation is the common lack of fishery data before establishment of MPAs, which often also lack appropriate spatial replication (Palumbi, 2001; Willis *et al.*, 2003a; Pelletier *et al.*, 2008). Yet non-existence of appropriate replication and of independent control sites is a common issue because MPAs are frequently sited in outstanding areas or protect unique ecosystems. Unfortunately, this problem cannot be solved once MPAs are established, and this dilemma underscores the importance of conducting baseline studies before MPAs are created. In addition, only a few studies encompass evaluations of MPA effects on fisheries over large temporal scales (Russ *et al.*, 2004; Murawski *et al.*, 2005; Stobart *et al.*, 2009; Goñi *et al.*, 2010). Thus, although there is now a wide consensus on the effectiveness of MPAs for rebuilding density and biomass of target species within their boundaries and on the benefits of spillover at local scales, uncertainty and low predictive power remain due to small sample sizes and possible confounding factors, such as habitat distribution and quality.

Another underlying process on which MPA effects on fisheries depend is connectivity. Understanding and quantifying the dispersal characteristics of populations at different life history stages remains the most difficult and challenging issue in employing MPAs, and is the least developed and the greatest source of uncertainty (Fogarty *et al.*, 2000; Jones *et al.*, 2009). To effectively enhance or help stabilize fisheries, MPAs must not only preserve minimum viable populations but must also export larvae or harvestable adults to adjacent areas (Bostford *et al.*, 2009). To do so, MPAs cannot function as islands but must interact with areas open to fishing, or with reserves in the case of networks. Thus, design requirements for MPAs for fisheries management must incorporate information on species life history and ecology, larval sources and sinks, and metapopulation dynamics. Theoretical models can help in this respect (Walters, 2000).

Even if MPA effects on fisheries evidenced by existing empirical studies seem scanty and limited in their potential to reverse the outlook of fisheries, MPAs can be used as controls to assess the effects of exploitation of marine living resources. They are an essential tool to tease out the complicated interactions between natural and human-induced alteration of these resources (Parrish, 1999). Therefore, more MPAs are needed for proper fisheries research, assessment, and management.

References

Abesamis, R. A. and Russ, G. R. (2005). Density-dependent spillover from a marine reserve: long-term evidence. *Ecological Applications*, **15**, 1798–812.

Abesamis, R. A., Alcala, A. C., and Russ, G. R. (2006). How much does the fishery at Apo Island benefit from spillover of adult fish from the adjacent marine reserve. *Fishery Bulletin*, **104**, 360–75.

Acosta, C. A. (2002). Spatially explicit dispersal dynamics and equilibrium population sizes in marine harvest refuges. *ICES Journal of Marine Science*, **59**, 458–68.

Alcala, A. C., Russ, G. R., Maypa, A. P., and Calumpong, H. P. (2005). A long-term, spatially replicated experimental test of the effect of marine reserves on local fish yields. *Canadian Journal of Fisheries and Aquatic Sciences*, **62**, 98–108.

Allison, G. W., Lubchenco, J., and Carr, M. H. (1998). Marine reserves are necessary but not sufficient for marine conservation. *Ecological Applications*, **8**, S79–S92.

Almany, G. R., Connolly, S. R., Heath, D. D., *et al.* (2009). Connectivity, biodiversity conservation and the design of marine reserve networks for coral reefs. *Coral Reefs*, **28**, 339–51.

Attwood, C. G. and Bennett, B. A. (1994). Variation in dispersal of galjoen (*Coracinus capensis*) (Teleostei: Coracinidae) from a Marine Reserve. *Canadian Journal of Fisheries and Aquatic Sciences*, **51**, 1247–57.

Badalamenti, F., D'anna, G., Pinnegar, J. K., and Polunin, N. V. C. (2002). Size-related trophodynamic changes in three target fish species recovering from intensive trawling. *Marine Biology*, **141**, 561–70.

Badalamenti, F., Sweeting, C. J., Polunin, N. C. V., *et al.* (2008). Limited trophodynamics effects of trawling on three Mediterranean fishes. *Marine Biology*, **154**, 765–73.

Barrett, N., Buxton, C., and Gardner, C. (2009). Rock lobster movement patterns and population structure within a Tasmanian Marine Protected Area inform fishery and conservation management. *Marine and Freshwater Research*, **60**, 417–25.

Beukers-Stewart, B. D., Vause, B. J., Mosley, M. W. J., Rossetti, H. L., and Brand, A. R. (2005). Benefits of closed area protection for a population of scallops. *Marine Ecology Progress Series*, **298**, 189–204.

Blyth-Skyrme, R. E., Kaiser, M. J., Hiddink, J. G., Edwards-Jones, G., and Hart P. J. B. (2006). Conservation benefits of temperate marine protected areas: variation among fish species. *Conservation Biology*, **20**, 811–20.

Botsford, L. W., White, J. W., Coffroth, M.-A., *et al.* (2009). Connectivity and resilience of coral reef metapopulations in marine protected areas: matching empirical efforts to predictive needs. *Coral Reefs*, **28**, 327–37.

Bradshaw, C., Veale, L. O., Hill, A. S., and Brand, A. R. (2001). The effect of scallop dredging on Irish Sea benthos: experiments using a closed area. *Hydrobiologia*, **465**, 129–38.

Buxton, C. D. and Allen, J. C. (1989). Mark and recapture studies of two reef sparids in the Tsitsikamma Coastal National Park. *Koedoe*, **32**, 39–45.

Chapman, M. R. and Kramer, D. L. (1999). Gradients in coral reef fish density and size across the Barbados Marine Reserve boundary: effects of reserve protection and habitat chaacteristics. *Marine Ecology Progress Series*, **181**, 81–96.

Claudet, J., Osenberg, C. W., Benedetti-Cecchi, L., *et al.* (2008). Marine reserves: size and age do matter. *Ecology Letters*, **11**, 481–9.

Claudet, J., Osenberg, C., Domenici, P., *et al.* (2010). Marine reserves: Fish life history and ecological traits matter. *Ecological Applications*, **20**, 830–9.

Cole, R. G., Villouta, E., and Davidson, R. J. (2000). Direct evidence of limited dispersal of the reef fish *Parapercis colias* (Pinguipedidae) within a marine reserve and adjacent fished areas. *Aquatic Conservation: Marine and Freshwater Ecosystems*, **10**, 421–36.

Davidson, R. J., Villouta, E., Cole, R. G., and Barrier, R. G. F. (2002). Effects of marine reserve protection on spiny lobster (*Jasus edwardsii*) abundance and size at Tonga Island Marine Reserve, New Zealand. *Aquatic Conservation: Marine and Freshwater Ecosystems*, **12**, 213–27.

Davis, G. E. and Dodrill, J. W. (1989). Recreational fishery and population dynamics of spiny lobsters, *Panulirus argus*, in Florida Bay, Everglades National Park, 1977–1980. *Bulletin of Marine Science*, **44**, 78–88.

DeMartini, E. E. (1993). Modeling the potential of fishery reserves for managing Pacific coral reef fishes. *Fishery Bulletin*, **91**, 414–17.

Dugan, J. E., and Davis, G. E. (1993). Applications of marine refugia to coastal fisheries management. *Canadian Journal of Fisheries and Aquatic Sciences*, **50**, 2029–42.

Ewers, R. M. and Rodrigues, A. S. L. (2008). Estimates of reserve effectiveness are confounded by leakage. *Trends in Ecology and Evolution*, **23**, 113–16.

Fanelli, E., Badalamenti, F., D'anna, G., and Pipitone, C. (2009). Diet and trophic level of scaldfish *Arnoglossus laterna* in the southern Tyrrhenian Sea (western Mediterranean): contrasting trawled vs. untrawled areas. *Journal of the Marine Biological Association of the U.K.*, **89**, 817–28.

Fanelli, E., Badalamenti, F., D'Anna, G., Pipitone, C., and Romano, C. (2010). Trophodynamic effects of trawling on the feeding ecology of pandora, *Pagellus erythrinus* off the northern Sicily coast (Mediterranean Sea). *Marine and Freshwater Research*, **61**, 408–17.

Fiorentino, F., Badalamenti, F., D'anna, G., *et al.* (2008). Changes in spawning-stock structure and recruitment pattern of red mullet, *Mullus barbatus*, after a trawl ban in the Gulf of Castellammare (central Mediterranean Sea). *ICES Journal of Marine Science*, **65**, 1175–83.

Fisher, J. A. D. and Frank, K. T. (2002). Changes in finfish community structure associated with an offshore fishery closed area on the Scotian Shelf. *Marine Ecology Progress Series*, **240**, 249–65.

Fogarty, M., Bonshack, J. A., and Dayton, P. K. (2000). Marine reserves and resource management. In *Seas at the Millennium: An Environmental Evaluation*, vol. 3, ed. C. Sheppard. New York: Elsevier, pp. 375–92.

Forcada, A., Valle, C., Bonhomme, P., *et al.* (2009). Effects of habitat on spillover from marine protected areas to artisanal fisheries. *Marine Ecology Progress Series*, **379**, 197–211.

Francini-Filho, R. B. and Moura, R. L. (2008). Evidence for spillover of reef fishes from a no-take marine reserve: an evaluation using the before–after control–impact (BACI) approach. *Fisheries Research*, **93**, 346–56.

Fretwell, S. D. and Lucas, H. L. (1970). On territorial behaviour and other factors influencing habitat distribution in birds. I. Theoretical development. *Acta Biotheoretica*, **19**, 16–36.

Gitschlag, G. R. (1986). Movement of pink shrimp in relation to the Tortugas Sanctuary. *North American Journal of Fisheries Management*, **6**, 328–38.

Goñi, R., Quetglas, A., and Reñones, O. (2006). Spillover of lobster *Palinurus elephas* (Fabricius 1787) from a Western Mediterranean marine reserve. *Marine Ecology Progress Series*, **308**, 207–19.

Goñi, R., Adlerstein, S., Alvarez-Berastegui, D., *et al.* (2008). Evidence of biomass export from six Western Mediterranean marine protected areas as measured from artisanal fisheries. *Marine Ecology Progress Series*, **366**, 159–74.

Goñi, R., Hilborn, R., Díaz, D., Mallol, S., and Adlerstein, S. (2010). Net contribution of spillover from a marine reserve to fishery catches. *Marine Ecology Progress Series*, **400**, 233–43.

Guidetti, P. and Claudet, J. (2010). Co-management practices enhance fisheries in marine protected areas. *Conservation Biology*, **24**, 312–18.

Halpern, B. S. (2003). The impact of marine reserves: do reserves work and does reserve size matter? *Ecological Applications*, **13**, S117–S137.

Hermsen, J. M., Collie, J. S., and Valentine, P. C. (2003). Mobile fishing gear reduces benthic megafaunal production on Georges Bank. *Marine Ecology Progress Series*, **260**, 97–108.

Hilborn, R. (2006). Faith-based fisheries. *Fisheries*, **31**, 554–5.

Hilborn, R., Stokes, K., Maguire, J. J., (2004). When can marine reserves improve fisheries management? *Ocean and Coastal Management*, **47**, 197–205.

Holland, K. N., Lowe, C. G., and Wetherbee, B. M. (1996). Movements and dispersal patterns of blue trevally (*Caranx melampygus*) in a fisheries conservation zone. *Fisheries Research*, **25**, 279–92.

Jennings, S. (2001). Patterns and prediction of population recovery in marine reserves. *Reviews in Fish Biology and Fisheries*, **10**, 209–31.

Jones, G. P., Almany, G. R., Steneck, R. S., *et al.* (2009). Larval retention and connectivity among populations of corals and reef fishes: history, advances and challenges. *Coral Reefs*, **28**, 307–25.

Jones, P. J. S. (2008). Fishing industry and related perspectives on the issues raised by no-take marine protected area proposals. *Marine Policy*, **32**, 749–58.

Kaiser, M. J., Blyth-Skyrme, R. E., Hart, P. J. B., Edwards-Jones, G., and Palmer, D. (2007). Evidence for greater reproductive output per unit area in areas protected from fishing. *Canadian Journal of Fisheries and Aquatic Sciences*, **64**, 1284–9.

Kaunda-Arara, B. and Rose, G. A. (2004). Out-migration of tagged fishes from marine reef National Parks to fisheries in coastal Kenya. *Environmental Biology of Fishes*, **70**, 363–72.

Kellner, J. B., Tetreault, I., Gaines, S. D., and Nisbet, R. M. (2007). Fishing the line near marine reserves in single and multispecies fisheries. *Ecological Applications*, **17**, 1039–54.

Kelly, S., Scott, D., and MacDiarmid, A. B. (2002). The value of a spillover fishery for spiny lobsters around a marine reserve in New Zealand. *Coastal Management*, **30**, 153–66.

McClanahan, T. R. and Kaunda-Arara, B. (1996). Fishery recovery in a coral-reef marine park and its effect on the adjacent fishery. *Conservation Biology*, **10**, 1187–99.

McClanahan, T. R. and Mangi, S. (2000). Spillover of exploitable fishes from a marine park and its effects on the adjacent fishery. *Ecological Applications*, **10**, 1792–805.

McClanahan, T. R., Graham, N. A. J., Calnan, J. M., and MacNeil, M. A. (2007). Toward pristine biomass: reef fish recovery in coral reef marine protected areas in Kenya. *Ecological Applications*, **17**, 1055–67.

Meyer, C. G. and Holland, K. N. (2005). Movement patterns, home range size and habitat utilization of the bluespine unicornfish, *Naso unicornis* (Acanthuridae) in a Hawaiian marine reserve. *Environmental Biology of Fishes*, **73**, 201–10.

Millar, R. B. and Willis, T. J. (1999). Estimating the relative density of snapper in and around a marine reserve using a log-linear mixed-effects model. *Australian and New Zealand Journal of Statistics*, **41**, 383–94.

Moffitt, E. A., Botsford, L. W., Kaplan, D. M., and O'Farrell, M. R. (2009). Marine reserve networks for species that move within a home range. *Ecological Applications*, **19**, 1835–47.

Molloy, P. P., McLean, I. B., and Côté, I. M. (2009). Effects of marine reserve age on fish populations: a global meta-analysis. *Journal of Applied Ecology*, **46**, 743–51.

Murawski, S. A., Brown, R., Lai, H. L., Rago, P. J., and Hendrickson, L. (2000). Large-scale closed areas as a fishery-management tool in temperate marine systems: the Georges Bank experience. *Bulletin of Marine Science*, **66**, 775–98.

Murawski, S., Rago, P., and Fogarty, M. (2004). Spillover effects from temperate marine protected areas. *American Fishery Society Symposium*, **42**, 167–84.

Murawski, S. A., Wigley, S. E., Fogarty, M. J., Rago, P. J., and Mountain, D. G. (2005). Effort distribution and catch patterns adjacent to temperate MPAs. *ICES Journal of Marine Research*, **62**, 1150–67.

National Research Council. (2001). *Marine Protected Areas: Tools for Sustaining Ocean Ecosystems*. Washington, DC: National Academy Press.

Palumbi, S. (2001). The ecology of marine protected areas. In *Marine Community Ecology*, eds. M. D. Bertness, S. D. Gaines, and M. E. Hay. Sunderland, MA: Sinauer Associates, pp. 509–30.

Parnell, P. E., Dayton, P. K., and Margiotta, F. (2007). Spatial and temporal patters of lobster trap fishing: a survey of fishing effort and habitat structure. *Bulletin of the Southern California Academy of Sciences*, **106**, 27–37.

Parrish, R. (1999). Marine reserves for fisheries management: why not. *California Cooperative Oceanic Fisheries Investigations Report*, **40**, 77–86.

Parsons, D. M., Babcock, R. C., Hankin, R. K. S., *et al.* (2003). Snapper *Pagrus auratus* (Sparidae) home range dynamics: acoustic tagging studies in a marine reserve. *Marine Ecology Progress Series*, **262**, 253–65.

Pelc, R. A., Baskett, M. L., Tanci, T., Gaines, S., and Warner, R. (2009). Quantifying larval export from South African marine reserves. *Marine Ecology Progress Series*, **394**, 65–78.

Pelletier, D. and Mahevas, S. (2005). Spatially explicit fisheries simulation models for policy evaluation. *Fish and Fisheries*, **6**, 307–49.

Pelletier, D., Claudet, J., Ferraris, J., Benedetti-Cecchi, L., and García-Charton, J. A. (2008). Models and indicators for assessing conservation and fisheries–related effects of Marine Protected Areas. *Canadian Journal of Fisheries and Aquatic Sciences*, **65**, 765–79.

Piet, G. J. and Rijnsdorp, A. D. (1998). Changes in the demersal fish assemblage in the south-eastern North Sea following the establishment of a protected area ("plaice box"). *ICES Journal of Marine Science*, **55**, 420–9.

Pipitone, C., Badalamenti, F., D'anna, G., and Patti, B. (2000). Fish biomass increase after a four year trawl ban in the gulf of Castellammare (N/W Sicily, Mediterranean Sea). *Fisheries Research*, **48**, 23–30.

Pipitone, C., Badalamenti, F., D'anna, G., *et al.* (2004). Research and management of marine coastal fisheries in the Gulf of Castellammare Fishery Reserve. *Biologia Marina Mediterranea*, **11**, 1–11.

Planes, S., Galzin, R., García-Rubies, A., *et al.* (2000). Effects of marine protected areas on recruitment processes with special reference to Mediterranean littoral ecosystems. *Environmental Conservation*, **27**, 126–43.

Planes, S., Jones, G. P., and Thorrold, S.R. (2009). Larval dispersal connects fish populations in a network of marine protected areas. *Proceedings of the National Academy of Sciences of the United States of America*, **106**, S693–7.

Polacheck, T. (1990). Year-round closed areas as a management tool. *Natural Resources Modelling*, **4**, 327–54.

Rakitin, A. and Kramer, D. L. (1996). Effect of a marine reserve on the distribution of coral reef fishes in Barbados. *Marine Ecology Progress Series*, **131**, 97–113.

Rhodes, K. L. and Tupper, M. (2008). The vulnerability of reproductively active squaretail coral grouper (*Plectropomus areolatus*) to fishing. *Fishery Bulletin*, **106**, 194–203.

Roberts, C. M., Bohnsack, J. A., Gell, F., Hawkins, J. P., and Goodridge, R. (2001). Effects of marine reserves on adjacent fisheries. *Science*, **294**, 1920–3.

Rodriguez-Cabello, C., Sanchez, F., Serrano, A., and Olaso, I. (2008). Effects of closed trawl fishery areas on some elasmobranch species in the Cantabrian Sea. *Journal of Marine Systems*, **72**, 418–28.

Rowe, S. (2001). Movements and harvesting mortality of American lobsters (*Homarus americanus*) tagged inside and outside no-take reserves in Bonavista Bay, Newfoundland. *Canadian Journal of Fisheries and Aquatic Sciences*, **58**, 1336–46.

Russ, G. R. (2002). Yet another review of marine reserves as reef fishery management tools. In *Coral Reef Fishes*, ed. P. Sale. San Diego, CA: Academic Press, pp. 421–43.

Russ, G. R., Alcalá, A. C., Maypa, A. P., Calumpong, H. P., and White, A. T. (2004). Marine reserve benefits local fisheries. *Ecological Applications*, **14**, 597–606.

Russ, G. R., Stockwell, B., and Alcalá, A. C. (2005). Inferring versus measuring rates of recovery in no-take marine reserves. *Marine Ecology Progress Series*, **292**, 1–12.

Saenz-Agudelo, P., Jones, G. P., Thorrold, S. R., and Planes, S. (2009). Estimating connectivity in marine populations: an empirical evaluation of assignment tests and parentage analysis under different gene flow scenarios. *Molecular Ecology*, **18**, 1765–76.

Sánchez-Lizaso, J. L., Goñi, R., Reñones, O., *et al.* (2000). Density dependence in marine protected populations: a review. *Environmental Conservation*, **27**, 144–58.

Stobart, B., Warwick, R., González, C., *et al.* (2009). Long-term and spillover effects of a marine protected area on an exploited fish community. *Marine Ecology Progress Series*, **384**, 47–60.

Sweeting, C. J., Badalamenti, F., D'anna, G., Pipitone, C., and Polunin, N. V. C. (2009). Steeper biomass spectra of demersal fish communities after trawler exclusion in Sicily. *ICES Journal of Marine Science*, **66**, 195–202.

Tilney, R. L., Nelson, G., Radloff, S. E., and Buxton, C. D. (1996). Ichthyoplankton distribution and dispersal in the Tsitsikamma National Park Marine Reserve. *South African Journal of Marine Science*, **17**, 1–14.

Tupper, M. (2007). Identification of nursery habitats for commercially valuable humphead wrasse (*Cheilinus undulatus*) and large groupers (Pisces: Serranidae) in Palau. *Marine Ecology Progress Series*, **332**, 189–99.

Tupper, M. and Juanes, F. (1999). Effects of a marine reserve on recruitment of grunts (Pisces: Haemulidae) at Barbados, West Indies. *Environmental Biology of Fishes*, **55**, 53–63.

Tupper, M. and Rudd, M. A. (2002). Species-specific impacts of a small marine reserve on reef fish production and fishing productivity in the Turks and Caicos Islands. *Environmental Conservation*, **29**, 484–92.

Walters, C. (2000). Impacts of dispersal, ecological interactions and fishing effort dynamics on efficacy of marine protected areas: how large should protected areas be? *Bulletin of Marine Science*, **6**, 745–57.

Walters, C., Hilborn, R., and Parrish, R. (2007). An equilibrium model for predicting the efficacy of marine protected areas in coastal environments. *Canadian Journal of Fisheries and Aquatic Sciences*, **64**, 1009–18.

Wetherbee, B. M., Holland, K. N., Meyer, C. G., and Lowe, C. G. (2004). Use of a marine reserve in Kaneohe Bay, Hawaii by the giant trevally, *Caranx ignobilis*. *Fisheries Research*, **67**, 253–63.

Wilcox, C. and Pomeroy, C. (2003). Do commercial fishers aggregate around marine reserves? Evidence from Big Creek Marine Ecological Reserve, central California. *North American Journal of Fisheries Management*, **23**, 241–50.

Willis, T. J., Millar, R. B., Babcock, R. C., and Tolimieri, N. (2003a). Burdens of evidence and the benefits of marine reserves: putting Descartes before des horse? *Environmental Conservation*, **30**, 97–103.

Willis, T. J., Millar, R. B., and Babcock, R. C. (2003b). Protection of exploited fish in temperate regions: high density and biomass of snapper *Pagrus auratus* (Sparidae) in northern New Zealand marine reserves. *Journal of Applied Ecology*, **40**, 214–27.

Yamasaki, A. and Kuwahara, A. (1989). Preserved area to effect recovery of over-fished zuwai crab stocks off Kyoto Prefecture. *Proceedings of the International Symposium on King and Tanner Crabs*, November 1989, Anchorage, Alaska: pp. 575–85.

Zeller, D. C. and Russ, G. R. (1998). Marine reserves: patterns of adult movement of the coral trout *Plectropomus leopardus* (Serranidae). *Canadian Journal of Fisheries and Aquatic Sciences*, **55**, 917–24.

Zeller, D. C., Stoute, S. L., and Russ, G. R. (2003). Movements of reef fishes across marine reserve boundaries: effects of manipulating a density gradient. *Marine Ecology Progress Series*, **254**, 269–80.

4 · BIOECONOMY – Economically optimal spatial and inter-temporal fishing patterns in a metapopulation

JAMES N. SANCHIRICO

4.1 Introduction

Over the past two decades, support for the creation of no-take areas as a means to curtail fishing, provide sources of relatively undisturbed habitats, and hedge against the uncertainties inherent in managing complex coupled human–natural systems has grown exponentially (Carr and Reed, 1993; Allison *et al.*, 1998; National Research Council, 2001; Botsford *et al.*, 2003; Gerber *et al.*, 2003). Vocal opponents of marine reserves (i.e., no-take zones) are commercial and recreational fishermen, who already feel overburdened with regulations and are wary of the stated gains from marine reserves (Bernstein *et al.*, 2004). Developing bioeconomic models that illuminate the trade-offs involved in creating a marine reserve can help reduce conflict over contentious sites and avoid disenfranchising various groups in the negotiation process.

Bioeconomic research on the value of using marine reserves for fishery management has focused on measuring the trade-offs in different governance regimes. Under open-access conditions, a typical assessment consists of comparing catch and biomass levels before and after the reserve is created (e.g., Beverton and Holt, 1957; Hannesson, 1998; Pezzey *et al.*, 2000; Sanchirico and Wilen, 2001a; Rodwell *et al.*, 2002; Sanchirico, 2005). Anderson (2002) and Hilborn *et al.* (2006) analyzed managing fisheries with closed areas and total allowable catches, which is a regulated open-access setting. Other research has investigated creating reserves in limited-entry fisheries where the amount of fishing effort is

Marine Protected Areas: A Multidisciplinary Approach, ed. Joachim Claudet. Published by Cambridge University Press. © Cambridge University Press 2011.

restricted (e.g., Holland and Brazee, 1996; Hastings and Botsford, 1999; Sanchirico, 2004) and the effects include catches along with profitability of the fishery. Across all of the governance regimes, reserves are beneficial for fishery management when the dispersal benefits (spillover of fish from the reserve to open areas) are greater than the opportunity cost of closing the area (lost catch or profit).

In this chapter, we develop a spatial and dynamic bioeconomic model of a metapopulation to address the following questions. (1) When does closing off areas to fishing lead to greater fishing profits than when all areas are open to fishing? (2) How does the inclusion of a broader set of values, such as non-consumptive use value derived from the populations intrinsic value, or e.g., recreation, affect the likelihood that closures emerge as an economically efficient solution? And (3) how do larval settlement processes for different species of fish affect that likelihood (Gerber et al., 2003)?

Following a long tradition in bioeconomic modeling (Clark 1990), we assume that a regulator chooses the fishing effort level in each patch and period to maximize the present discounted value from the time path of fishery profits and non-consumptive use values from the *entire* metapopulation. Discounting leads to future profits being worth less than current profits. Using our framework, we solve for the optimal spatial and inter-temporal distribution of fishing effort across the metapopulation. Therefore, rather than impose a reserve on the system (as many previous bioeconomic studies do) and ask what is its effect, we solve for the optimal distribution of fishing effort (location and level) and ask when is setting fishing effort to zero in a particular patch part of the optimal solution.

Closely related papers include Tuck and Possingham (1994, 2000), Neubert (2003), Sanchirico et al. (2006), White et al. (2008), and Hart and Sissenwine (2009). Neubert (2003) investigated the issue of how to manage sustainable yield in a spatially continuous dynamic system with dispersal. He reached the conclusion that the spatial pattern of catch rates that optimizes system-wide yield contains areas that are completely closed, as a necessary condition for optimality. Sanchirico et al. (2006) found that reserves are potentially part of the economically optimal solution depending on the nature of the settlement process, dispersal rates, and relative costs of fishing. The finding that reserves can be economically optimal is controversial (White et al., 2008; Hart and Sissenwine, 2009), and further research is needed to help define the set of cases where it is more likely to occur.

Understanding ecological and economic trade-offs in complex coupled human–natural systems is a difficult task even in highly stylized settings, like the framework developed in this chapter. In accordance with previous studies, we find potential circumstances where a reserve can be part of the optimal solution. Unlike the previous literature that considered values only from fishing, we find that incorporating non-consumptive use values can have a significant implication for when and where one or more fishing closures are optimal. For example, we find that non-consumptive use values can lead to closing two of the three patches that were optimal to fish when only fishing returns were considered.

The chapter is organized as follows. We introduce the metapopulation and economic components of the model in the next two sections. We then discuss numerical results for a base case and sensitivity analysis on the costs of fishing and ecological value with and without non-consumptive use values. We conclude with a discussion of our findings.

4.2 Metapopulation dynamics

Information generated from new technologies (e.g., remote sensing, acoustic Doppler systems, unmanned submersible vehicles, and electronic tags) has greatly improved our understanding of oceanographic processes that operate on a variety of spatial and temporal scales (Hilborn *et al.*, 2003). Oceanographic processes, such as the Pacific Decadal Oscillation (PDO) and El Niño in turn interact with larval production, dispersal, and settlement processes in complex ways (Caley *et al.*, 1996). For example, annual recruitment of red sea urchins on the west coast of North America is determined by wind conditions and oceanographic currents during a window of a few days or a week (Botsford *et al.*, 1994). Furthermore, larvae are not necessarily passive in this process (Cowen *et al.*, 2000; Warner and Cowen, 2002; Cowen *et al.*, 2006).

Such new and exciting advances are revealing a patchy distribution of marine populations and the determinants of that patchy distribution. Consequently, the conventional aspatial paradigm for describing the nature of marine systems is giving way to a new spatial paradigm. One conceptual framework for this new paradigm is a metapopulation, a system consisting of local populations occupying discrete habitat patches with significant demographic connectivity between patches (Kritzer and Sale, 2004).

We employ a simple yet flexible metapopulation model that combines the features of an implicit larval dispersal process (Polacheck, 1990;

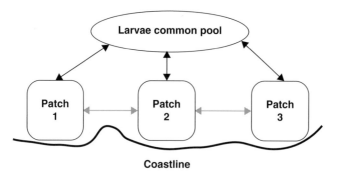

Figure 4.1 Metapopulation system. The gray arrows represent the potential dispersal of adults and the black arrows represent the movement of larvae in the system. Larvae are transported to the common pool where they perfectly mix and are then redistributed to the three patches.

Brown and Roughgarden, 1997; Tuck and Possingham, 2000) with (adult) movements (Sanchirico and Wilen, 1999, 2001a; 2001b). Following Sanchirico *et al.* (2006), we differentiate between "juvenile" and "adult" movement in terms of the density dependence in settlement. In particular, adult dispersal is characterized by density-independent settlement and juvenile dispersal is modeled with a density-dependent settlement process.

For simplicity, we limit the analysis to three patches. The patches are assumed to be aligned along a coastline (Figure 4.1). Adult dispersal movements are between neighboring patches, whereas larvae are transported to a common pool and are then redistributed to the patches.

In each patch i, the instantaneous rate of change of biomass is:

$$\frac{dx_i}{dt} = F_i(x_1, x_2, x_3)$$
$$= f_i(x_1, x_2, x_3) + ND_i(x_1, x_2, x_3) - h_i(e_i, x_i) \ \forall i = 1, 2, 3.$$
$$(4.1)$$

Growth in each patch depends upon the own growth function in patch i, $f_i(x_1, x_2, x_3)$, generally assumed to be a density-dependent process, and also on net dispersal, ND_i, of adult biomass into and out of patch i, which may depend upon own biomass as well as biomass in any or all of the other patches. In this formulation, the adult dispersal process is flexibly modeled via appropriate choice of the net dispersal function, and the juvenile or larval dispersal stage is modeled via interactions that occur in the growth function.

For the most part, the literature utilizing a formulation similar to Equation (4.1) has employed a linear net dispersal function of the general form:

$$\text{ND}_i(x_1, x_2, x_3) = d_{ii}x_i + \sum_{\substack{j=1 \\ i \neq j}}^{3} d_{ij}x_j \quad \forall i = 1, 2, 3 \qquad (4.2)$$

where d_{ii} is the rate of emigration from patch i ($d_{ii} < 0$), and d_{ij} is the dispersal rate from patch j to patch i. We make an "adding up" assumption that whatever leaves patch i for patch j arrives in patch j from patch i (Sanchirico and Wilen, 1999). This assumes no mortality in the "adult" dispersal process and no deviations in movement along the dispersal route. Typically, the net dispersal function captures the case where species redistribute themselves among the patches based on relative densities of the patch populations. For our system, the net dispersal function for each patch is:

$$\text{ND}_1 = d_{11}x_1 + d_{12}x_2 = b\left(\frac{x_2}{k_2} - \frac{x_1}{k_1}\right)$$

$$\text{ND}_2 = d_{22}x_2 + d_{21}x_1 + d_{23}x_3 = b\left(\frac{x_1}{k_1} - \frac{x_2}{k_2}\right) + b\left(\frac{x_3}{k_3} - \frac{x_2}{k_2}\right)$$

$$\text{ND}_3 = d_{33}x_3 + d_{32}x_2 = b\left(\frac{x_2}{k_2} - \frac{x_3}{k_3}\right) \qquad (4.3)$$

where b is a common dispersal rate. In Equation (4.3), the rate of dispersal (b) is independent of the location but the flow of dispersal depends on the relative densities of patches.

To depict own growth and the role played by larval dispersal processes, we use one of the models developed in Sanchirico (2005) based on Pezzey *et al.* (2000). The growth function in each patch is:

$$f_i(x_1, x_2, x_3) = r_i[\alpha_i x_i + \beta_i \sum_{j=1}^{3}(1 - \alpha_j)x_j]\left(1 - \frac{x_i}{k_i}\right) \qquad (4.4)$$

where r_i is the intrinsic growth rate in patch i, k_i is the carrying capacity in patch i, α_i is the probability that larvae remain and successfully settle in patch i, $1 - \alpha_i$ is the probability that larvae leave patch i and enter a larval common pool, and β_i is the probability that larvae survive the journey to and from the larval pool to resettle in patch i. Assuming that $\beta_i = m/3$ where m is the survival probability, all larvae that do not settle in their local area [$(1 - \alpha_i)x_i$] are assumed perfectly mixed in a larval pool and evenly redistributed among all the patches (Hastings and Botsford, 1999; Gerber *et al.*, 2003). This implies that the distribution of larvae covers the entire range of patches (Hastings and Botsford, 1999). Equation (4.4) does permit other formulations and asymmetries in larval settlement rates that might be due to ocean and wind circulation patterns (e.g., gyres).

Equation (4.4) captures a process whereby regional larval *production* is density-independent but larval *settlement* is subject to local density-dependent mechanisms. For example, consider the situation where all dispersal enters the common pool ($\alpha_i = 0$). Then the larvae that are produced and enter the common pool are a function of the population level in the patch, but the overall growth in the population is driven by the local density-dependent effect $(1 - x_i/k_i)$, all else being equal. The post-dispersal density-dependence formulation predicts higher marginal and total biological growth than if the patches were not connected via larval dispersal, and it predicts that the effect of the population in patch j on patch i's production is greatest when patch i's population is low (Gerber *et al.*, 2003; Sanchirico, 2005). At the other extreme, if patch i is close to its carrying capacity, the effect of other patches' population levels is dampened because of competition for limited space and food in patch i. When all larvae are retained locally ($\alpha_i = 1$ for all i), the growth function in patch i reduces to the standard logistic growth function.

The final piece in Equation (4.1) that determines whether the population increases or decreases in any period t is the catch function, $h_i(e_i,x_i)$ in each patch i. The catch is a function of the amount of fishing effort e_i applied in the patch and the level of the population or biomass in patch i. Properties of the catch function include $h_i(e_i,0) = 0$ and that the catch increases with increasing effort level ($\partial h_i/\partial e_i > 0$).

The model is capable of depicting a variety of behavioral characteristics of a metapopulation and a range of productivity assumptions. Some patches may have higher biological productivity than others; some, like larval pools that receive and disperse larvae from other patches, may have no inherent productivity. By embedding larval dispersal within a lumped-parameter model, we capture many of the essential features of more complex larval processes without adding the complexity of another set of n state variables.

It is important to note, however, that a lumped-parameter representation is highly stylized. It ignores important aspects of real population growth and dispersal dynamics, including age- and size-specific mechanisms, selectivity issues, egg production per recruit, and more complicated recruitment processes. Furthermore, this is a deterministic metapopulation model. Bioeconomic analyses that investigate reserve creation in the presence of stochastic shocks and uncertainty include Grafton *et al.* (2005) and Costello and Polasky (2008).

4.3 Economic model

There are many possible economic models that one could consider (Clark, 1990). We abstract from many institutional issues that confound current-day fishery management, such as incomplete rights to harvest a share of the resource (Wilen, 2006) to focus on finding conditions when a patch closed to fishing maximizes economic returns, including values from fishing and non-consumptive use. Our approach follows the long tradition in the bioeconomic literature (Clark, 1990) that considers a fishery where a regulator has direct and complete control of fishing effort levels in each patch.

The main conclusions from this literature are as follows (e.g., Scott, 1955; Crutchfield and Zellner, 1962; Clark and Munro, 1975). First, as long as economic and ecological parameters are constant over time, there is an optimal long-run steady state to which the optimal dynamic trajectories of fishing effort and fish stocks should converge. Second, it is desirable to get to this steady state as quickly as possible, where the nature of the optimal path depends on the costs of adjusting fishing effort over time.

We assume, as does most of the previous work, that the regulator (benevolent social planner) is knowledgeable, understands biological population dynamics and dispersal mechanics, and has perfect foresight. In other words, the regulator is able in period t to predict the implications of different scenarios of fishing effort levels on the economic returns of the fishery in the future. For example, if the regulator increases catch in patch i in period t, he or she knows how the corresponding lower biomass in patch i affects its own growth and the levels of the population throughout the system for *all* future periods. Of course, these assumptions do not hold in practice, but they are more likely to predict that closing off areas to fishing is not economically sensible unless the cost of fishing is so high that it does not pay to fish at all. Therefore, if there are conditions – as Sanchirico *et al.* (2006) and White *et al.* (2008) found – when closing off areas is optimal, then it is very likely that when we add in the complexities reflecting current institutional, economic, and ecological settings, the argument for setting aside areas will be stronger.

The objective function of the regulator is to maximize the present discounted value of fishing returns (total revenue minus total cost) across the patches along with the non-consumptive use value associated with the fish stock. To accomplish the objective, the regulator chooses the level of fishing effort in each patch and period. The objective function is:

$$
J = \max_{e_1(t),e_2(t),e_3(t)} \int_0^\infty e^{-\delta t}
$$

$$
\times \left[\sum_{i=1}^{3} \left(\underbrace{p_i h_i (e_i(t), x_i(t))}_{\text{total revenue}} - \underbrace{c_i (e_i(t))}_{\text{total cost}} \right) + \underbrace{V(x_1, x_2, x_3)}_{\substack{\text{non-consumptive} \\ \text{value}}} \right] dt
$$

$$(4.5)$$

where δ is the discount rate, p_i is the price of fish at the dock in patch i, $c_i(e_i)$ is the cost of fishing in patch i, and V is the total willingness to pay (WTP) function for the fish stock, which depends on the total population size. Willingness to pay captures society's non-consumptive value of the fish stock *in situ* that includes the species' intrinsic value, returns to scuba-diving, and other non-consumptive activities that value the stock.

The price of fish at the dock is allowed to vary based on the location where it is caught (e.g., a patch closer to a port results in fresher fish) but is held constant over time and unresponsive to catches. The assumption that price is not a function of the catch level captures a fishery that is selling fish in the world market. We also abstract away from considering price differentials for older and/or larger fish. Hart and Sissenwine (2009) found that considering these price differentials reduces the likelihood for optimal prohibitions on fishing. Costs of fishing increase with fishing effort and can vary across the patches because of travel costs, topographical features, and ocean currents.

The maximization of Equation (4.5) is subject to the metapopulation dynamics represented in Equation (4.1) and a set of initial population levels $(X_1(0), X_2(0), X_3(0))$ with $0 \leq X_i$ and $0 \leq e_i$. We do not present a discussion of the method, because beyond the additional complexity of three patches, the solution methodology is standard (e.g., Clark, 1990; Kamien and Schwartz, 1991; Bryson, 1999).

4.4 Results

In general, an analytical closed-form solution for all patches and periods is not possible because of the complexity of the system. We can, however, qualitatively illustrate the interplay between the economic and the ecological processes. We do so by focusing on the optimal steady state because it illuminates the essential trade-offs between resource use and non-consumptive values. Specifically, the following nine equations define the steady-state equilibrium levels:

$$\underbrace{f_i(x_1, x_2, x_3) + ND_i(x_1, x_2, x_3)}_{\text{net growth rate of the population}} = \underbrace{h_i(e_i, x_i)}_{\text{fishing rate}} \, i = 1, 2, 3 \quad (4.6)$$

$$\underbrace{(p_i - \lambda_i)\frac{\partial h_i(e_i, x_i)}{\partial e_i}}_{\substack{\text{net marginal} \\ \text{benefit from fishing}}} = \underbrace{\frac{\partial c_i(e_i)}{\partial e_i}}_{\substack{\text{marginal cost} \\ \text{of fishing}}} \quad i = 1, 2, 3 \quad (4.7)$$

$$\underbrace{(p_i - \lambda_i)\frac{\partial h_i(e_i, x_i)}{\partial x_i} + \frac{\partial v}{\partial x_i}}_{\substack{\text{net return from fishing and} \\ \text{non-consumptive use}}}$$

$$= \underbrace{\lambda_i \left(\delta - \frac{\partial f_i}{\partial x_i} - \frac{\partial ND_i}{\partial x_i} \right) - \sum_{\substack{j=1 \\ j \neq i}}^{n} \lambda_j \left(\frac{\partial f_j}{\partial x_i} + \frac{\partial ND_j}{\partial x_i} \right)}_{\text{user cost}} \quad i = 1, 2, 3$$

$$(4.8)$$

where λ_i is the shadow price or adjoint variable for each patch i. The shadow price is the (marginal) change in the value of the objective function [Equation (4.5)] resulting from a (marginal) change in the fish stock in patch i. In other words, it represents the amount of money the planner is willing to pay (or forgo) to increase (decrease) the fish stock in a given patch, which is determined by how much the additional unit increases fishing returns and non-consumptive use values. The term shadow is used, because there is no actual outlay.

The steady-state solution depends critically on the characteristics of the biological dispersal processes, as illustrated by the set of connectivity and dispersal terms in Equations (4.6) and (4.8). Equation (4.6) says that at the optimal steady state, the biological equations of motion are at rest [Equation (4.1)] with catch offsetting biological growth and dispersal. The choice of fishing effort levels in each t is determined such that the net marginal benefit from an additional unit of fishing effort is equal to the marginal cost of fishing effort in each patch [Equation (4.7)].

Equation (4.8) shows that the equilibrium biomass in each patch is chosen to satisfy a relationship that balances the direct value of another unit of biomass stemming from fishing and in the generation of non-consumptive use values (the left-hand side) with its marginal user cost (the right-hand side). The marginal user cost, in turn, represents the cost of taking another unit of fish stock out of the water via harvesting, which depends on the biological growth rates and dispersal process along with the discount rate. For example, if the planner takes an additional unit of biomass out of the water today, then there is one less unit of fish in the water to reproduce and disperse throughout the system. Because this relationship holds at the steady state, there is one less unit of fish *in situ* forever. The discount rate is part of the user costs, because it captures the opportunity cost of leaving more fish in the water today. That is, the planner could harvest an additional fish and invest the proceeds from the sale of the fish in a bank account to earn a rate of return forever.

In general, the marginal user cost in each patch may be adjusted upward or downward by dispersal. The regulator, therefore, needs to trade off not just the local value of biomass (own growth, economic conditions), but also the value of allowing "nature" to reallocate the biomass (e.g., dispersing from low-profitability to high-profitability patches). For example, in a system where dispersal depends on relative densities, the own dispersal effect would be negative (higher biomass levels cause out-migration from patch i) and the other dispersal effects would be positive (higher biomass levels in patch i cause in-migration to other patches j). The last unit of biomass added to patch i balances its immediate value in production with its contribution to the economic value at the steady state, which includes its role in dispersal over the whole system [last term on the right-hand side of Equation (4.8)].

4.4.1 Numerical analysis

In this section, we provide numerical solutions of the steady-state (x_i^{ss}, e_i^{ss}) and dynamic solution $[x_i(t), e_i(t)]$. Equations (4.6)–(4.8) were derived under the assumption that fishing effort levels are non-zero at the steady state. Because our objective is to find cases where one or more of the effort levels is exactly equal to zero (no fishing in the patch), we permit boundary solutions in the numerical analysis.

To solve for a particular solution, we need to specify the harvest, cost, and non-consumptive use value functions. With respect to catch, we utilize the Schaefer (1957) function, which is often employed in bioeconomic analysis of fisheries. Catch in patch i is $h(e_i,x_i) = q_i e_i x_i$ where q_i is the catchability coefficient. We assume that the cost function is quadratic with respect to fishing effort. Specifically, fishing cost in patch i is equal to $c_i(e_i) = c_{i,0}\, e_i + c_{i,1}\, e_i^2$, where $c_{i,0}$ and $c_{i,1}$ are cost parameters. This cost function embeds the realistic assumption that the average (and marginal) cost of fishing effort is increasing (linearly) as more fishing effort is applied and that the first infinitesimal unit of fishing effort applied incurs a cost equal to $c_{i,0}$.

We assume that the non-consumptive use value increases with the aggregate population at a decreasing rate. For example, when the metapopulation is close to zero, an increase in the patch populations has a much greater effect on the total WTP than an increase in the aggregate population when it is close to the carrying capacity of the system. A simple functional representation that captures this behavior is $V(x_1, x_2, x_3) = v(\sum_{i=1}^{3} x_i)^{1/2}$, where v is the non-consumptive value (per unit) of the fish population. Our formulation assumes that individuals do not put a specific value on the stock in a particular location but rather value the entire metapopulation system. This is unlikely, for example, for resources located far from each other (e.g., in different oceans), but seems like a reasonable assumption for the scale of a metapopulation that fits the depiction of Figure 4.1.

Table 4.1 lists the economic and ecological parameters. We choose levels that are consistent with previous bioeconomic studies (e.g., Sanchirico et al., 2006). The economic parameters result in unmanaged population levels (under open access) in each patch in the neighborhood of 20% of their carrying capacity. Our base case also assumes that there is no difference in carrying capacity, prices, and costs. The two sources of heterogeneity in the base case include higher intrinsic growth rates in patch 2 and the connectivity structure. The linear coastline creates an asymmetry with respect to adult dispersal flows, since patches 1 and 3 (edge patches) are connected to patch 2 (center patch). We utilize a 5% discount rate, where higher rates result in lower steady-state populations. With little information on the magnitude of the non-consumptive value, we measure v as a share of the price of fish at the dock. In doing so,

Table 4.1 *Ecological and economic parameters in the base case*

	Parameter	Level	Notes
Ecology	Intrinsic growth rate, r_i	$r_2 = 0.5$, $r_{1 \text{ and } 3} = 0.45$	Captures moderate rate of growth
	Carrying capacity, k_i	5	Scales population to level that improves numerical convergence
	Common dispersal rate, b	0.15	Set at 30% of max. intrinsic growth rate
	Dispersal rate in each patch, d_{ij}	$d_{11} = -b/k_1$, $d_{22} = -2 \star b/k_2$, $d_{33} = -b/k_3$, and $d_{ij} = b/k_i \; i \neq j$	Set such that adding up restrictions on d_{ij} hold. No mortality in "adult" dispersal and movement based on relative densities
	Larval mixing, α	Varies based on run	$\alpha = 1$ all larvae retained locally $\alpha = 0$ all larvae go to common pool
	Larval survival rate, m	1	No mortality in larval dispersal
Economics	Price received at dock, p_i	1.5	Price per unit of catch
	Cost of fishing	$c_{i,0} = 3$, $c_{i,1} = 0.5$	Costs increase at increasing rate
	Catchability coefficient, q_i	0.95	Units are (time $\star$ effort)$^{-1}$
	Discount rate	0.05	Rates often fall between 0% and 10%
	Non-consumptive use value, v	1.86	125% percent of price of fish

we can put bounds on the size of the value necessary to change optimal management of the system.

4.4.2 Base case

We start by investigating how larval and adult dispersal processes affect the optimal distribution of fishing effort in the steady state. We measure the percentage differences between the patch fishing effort levels at the steady state with either larval dispersal ($\alpha = 0$ and $b = 0$) or adult dispersal

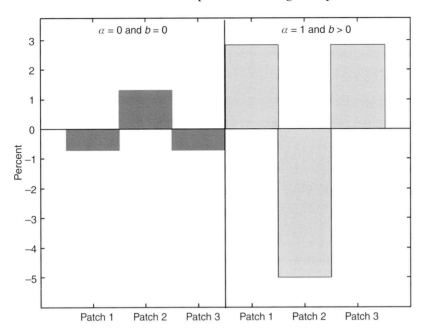

Figure 4.2 Percentage deviations of optimal steady-state effort levels with and without connectivity. The optimal steady-state effort levels for the case with no connectivity are compared with the cases with connectivity. A positive percentage implies that the level with connectivity is greater than without.

($\alpha = 1$ and $b > 0$) and the optimal steady state when the patches are not connected ($\alpha = 1$ and $b = 0$). To highlight the role of connectivity and settlement processes, we assume that non-consumptive use values are not part of the objective function ($\nu = 0$).

Overall the deviations at our base set of parameters are within plus or minus 5% (see Figure 4.2). Interestingly, the pattern switches based on the type of connectivity. With only larval dispersal, where 100% of the larvae leave the common pool and are redistributed uniformly, we find that the effort level in patch 2 increases relative to the independent system. On the other hand, the regulator optimally sets fishing effort levels lower in patch 2 in the case of adult dispersal. Patch 2, therefore, has a greater relative density of biomass than patches 1 and 3 and is a source of biomass at the steady state. The differences arise because patch 2 has a more fundamental role in the system in the presence of only adult dispersal (center patch) than it does in the larval dispersal system, where each patch contributes equally to the system (see Figure 4.1).

The regulator, who is assumed to know the dispersal mechanisms and these differences, manipulates fishing effort levels in order to influence dispersal direction and flows to get the greatest economic return from the system (Sanchirico and Wilen, 2005).

What are the differences in the path to the steady state? We assume that each patch is overfished and needs to be rebuilt. Consistent with the assumption on the differences in intrinsic growth rates, we assume that patch 2's initial population level is greater than that of the others. The initial population levels are $X_1(0) = 0.15 \star k_1$, $X_2(0) = 0.25 \star k_2$, $X_3(0) = 0.15 \star k_3$.

This is a high–dimension non–linear optimal control problem. One solution approach would be to use a (reverse or forward) shooting algorithm (Bryson, 1999). An often more robust method involves collocation techniques (Ascher and Petzold, 1998) that are based on minimizing a set of residual functions at a set of collocation points, or nodes. We utilized 100 Gaussian collocation points that span our solution space. The resulting system of residual equations is a large-scale non–linear constrained optimization problem that is solved using the KNITRO solvers within the TOMLAB state-of-the-art optimization package for Matlab (release 2009a; http://tomopt.com). All constraints were met at $10e^{-7}$ or higher resolution and convergence took on average 10 to 20 iterations. Our methods also permit us to consider the case where boundary solutions (temporary or permanent moratoriums on fishing effort) are optimal. This is an important advance, because most numerical analyses include either non–negativity constraints in an *ad hoc* manner or consider optimal solutions that are interior only.

In the independent system, we find that the optimal economic solution is to impose a temporary moratorium in each patch to let the population rebuild at the fastest rate possible (see Figure 4.3). The length of the moratorium varies across the three patches with the shortest being in patch 2 (about 37% shorter), whose higher intrinsic growth rate leads to a faster recovery. The temporary moratorium in patch 2 is approximately 10% longer in the case of adult dispersal than in the independent system because the outflow of dispersal from patch 2 reduces the net growth rate. Furthermore, by holding off on harvesting in patch 2, the regulator utilizes dispersal from patch 2 to speed up the recovery of the metapopulation. With the larval dispersal mechanism, the temporary moratorium is shorter in patches 1 and 3 and longer in patch 2. The longer moratorium in patch 2 is maintained to speed up the recovery of the system, since patch 2 has both a higher initial population and a higher intrinsic

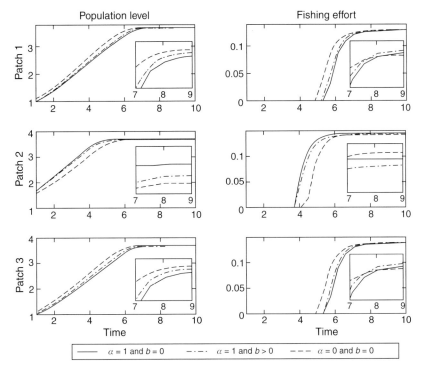

Figure 4.3 Optimal solution of path to steady state across three connectivity systems. The optimal paths for each of the connectivity scenarios: independent ($\alpha = 1$ and $b = 0$), larval dispersal only with 100% going to the common pool ($\alpha = 0$ and $b = 0$), and adult dispersal ($\alpha = 1$ and $b > 0$) are illustrated.

growth rate. Higher dispersal rates or more economic or ecological heterogeneity increases the differences in the dynamic solutions (Sanchirico and Wilen, 2010).

In each scenario, the steady-state population is "reached" within about 10 periods. At the current set of parameters, when we combine the adult dispersal with 100% of the larvae going to a common pool, the solution path follows almost exactly the same path as with larval dispersal only.

4.4.3 Permanent moratorium

Although our base case analysis did not yield a permanent moratorium, at other parameter configurations such a moratorium could be part of the solution (Neubert, 2003; Sanchirico *et al.*, 2006; White *et al.*, 2008; Hart and Sissenwine, 2009). Following Sanchirico *et al.* (2006), we investigate how the cost of fishing can lead to the possibility of optimal fishery closures. We extend their analysis by considering how non-consumptive use values either increase or decrease the likelihood that closures are part of the optimal solution.

Specifically, we vary the linear portion of the cost function in patch 2 ($c_{2,0}$) holding all of the other parameters constant. We know, for example, that the higher the cost of fishing the less profitable it is to fish. There is, therefore, a level of cost where it no longer pays to fish in patch 2. In many respects, this cost level is not interesting. What is interesting, however, is how connectivity can make an otherwise profitable activity (fishing) no longer the most valuable activity for that patch. That is, we are interested in discovering when connectivity results in a patch or patches that are more valuable for the production of biomass for the system than as a direct source of catch.

We find the cost where it no longer pays to fish patch 2 by varying the cost in the independent system ($\alpha = 1$ and $b = 0$ in Figure 4.4B). The cost where the optimal fishing effort level is equal to zero at the steady state is $c_{2,0} = 7.114$ (or more than 200% of the cost in the base case). Figure 4.4B depicts the inverse relationship between the optimal effort level and fishing costs. In the independent system, patch 1 and patch 3 effort levels are constant as we vary $c_{2,0}$ (Figure 4.4A and C).

How does connectivity affect the threshold level of costs such that a permanent moratorium is part of the optimal solution? In the case of "adult" dispersal, the cost threshold for an optimal permanent moratorium is equal to 6.9, which is just 2% below the threshold in the independent case. When all larvae enter the common pool and there is no adult dispersal, the threshold is 5% below the independent case, or 6.7. Although this difference is small, the results illustrate the potential for connectivity to make permanent moratorium optimal.

Non-consumptive use values have a more dramatic effect on the spatial distribution of fishing effort. In the analysis, v_i is equal to 1.25 times the price of fish at the dock (ex-vessel price). In general, the cost threshold for patch 2 decreases in all scenarios (Figure 4.4E). We find that the difference between the cases goes down but the qualitative patterns are the same. What is surprising, however, is that when the cost in patch 2 drops below $c_{2,0} = 1.44$ (or about 41% below the base case), the manager optimizes economic value of the system by closing patches 1 and 3. These patches specialize in producing standing biomass for two reasons. First, the standing biomass has value in and of itself because of the inclusion of non consumptive use values. Second, the standing biomass produces

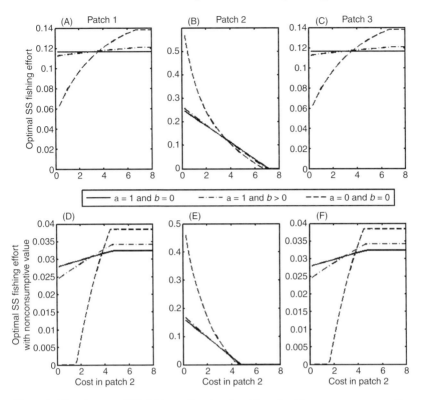

Figure 4.4 Steady-state (SS) fishing effort levels with and without non-consumptive use values. For each connectivity scenario, we vary the linear cost term in patch 2, holding all other parameters constant, and solve for the optimal steady state of fishing effort. A steady-state level of zero corresponds to a permanent moratorium.

a significant number of larvae that contribute to the biomass in patch 2 and the economic returns derived from patch 2. We find, therefore, that with non-consumptive use values, the optimal solution is to close two of the three patches to fishing on a permanent basis.

When we lower the value of v_i, the area where fishing is optimal in all three patches increases. The limit, of course, is when $v_i \rightarrow 0$ and the results converge to the scenario with no non-consumptive use. We also investigated changing the relative biological value of patch 2 by increasing its intrinsic growth rate to 50% over the growth rate in patches 1 and 2. Because we measure the dispersal rate as a percentage of the maximum growth rate, the dispersal rate also increases. The runs with and without non-consumptive use value are qualitatively similar in this case. One quantitative difference, however, is that the region where fishing is optimal in patches 1 and 2 with non-consumptive use value decreases (the lower threshold is approximately 2, and upper threshold is approximately 5). The region is smaller because the gains in the biomass (due to the higher growth rate in patch 2 and resulting more larvae in the system) are sufficient to meet the non-consumptive objective, everything else being equal. The need to specialize in standing stock, therefore, is lower.

4.5 Discussion

Unlike much of the previous literature on the ecological and economic effects of marine reserves, we do not impose where to put a reserve. Rather, we ask, when does using spatial management to maximize fishing profits and non-consumptive use values from a metapopulation *imply* that a reserve should be created and indicate where the reserve should be placed? Spatial fishery closures that are part of the economically optimal solution are less likely to meet resistance from the stakeholders who perceive they have the most to lose from reserve creation.

We extend Sanchirico *et al.* (2006) by considering a three-patch metapopulation, solving for the dynamic optimal solution, and including multiple objectives (fishery profits and non-consumptive use values). Because the fishery effects of marine reserves depend critically on the nature of the ecological connectivity, we model within one framework both juvenile and adult movement, with density dependence in settlement differentiating between the two types of dispersal.

In many respects, our findings are consistent with Neubert (2003), Sanchirico *et al.* (2006), White *et al.* (2008), and Hart and Sissenwine (2009) and the discussion in Gerber *et al.* (2003). We find, for example, that the relative economic return from harvesting fish across space is a fundamental driver of the potential opposition to marine reserve creation (see also Sanchirico, 2005). We also find that the nature of density dependence relative to the timing of the dispersal process is a critical component in determining when, where, and whether marine reserves are part of an optimal fishery policy (White, 2009). Our findings suggest that there is considerable value in understanding the characteristics of dispersal at different ages within a species (Shanks *et al.*, 2003) and how the post-settlement success of the recruits depends on scale- and context-dependent demographic factors and population regulation mechanisms (Steele, 1997; Quinn and Deriso, 1999).

Unlike the previous analyses, we find that even if a permanent closure is not optimal, a temporary moratorium can be the best way to rebuild the metapopulation as fast as possible. The optimal rebuilding plan takes into account the dispersal process: we find that the planner maintains a longer moratorium in patch 2 with adult dispersal than in the independent system (Sanchirico and Wilen, 2010). It is worth repeating that a caveat of our analysis is the assumption of an omniscient and omnipotent regulator or benevolent planner. A fruitful area of research is to relax the model assumptions (deterministic, single species, no management costs, centralized control, etc.) as a means to test the robustness of the model predictions. For example, Clark (1990) discusses how introducing fixed costs of fishing into a similar set-up can lead to optimal pulse fishing in a single patch fishery. An interesting question is whether it is ever optimal to rotate your fishing effort across the patches (e.g., rotating harvest zones), which is the spatial analog to pulse fishing.

We also show that the inclusion of non-fishery values can dramatically affect the optimality of marine reserves. If marine reserves represent the preferences of society for conservation (e.g., as expressed in our model in terms of a positive non-consumptive use value), then the debate surrounding marine reserves should be less about the merit of them as a fishery management tool and more about the trade-off between extractive values and non-consumptive values. We show that marine reserves are a potential valuable use of ocean resources from an economical *and* ecological perspective.

In the past 5 years, ocean policy debates have begun to evolve from focusing on marine reserves into a more general discussion on how to use ocean resources to achieve sustainable and wise use of ocean ecosystems. The ecosystem-based management movement is evidence of such a shift, where the focus of managing a single resource and/or sector, such as trawl fisheries or wind farms, is being subsumed into a more holistic framework (Browman and Stergiou, 2004; McLeod *et al.*, 2005; Murawski, 2007). For example, the US National Oceanographic and Atmospheric Administration is charged with developing integrated ecological assessments (IEAs) for marine and coastal ecosystem management (Levin *et al.*, 2009). These IEAs in turn require the development of trade-off tools for decision support to help make scientifically informed decisions on how to allocate the ocean to different uses (Levin *et al.*, 2009). Bioeconomic models and analysis, such as we presented here, can play an important part in this transition: they are a readily available tool that can illuminate the benefits and costs of different allocation scenarios.

References

Allison, G. W., Lubchenco, J., and Carr, M. H. (1998). Marine reserves are necessary but not sufficient for marine conservation. *Ecological Applications*, **8**, S79–S92.

Anderson, L. (2002). A bioeconomic analysis of marine reserves. *Natural Resource Modeling*, **15**, 311–34.

Ascher, U. M. and Petzold, L. R. (1998). *Computer Methods for Ordinary Differential Equations and Differential-Algebraic Equations*. Philadelphia, PA: Society for Industrial and Applied Mathematics (SIAM).

Bernstein, B., Iudicello, S., and Stringer, C. (2004). *Lessons Learned from Recent Marine Protected Area Designations in the United States*, a report to the National Marine Protected Areas Center. Ojai, CA: National Fisheries Conservation Center.

Beverton, R. J. H. and Holt, S. J. (1957). *On the Dynamics of Exploited Fish Populations*. London: Ministry of Agriculture, Fisheries and Food.

Botsford, L. W., Smith, B. D., and Quinn, J. F. (1994). Bimodality in size distributions: red sea urchin *Stronylocentrotus franciscanus* as an example. *Ecological Applications*, **4**, 42–50.

Botsford, L. W., Micheli, F., and Hastings, A. (2003). Principles for the design of marine reserves. *Ecological Applications*, **13**, 25–31.

Browman, H. I. and Stergiou, K. I. (2004). Perspectives on ecosystem-based approaches to the management of marine resources. *Marine Ecology Progress Series*, **274**, 269–70.

Brown, G. M. and Roughgarden, J. (1997). A metapopulation model with private property and a common pool. *Ecological Economics*, **22**, 65–71.

Bryson, A. E., Jr. (1999). *Dynamic Optimization*. Reading, MA: Addison Wesley.

Caley, M. J., Carr, M. H., Hixon, M. A., *et al.* (1996). Recruitment and the population dynamics of open marine populations. *Annual Review of Ecology and Systematics*, **27**, 477–500.

Carr, M. H. and Reed, D. C. (1993). Conceptual issues relevant to marine harvest refuges: examples from temperate reef fishes. *Canadian Journal of Fisheries and Aquatic Sciences*, **50**, 2019–28.

Clark, C. W. (1990). *Mathematical Bioeconomics: The Optimal Management of Renewable Resources*, 2nd edn. New York: John Wiley.

Clark, C. W. and Munro, G. (1975). Economics of fishing and modern capital theory: a simplified approach. *Journal of Environmental Economics and Management*, **2**, 92–106.

Costello, C. and Polasky, S. (2008). Optimal harvesting of stochastic spatial resources. *Journal of Environmental Economics and Management*, **56**, 1–18.

Cowen, R. K., Lwiza, K. M. M., Sponaugle, S., Paris, C. B., and Olson, D. B. (2000). Connectivity of marine populations: open or closed? *Science*, **287**, 857–9.

Cowen, R. K., Paris, C. B., and Srinivasan, A. (2006). Scaling connectivity in marine populations. *Science*, **311**, 522–7.

Crutchfield, J. A. and Zellner, A. (1962). *Economic Aspects of the Pacific Halibut Fishery*. Washington, DC: US Department of the Interior.

Gerber, L. R., Botsford, L. W., Hastings, A., *et al.* (2003). Population models for marine reserve design: a retrospective and prospective synthesis. *Ecological Applications*, **13**, S47–S64.

Grafton, R. Q., Kompas, T., and Lindenmayer, D. (2005). Marine reserves with ecological uncertainty. *Bulletin of Mathematical Biology*, **67**, 957–71.

Hannesson, R. (1998). Marine reserves: what will they accomplish? *Marine Resource Economics*, **13**, 159–70.

Hart, D. R. and Sissenwine, M. P. (2009). Marine reserve effects on fishery profits: a comment on White *et al.* (2008). *Ecology Letters*, **12**, E9–E11.

Hastings, A. and Botsford, L. (1999). Equivalence in yield from marine reserves and traditional fisheries management. *Science*, **284**, 1537–8.

Hilborn, R., Quinn, T. P., Schindler, D. E., and Rogers, D. E. (2003). Biocomplexity and fisheries sustainability. *Proceedings of the National Academy of Sciences of the United States of America*, **100**, 6564–8.

Hilborn, R., Micheli, F., and Leo, G. D. (2006). Integrating marine protected areas with catch regulation. *Canadian Journal of Fisheries and Aquatic Sciences.*, **63**, 642–9.

Holland, D. S. and Brazee, R. J. (1996). Marine reserves for fisheries management. *Marine Resource Economics*, **11**, 157–71.

Kamien, M. L. and Schwartz, N. L. (1991). *Dynamic Optimization: The Calculus of Variations and Optimal Control in Economics and Management*, 2nd edn. New York: North-Holland.

Kritzer, J. P. and Sale, P. F. (2004). Metapopulation ecology in the sea: from Levins' model to marine ecology and fisheries science. *Fish and Fisheries*, **5**, 131–40.

Levin, P. S., Fogarty, M. J., Murawski, S. A., and Fluharty, D. (2009). Integrated ecosystem assessments: developing the scientific basis for ecosystem-based management of the ocean. *PLoS Biol*, **7**, e1000014.

McLeod, K. L., Lubchenco, J., Palumbi, S. R., and Rosenberg, A. (2005). *Scientific Consensus Statement on Marine Ecosystem-Based Management*. Portland, OR: COMPASS (Communication Partnership for Science and the Sea).

Murawski, S. A. (2007). Ten myths concerning ecosystem approaches to marine resource management. *Marine Policy*, **31**, 681–90.

National Research Council (2001). *Marine Protected Areas: Tools for Sustaining Ocean Ecosystems*. Washington, DC: National Academy Press.

Neubert, M. G. (2003). Marine reserves and optimal harvesting. *Ecology Letters*, **6**, 843–9.

Pezzey, J. C. V., Roberts, C. M., and Urdal, B. T. (2000). A simple bioeconomic model of a marine reserve. *Ecological Economics*, **33**, 77–91.

Polacheck, T. (1990). Year round closed areas as a management tool. *Natural Resource Modeling*, **4**, 327–54.

Quinn, T. J. II and Deriso, R. B. (1999). *Quantitative Fishery Dynamics*. New York: Oxford University Press.

Rodwell, L., Barbier, E., Roberts, C., and McClanahan, T. (2002). A model of tropical marine reserve–fishery linakges. *Natural Resource Modeling*, **15**, 453–86.

Sanchirico, J. N. (2004). Designing a cost-effective marine reserve network: a bioeconomic metapopulation analysis. *Marine Resource Economics*, **19**, 46–63.

Sanchirico, J. N. (2005). Additivity properties in metapopulation models: implications for the assessment of marine reserves. *Journal of Environmental Economics and Management*, **49**, 1–25.

Sanchirico, J. N. and Wilen, J. E. (1999). Bioeconomics of spatial exploitation in a patchy environment. *Journal of Environmental Economics and Management*, **37**, 129–50.

Sanchirico, J. N. and Wilen, J. E. (2001a). A bioeconomic model of marine reserve creation. *Journal of Environmental Economics and Management*, **42**, 257–76.

Sanchirico, J. N. and Wilen, J. E. (2001b). Dynamics of spatial exploitation: a metapopulation approach. *Natural Resource Modeling*, **14**, 391–418.

Sanchirico, J. N. and Wilen, J. E. (2005). Optimal spatial management of renewable resources: matching policy scope to ecosystem scale. *Journal of Environmental Economics and Management*, **50**, 23–46.

Sanchirico, J. N. and Wilen, J. E. (2010). Economically optimal management of a metapopulation. In *Spatial Ecology*, eds. S. Cantrell, C. Cosner, and S. Ruan. London: Chapman and Hall, pp. 317–33.

Sanchirico, J. N., Malvadkar, U., Hastings, A., and Wilen, J. E. (2006). When are no-take zones an economically optimal fishery management strategy? *Ecological Applications*, **16**, 1643–59.

Schaefer, M. B. (1957). Some considerations of population dynamics and economics in relation to management of marine fisheries. *Journal of the Fisheries Research Board of Canada*, **14**, 669–81.

Scott, A. D. (1955). The fishery: the objectives of sole ownership. *Journal of Political Economy*, **63**, 116–24.

Shanks, A., Grantham, B., and Carr, M. (2003). Propagule dispersal distance and the size and spacing of marine reserves. *Ecological Applications*, **13**, S159–S69.

Steele, M. A. (1997). Population regulation by post-settlement mortality in two temperate reef fishes. *Oecologia*, **112**, 64–74.

Tuck, G. N. and Possingham, H. P. (1994). Optimal harvesting strategies for a metapopulation. *Bulletin of Mathematical Biology*, **56**, 107–27.

Tuck, G. N. and Possingham, H. P. (2000). Marine protected areas for spatially structured exploited stocks. *Marine Ecology Progress Series*, **192**, 89–101.

Warner, R. R. and Cowen, R. K. (2002). Local retention of production in marine populations: evidence, mechanisms, and consequences. *Bulletin of Marine Science*, **70**, 245–9.

White, C. (2009). Density dependence and the economic efficacy of marine reserves. *Theoretical Ecology*, **2**, 127–38.

White, C., Kendall, B. E., Gaines, S., Siegel, D. A., and Costello, C. (2008). Marine reserve effects on fishery profit. *Ecology Letters*, **11**, 370–9.

Wilen, J. E. (2006). Why fisheries management fails: treating symptoms rather than causes. *Bulletin of Marine Science*, **78**, 529–46.

5 · SOCIO-ECONOMY – Social dynamics of scaling-up marine protected area declarations and management

PATRICK CHRISTIE AND RICHARD POLLNAC

5.1 Introduction

Marine protected areas (MPAs) are increasingly used for multiple goals – sustainable fisheries, economic development, and biodiversity conservation being among the most important. As such, they involve a wide variety of constituencies and spawn complex management processes (Pollnac *et al.*, 2001; Jones, 2006; Christie *et al.*, 2009a). Social research, ideally integrated with biophysical research, plays an important role in the design, adaptive management, and evaluation of MPAs. The field of MPA-related social research is rapidly expanding (Jones, 2006; Cinner, 2007; Pollnac *et al.*, 2010), and has the potential to improve theories of environmental management and MPA management effectiveness. Currently, there appears to be growing interest among donors, non-governmental organizations, government agencies, and academics to fill the once notable gap in understanding.

Social research on MPAs appropriately consists of both basic and applied, mandate-responsive and mandate-independent research (Christie *et al.*, 2003). As reviewed in this volume, it utilizes a variety of research methods, generating quantitative and qualitative information which can provide broad and specific analyses. Increasingly, integrated approaches are providing socio-ecological analyses either through integration (Aswani and Hamilton, 2004; Christie, 2005; Pollnac *et al.*, 2010) or serial analysis (Stoffle *et al.*, 2010) of social and ecological data (Christie, 2011). Ideally, these analyses are integrated into MPA management and

Marine Protected Areas: A Multidisciplinary Approach, ed. Joachim Claudet. Published by Cambridge University Press. © Cambridge University Press 2011.

evaluation within an adaptive planning framework, a practice which is complex but results in better MPA management, convincing documentation of MPA impacts, and learning (McClanahan et al., 2005; Armada et al., 2009; Eisma-Osorio et al., 2009; Lowry et al., 2009). There is little doubt that socio-economic considerations and effective MPA management determine the long-term success of any MPA.

The integration of ecological and social processes is at the heart of how people come to support or reject MPAs. Fishers are generally keen observers of the ocean and fishery resources – their livelihoods and protein intake are dependent on it. Similarly, environmentalist MPA advocates are keen observers of ocean and fishery resources trends. However, each social group is likely to have distinct goals for any one MPA – a predictable outcome of their varying social constructions of the ocean (Steinberg, 2004; Christie, 2011). Their goals may overlap, but not fully. Empirical research in the Philippines demonstrates that environmentalists primarily value biodiversity and the existence value of marine ecosystems while fishers primarily value livelihoods and healthy fisheries (Christie et al., 2005). The goals are not mutually exclusive, but are not always obviously or fully commensurate (Jones, 2006). More importantly, each group acts based on its perceptions of the ocean and associated marine resources. Fishers are motivated to support an MPA if they perceive a threat to the condition of reefs and fisheries (Pollnac et al., 2001; Christie et al., 2009a) as are international conservation organizations interested in preserving coral reefs. But the perception of fishers is mainly local, whereas the perception of the international NGOs is frequently global (Johannes, 1981). The fisher, especially an impoverished one, is likely to be mainly interested in local fisheries and MPA management that will not further reduce an already modest income. The environmentalist is likely to advocate for large-scale no-take MPAs which provide, if well implemented, the greatest protection to the widest array of organisms. Proponents of sustainable fisheries and MPAs must acknowledge this dilemma and propose realistic and meaningful means to resolve this tension, otherwise plans for global networks of MPAs are almost certain to fail. Coercive strategies may work in the short term, but will unravel once external sources of technical assistance or funding are withdrawn (Christie et al., 2005).

No social construction, perception, or motivation is necessarily wrong, but they tend to lead to different MPA interventions and expectations. Clear and transparent communication surrounding these issues is essential to long-term success of MPAs, fisheries management, or new frameworks such as ecosystem-based management (Christie et al., 2009b; Christie, 2011; Aswani et al., 2011). As borne out of large-scale, multi-national empirical studies, compliance with MPA rules is directly reliant on the perception of legitimacy of rules and a sense of ownership and engagement in the design, implementation and evaluation of MPAs (Kuperan and Sutinen, 1998; Ostrom, 1992; Pollnac *et al.*, 2001; Pollnac and Pomeroy, 2005; Christie *et al.*, 2009a). Long-term commitment to MPA implementation is based not only on ecological and social benefits and their equitable distribution (i.e., outcomes), but also on the process by which these outcomes are generated. Developing effective MPA management processes requires attention to governance, capacity development, culture, and many other considerations. Social research documents, contextualizes, and qualifies these outputs and processes that determine MPA success.

This chapter presents findings from the Philippines in which two important dimensions of MPA and MPA network management are examined – (a) MPA effectiveness and (b) the scaling-up of MPAs and MPA networks to ecological relevant but socially feasible levels. Calls to scale up MPA establishment are ubiquitous in environmentalist and scientific communities (World Bank, 2006). Some have argued, primarily from a conceptual point of view, that overly ambitious and rapidly evolving MPA targets may be problematic (Agardy *et al.*, 2003), while others portray the current array of MPAs as woefully lacking, based primarily on ecological principles (Mora *et al.*, 2006). This analysis will disengage from these polemics and investigate primarily from an empirical position the processes affecting MPA performance and what are the conditions and dynamics which influence the MPA performance and receptiveness to scaling-up of MPA systems. Finally, this analysis concludes with an empirically grounded discussion as to whether plans for scaling-up MPA systems are feasible in tropical contexts. The analysis draws from two large data sets from the Philippines, but the conclusions are analyzed with an eye to other tropical contexts. Conclusions are relevant to non-tropical contexts as well, but readers should realize that the socio-political, historical, and cultural context of each location will influence MPA implementation (Pollnac *et al.*, 2010; Christie, 2011). As such, this analysis also highlights the need for such research in many locations.

5.2 Methods and research site descriptions

This analysis uses a multi-methods approach drawing from quantitative analysis of survey results and qualitative analysis of semi-structured interviews. This analysis draws first from a 2000 data set which is analyzed

Figure 5.1 Locations of the marine protected areas examined in four provinces of the Philippines (Central Visayas, sampled in 2000).

to elucidate MPA performance dynamics, then second from a 2007 data set which is analyzed to elucidate the dynamics influencing the scaling up of MPAs. These data sets are comparable since the survey instruments include identical questions for many variables and data collection by Filipino research assistants was supervised by the authors. Since most MPAs in the Philippines are established through a community-based management process (Pollnac *et al.*, 2001; Christie and White, 2007), the term community-based MPA (CB-MPA) is used.

5.2.1 Research sites

5.2.1.1 Central Visayas 2000 research sites

Philippines CB-MPAs examined in 2000 includes a quota sample of 45 CB-MPAs on small islands adjacent to and on the coastlines of the Visayan region of Negros Oriental, Cebu, Bohol, and Leyte (CB-MPAs ranged from 0.012 to 2.22 km^2, median 0.072 km^2, mean 0.19 km^2, SD 0.38 positively skewed) (Figure 5.1). The sample includes only CB-MPAs which include coral reef area, allow no fishing within the boundary, and were officially recognized by municipal ordinance for at least 3 years. Sites were selected to manifesting a range of "success" based on informal testimonies collected prior to interviews, with a stress on geographic representativeness across the four provinces. The final sample is composed of 14 CB-MPAs located in Bohol, 12 in Leyte, 8 in Cebu, and 11 in Negros Oriental. Interviews were conducted with 495 local government officials (one per site), community leaders (two per site), and fishers (eight per site) in the villages associated with the 45 MPAs.

5.2.1.2 South-east and south-west Cebu and northern Bohol 2007 research sites

In 2007, 36 CB-MPAs in south-east and south-west Cebu and northern Bohol (MPAs ranged from 0.042 to 0.76 km^2, median 0.208 km^2, mean 0.27, SD 0.20) were surveyed (some overlapping with sites sampled in 2000) (Figure 5.2). Conservation organizations (www.coast.ph), local government units, a US Agency for International Development-funded program (www.oneocean.org), and coastal communities are engaged in the development of two MPA networks in south-east Cebu and northern Bohol (Armada et al., 2009; Christie et al., 2009a; Eisma et al., 2009). These CB-MPAs were originally established independently with limited consideration of relation to other CB-MPAs in the region. Currently, coordination amongst seven Cebu municipalities resulting in a network of 21 CB-MPAs along 118 km of shoreline, and coordination amongst four municipalities in Bohol is resulting in a network of 20 CB-MPAs along approximately 268 km of coastline. Additionally, new MPA declarations are being considered to include critical and underrepresented habitats (e.g., mangroves) within the current MPAs. Social surveys of 468 local government officials (one per site), community leaders (two per site), and fishers (ten per site) in the 11 municipalities and 101 in-depth semi-structured interviews were conducted.

The following subsections provide descriptions of how dependent and independent variables were measured and constructed from multiple metrics in some cases.

5.2.2 Dependent variables

5.2.2.1 Marine protected area performance

The success of an MPA is usually evaluated in terms of its biological impact or less frequently in terms of community members' perceptions.

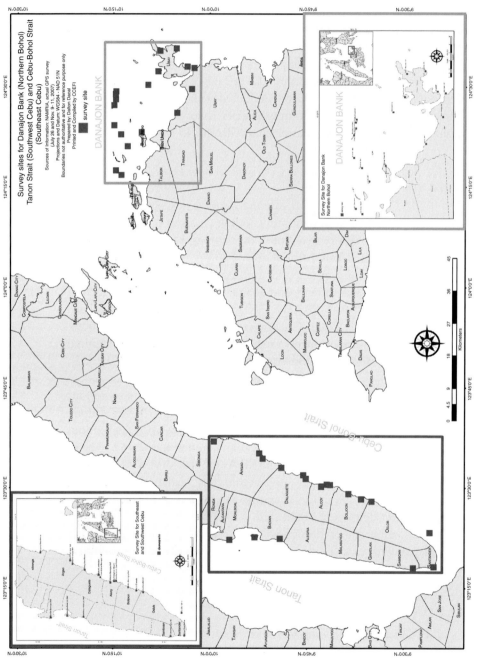

Figure 5.2 Locations of the marine protected areas examined in south–east and south–west Cebu and northern Bohol (sampled in 2007).

Table 5.1 *Principal component analysis of MPA performance variables*

Variable	Loading
Level of community empowerment	0.925
Level of MPA compliance	0.922
Number of MPA attributes present	0.743
Perceptions of resource abundance change	0.728
Biological differences in/out MPA	0.595
Percent variance	58.9

Success of a CB-MPA, however, can be conceptualized as complex of variables representing biological, physical, and social aspects of the institution (Pollnac *et al.*, 2001; Christie *et al.*, 2003; Christie and White, 2007). Successful CB-MPAs involve: (1) empowerment of community members; (2) compliance with MPA rules; (3) maintenance of a set of MPA attributes (e.g., marker buoys, guard house, community sign boards); (4) perceived increased marine resources; and (5) directly observed improved biological conditions. For this analysis the five variables were standardized and subjected to a principal component analysis with component scores (Table 5.1). The resultant variable is used as a key dependent variable. The following are descriptions of how each of these five variables was measured.

Level of community empowerment Since CB-MPAs involve empowering community members to manage their own resources, the degree to which this empowerment is realized is a component of success. This is also difficult to measure. It was decided to have an "expert panel" rank the communities on a scale of from 0 to 5 concerning the degree of community member empowerment to manage resources. The "expert panel" consisted of the researcher, his research associate, and the three to five experienced field workers who were involved in the data collection process. Following completion of data collection at each site the team assembled (all were involved in the data collection process) and ranked each site in relation to the others (range = 0 to 5, median = 2, mean = 2.3, SD = 1.8).

Level of MPA compliance Degree of adherence to CB-MPA rules is not easy to measure. Violation rates (if records are kept) are not a good indicator. You may have a relatively high officially recorded violation rate where strict enforcement is practiced and a low or no official violation rate where the enforcement is weak or non-existent. The same "expert panel" ranked the communities in relation to other sites on a scale of from 0 to 5 concerning the degree of adherence to MPA rules (range = 0 to 5, median = 2, mean = 2.2, SD = 1.7).

Number of MPA attributes present Another indicator of success is the establishment and maintenance of a set of features inherent to a functioning CB-MPA, such as marker buoys, community signboards, a management plan, a management committee, a file of documents concerning the CB-MPA, a monitoring program, and a guard house. The CB-MPA sites were assigned a score of 1 if a specific feature were present and 0 if not. These scores were summed (range = 0 to 7, mean = 3.9, SD = 2.2).

Perceptions of resource abundance change Community members' perceptions will influence their behavior regarding the CB-MPA. Fishers representing all the different gear types deployed in the community were requested to evaluate the coral cover, the fish numbers, and fish biodiversity in the CB-MPA as well as the numbers of fish adjacent to the CB-MPA. The evaluation was a three-point scale – "worse," "the same," or "better" than before the establishment of the CB-MPA. If all of the fishers replied that a specific aspect of the resource (e.g., number of fish in the MPA) improved (e.g., was "better"), the MPA would receive a score of 1 for that aspect. Otherwise, it would receive a score of 0. The scores for each of the four aspects of the resource were summed, resulting in a scale with a range from 0 to 4 (range = 0 to 4, mean = 2.0, SD = 1.6).

Biological differences in/out MPA This variable is composed of observed differences inside and outside the CB-MPA with regard to coral health (mortality index), numbers of fish families observed, and numbers of top predators (large groupers) observed. Data concerning these indicators were obtained using a systematic snorkel method that required the observer to snorkel over a shallow (1–5 meters deep) imaginary transect line 500 to 1000 meters in total length. The observer visualized a square meter area on the substrate and noted the percent cover of each parameter within the imaginary square as seen from the surface. The squares were approximately 50 meters apart (based on fin kicks); hence, 10–20 50-meter interval observations were accomplished. This was done both inside and outside (adjacent to) the CB-MPA. Differences for each of the three indicators inside and outside the CB-MPA were calculated, standardized, and summed.

5.2.2.2 Scaling-up
The measure of tendency toward scaling-up (variable name: Scale-up) is composed of the total of positive responses to six questions posed to CB-MPA management committee members in each of the 36 communities in 2007. The questions were:

(1) Should the MPA be larger than it is now?
(2) Are there benefits of managing the sanctuary as a network?
(3) Within the current context what is the degree of difficulty of making the MPA larger (three-point scale: very unlikely, difficult, possible)?
(4) Does the sanctuary management committee collaborate with other sanctuary management committees?
(5) Do you coordinate sanctuary enforcement with neighboring villages?
(6) Is there collaboration between mayors to improve sanctuary management?

The assumption is that receptivity to scaling-up MPAs will have a significant effect on the success of larger and networked MPAs. The first three variables within this composite variable measure this receptivity. The last three variables measure scaling-up from a governance point of view. Larger and networked MPAs will require collaboration among CB-MPA management committees, enforcement groups, and mayors. Municipal governments have jurisdiction over nearshore MPAs within 15 km of the shore.

5.2.3 Independent variables

Various contextual, outcome, and process phenomena were measured and the means of measurement is described below.

(a) Participation component score. This score was derived from a principal component analysis of seven project activities related to CB-MPA project participation (Table 5.2). The scree test indicated that extraction of a single component was appropriate. Standardized component scores were calculated for each site.
(b) Training component score. This score was derived from a principal component analysis of six project activities related to project training (Table 5.3). The scree test indicated that extraction of a single component was appropriate. Standardized component scores were calculated for each site.

Table 5.2 *Principal component analysis of project participation variables*

Variable	Loading
Consultations with villagers about MPA	0.884
Formal MPA consultations (meetings)	0.882
Core participant group formed early	0.743
Villagers voted on MPA	0.728
Villagers contributed to MPA project	0.688
Informal MPA consultations	0.621
Village influenced size and location of MPA	0.595
Percent variance	55.5

Table 5.3 *Principal component analysis of project training variables*

Variable	Loading
MPA advice continued after implementation	0.833
Number of initial trainings	0.827
Villagers can go to organization for advice	0.733
Village received external advice for MPA	0.710
Villagers visited other MPAs (cross-visits)	0.611
Number of ongoing trainings	0.511
Percent variance	50.9

In addition to the above scores, various other independent variables were measured. Population figures, density of fishers, number of community organizations, distance of CB-MPA from municipal center, and MPA size (in ha) were obtained from village and municipal statistics. The population figure refers to the total population of the village associated with the CB-MPA. Classification of an island as a small island was subjective but clear to the researchers. In the Philippines, small islands, many below 10 km², are scattered between large islands such as Cebu, Bohol, and Negros. These were classified as "small." The MPA fisher density was obtained by dividing number of fishers by the size of an MPA. Village heterogeneity was determined with the use of an indicator – number of religions. Village officials provided information on strength of the MPA management committee (a scale of 1 to 4 ranging from very weak to very strong). The MPA committee members interviewed were able to indicate the percent of alternative income projects associated with the MPA project that were successful, and whether or not the community was involved in monitoring MPA biological status. Finally, resource users (fishers) evaluated level of conflict over the establishment of the MPA (scale from 1 to 3 ranging from minor, serious, to very serious), compliance with MPA rules (five-point scale ranging from none to everyone complies) and community support (a three-point ordinal scale classified as no support, about half the community members support, and all support).

5.2.4 Qualitative research methods

In addition to quantitative analyses of the above variables, qualitative social data provide contextual and explanatory information to explain general patterns. Triangulation of quantitative and qualitative methods and data results in greater certainty and completeness of analysis (Miles and Huberman, 1994). This approach, combined with the quantitative analysis, provides a broader and deeper conceptual and practical understanding of effective MPA management processes. The qualitative analysis of scaling-up draws from a selection of quotes from 101 in-depth, semi-structured interviews conducted in the Philippines between 2002 and 2007. Analysis of qualitative social data requires consistent and transparent methods. Software programs such as Atlas.ti (http://www.atlasti.com/) provide a tool to organize transcripts, develop code categories inductively based on interview content, easily code data into one or multiple categories, query the interviews to explore linkages between types of responses, create memos affixed to portions of transcript or to code categories, and display results of analysis. The process of developing code categories and application of these categories is an iterative process requiring the constant comparison of content of categories with other categories (Strauss and Corbin, 1990; Miles and Huberman, 1994). Data are coded into categories that are abstractions of direct interview quotes (e.g., "perception that the environment is improving"). With some quotes falling into multiple categories, search commands were used to scan all interviews for quotes meeting two or more criteria (e.g., "leadership" and "perception that the environment is improving" or "motivations to support MPA") which are explanatory of relationships identified with survey data. This approach allows researchers to create an explicit "analytic trail" which demonstrates how conclusions are reached. The strength of

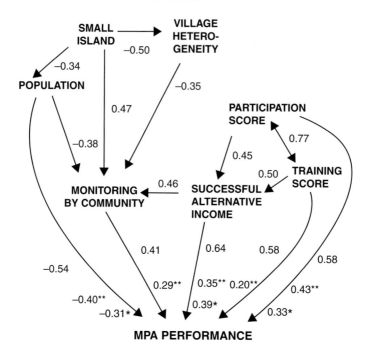

Figure 5.3 Examination of a correlation matrix of data derived from the Central Visayas sample (adapted from Pollnac and Seara, 2011). Numbers without asterisks are bivariate Pearson's *r*. ★, standardized beta coefficients; ★★, partial coefficients.

qualitative research is not in providing generalized results, rather it offers rich and convincing narratives in informants' voices which, in this application with quantitative analysis, may help to explain *why* particular statistical relationships between variables emerge.

5.3 Results and Discussion

5.3.1 Analysis of MPA performance

Figure 5.3 is based on examination of a correlation matrix of data derived from the Central Visayas sample (see Pollnac and Seara 2011). The arrows in Figure 5.3 illustrate hypothesized causal relationships based on the size of the correlation, social science theory, and MPA management experience. The heuristic model provides insights as to which context and management processes are most directly related to MPA performance, as well as how other variables are related indirectly through proximate variables. As described above, MPA performance is a composite variable derived from a principal component analysis.

Village population size is negatively correlated with MPA performance ($r = -0.54$, $p < 0.001$). Population also manifests a negative correlation with involvement of community in MPA monitoring ($r = -0.38$, $p < 0.05$) which is positively correlated with MPA performance ($r = 0.41$, $p < 0.01$). In an attempt to separate out the independent effects of population on MPA performance, the data set was examined to find other variables significantly correlated with at least one of the two independent variables examined so far, resulting in the net of relationships depicted in Figure 5.3.

Partial correlations (coefficients with double asterisk in Figure 5.3) of each of the proximate independent variables, holding all other proximate variables constant, identify population, percent successful alternative income projects, and participation as significant predictors ($p < 0.05$). Backward and forward stepwise regression provide identical results, eliminating both involvement of community in MPA monitoring and training score with the stepwise procedure (standardized beta coefficients indicated with single asterisk in Figure 5.3). The remaining three variables account for 61% of the variance in MPA Performance (Figure 5.3).

Participatory processes are key to MPA Performance in the Philippines and elsewhere. These survey results are further explored with narrative information derived from independently collected semi-structured interviews. In the Philippines, where participatory planning processes are relied on heavily and mandated by law, a former Under-Secretary of the Department of Environment and Natural Resources notes the shift in management standards:

There is a move towards decentralization – the paradigm has really shifted from a more state-based system towards one which is more participatory, involving the community and various stakeholders ... In the past, the degree of control of the state was very high relative to the public. Over the years, we are moving towards a situation where government is trying to diminish its control and elevate the control of the communities or what is known as community based resource management ... At least, it's a compromise because the state has control while the local community is also able to participate more ... So what we are saying is that let's elevate decision making into a societal process, rather than merely a governmental [one]. (May, 2002)

The link between participatory planning processes and compliance appears to be due to mixture of awareness raising and sense of agency within the planning process, a finding in other studies for the Philippines (Pollnac *et al.*, 2001; Christie *et al.*, 2009a).

Interviewer: What about illegal fishing? Has it declined?
Interviewee: Yes, it has really declined because of the increase in awareness of the people of the effects of destructive fishing. Also because they have been part of the planning process . . . *(Philippine local government official, June, 2002)*

In a context of limited government resources, participatory processes also can be used to improve enforcement.

Interviewer: Is the MPA network management committee generating community participation on sanctuary planning?
Interviewee: The MPA network management committee has invited community participation during the planning stage of the MPA . . . To have effective law implementation in the community level, the concerned community leaders must be involved. Without them, implementation of the law would be difficult. *(Philippine local government official, September, 2007)*

Community members are directly involved in marking their local MPAs and consult with local officials on appropriate material selection and placement.

For example with the making and setting of MPA buoys – we have to plan for what kind of materials can be used as buoys and are locally available. We teach them [community members] how to fix and install the buoys themselves. They volunteer the setting up of the buoys . . . *(Philippine local government official, June, 2007)*

And finally, community members are increasingly involved in MPA monitoring, a strategy that has led to increased material support from local governments, a key consideration in long-term sustainability of MPA implementation.

The local municipal government provides the boat during the MPA underwater assessment. We invite fisher folks to be with us. So when we are no longer there, they would know how to go about monitoring their reef . . . to see what happened with the biodiversity, population of the fish stock . . . *(Philippine Bureau of Fisheries and Aquatic Resources official, 2002)*

5.3.2 Analysis of scaling-up marine protected areas

The potential of properly implemented MPAs has been demonstrated in the Philippines and elsewhere, but they cover a limited area and cannot address all marine resource management concerns (World Bank, 2006).

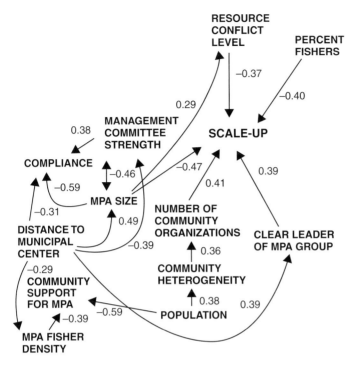

Figure 5.4 Interrelationships between selected variables and attitudes towards scaling-up marine protected areas in south-east/south-west Cebu and northern Bohol. Spearman's ρ correlation coefficients; $p < 0.05$.

This has led to management efforts to increase protected area coverage, to network existing MPAs, and to complement them with other management tools (Christie *et al.*, 2009b). This can be accomplished by increasing MPA numbers and/or sizes. In the Philippines context most are small, community-based MPAs, and increasing size would in some cases result in increasing the number of communities and populations associated with each MPA. In other cases, size increases with population held constant or growing would result in increasing pressure on available (i.e., outside MPA) resources. Figure 5.4 is a heuristic model of how contextual and MPA management variables are related to a composite measure of MPA scaling-up. The arrows indicate hypothesized direction of influence of one variable on another. The model provides insights as to which context and management processes are most directly related to this measure of MPA scaling-up, as well as how other variables are related indirectly through proximal variables.

The presence of a clear leader for the MPA management committee and number of community organizations, measures of the creation of social capital within communities and institutions, are proximally and positively correlated with Scale-up. The presence of social and institutional capital provides a positive context allowing for MPA scaling-up to occur. Size of the MPA, perceived conflict over marine resources, and percentage of fishers in a community are inversely correlated with Scale-up. Resource users may feel that relatively large MPAs are sufficient and cannot afford larger MPAs. Communities with a high reliance on fisheries are also reluctant to scale up MPAs. The inverse relation between perceived conflict associate with the establishment of the MPA and potential for scaling-up MPAs requires further research, but suggests that if conflict surrounding existing MPAs is high then receptivity to scaling-up MPAs may be reduced (Christie et al., 2009a). However, the presence of conflict should not be perceived as a shortcoming of MPAs or an insurmountable barrier to MPAs, but rather as a dynamic that requires careful response (Christie et al., 2009a).

This model identifies other relationships which should be noted by proponents of scaling-up MPAs. Size of MPA is negatively related to management committee strength and compliance with MPA rules. Both population size and fisher density are negatively related to community support for the MPA. Increased population size is, however, positively correlated with the number of community organizations, which is, in turn, positively correlated with measurement of tendency for MPA scaling-up – the organizations probably functioning to reduce the effects of heterogeneity associated with larger populations. These survey results are further explored with narrative information derived from independently collected semi-structured interviews.

Examples of coordination for improved MPA enforcement is a component of the Scale-up variable in Figure 5.4. The following is an example of how managers are coordinating management efforts.

In this community, patrollers had agreed that they will call the municipality in which the illegal fishers are heading since they already have a radio for communication. If they need help, they will communicate with each other. There's a need to be alert always because the boats of illegal fishers are very fast. *(Fisheries technician, September, 2007)*

Narratives also provide an example of how leaders emerge and why they are committed to MPA implementation – providing insight into causal relations between variables in Figure 5.4.

The number one reason I am active in the sanctuary network: I understand and foresee what our future would be. The main purpose of the sanctuary is to maintain the parent stock of fish. What we catch is only the spillover. What we are concerned about is the future and our children. I have already taken protecting our seas to heart. I used to be an illegal fisher before. And I'm greatly thankful to the non-governmental organization. So, that's why during my second term, I sold my gears, trawl nets, and decided to go after illegal fishers. *(Local government employee, September, 2007)*

5.4 Conclusions

This multi-method analysis clearly demonstrates that while there are global targets for larger MPAs, more MPAs, and networks of MPAs there are important considerations of social acceptance and, therefore, feasibility. In these communities, potential for scaling-up MPAs is inversely related to the current MPA size, conflict over marine resources, and the number of fishers in a community. Within current implementation terms, fishers may be reluctant to give up more fishing grounds to MPAs, especially when there are high numbers of fishers. This analysis also demonstrates that continued investment in social and institutional capacity should be a high priority if scaling-up is the goal (e.g., developing local organization to counteract the social heterogeneity associated with the increase in population associated with scaling-up). In short, comparative and in-depth social research demonstrates that scaling-up MPAs within the Philippines will be challenging given the high reliance on marine resources, but investing in human and institutional capacity development increases the possibilities of successful scaling-up of MPAs. Challenges to scaling-up are noted in other contexts such as the Caribbean, but for distinct reasons including multi-country contexts with distinct governance regimes (Fanning *et al.*, 2009). Planning and implementation of MPAs will be complex for multi-national initiatives such as the Coral Triangle Initiative (http://www.cti-secretariat.net/). Independent of the context, this study strongly suggests that the effectiveness of MPA scaling-up will depend on knowledge of and consideration of complex local dynamics (Christie *et al.*, 2009a; Christie *et al.*, 2009b; Pollnac *et al.*, 2010).

More comparative social research should be conducted in various sites in order to improve the likelihood that MPA investments are likely to succeed. Few global studies exist and those which have been conducted either ignore contextual considerations and use highly simplified measures of MPA effectiveness (e.g., Mora *et al.*, 2006) or suggest that generating globalized recommendations for MPA implementation may be difficult since governance contexts and management approaches vary tremendously (Pollnac *et al.*, 2010). Investment in global or regional studies whereby social and governance context are carefully considered will improve social theory and MPA implementation. These studies should, as above, utilize multiple measures. When possible, social and ecological information should be integrated. Critical research topics, highlighted in the above study, are: the opportunities and challenges of scaling-up MPA management in various contexts, the conditions leading to conflict and culturally appropriate conflict resolution mechanisms, means to identify and develop leaders and institutional capacity, and the means to develop context appropriate participatory processes.

5.5 Acknowledgments

The authors would like to acknowledge the staff of Coastal Conservation and Education Foundation (www.coast.ph) and Dr. Enrique Oracion for assistance with field research and Filipino coastal community members for working to sustainably manage marine resources against all odds. The manuscript also benefited from the comments of two reviewers and Pascal Raux.

References

Agardy, T., Bridgewater, P., Crosby, M. P., *et al.* (2003). Dangerous targets? Unresolved issues and ideological clashes around marine protected areas. *Aquatic Conservation: Marine and Freshwater Ecosystems*, **13**, 353–67.

Armada, N., White, A. T., and Christie, P. (2009). Managing fisheries resources in Danajon Bank, Bohol, Philippines: an ecosystem-based approach. *Coastal Management*, **37**, 275–99.

Aswani, S. and Hamilton, R. J. (2004). Integrating indigenous ecological knowledge and customary sea tenure with marine and social science for conservation of bumphead parrotfish (*Bolbometopon muricatum*) in the Roviana Lagoon, Solomon Islands. *Environmental Conservation*, **31**, 69–83.

Aswani, S., Christie, P., Muthiga, N. A. *et al.* (2011). The way forward with ecosystem-based management in tropical contexts: reconciling with existing management systems. *Marine Policy*, in press.

Christie, P. (2005). Observed and perceived environmental impacts of integrated coastal management in two Southeast Asia sites. *Ocean and Coastal Management*, **48**, 252–70.

Christie, P. (2011). Creating space for interdisciplinary marine and coastal research: five dilemmas and suggested resolutions. *Environmental Conservation*, **38**, 172–86.

Christie, P. and White, A. T. (2007). Best practices for improved governance of coral reef Marine Protected Areas. *Coral Reefs*, **26**, 1047–56.

Christie, P., McCay, B. J., Miller, M. L., *et al.* (2003). Toward developing a complete understanding: a social science research agenda for marine protected areas. *Fisheries*, **28**, 22–6.

Christie, P., Lowry, K., White, A. T., *et al.* (2005). Key findings from a multidisciplinary examination of integrated coastal management process sustainability. *Ocean and Coastal Management*, **48**, 468–83.

Christie, P. Pollnac, R. B.,Oracion, E. G., *et al.* (2009a). Back to basics: an empirical study demonstrating the importance of local-level dynamics for the success of tropical marine ecosystem-based management. *Coastal Management*, **37**, 350–74.

Christie, P., Pollnac, R. B., Fluharty, D. L., (2009b). Tropical marine EBM feasibility: a synthesis of case studies and comparative analyses. *Coastal Management*, **37**, 374–85.

Cinner, J. (2007). Designing marine reserves to reflect local socioeconomic conditions: lessons from long-enduring customary management systems. *Coral Reefs*, **26**, 1035–45.

Fanning, L., Mahon, R., and McConney, P. (2009). Focusing on living marine resource governance: the Caribbean Large Marine Ecosystem and adjacent areas project. *Coastal Management*, **37**, 219–34.

Eisma-Osorio, R. L., Amolo, R. C., Maypa, A. P., White, A. T., and Christie, P. (2009). Scaling-up local government initiatives towards ecosystem-based fisheries management in Southeast Cebu Island, Philippines. *Coastal Management*, **37**, 310–34.

Johannes, R. E. (1981). *Words of the Lagoon: Fishing and Marine Lore in the Palau District of Micronesia*. Berkeley, CA: University of California Press.

Jones, P. J. S. (2006). Collective action problems pose by no-take zones. *Marine Policy*, **30**, 143–56.

Kuperan, K. and Sutinen, J. G. (1998). Blue water crime: deterrence legitimacy and compliance in fisheries. *Law and Society Review*, **32**, 309–38.

Lowry, G. T., White, A. T., and Christie, P. (2009). Scaling up to networks of marine protected areas in the Philippines: biophysical, legal, institutional and social considerations. *Coastal Management*, **37**, 335–49.

McClanahan, T. R., Mwaguni, S., and Muthiga, N. A. (2005). Management of the Kenyan coast. *Ocean and Coastal Management*, **48**, 901–31.

Miles, M. B. and Huberman, A. M. (1994). *Qualitative Data Analysis*, 2nd edn. Thousand Oaks, CA: Sage.

Mora, C., Andréfouët, S., Costello, M. J., *et al.* (2006). Coral reefs and the global network of marine protected areas. *Science*, **312**, 1750–1.

Ostrom, E. (1992). *Governing the Commons: The Evolution of Institutions for Collective Action*. New York: Cambridge University Press.

Pollnac, R. B. and Pomeroy, R. S. (2005). Factors affecting the long-term sustainability of integrated coastal management projects in the Philippines and Indonesia. *Ocean and Coastal Management*, **48**, 233–51.

Pollnac, R. B. and Seara, T. (2011). Factors influencing success of marine protected areas in the Visayas, Philippines as related to increasing protected area coverage. *Environmental Management*, **47**, 584–92.

Pollnac, R. B., Crawford, B. R., and Gorospe, M. L. G. (2001). Discovering factors influencing the success of community-based marine protected areas in the Visayas, Philippines. *Ocean and Coastal Management*, **44**, 683–710.

Pollnac, R. B., Christie, P., Cinner, J. E., *et al.* (2010). Evaluation of marine reserve success using social and ecological indicators. *Proceedings of the National Academy of Sciences of the United States of America*, **107**, 18262–5.

Steinberg, P. E. (2001). *The Social Construction of the Ocean.* Cambridge, UK: Cambridge University Press.

Stoffle, R. W., Minnis, J., Murphy, A., *et al.* (2010). Two-MPA model for siting marine protected areas: Bahamian case. *Coastal Management*, **38**, 501–17.

Strauss, A. and Corbin, J. (1990). *The Basics of Qualitative Research: Grounded Theory Procedures and Techniques.* Thousand Oaks, CA: Sage.

World Bank (2006). *Scaling Up Marine Management: The Role of Marine Protected Areas*, Report 36635-GLB. Washington, DC: World Bank.

Part III

Assessment of the effectiveness of marine protected areas

6 · ECOLOGY – Assessing effects of marine protected areas: confounding in space and possible solutions

CRAIG W. OSENBERG, JEFFREY S. SHIMA, SONJA L. MILLER, AND ADRIAN C. STIER

6.1 Introduction

Marine protected areas (MPAs) are increasingly used as tools to conserve biodiversity, manage fishing effort, and facilitate recovery of degraded ecosystems (Roberts *et al.*, 2001; Sale, 2002; Hastings and Botsford, 2003; Cinner *et al.*, 2006). Marine protected areas are expected to produce long-lasting local increases in the density, size, diversity, and/or productivity of marine organisms within MPA boundaries (Russ and Alcala 1996; Claudet *et al.*, 2006; Chapter 2), as well as regional increases outside of the MPA via spillover from the MPA to sites that continue to be fished (Chapter 3). Assessment of the *actual* effects of MPAs relative to these goals is essential for adaptive management and decision-making. Despite a large number of assessments, however, there remains considerable uncertainty about the actual effects of MPAs (e.g., Osenberg *et al.*, 2006).

The central question (and challenge) that underlies the assessment of any MPA is easy to express but difficult to measure: "How does the state of the system (e.g., density or size of a target organism) within the MPA compare to the state that would have existed had the MPA never been established?" The former can be directly observed; however, the latter cannot and must therefore be estimated through indirect means (Stewart-Oaten *et al.*, 1986; Osenberg and Schmitt, 1996; Stewart-Oaten, 1996a,

Marine Protected Areas: A Multidisciplinary Approach, ed. Joachim Claudet. Published by Cambridge University Press. © Cambridge University Press 2011.

1996b; Stewart-Oaten and Bence, 2001; Osenberg *et al.*, 2006). Several different approaches have been proposed to estimate this baseline (Box 6.1; see also Osenberg *et al.*, 2006), yet, considerable controversy still exists (Box 6.2).

Box 6.1 *Types of assessment designs*

ASSESSMENTS, in contrast to experiments, aim to quantify site-specific effects (e.g., due to a particular MPA) rather than average effects (e.g., across many MPAs). General goals and approaches are described by Stewart-Oaten *et al.* (1986), Stewart-Oaten (1996a, 1996b), Stewart-Oaten and Bence (2001); issues specific to MPAs are addressed by Osenberg *et al.* (2006). The basic designs are summarized below. We assume there are two sites: an "Impact" site (e.g., the region within an MPA boundary) and a "Control" site (a region outside of the MPA). Each site may consist of multiple subsites.

CONTROL–IMPACT (or After-only): The Control and MPA site are assumed to be identical in the absence of an effect of the MPA. Under this assumption, the difference between the Control and MPA site after the establishment of the MPA provides an estimate of the effect of the MPA. In reality this estimated effect confounds the effect of the MPA with other sources of spatial variation (e.g., due to pre-existing differences in habitat). This is the most common assessment design.

BEFORE–AFTER (Box and Tiao, 1975): An MPA site is sampled Before and After enforcement. In the simplest approach, the difference from Before to After is a measure of the effect of the MPA. If the MPA site is sampled only once Before and once After, then the effect of the MPA is confounded with other sources of temporal variation (e.g., larval supply). If a time-series is obtained, and serial correlation is accounted for, then better estimates can be obtained; however, because ecological time-series are noisy, this approach is often problematic.

BEFORE–AFTER–CONTROL–IMPACT (BACI): the Control and Impact sites are sampled both Before and After establishment of the MPA. The change in the MPA site from Before to After, relative to the change at the Control site, provides a measure of the effect. In general, BACI designs (especially BACIPS; see below) provide more reliable measures of effects than either Control–Impact or Before–After designs. There are several variants of this approach.

- BACI (WITHOUT TIME SERIES) (Green, 1979): This design uses only a single sampling time Before and After. Thus, it assumes that the Impact and Control site will respond identically through time in the absence of an MPA effect, and therefore confounds the effect of the MPA with other sources of spatiotemporal variation. The other BACI designs use time-series Before and After to avoid this problem.
- BACI PAIRED SERIES (BACIPS) (Stewart-Oaten *et al.*, 1986): The Control and MPA sites are sampled at the same times (or nearly so) so that shared temporal effects can be removed by differencing (e.g., Equation 6.1). A change in the differences from Before to After provides one possible measure of the effect.
- BEYOND BACI (Underwood, 1992, 1994): Multiple Control and MPA sites are sampled multiple times Before and After, but the sites are not sampled at the same points in time. Although championed for introducing spatial replication, this design-based approach assumes random sampling (see Box 6.2).
- PREDICTIVE BACIPS (Bence *et al.*, 1996): Similar to BACIPS, this design provides estimates of effects that can vary with the ambient environmental conditions (as indexed by the state of the Control).

Box 6.2 *Design-based versus model-based assessment frameworks*

Two general frameworks have been discussed in assessments of ecological impacts and/or restorations: *design-based* and *model-based* approaches (see Edwards, 1998; Stewart-Oaten and Bence 2001; Benedetti-Cecchi and Osio, 2007; Stewart-Oaten, 2008).

Before–After and BACIPS designs are typically model-based. Box and Tiao (1975) provide the classic application of the Before–After approach, in which they modeled the dynamics of ozone in downtown Los Angeles and quantified the effects of two interventions (e.g., the opening of the 405 Freeway which diverted traffic around the city). Because data were plentiful and ozone dynamics were well behaved, the Before–After approach worked well. In contrast, ecological time-series are notoriously noisy and sparse, and ecological parameters are poorly behaved. In BACIPS, a Control site is therefore used to improve the modeled dynamics of the Impact site; the Control plays the role of a covariate (Bence *et al.*, 1996; Stewart-Oaten and Bence, 2001;

Osenberg *et al.* 2006). This approach is flexible and allows a variety of functional forms of impacts to be modeled: e.g., step changes vs. gradual temporal responses (Box and Tiao, 1975) or effects that vary with environmental conditions (Bence *et al.*, 1996).

These model-based analyses have been criticized because they do not explicitly incorporate spatial replication (Hurlbert, 1984; Underwood, 1992, 1994; Bulleri *et al.*, 2008). Before–After and BACIPS analyses *can* use data from multiple Control sites, but they do not require it (Stewart-Oaten 1996b). Design-based approaches are appealing because they fit into classic experimental design contexts (e.g., using analysis of variance [ANOVA]) with which most field ecologists are familiar. Most Control–Impact and Beyond-BACI designs, which rely upon spatial replication, are examples of this school of thought. However, such design-based approaches assume random assignment. In a classic experiment, sites are assigned at random to the two treatments. In our context, that is not the case: the MPA site is not selected at random from candidate sites that define the pool of all possible sites. Instead, the MPA site is usually selected for very specific reasons, many of which cannot be clearly articulated. Control sites are often then selected a posteriori by the investigator. Put differently, the MPA site and Control site(s) are not expected (in the statistical sense) to be the same in the absence of an "effect," unlike the situation in standard experiments with random assignment.

These philosophical issues are not simple, and we doubt the underlying issues will be resolved in the short term (e.g., see the debate between Stewart-Oaten [2008] and Bulleri *et al.* [2008]). Benedetti-Cecchi and Osio (2007) have attempted to integrate the design- and model-based approaches for impact assessments. We applaud their effort, but note that their approach remains design-based with random assignment assumed (albeit with covariates, not unlike our habitat-based adjustments). Furthermore, measures of effect sizes are difficult to extract from their ANOVA results. One notable advantage of the model-based approach is that it provides direct estimates of effect sizes, usually as specific parameters in the fitted model (e.g., Box and Tiao [1975]; see also Osenberg *et al.* [2006] for a simple Before–After example using MPA data). Future resolution of these debates will likely come as ecologists embrace model-based approaches and estimation more generally (Clark, 2007; Bolker, 2008).

Most assessments of MPAs rely upon a Control–Impact design (Cole *et al.*, 1990; Roberts, 1995; McClanahan *et al.*, 1999; Halpern, 2003; Westera *et al.*, 2003; Osenberg *et al.*, 2006), in which the MPA (i.e., "Impact" or unfished) site is compared to a nearby Control (i.e., fished) site(s). A difference in response (e.g., in fish density) is taken as evidence of an effect of the MPA. In a well-known and influential meta-analysis of MPA effects, Halpern (2003) reported a 91% increase in the density and a 192% increase in biomass of target species inside MPAs relative to Controls. This finding has been heralded as strong evidence for the effectiveness of MPAs. However, Control–Impact designs (which comprised over 70% of the studies summarized by Halpern: Osenberg *et al.*, 2006) implicitly assume that, in the absence of the MPA, measured variables will be identical in the MPA and Control sites. Yet for many reasons, the organisms present at any two sites are certain to vary in traits such as size, density, or diversity. Furthermore, siting of MPAs is a complex and challenging task, involving political, socio-economic, and ecological considerations: MPAs are not located at random among candidate sites and as a result, MPAs will differ in many ways from nearby areas. For example, MPAs may be established in places deemed to be ecologically valuable because the greater habitat complexity at the locale may provide important habitat to fishes. Assessments that do not take this potential variation into account (e.g., Control–Impact designs) may give misleading estimates of the effect of protection (Osenberg *et al.*, 2006).

Thus, despite considerable empirical effort, we are left with an unresolved question: are observed differences inside vs. outside of MPAs indicative of a positive effect of the MPA on local fish densities (or other variables), or do these differences reflect natural spatial variation that potentially existed prior to MPA establishment? Adding to this controversy is the observation that MPA effects appear to arise quickly, often being present at the very earliest sampling date after establishment of the MPA (Halpern and Warner, 2002). This result is exactly what would be expected by pre-existing site differences if particular types of sites (e.g., with greater initial fish density or greater habitat complexity) were selected for protection. Despite these obvious limitations, most of the available data to assess the efficacy of MPAs come from Control–Impact designs (Osenberg *et al.*, 2006). Unfortunately, there has been inadequate acknowledgment of these limitations.

In contrast to Control–Impact designs, BACIPS (Before–After–Control–Impact Paired Series) designs can provide less biased estimates of effects because they deal with many extraneous sources of spatial and temporal variability that limit other assessment designs (Stewart-Oaten *et al.*, 1986; Osenberg *et al.*, 2006). However, BACIPS studies have rarely been implemented (but see Castilla and Bustamante, 1989; Lincoln-Smith *et al.*, 2006; Shears *et al.*, 2006), due in part to the need for prior planning and the collection of a time-series of data from Before the establishment of the MPA (Osenberg *et al.*, 2006). Even studies with Before data tend to have, at most, only one sample taken prior to establishment of the MPA (e.g., Roberts *et al.*, 2001; McCook *et al.*, 2010). Better approaches are needed (Osenberg *et al.*, 2006).

Given the preponderance of Control–Impact studies in the literature, the continued opportunity for new Control–Impact studies (i.e., based on new studies of existing MPAs), and the obvious conceptual limitations of Control–Impact designs, it would be valuable to determine if existing conclusions about the beneficial effects of MPAs have been in error. The natural variability that contaminates Control–Impact studies not only has the potential to be confounded with MPA effects, but it may also add noise to more appropriate designs (e.g., BACIPS), thus limiting their ability to detect effects. Therefore, it also would be useful to ask if other approaches can be taken that could achieve more reliable results, even in the absence of Before data. Here, we have two goals: first, we determine whether past inferences of MPA effectiveness (e.g., Halpern, 2003) arose from the use of poor designs (Control–Impact assessments) that misattributed siting effects (i.e., spatial differences) to MPA effects (see also Halpern *et al.*, 2004). Second, we examine how the use of habitat covariates might improve assessment designs, for example, by removing the spatial variation that plagues studies lacking Before data.

6.2 "Effects": due to siting bias or protection?

6.2.1 Goals

To determine if results from Control–Impact designs have biased our conclusions about the effectiveness of MPAs, we compiled data from published assessments that included Before data (see Table 6.1). From these BACIPS studies, we estimated effect sizes using either the full data set (using Before and After data) or only the After data (i.e., ignoring information from the Before period and pretending the data came from a Control–Impact design). We also extracted data from Halpern's meta-analysis, which was based mostly on Control–Impact (CI) studies

Table 6.1 *Studies of MPA effects that included Before data and were used in our analyses*

Original paper	Marine reserve system(s)	Response: target group(s) (data source from original paper)	No. effect sizes (i.e., studies)	No. sampling dates (Before, After)	Other notes
Roberts *et al.* (2001)	St. Lucia	Biomass: commercially important fishes (Fig. 2)	1	1, 3	
Nardi *et al.* (2004)	Easter; Wallabi	Density: *Choerodon rubescens; Plectropomus leopardus* (Figs. 2d, 3d, 4d, 5d)	4	1, 4	
Francini-Filho and Moura (2008)	Marine Extractive Reserve of Morumbau	Biomass: *Mycteroperca bonaci; Carangoides crysos; Ocyurus chrysurus; Anisotremus surinamensis; A. virginicus; Scarus trispinosus; Sparisoma amplum; S. axillare* (Fig. 2); non-target fishes (Fig. 3)	9	1, 4	Due to zeros, analyses based on biomass + 0.07. Control data were means of unprotected sites at 400–800 m and 800–1200 m
Claudet *et al.* (2006)	Cote Bleu Marine Park (Couronne MPA)	Density: *Coris julis; Serranus cabrilla; Symphodus doderleini* (Fig. 4a, c, d and authors)	3	1, 2	Based on medians; due to zeros for *S. doderleini*, analyses based on density + 1
Lincoln-Smith *et al.* (2006)	Arnavon Islands	Density: *Holothuria atra; H. fuscogilva; H. fuscopunctata; Stichopus chloronotus; Tectus pyramis; Thelanota anax; Tridacna maxima; Trochus niloticus* (authors)	8	3, 3	

(*cont.*)

Table 6.1 (*cont.*)

Original paper	Marine reserve system(s)	Response: target group(s) (data source from original paper)	No. effect sizes (i.e., studies)	No. sampling dates (Before, After)	Other notes
Russ and Alcala (2004)	Sumilon Island	Biomass: large Serranidae (Epinephelinae), Lutjanidae, Lethrinidae, and Carangidae (Fig. 1a)	1	3, 7	
Shears *et al.* (2006)	Tawharanui Marine Park	Density: *Jasus edwardsii* (Fig. 2 and authors)	1	7, 6	Due to zeros, analyses based on density + 0.2
McClanahan and Kaunda-Arara (1996)	Mombasa Marine National Park	Biomass: Acanthuridae; Balistidae; Chaetontidae; Labridae; Lethrinidae; Pomacanthidae; Pomacentridae; Scaridae; others (Fig. 4)	9	1, 3	Due to zeros, analyses based on biomass + 0.07
Castilla and Bustamante (1989)	Punta El Lacho	Biomass and density: *Durvillaea antarctica* (Fig. 3a, b)	2	4, 12	
Castilla and Durán (1985)	Punta El Lacho	Density: *Concholepas concholepas* (Figs. 1 and 3)	1	1, 4	Combined density in center and lower sites
Samoilys *et al.* (2007)	Asinan; Batasan	Density: Chaetodontidae; Labridae; Pomacentridae; Scaridae; top trophic-level fishes (Figs. 3, 4, 5, 6, 7)	5	1, 4	Analyses contrasted "Inside" with the "Control" sites (not "Outside")

(i.e., that lacked Before data). Thus we had three different effect sizes: (1) CI comparisons from CI designs; (2) CI comparisons from BACIPS designs; and (3) BACIPS comparisons based on BACIPS designs. Halpern *et al.* (2004) previously noted the possible confounding of siting and MPA effects. They addressed this possibility by using the few existing BACIPS studies to determine if Control and Impact sites were similar *prior* to establishment of the MPA. Our approach differed from theirs in two important ways: we calculated effect sizes, and we recognized that by taking Before data, investigators might have been more likely to choose similar Control and Impact sites than in situations when Before data were not obtained. Thus, we hypothesized that:

(i) if siting is biased and MPAs are often located in the best locations, then the effect sizes estimated from Control–Impact studies will be larger than the effect sizes from BACIPS studies;

(ii) if sampling Before enables investigators to pick more "similar" sites (and thus reduce the pre-existing differences), then effect sizes using a Control–Impact comparison will be smaller for BACIPS studies than for Control–Impact studies (i.e., the BACIPS studies will have reduced siting bias relative to CI studies).

(iii) If siting bias exists even in BACIPS studies (a possibility that does not compromise the BACIPS analyses), then calculated effects will be greater using Control–Impact comparisons (relative to BACIPS comparisons) using the same data set.

6.2.2 Methods

We found 11 papers that sampled organismal or biomass density Before and After establishment of an MPA at sites both inside and outside of the MPA (Table 6.1). From the data in these papers, we estimated 44 effect sizes for different MPAs and/or species (herein called a "study"); 23 of these effects were based on density (e.g., number of individuals/m^2) and 21 were based on biomass (e.g., kg/m^2). Given the paucity of studies with Before data, we used multiple estimates for different target species from the same MPA investigation. We separated the studies using different response variables (biomass vs. density) because biomass responses were expected to be greater owing to the combined responses of density and organismal size (Halpern 2003).

For the ith study, sampled in the Pth Period (Before or After), during the tth sampling date, we calculated the difference in log-transformed densities between the MPA and Control site (if multiple subsites were available, we first averaged those):

$$D_{i,P,t} = \ln(F_{\text{MPA},i,P,t}) - \ln(F_{\text{Control},i,P,t})$$
$$= \ln(F_{\text{MPA},i,P,t}/F_{\text{Control},i,P,t}), \tag{6.1}$$

where F is density or biomass of the monitored group (e.g., a species of fish). In a few cases (Table 6.1), $F = 0$, so we added a constant to each estimate of F in that study (generally corresponding to one individual per sampling unit, or the smallest observed biomass in the data set). We then averaged those differences within each period for each study and response variable (i.e., density or biomass) and calculated effects and variances using either the After data only (i.e., mimicking a CI design) or using the After and Before data:

$$E_{i,\text{CI}} = \frac{\sum_{t=1}^{n_A} D_{i,A,t}}{n_A} \tag{6.2}$$

$$V(E_{i,\text{CI}}) = \left.\sum_{t=1}^{n_A} \left(D_{i,A,t} - \bar{D}_{i,A}\right)^2 \middle/ n_A(n_A - 1)\right. \tag{6.3}$$

$$E_{i,\text{BACIPS}} = \frac{\sum_{t=1}^{n_A} D_{i,A,t}}{n_A} - \frac{\sum_{t=1}^{n_B} D_{i,B,t}}{n_B} \tag{6.4}$$

$$V\left(E_{i,\text{BACIPS}}\right) = \left.\sum_{t=1}^{n_A} \left(D_{i,A,t} - \bar{D}_{i,A}\right)^2 \middle/ n_A(n_A - 1)\right.$$
$$+ \left.\sum_{t=1}^{n_B} \left(D_{i,B,t} - \bar{D}_{i,B}\right)^2 \middle/ n_B(n_B - 1)\right. \tag{6.5}$$

where n_P is the number of sampling dates in period P. If $n_B = 1$, Equation 6.5 was modified to reflect the lack of multiple observations in the Before period:

$$V\left(E_{i,\text{BACIPS}}\right) = \left[\frac{\sum_{t=1}^{n_A} \left(D_{i,A,t} - \bar{D}_{i,A}\right)^2}{n_A - 1}\right]\left[1 + \frac{1}{n_A}\right] \tag{6.6}$$

We then summarized these results by calculating weighted means across studies using a random effects model in which the weights were the inverse of the within-study variance and the among study variance. All means and confidence intervals were back-transformed with exponentiation to yield final relative effect sizes: e.g., an effect of 1 indicated no effect, and an effect of 2 indicated a doubling in density. Densities that required the addition of a constant were exponentiated, but the constant was retained (the influence of the constant was small relative to the overall effect). Equations (6.2) and (6.3) differ slightly from standard Control–Impact designs because the BACIPS studies we used all had >1 After sampling date. We therefore averaged the differences through time; the resulting confidence intervals will generally be larger than those reported in the original study because we used dates as replicates rather than spatial subsamples.

Finally, we also extracted effect sizes from Halpern's (2003) meta-analysis of effects on organismal density, which was based on MPA studies derived almost entirely from Control–Impact studies. We used this as a sample of Control–Impact effect sizes from studies that did not have any Before sampling. An overall mean and confidence interval was obtained based on unweighted analyses (because variances from individual studies were not provided). Use of unweighted effects from different studies should increase the variance of the average effects size (and the associated confidence interval), but not the expected effect size itself.

6.2.3 Results

Effects of MPAs were variable both within and among studies, giving rise to considerable uncertainly in patterns (Figures. 6.1 and 6.2). All meta-analyses (CI effect size from CI studies, CI effect size from BACIPS studies, and BACIPS effect size from BACIPS studies; for both density and biomass) indicated demonstrable beneficial effects of MPAs (i.e., confidence intervals that excluded the null hypothesis of equality inside and outside the MPA: Figure 6.1); however, individual studies varied in their effects and in the uncertainty of those effects (Figure 6.2). The high variability made it difficult to clearly assess our three core hypotheses.

Analysis of BACIPS effect sizes from BACIPS studies revealed an approximately 86% (95% confidence interval: 28–170%) increase in biomass within the MPAs relative to the Controls (Figure 6.1a). The effect size based on CI comparisons using the same BACIPS studies was larger but not demonstrably so (average effect: 128% increase in biomass). Both effect sizes calculated from BACIPS studies exclude the threefold increase that is often referred to in citations of Halpern's (2003) meta-analysis (i.e., primarily CI studies).

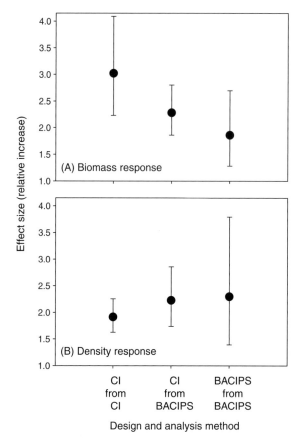

Figure 6.1 Effect sizes (ratio of reserve to non-reserve sites) based on (A) biomass and (B) density of study species from Control–Impact (CI) and Before–After–Control–Impact Paired Series (BACIPS) designs. The data for CI designs were digitized from Halpern (2003) and include a small number of Before–After studies. The data from BACIPS studies were used to calculate effect sizes based on both CI calculations (using only the After data) and BACIPS calculations (using data Before and After). Sample sizes are: (A) 32 (CI) and 21 (BACIPS), and (B) 65 (CI) and 23 (BACIPS). Plotted are means and 95% confidence intervals. For BACIPS studies, means were weighted based on the inverse of the variance of the individual effect sizes.

Based on the results for biomass responses, we conclude that BACIPS and CI studies likely yield different effect size estimates, although we caution that the high uncertainty precludes a definitive evaluation. The similarity in effects using CI and BACIPS comparisons from BACIPS

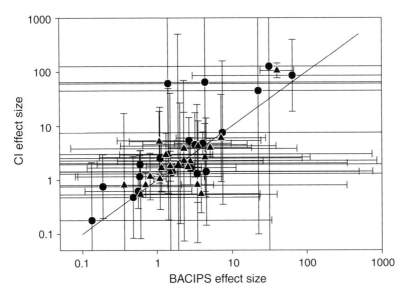

Figure 6.2 Effect sizes (ratio of MPA response to Control response) from studies of MPAs ($n = 44$) that included Before data, based on biomass (circles) and density (triangles) responses. Effect sizes for each species were estimated using data from the After period only (CI effect size) and using the full BACIPS design (BACIPS effect size). All BACIPS studies had >1 sampling date in the After period (range: 2–7), but only 12 studies had >1 sampling date in the Before period (range: 1–7). Plotted are the means and 95% confidence intervals, and the 1:1 line along which the two effect sizes are equal; excessively large error bars were truncated for presentation.

studies suggests that when investigators conduct Before sampling they tend to select sites that are relatively similar in initial conditions, presumably because they are able to see the sites during their planning phases and a priori select sites more similar in their biological and physical attributes. The apparent disparity in effects from BACIPS studies (~100% increase using both BACIPS and CI comparisons) vs. CI studies (~200% increase) suggests that either: (1) when investigators did not have the opportunity to sample Before MPA establishment (i.e., when they conducted CI studies), they tended to select sites that were more disparate in initial (but unknown) conditions; and/or (2) investigators are more likely to publish negative results in more recent years, and because BACIPS studies have generally been published since the publication of Halpern's review, the BACIPS studies may be more likely to include negative results. Both explanations likely play some role. If the first explanation is correct, then some of the results from previously published CI studies using biomass responses arose from a combination of MPA effects and pre-existing site differences. We suspect that previous CI studies may have overestimated the effectiveness of MPAs by about 100% – i.e., rather than generating an approximately 200% increase in biomass MPAs appear to lead to only a 100% increase. The effectiveness of MPAs remains well established – it just may not be as strong as previous analyses suggested.

The results based on density (instead of biomass) are even more ambiguous (Figure 6.1B). These data provide no support for siting effects, although the large uncertainty (e.g., the confidence interval for BACIPS effects from BACIPS studies ranges from a 39% to 279% increase) makes any inference problematic. No doubt, we could resolve some of this variation by considering attributes of the species that were studied (e.g., whether they are heavily fished, sedentary vs. mobile, herbivores vs. piscivores: Micheli *et al.*, 2004; Claudet *et al.*, 2010), but the limited number of studies preclude such an analysis.

The effect sizes based on CI and BACIPS comparisons from the same BACIPS study were positively correlated (Figure 6.2), and followed a 1:1 relationship. Further, BACIPS studies yielding larger effect sizes based on BACIPS comparisons tended also to yield larger effects using only the After data (i.e., based on a CI comparison). There was no indication that effects were smaller or absent in the BACIPS comparison relative to a CI comparison from these BACIPS studies. This suggests that siting biases were small or non-existent in the BACIPS studies. That said, there were few studies with Before data, so these results must be interpreted with caution.

Perhaps more important to the design of assessment studies is the substantial uncertainty in the effect estimated from any particular BACIPS study (Figure 6.2): only 9/44 effect sizes based on BACIPS had confidence intervals that excluded 1.0 (i.e., that led to the rejection of the null hypothesis of no effect), and many had confidence intervals that spanned several orders of magnitude in possible effects! This uncertainty reflects not only the tremendous spatiotemporal variation (i.e., variation in the difference: equation [6.1]) but also the limited number of sampling dates in the BACIPS studies (Table 6.1). This large uncertainty was rarely discussed in the original BACIPS papers because effect sizes were seldom determined (although some investigators carried out careful and thorough null hypothesis tests within a BACIPS framework: e.g., Lincoln-Smith *et al.*, 2006).

6.3 Habitat as a covariate: helpful or misleading?

Fishes and invertebrates often respond to the availability of habitat (e.g., Carr 1994; Holbrook *et al.*, 2000; Munday, 2002; Galst and Anderson, 2008). Thus, one source of pre-existing differences in the density of organisms (when measured per unit of transect without regard to substrate) could be the availability of their habitat. If variation in habitat explains variation in organism density then habitat could be used to adjust density,[1] possibly giving rise to more accurate assessments, even in the absence of Before data. Indeed, if siting effects bias CI assessments, and if these siting effects are manifest via differences in habitat availability, then the use of habitat-adjusted densities could eliminate much of the concern about CI designs.

The efficacy of using habitat-adjusted responses will ultimately depend upon the pathways that couple the MPA, organism, and habitat. We envision five scenarios (Figure 6.3), although others also are possible. These five scenarios all assume that the MPA has an effect, but they differ in whether the direct effect is on the organismal density, habitat, or both. They also differ in whether habitat affects organismal density (e.g., compare scenarios C and E).

Given these scenarios (Figure 6.3), we compared the effect sizes derived from CI or BACIPS studies using either raw densities (per unit area), or densities adjusted by habitat availability (Table 6.2). In all cases, we assumed that there were pre-existing differences among sites with the MPA starting out with higher densities of target organisms and more habitat.

In these scenarios, a CI design using unadjusted densities always overestimated the actual effect of the MPA because the pre-existing differences were incorrectly attributed to effects of the MPA. Habitat adjustment sometimes reversed and sometimes eliminated this bias. However, adjustment only worked if habitat affected organismal density because the adjustment corrected for site differences in habitat, thus putting all sites on equal footing. If habitat was unaffected by the MPA, then the effect on adjusted density correctly measured the effect of the MPA on the target population. However, if the MPA also increased habitat availability, then adjustment of density by habitat eliminated some of the effect of

---

[1] We assume that habitat adjustment is achieved by dividing organismal density by the areal extent of habitat (i.e., habitat availability), although more general, non-linear corrections might be more appropriate: e.g., Packard and Boardman (1988).

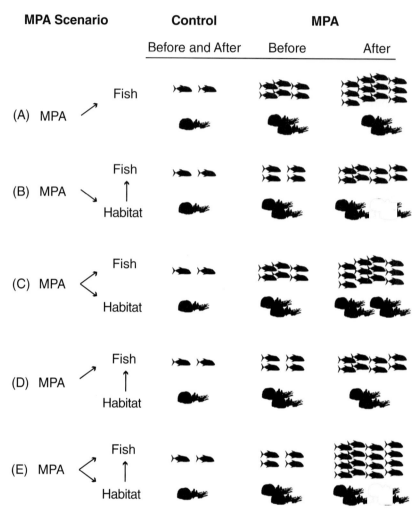

Figure 6.3 Models of fish and habitat responses to MPAs. (A) MPA increases fish abundance independent of habitat availability; (B) MPA increases fish abundance indirectly by increasing habitat availability; (C) MPA increases fish and habitat availability independently; (D) fish increase in response to MPA but also are habitat-dependent; (E) fish and habitat are positively affected by the MPA and fish are habitat-dependent. We assume a 2:1 fish:habitat relationship in scenarios where fish are habitat-dependent, that fish and habitat are more common at the MPA prior to MPA establishment (i.e., there are pre-existing site differences), that the Control site does not change from Before to After, and that the MPA has a twofold direct effect on fish (and/or habitat).

Table 6.2 *Illustration of the effects of assessment designs on effect sizes under different assumptions about the relationships between MPAs (M), fish (F), and habitat (H). We contrast Control–Impact and BACIPS designs, with two different response variables: unadjusted fish density (F) and density adjusted by habitat availability (H). We assume that MPAs are placed in sites with greater habitat and fish density (which creates the pre-existing differences in F and H), and that the MPA increases F and/or H (arrows indicate positive effects). Figure 6.3 provides the expected patterns of response at the MPA and Control sites*

Scenario Response variable Effect Formula	Control–Impact Fish $\dfrac{F_{A,MPA}}{F_{A,C}}$	Control–Impact Fish/Habitat $\dfrac{F_{A,MPA}/H_{A,MPA}}{F_{A,C}/H_{A,C}}$	BACIPS Fish $\dfrac{F_{A,MPA}/F_{A,C}}{F_{B,MPA}/F_{B,C}}$	BACIPS Fish/Habitat $\dfrac{F_{A,MPA}/H_{A,MPA}}{F_{A,C}/H_{A,C}}\bigg/\dfrac{F_{B,MPA}/H_{B,MPA}}{F_{B,C}/H_{B,C}}$	Reality
(A) F ↑ M	$\dfrac{12}{2}=6$ Biased High	$\dfrac{12/2}{2/1}=3$ Biased High	$\dfrac{12/2}{6/2}=2$ **Correct**	$\dfrac{12/2}{2/1}\bigg/\dfrac{6/2}{2/1}=2$ **Correct**[a]	2× increase
(B) F ← H M	$\dfrac{8}{2}=4$ Biased High	$\dfrac{8/4}{2/1}=1$ Biased Low	$\dfrac{8/2}{4/2}=2$ **Correct**	$\dfrac{8/4}{2/1}\bigg/\dfrac{4/2}{2/1}=1$ Biased Low	2× increase
(C) F ↗ ↖ H M	$\dfrac{12}{2}=6$ Biased High	$\dfrac{12/4}{2/1}=1.5$ Biased Low	$\dfrac{12/2}{6/2}=2$ **Correct**	$\dfrac{12/4}{2/1}\bigg/\dfrac{6/2}{2/1}=1$ Biased Low	2× increase

(cont.)

Table 6.2 (*cont.*)

Scenario		Control–Impact		BACIPS		Reality
Response variable		Fish	Fish/Habitat	Fish	Fish/Habitat	
Effect Formula		$\dfrac{F_{A,MPA}}{F_{A,C}}$	$\dfrac{F_{A,MPA}/H_{A,MPA}}{F_{A,C}/H_{A,C}}$	$\dfrac{F_{A,MPA}/F_{A,C}}{F_{B,MPA}/F_{B,C}}$	$\dfrac{F_{A,MPA}/H_{A,MPA}}{F_{A,C}/H_{A,C}} \Big/ \dfrac{F_{B,MPA}/H_{A,MPA}}{F_{B,C}/H_{B,C}}$	
(D) M ← F/H		$\dfrac{8}{2}=4$ Biased High	$\dfrac{8/2}{2/1}=2$ Correct	$\dfrac{8/2}{4/2}=2$ Correct[b]	$\dfrac{8/2}{2/1}\Big/\dfrac{4/2}{2/1}=2$ Correct[b]	2× increase
(E) M ← F/H		$\dfrac{16}{2}=8$ Biased High	$\dfrac{16/4}{2/1}=2$ Biased Low	$\dfrac{16/2}{4/2}=4$ Correct	$\dfrac{16/4}{2/1}\Big/\dfrac{4/2}{2/1}=2$ Biased Low	4× increase

[a] Habitat-adjusted and unadjusted BACIPS approaches give correct answers, although the adjusted analysis will likely have lower power (by introducing noise produced by variation in habitat).

[b] Habitat-adjusted and unadjusted BACIPS approaches give correct answers, although the adjusted analysis will likely have higher power (by reducing noise produced by variation in habitat-driven fluctuations in fish abundance).

the MPA (mediated via habitat) and therefore underestimated the MPA effect (scenario E).

There were different results from BACIPS using raw or adjusted densities. Raw densities always gave the correct expected effect size (Table 6.2), because the habitat adjustment was unnecessary with Before data (the effect of habitat differences was already included in the analysis): the Before period was used to estimate the existing difference between the Control and Impact sites and BACIPS therefore already incorporated the average spatial variation between the two sites (Stewart-Oaten et al., 1986; Osenberg et al., 1996). Adjustment actually led to misleading effect sizes in some cases (Table 6.2: scenarios B, C, and E). If habitat did not affect density, but the MPA increased habitat availability, then adjustment led to a decrease in the response variable, leading to an underestimation of the MPA effect (scenario C). If, on the other hand, the MPA increased habitat and this change also increased organismal density, then habitat adjustment underestimated the MPA effect. The problem here was that the portion of the MPA effect on the target population that was mediated through habitat was "removed" via the habitat adjustment and therefore was not included in the final effect size.

Even when adjusted and unadjusted BACIPS analyses gave the correct effect sizes (scenarios A and D), they potentially differed in their statistical power (Table 6.2). If MPAs increased density directly, but had no effect on habitat, *and* if habitat varied (among subsites within a site or through time) but had no effect on the target population (scenario A), then habitat adjustment would increase variance in adjusted densities and reduce statistical power. In contrast if both the MPA and habitat affected the target population (but not one another: scenario D), then adjustment by habitat would reduce nuisance variation in density, leading to a more powerful analysis.

In general, this discussion suggests that in the absence of more precise information about the dynamics of the system and the likely linkages, BACIPS analyses with unadjusted response variables, may be the most effective. Although CI and BACIPS designs using adjusted density can work (and be more powerful), this is only likely when MPAs do *not* affect habitat, when habitat plays a strong role in determining organismal abundance, and when habitat varies spatiotemporally.

6.4 Discussion and conclusions

Marine protected areas are a potentially powerful management tool. However, their effectiveness may have been overestimated due to the reliance on assessment designs that confound pre-existing differences with intended effects of protection. Unfortunately, spatial variation always exists (any two sites can be shown to be different if sampled sufficiently), and therefore CI designs will always be problematic. This is true in assessments as well as experiments, where replication and random assignment overcome problems posed by spatial variation. For example, Halpern (2003) saw consistent effects among CI studies. However, these "treatments" were not randomly assigned. Is the observed consistency in effects a reflection of consistent bias in siting or a consistent effect of MPAs? Our analysis (albeit with limited and noisy data) suggests the answer to both questions is an equivocal yes.

One approach to help with future CI assessments is to adjust densities (e.g., counts per transect area) by habitat variables (e.g., percent cover by preferred substrates) to remove sources of spatial variation unrelated to the MPA. This can work, but only in a limited number of situations (Table 6.2). In other situations, it may lead to new sources of bias. For example, fish are known to respond to the amount of biogenic habitat, such as live coral (e.g., Holbrook *et al.*, 2000; Munday, 2002; Graham *et al.*, 2008), seagrass (Galst and Anderson, 2008), and large kelps (Carr 1994), suggesting that adjusting for the amount of this habitat might be advantageous. However, if MPAs alter dynamics of these biogenic habitats (Selig and Bruno, 2010) then habitat adjustment may obscure the beneficial effects of the MPAs on the target organisms (Table 6.2). In cases where the habitat is unaffected by MPA protection, or where habitat recovers but on a very slow timescale, CI analyses using habitat adjustment *might* work (see Miller [2008] for an example of a CI assessment of MPAs where fish and invertebrate densities were adjusted by an index of habitat selectivity). The problem of course is that we cannot know *a priori* which situation we are in (i.e., does the MPA affect the habitat or not?). So, instead of "fixing" the CI approach, why not just use a more appropriate design to start with?

The obvious answer is that we cannot always obtain Before data. Doing so requires extensive planning and funding. But rather than continue to rely on flawed designs, it is vital that we collect such data when possible (e.g., as in Lincoln-Smith *et al.*, 2006 and de Loma *et al.*, 2008). Interestingly, even in cases where there has been extensive planning of MPAs (e.g., California, Florida Keys, Great Barrier Reef), assessments still have only a few Before samples, typically from a single date (e.g., Babcock *et al.*, 2010; McCook *et al.*, 2010). A single Before sample is insufficient for model development in BACIPS designs, which is a critical step that can avoid confounding of true effects with other sources of spatiotemporal variability (Stewart-Oaten et al., 1986, 1995). The limited number of Before dates also limits the power of any subsequent analysis and therefore increases the uncertainty of any effect size estimate (Osenberg et al., 1996b).

Finally, we note that our analyses are predicated upon the detection of local effects: comparisons of inside and outside MPAs. These local effects, while important, are perhaps the least important effect of MPAs. Regional effects (Chapter 3) arising from spillover provide the mechanism that underlies promised improvements in fisheries and regional biodiversity. Regional assessments remain rare, because they require a sampling scale that is hard to achieve: e.g., comparing a region with an MPA to a region lacking MPAs (Osenberg et al., 2006). Designs that rely on comparisons at even larger spatial scales may lead to even greater pre-existing differences, further necessitating the need for Before data.

6.5 Acknowledgments

We thank Joachim Claudet for the invitation to write this chapter and for his endless assistance and patience during the process. We also thank Joachim Claudet, Nick Shears, and Marcus Lincoln-Smith for providing data from their studies that allowed us to estimate effect sizes, Suzanne Stapleton for editorial help, and Joachim Claudet and Simonetta Fraschetti for helpful reviews that improved this chapter. Support from the NSF (OCE-0242312) and the Ocean Bridges program (French–American Cultural Exchange) contributed to the development of these ideas.

References

Babcock, R. C., Shears, N. T., Alcala, A. C., et al. (2010). Decadal trends in marine reserves reveal differential rates of change in direct and indirect effects. *Proceedings of the National Academies of Sciences*, doi/10.1073/pnas.0908012107

Bence, J. R., Stewart-Oaten, A. and Schroeter, S. C. (1996). Estimating the size of an effect from a before–after-control–impact paired series design: the predictive approach applied to a power plant study. In *Detecting Ecological Impacts: Concepts and Applications in Coastal Habitats*, ed. R. J. Schmitt and C. W. Osenberg: Academic Press, pp. 133–149.

Benedetti-Cecchi, L. and Osio, G. C. (2007). Replication and mitigation of effects of confounding variables in environmental impact assessment: effect of marinas on rocky-shore assemblages. *Marine Ecology Progress Series*, **334**, 21–35.

Bolker, B. M. (2008). *Ecological Data and Models in R.* Princeton, NJ: Princeton University Press.

Box, G. E. P. and Tiao, G. C. (1975). Intervention analysis with applications to economic and environmental problems. *Journal of the American Statistical Association*, **70**, 70–79.

Bulleri, F., Underwood, A. J., and Benedetti-Cecchi, L. (2008). The analysis of ecological impacts in human-dominated environments: reply to Stewart-Oaten (2008). *Environmental Conservation*, **35**, 11–13.

Carr, M. H. (1994). Effects of macroalgal dynamics on recruitment of a temperate reef fish. *Ecology*, **75**, 1320–33.

Castilla, J. C. and Bustamante, R. H. (1989). Human exclusion from rocky intertidal of Las Cruces, central Chile: effects on *Durvillaea antarctica* (Phaeophyta, Durvilleales). *Marine Ecology Progress Series*, **50**, 203–14.

Castilla, J. C. and Durán, L. R. (1985). Human exclusion from the rocky intertidal zone of central Chile: the effects on *Concholepas concholepas* (Gastropoda). *Oikos*, **45**, 391–9.

Cinner, J., Marnane, M. J., McClanahan, T. R., and Almany, G. R. (2006). Periodic closures as adaptive coral reef management in the Indo-Pacific. *Ecology and Society*, **11**, 1–31.

Clark, J. S. (2007). *Models for Ecological Data.* Princeton, NJ: Princeton University Press.

Claudet, J., Pelletier, D., Jouvenel, J.-Y., Bachet, F., and Galzin, R. (2006). Assessing the effects of marine protected area (MPA) on a reef fish assemblage in a northwestern Mediterranean marine reserve: identifying community-based indicators. *Biological Conservation*, **130**, 349–69.

Claudet, J., Osenberg, C. W., Domenici, P., *et al.* (2010). Marine reserves: fish life history and ecological traits matter. *Ecological Applications*, **20**, 830–9.

Cole, R. G., Ayling, A. M., and Creese, R. G. (1990). Effects of marine protection at Goat Island, northern New Zealand. *New Zealand Journal of Marine and Freshwater Research*, **24**, 197–210.

de Loma, T. L., Osenberg, C. W., Shima, J. S., *et al.* (2008). A framework for assessing the impacts of marine protected areas in Moorea (French Polynesia). *Pacific Science*, **62**, 431–41.

Edwards, D. (1998). Issues and themes for natural resources trend and change detection. *Ecological Applications*, **8**, 323–5.

Francini-Filho, R. B. and Moura, R. L. (2008). Evidence for spillover of reef fishes from a no-take marine reserve: an evaluation using the before–after–control–impact (BACI) approach. *Fisheries Research*, **93**, 346–56.

Galst, C. J. and Anderson, T. W. (2008). Fish–habitat associations and the role of disturbance in surfgrass beds. *Marine Ecology Progress Series*, **365**, 177–86.

Graham, N. A. J., McClanahan, T. R., MacNeil, M. A., *et al.* (2008). Climate warming, marine protected areas and the ocean-scale integrity of coral reef ecosystems. *PLoS One*, 3, e3039, doi:10.1371/journal.pone.0003039.

Green, R. H. (1979). *Sampling Design and Statistical Methods for Environmental Biologists*. New York: John Wiley.

Halpern, B. S. (2003). The impact of marine reserves: do reserves work and does reserve size matter? *Ecological Applications*, **13**, S117–S137.

Halpern, B. S. and Warner, R. R. (2002). Marine reserves have rapid and lasting effects. *Ecology Letters*, **5**, 361–6.

Halpern, B. S., Gaines, S. D. and Warner, R. R. (2004). Confounding effects of the export of production and the displacement of fishing effort from marine reserves. *Ecological Applications*, **14**, 1248–56.

Hastings, A. and Botsford, L. W. (2003). Comparing designs of marine reserves for fisheries and for biodiversity. *Ecological Applications*, **13**, S65–S70.

Holbrook, S. J., Forrester, G. E., and Schmitt, R. J. (2000). Spatial patterns in abundance of a damselfish reflect availability of suitable habitat. *Oecologia*, **122**, 109–20.

Hurlbert, S. J. (1984). Pseuoreplication and the design of ecological field experiments. *Ecological Monographs*, **54**, 187–211.

Lincoln-Smith, M. P., Pitt, K. A., Bell, J. D., and Mapstone, B. D. (2006). Using impact assessment methods to determine the effects of a marine reserve on abundances and sizes of valuable tropical invertebrates. *Canadian Journal of Fisheries and Aquatic Sciences*, **63**, 1251–66.

McClanahan, T. R. and Kaunda-Arara, B. (1996). Fishery recovery in a coral-reef marine park and its effect on the adjacent fishery. *Conservation Biology*, **10**, 1187–99.

McClanahan, T. R., Muthiga, N. A., Kamukuru, A. T., Machano, H., and Kiambo, R. W. (1999). The effects of marine parks and fishing on coral reefs of northern Tanzania. *Biological Conservation*, **89**, 161–82.

McCook, L. J., Ayling, T., Cappo, M., *et al.* (2010). Adaptive management of the Great Barrier Reef: a globally significant demonstration of the benefits of networks of marine reserves. *Proceedings of the National Academies of Sciences of the United States of America*, **107**, 18 278–85.

Micheli, F., Halpern, B. S., Botsford, L. W., and Warner, R. R. (2004). Trajectories and correlates of community change in no-take marine reserves. *Ecological Applications*, **14**, 1709–23.

Miller, S. L. (2008). A quantitative assessment of Ra'ui (a traditional approach to marine protected areas) on the fishes and invertebrates of Rarotonga, Cook Islands. Ph.D. thesis, Victoria University of Wellington. Wellington, New Zealand.

Munday, P. L. (2002). Does habitat availability determine geographical-scale abundances of coral-dwelling fishes? *Coral Reefs*, **21**, 105–16.

Nardi, K., Jones, G. P., Moran, M. J., and Cheng, Y. W. (2004). Contrasting effects of marine protected areas on the abundance of two exploited reef fishes at the sub-tropical Houtman Abrolhos Islands, Western Australia. *Environmental Conservation*, **31**, 160–68.

Osenberg, C. W. and Schmitt, R. J. (1996). Detecting ecological impacts caused by human activities, In *Detecting Ecological Impacts: Concepts and Applications in Coastal Habitats*, eds. R. J. Schmitt and C. W. Osenberg. San Diego, CA: Academic Press, pp. 3–16.

Osenberg, C. W., Schmitt, R. J., Holbrook, S. J., Abu-Saba, K. E., and Flegal, A. R. (1996). Detection of environmental impacts: natural variability, effect size, and power analysis. In *Detecting Ecological Impacts: Concepts and Applications in Coastal Habitats*, eds. R. J. Schmitt and C. W. Osenberg. San Diego, CA: Academic Press, pp. 83–108.

Osenberg, C. W., Bolker, B. M., White, J. S., St Mary, C. M., and Shima, J. S. (2006). Statistical issues and study design in ecological restorations: lessons learned from marine reserves. In *Foundations of Restoration Ecology*, eds. D. A. Falk, M. A. Palmer, and J. B. Zedler. Washington, DC: Island Press, pp. 280–302.

Packard G. C. and Boardman, T. C. (1988). The misuse of ratios, indices, and percentages in ecophysiological research. *Physiological Zoology*, **61**, 1–9.

Roberts, C. M. (1995). Rapid build-up of fish biomass in a Caribbean marine reserve. *Conservation Biology*, **9**, 815–26.

Roberts, C. M., Bohnsack, J. A., Gell, F., Hawkins, J. P., and Goodridge, R. (2001). Effects of marine reserves on adjacent fisheries. *Science*, **294**, 1920–3.

Russ, G. R. and Alcala, A. C. (1996). Marine reserves: rates and patterns of recovery and decline of large predatory fish. *Ecological Applications*, **6**, 947–61.

Russ, G. R. and Alcala, A. C. (2004). Marine reserves: long-term protection is required for full recovery of predatory fish populations. *Oecologia*, **138**, 622–7.

Sale, P. F. (2002). The science we need to develop for more effective management. In *Coral Reef Fishes: Dynamics and Diversity in a Complex Ecosystem*, ed. P. F. Sale. San Diego, CA: Academic Press, pp. 361–76.

Samoilys, M. A., Martin-Smith, K. M., Giles, B. G., *et al.* (2007). Effectiveness of five small Philippines coral reef reserves for fish populations depends on site-specific factors, particularly enforcement history. *Biological Conservation*, **136**, 584–601.

Selig, E. R. and Bruno, J. F. (2010). A global analysis of the effectiveness of marine protected areas in preventing coral loss. *PLoS One*, **5**, e9278, doi:10.1371/journal.pone.0009278.

Shears, N. T., Grace, R. V., Usmar, N. R., Kerr, V., and Babcock, R. C. (2006). Long-term trends in lobster populations in a partially protected vs. no-take marine park. *Biological Conservation*, **132**, 222–31.

Stewart-Oaten, A. (1996a). Goals in environmental monitoring. In *Detecting Ecological Impacts: Concepts and Applications in Coastal Habitats*, eds. R. J. Schmitt and C. W. Osenberg. San Diego, CA: Academic Press, pp. 17–27.

Stewart-Oaten, A. (1996b). Problems in the analysis of environmental monitoring data. In *Detecting Ecological Impacts: Concepts and Applications in Coastal Habitats*, eds. R. J. Schmitt and C. W. Osenberg. San Diego, CA: Academic Press, pp. 109–31.

Stewart-Oaten, A. (2008). Chance and randomness in design versus model-based approaches to impact assessment: comments on Bulleri *et al.* (2007). *Environmental Conservation*, **35**, 8–10.

Stewart-Oaten, A. and Bence, J. R. (2001). Temporal and spatial variation in environmental impact assessment. *Ecological Monographs*, **71**, 305–39.

Stewart-Oaten, A., Murdoch, W. W., and Parker, K. R. (1986). Environmental impact assessment: "pseudoreplication" in time? *Ecology*, **67**, 929–40.

Underwood, A. J. (1992). Beyond BACI: the detection of environmental impacts on populations in the real, but variable, world. *Journal of Experimental Marine Biology and Ecology* **161**, 145–78.

Underwood, A. J. (1994). On beyond BACI: sampling designs that might reliably detect environmental disturbances. *Ecological Applications*, **4**, 3–15.

Westera, M., Lavery, P., and Hyndes, G. (2003). Differences in recreationally targeted fishes between protected and fished areas of a coral reef marine park. *Journal of Experimental Marine Biology and Ecology*, **294**, 145–68.

7 · FISHERIES – Monitoring fisheries effects of marine protected areas: current approaches and the need for integrated assessments

VANESSA STELZENMÜLLER AND
JOHN K. PINNEGAR

7.1. Marine protected areas as fisheries management tools

In the past MPAs have mainly been implemented in coastal areas to preserve marine habitats and to conserve biodiversity. However, in recent years there have been an increasing number of calls for interdisciplinary approaches to marine management, such as the widely cited "ecosystem approach to fisheries" (EAF), and MPAs are now increasingly being advocated to safeguard declining coastal fish stocks as well (Halpern, 2003; Hilborn et al., 2004). Coastal multiple-use MPAs can be found, e.g., in the tropics (Russ and Alcala, 1996; Abesamis and Russ, 2005), the north Pacific (Schroeter et al., 2001), and the Mediterranean and Atlantic regions (Dulvy et al., 2008; García-Charton et al., 2008). Often these coastal MPAs have a year-round no-take zone where all kinds of fishing activities are prohibited. Such a no-take zone is sometimes surrounded by a buffer zone or partial-take zone where commercial fishing is restricted to only small-scale or artisanal fishing (Claudet et al., 2008).

In contrast, in many temperate regions such as the Georges Bank (Stokesbury et al., 2007) in North America, the Emerald/Western Bank on the Scotian Shelf (Frank et al., 2000), or parts of the North Sea, known to be productive fishing grounds, areas are either temporarily

Marine Protected Areas: A Multidisciplinary Approach, ed. Joachim Claudet. Published by Cambridge University Press. © Cambridge University Press 2011.

or permanently closed for fishing by the respective fisheries management authorities, with the aim of enhancing survivorship of spawning adults or juveniles on nursery grounds. According to the life history of the respective target species, some fisheries closures or exclusive fisheries MPAs such as, e.g., the hake closures in north-west Spain can have a strong seasonal component with fishery exclusion only lasting a few weeks or months each year. Besides the seasonal banning of fishing activity, other management measures can include restrictions on the gear types permissible within designated areas (Frank *et al.*, 2000) or the type of fishing vessels (e.g., the Maltese 25-mile zone). Many closures established, e.g., in Europe under the Common Fisheries Policy (CFP) were implemented as part of a package of measures to achieve a wider objective, for example recovery and replenishment of a particular stock (Scientific, Technical and Economic Committee for Fisheries, 2007).

Due to global commitments to conserve natural resources an increasing number of marine habitats are coming under legislative protection. In Europe a significant part of this effort is associated with the European Habitat and Birds Directives (European Union, 1979; European Union, 1992) although other closures are mandated under the revised CFP, as well as national and regional by-laws. Sites for protecting marine habitats are known as Special Areas of Conservation (SACs), and those for protecting birds are known as Special Protection Areas (SPAs). A comprehensive (Natura 2000) network of such sites in coastal and offshore waters, accompanied by pre-agreed management measures, is required to be in place by the year 2012. Such management measures will include new restrictions on fisheries, and there may well be secondary fisheries objectives agreed for such sites, although this is not their primary purpose.

Despite this great variety of implemented MPAs aiming to enhance fisheries, our ability to measure the success or failure of these MPAs against clearly stated objectives remains problematical and is often overlooked (Ward, 2004). In general, MPA objectives are stated at a local level, but when an MPA is established as part of a regional scheme then the local objectives can be nested within the respective regional objectives (Jennings, 2009). For instance, if at a local level the overarching goal for an exclusive fisheries MPA is the sustainable use of local marine resources, or the protection of a particular spawning area, an associated and complementary large-scale fisheries objective could be, e.g., "maintaining spawning biomass at 50% of virgin spawning stock," making use of MPAs as a source of larvae, and a refuge for mature adults. In practice, many multiple-use MPAs have multiple and sometimes conflicting objectives ranging, e.g., from fisheries objectives for the no-take zone to ecological and socio-economic objectives for the no-take and buffer zone (Ward, 2004).

A key part of any MPA performance assessment system (PAS) involves the setting of objectives and goals (Hilborn *et al.*, 2004). Other important steps comprise the identification of performance indicators with realistic benchmarks and thresholds, and the implementation of an appropriate monitoring program (Hockings *et al.*, 2000; Jameson *et al.*, 2002; Pomeroy *et al.*, 2004).

A vast literature discusses the appropriate choice of indicators within the context of achieving stated fisheries objectives (Ward, 2000; Ward, 2004; Pelletier *et al.*, 2008). In general, performance indicators describe quantitative, qualitative, direct, and indirect phenomena and are defined based on assumed cause–effect pathways between the change in anthropogenic pressure (usually fishing) and the response of the indicator in the particular MPA system (Ward, 2004). Cause–effect pathways can be established with the help of a driver–pressure–state–impacts–response (DPSIR) framework (Elliott, 2002; Mangi *et al.*, 2007), and an example application of this approach to MPAs is provided by Ojeda-Martínez *et al.* (2009). These authors concluded that the DPSIR framework can help to simplify the complexity of MPA management, and that it can be a very effective tool to organize participation processes to better involve stakeholders, managers, and scientists.

7.2 Fisheries effects of marine protected areas: mechanisms involved and monitoring approaches

7.2.1 Mechanisms involved that can enhance fisheries

Fisheries effects can be generally categorized by their spatial dimension (inside MPA, outside MPA), temporal dimension (short term, medium term, long term), biological component (population, reproduction, genetics), system (stock, general environment, ecosystem) and causal dimension (direct or indirect effect) (see Ward *et al.*, 2001; García-Charton *et al.*, 2008 for more detailed list). In the following section we give some examples of fisheries effects and their underlying mechanisms rather than offering a fully comprehensive overview (see Figure 7.1 and Chapter 3).

Due to the protection from fishing pressure inside an MPA direct effects include, e.g., an increase in the abundance of target species, an increase in mean size/age (i.e., survivorship) for the target species, increased spawning stock, and hence larval supply for the target species (Halpern, 2003). Expected direct medium-term benefits for the fisheries are largely due to the export of adult/juvenile individuals over the boundaries of the MPA, i.e., "spillover" (McClanahan and Mangi, 2000), and eggs and larvae that are transported from the MPA outwards by currents and advection (Planes et al., 2000; Almany et al., 2007). The spillover of adult biomass can be due to random movement, density-dependent out-migration, directed movements (daily or seasonal migrations), and ontogenic habitat shifts (see, e.g., Sánchez Lizaso et al., 2000). By contrast the outflux of eggs and larvae will depended on currents, tides, and frontal dynamics, but also larval duration and swimming capabilities (see Planes et al., 2000).

Spillover can sometimes manifest itself in an increase in fisheries recruitment locally and regionally, and consequently in increased catches and yields overall (Roberts et al., 2001; Alcala et al., 2005). In such circumstances increased fisheries yield will be the result of an increase in the number of fish but also an improvement in the quality and/or size of target fish available (see Figure 7.1).

At the level of species communities and the exploited stock, the consequences of establishing an MPA can include, e.g., the enhancement of species of diversity and richness (Gladstone, 2007), an apparent increase in stock size overall (Horwood et al., 1998), or preservation of genetic diversity within the target stock, which is linked to the vulnerability of populations to anthropogenic pressures and the ability to recover afterwards (Hughes et al., 2003; Roberts et al., 2005; Pérez-Ruzafa et al., 2006). The restoration of species diversity and richness is likely to contribute to increased diversity in fisheries catches (e.g., Stelzenmüller et al., 2009). A diverse fishery is thought to be more sustainable in the long run and may help to buffer against natural fluctuations in catch and revenues, and hence can reduce the years of "boom" and "bust" in fisheries (Ward et al., 2001). Increasing stock size, and allowing some individuals to reach older ages, reduces the catch variability and the susceptibility to occasional poor year-classes, which can contribute to an economically more viable fishery (Horwood et al., 1998; Roberts et al., 2005) that is able to withstand infrequent shock events. The lack of fishing pressure

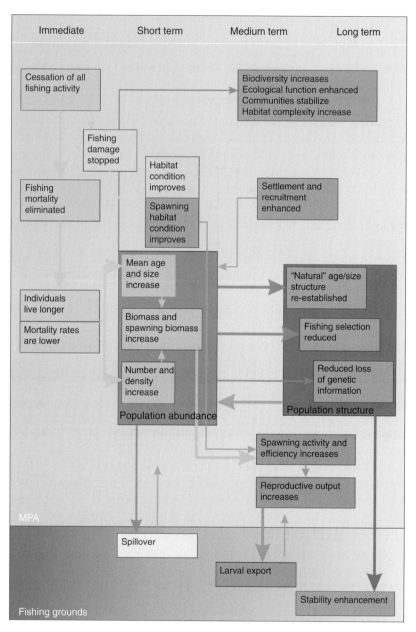

Figure 7.1 This conceptual model shows the pathways by which an MPA establishment could lead to environmental enhancement within the MPA, and potential fisheries benefits outside the MPA through the processes of spillover, larval export, and stability enhancement. The large upper box represents an MPA, and the lower box represents the fished areas outside the MPA. The size of arrows roughly indicates the hypothesized importance of pathway to the potential fisheries

should provide some protection for genetic diversity (an "insurance policy") which prevents low-population bottlenecks (Jennings *et al.*, 1999). This buffering of genetic impacts of fishing should result in improved resilience of the system. However, the recovery of key predators within a system (e.g., within an MPA) can lead to "trophic cascades" (Pinnegar *et al.*, 2000). For example, one might expect an increase of predators in a system due to protection, and this in turn might result in the loss or depletion of other species that are prey or competitors, some of which might themselves be targeted by humans (e.g., sea urchins or cephalopods).

7.2.2 Empirical approaches to assess fisheries effects

Current approaches to assess fisheries effects comprise empirical approaches based on statistical modeling of field data and dynamic models describing spatiotemporal dynamics of populations and fisheries (Pelletier *et al.*, 2008). While dynamic models can support the design of MPAs and assess the theoretical consequences for both populations and fisheries (see review of Higgins *et al.*, 2008), empirical approaches can support the ongoing assessment of MPA indicators and be integrated as a component of long-term monitoring programs.

Based on the assumption that ecological responses due to protection will translate directly into benefits for the adjacent fisheries, most empirical studies that monitor and assess fisheries effects tend to focus on the population and ecosystem level, and use ecological measures such as abundance and biomass retrieved from biological sampling (Halpern, 2003; Micheli *et al.*, 2004). As discussed by Higgins *et al.* (2008), this is especially the case for tropical and subtropical case studies in and around multiple use MPAs. In contrast, case studies of fisheries MPAs and fisheries closures in temperate waters have tended to emerge from a fisheries management perspective and hence use complex statistical models (stock assessments) to assess whether any benefits have accrued at the wider stock level (Horwood *et al.*, 1998; Fisher and Frank, 2002; Murawski *et al.*, 2003; Kjærsgaard and Frost, 2008). Regardless of the geographic setting, as yet only a few empirical studies have convincingly been able to quantify the benefits for the respective fisheries. In Table 7.1 we compiled

---

effects, and the timeframe (immediate to long term) indicates roughly when these benefits might be expected to occur. Redrawn from Ward *et al.* (2001). *The Role of Marine Reserves as Fisheries Management Tools: A Review of Concepts, Evidence and International Experience.* Canberra, ACT: Bureau of Rural Sciences.

Table 7.1 *Example case studies of empirical approaches to assess fisheries benefits of MPAs such as increased catches, catch per unit effort (CPUE), income per unit effort (IPUE), and yields; with the category of the fisheries effect, the variables measured, the biological component (reflecting the level at which the effects are studies), a brief description of the approach, the information on the enhancement of the fisheries yield, the maximum distance where the MPA effect has been measured (km), the type of fisheries, the case study location, and the respective references*

Fisheries effects	Variable measured	Biological component	Approach	Enhanced yield	Distance of influence (km)	Type of fisheries	Location	Reference
Biomass export	CPUE, IPUE, fishing effort	Population	Temporal pattern, frequency distribution, spatially structured	Yes	<1	Artisanal	Kenya	Abesamis et al., 2006
Biomass export	CPUE, fishing effort	Population	Temporal pattern, frequency distribution, spatially structured	Yes	—		Philippines	Russ et al., 2004
Biomass export	Catch, fishing effort	Population	Temporal pattern, statistical tests	Yes	—	Artisanal	USA – Florida	Roberts et al., 2001
Biomass export	CPUE, yield	Population	Temporal pattern, statistical tests	Yes	—	Artisanal	Philippines	Alcala et al., 2005
Biomass export	CPUE, revenue, fishing effort	Population	Regression analysis (GAMs, GLMs)	Yes	0.7–2.5	Artisanal	Mediterranean	Goñi et al., 2008
Biomass export	CPUE, fish size	Population	Spatial modeling with GIS and geostatistics	Yes (for some species)	2	Artisanal	Mediterranean	Stelzenmüller et al., 2007

Biomass export	CPUE, fishing effort	Population	Density gradient, regression analysis (GLMs)	Yes (for some species)	<20	Bottom-trawling	USA – New England coast	Murawski et al., 2003
Biomass export	CPUE, fishing effort	Population	Density gradient, regression analysis (GAMs, GLMs)	Yes	1.5	Artisanal	Mediterranean	Goñi et al., 2006
Biomass export	CPUE, fish size	Population	Before–after design, statistical tests	Yes	—	Artisanal	Egypt, Red Sea	Galal et al., 2002
Biomass and larvae export	Biomass, egg production	Population	Temporal and spatial replicates, ordination techniques, ANOVA	Yes (for target species)	—	Artisanal	USA – California	Tetreault and Ambrose, 2007
Increased species diversity	CPUE, IPUE, species diversity, functional diversity	Population and community	Spatial modeling with GIS and geostatistics	Yes	<2	Artisanal	Mediterranean	Stelzenmüller et al., 2009
Protection of recruitment	CPUE, fishing effort, survival index, condition index	Exploited fish stock	BACIP design, time-series of variables	—	—	Bottom trawling	Scotian shelf	Frank et al., 2000
Egg and larvae export	CPUE, IPUE, larvae density	Population	Habitat suitability modeling (GAMs)	Yes (for target species)	—	Artisanal	Mediterranean	Crec'hriou et al., 2008

Note that this is not a comprehensive review. GIS, geographic information system; GAMs, generalized algebraic models; GLMs, generalized linear models.

examples of empirical studies assessing effects of MPAs on the adjacent fisheries such as an increased catch per unit effort (CPUE), income per unit effort (IPUE), and yield. Although we did not conduct an exhaustive review, the set of studies reveal that monitoring approaches primarily focus on the assessment of export of biomass.

Often the fisheries involved are small-scale or artisanal. In the cases where spillovers have been measured, effects were particularly evident close to the border of the MPA, within 5 km. However, in some instances effects have been measured up to 30 km from the MPA. This highlights the need for case-by-case design and monitoring based on the life history of the respective target species. Environmental variability due to habitat heterogeneity or depth gradients and the distribution of fishing effort have not always taken into account possible gradients in catch and yield (see next section for more detailed discussion). Our review revealed that there is a lack of empirical research deploying integrative approaches to assess a set of fisheries performance indictors such as CPUE, catch rates, larvae export, and fishing effort. Also we found that the current body of literature lacks an assessment of long-term fisheries effects on regional scales or at the level of fish stocks, despite this being a stated objective in some instances (Scientific, Technical and Economic Committee for Fisheries, 2007).

7.3 Finding an appropriate baseline for assessing fisheries effects

Common reasons for the lack of empirical evidence of fisheries benefits of MPAs (and fisheries closures) that are discussed in the literature include the absence of rigorous and planned "Before–After–Control–Impact" designs for monitoring (BACI design) (Mosquera *et al.*, 2000; Jennings, 2001; Sale *et al.*, 2005), inadequate sampling strategies (Fraschetti *et al.*, 2002), the disregard of spatiotemporal variability in fish populations and/or habitat heterogeneity (García-Charton and Pérez-Ruzafa, 1999; García-Charton *et al.*, 2004), and the selection of methods that are only capable of detecting linear biomass gradients (Murawski *et al.*, 2003).

There are two approaches to analyze the impacts of MPAs on living resources (Houde, 2001). In the first approach, changes within the MPA are evaluated temporally such that conditions are documented before the implementation and then compared to conditions following implementation (before vs. after). A limitation of this approach is that environmental variation in the years before and after the establishment of the MPA may obscure trends resulting from protection. In the second approach, changes in the MPA are evaluated spatially such that conditions inside the MPA are compared to conditions in a similar "reference" area outside (inside vs. outside). The limitation of this approach is that MPAs often encompass unique habitats and are set up because the area is distinctive or "special" in the first place (García-Charton *et al.*, 2004); hence, there are few situations in which comparison areas accurately represent the features found within the MPA. The worst-case scenario occurs when only one MPA has been established long before an evaluation program was initiated and only post-establishment monitoring takes place (Table 7.2). Thankfully such circumstances are rare and in most cases the MPA is compared to some "non-MPA" reference site or sites, although in such cases, it is never clear whether observed differences (MPA vs. non-MPA) are caused by the MPA or if these differences already existed before the MPA was established (Syms and Carr, 2002).

Recently, empirical studies comprising artisanal (Stelzenmüller *et al.*, 2008a) and industrial bottom-trawling fishing effort (Murawski *et al.*, 2005) showed a concentration of effort density in the close vicinity of the MPA boundaries. This concentration of effort can reduce spillover of fish to the surrounding area and can have major implications for the effectiveness of reserves in achieving ecological and socio-economic goals (Wilcox and Pomeroy, 2003), particularly those concerning wider stock replenishment. For illustration purposes we explored the phenomenon of "fishing the line" (Kellner *et al.*, 2007) around the Rockall haddock box and north-west Rockall flank which are closed to demersal fishing to protect the haddock recruitment (haddock box) and habitat features (north-west Rockall flank) (see Newton *et al.*, 2008) (Figure 7.2A). From the EC Vessel Monitoring System (i.e., satellite surveillance) database we extracted and filtered for those areas the fishing activity of UK vessels ≥ 18 m deploying bottom otter trawl gears in 2007 (for details on the methods see Stelzenmüller *et al.*, 2008b). In Figure 7.2B a histogram shows for the indicated area the linear distance (m) of the fishing activity to the western border of the MPA/closure area. The greater part of the fishing activity occurred within 1 km distance from the border of haddock box.

Beyond this, there are other factors that could potentially hamper a sound evaluation of MPAs as a wider tool in fisheries management, which generally receive little attention. For instance, recent studies highlight the need to take account for gear catchability when merging survey data to designate (Fraser *et al.*, 2009) or to evaluate MPAs (Stelzenmüller *et al.*,

Table 7.2 *Sampling designs that have been used to measure MPA effectiveness*

Design	Frequency of application	Comments
Impact only: Samples taken only within MPA, after MPA establishment	Uncommon	Very poor inferential ability
Control–Impact: Samples taken both within MPA and "control" areas, after MPA establishment	Very common	Poor inferential ability confounds spatial patterns with MPA effects
Before–After: Samples taken before and after MPA establishment, only within MPA	Uncommon	Poor inferential ability confounds natural temporal patterns/ variability with MPA effects
Before–After–Control–Impact (BACI): Samples taken before and after MPA establishment, within MPA and "control" site(s)	Uncommon	If temporally replicated, strong design to make statements of effects of particular MPAs; weaker ability to make global statements of effectiveness; conditional on MPA and non-MPA sites having correlated dynamics
Impact vs. Reference sites: Samples taken before and after MPA establishment, within multiple MPA and "control" site(s)	Uncommon	If replicated, strong design to make global statements of effectiveness; weak design to evaluate particular MPAs; conditional on MPA and non-MPA sites having uncorrelated dynamics, and MPA "treatment" being allocated randomly to sites

Source: From Syms and Carr (2002).

2007). The lack of data standardization can confound the estimation of fish abundance (Fraser *et al.*, 2009) and lead to misinterpretation of spatial patterns in catch data (Stelzenmüller *et al.*, 2006). Furthermore, experience from terrestrial studies showed that using data from sources with different resolutions introduced uncertainty in the evaluation of reserve effectiveness (Araujo and Guisan, 2006).

Marine protected areas can be extremely spatially heterogeneous, which results in the uneven distribution of fishing activities which is

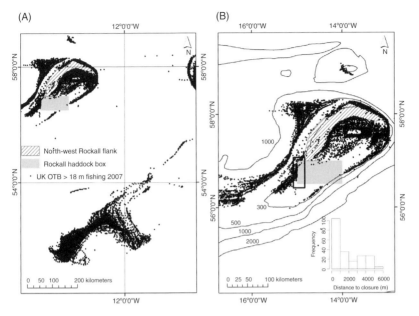

Figure 7.2 (A) The Rockall haddock box (gray) and north-west Rockall flank (striped box) which are closed for demersal fishing to protect the haddock recruitment (haddock box) and the habitat (north-west Rockall flank) (see Newton *et al.*, 2008). The points represent fishing activity of UK vessels >18 m deploying otter trawls in 2007 derived from satellite surveillance (VMS) data (see Stelzenmüller *et al.* [2008b] for methods). (B) As an example within the indicated area we calculated the frequency distribution of the distance (m) of the VMS points indicating fishing activity to the haddock box. The majority of the fishing activity within this area occurred within 1 km distance from the border of haddock box.

in turn linked to a "patchy" distribution of the resources. Spatial heterogeneity is often accounted for through the standardization of catch data, e.g., by means of a generalized linear model (GLM) that estimates the effect of area, season, and year (Babcock *et al.*, 2005). However, data standardization does not eliminate the influence of spatial autocorrelation (Legendre and Fortin, 1989; Legendre, 1993) on biomass estimates (Simard *et al.*, 1992; Babcock *et al.*, 2005). Spatial autocorrelation is caused by inadequate sampling designs, i.e., statistical non-independence of nearby samples, and can be analyzed and modeled mathematically using geostatistics (Cressie, 1991). Hence, for spatially explicit questions such as the export of biomass spillover from an MPA or the spatial pattern of CPUE and IPUE adequate approaches are necessary. From our review of empirical approaches we recognized that the methods deployed are rarely designed to deal with spatial data although many studies use spatial replicates (Table 7.1).

As with spatial data, temporal replicates or samples can be autocorrelated, which in turn can result in invalid estimations of uncertainty and significance (e.g., Olden and Neff, 2001; Panigada *et al.*, 2008). The adequate length of a time-series to detect a decline and/or recovery of species that are vulnerable to fishing was studied by Dinmore *et al.* (2003). These authors found that although the English North Sea bottom-trawl survey is one of the largest and best-resourced trawl surveys in the northeast Atlantic, the power to detect declines in abundance of vulnerable and rare species (elasmobranchs, cod, etc.) on timescales of <10 years was low. Furthermore, the study showed that if conservation measures were effective, and vulnerable populations recovered at maximum potential rate, 5–10 years of monitoring would often be required to statistically detect recovery. Unfortunately, many surveys and monitoring schemes are established with little prior assessment of power, and others are used to study species that were not their original focus. This has become increasingly the case in recent years, given the current focus on the integration of conservation concerns into fisheries management. Fisheries surveys are often the only source of time-series distribution and abundance data for species, particularly in offshore waters (Dinmore *et al.*, 2003).

While the effect of habitat variability on the potential yield associated with MPAs is discussed on the literature and partly accounted for, the impact of environmental change on the latter is barely understood (e.g., Frank *et al.*, 2000). One aspect to consider is if climate change related effects can really be separated from the "reserve effect" (i.e., the consequences of establishing an MPA). Blanchard *et al.* (2008) simulated the power of different survey designs to detect known trends in the abundance and to attribute causality, when both fisheries and climatic factors were varied in concert. Temperature preferences and local patchiness had a significant impact on the power of surveys to detect increases in abundance, and in some scenarios, indices would consistently underestimate or overestimate trends in overall abundance when these factors were included. With climate change, it could take 30 years of monitoring with a fixed stratified design to detect a trend for cold-water, patchy populations. This compares to 15–20 years with no assumed climate change. This leads to the question of the effect of background climate change on the functioning of designated MPAs.

An example of this in practice can be glimpsed from studies at the Medes Islands in the Mediterranean, where authors had supposedly provided incontrovertible evidence for the reserve effect (i.e., an increase in fish numbers and a corresponding decrease in sea urchins, within the MPA) over a number of years (see Garrabou *et al.*, 1998), but such results were later called into question when it was found that sea urchin populations exhibit striking short-term fluctuations in abundance in both protected and unprotected sites, as a result of climate variability (Garrabou *et al.*, 1998). Similarly a review by ICES (2004) indicated that in some years the Bornholm cod closure area in the Baltic protects the vast majority of cod larvae (the main objective of this MPA was to enhance the Baltic cod stock), whereas in other years, with markedly different hydrodynamic conditions, very little of the population is protected.

Furthermore an increasing number of studies deal with changes in species distribution due to long-term environmental change. As seawater temperatures warm up, fish species are expected to retreat northwards but also into deeper waters in search of cooler conditions (Dulvy *et al.*, 2008; Rijnsdorp *et al.*, 2009) and this can have consequences for the effectiveness of MPAs since the "center of gravity" of a species' population range may shift gradually until it lies outside the boundaries of the original protected area. In recent years juvenile plaice in the North Sea have been distributed more offshore (van Keeken *et al.*, 2007) than was the case previously. This change in distribution has been suggested as one of the main reasons that the North Sea "Plaice Box" has failed to be successful as a fishery conservation tool in the region (van Keeken *et al.*, 2007).

7.4 The need for integrated assessments of marine protected areas as fisheries management tools

In the following section we discuss the need for integrated assessments from two perspectives. One is the integration of MPA monitoring in the wider context of environmental management, and the other perspective relates to integrated monitoring approaches to assess MPAs as fisheries management tools.

Worldwide the increasing human pressure on coastal and offshore areas has highlighted the need for strategic, integrated and future-oriented frameworks for management of the seas generally, to allow for sustainable development of marine resources without irrevocably damaging ecosystems. Marine spatial planning (MSP) is an ecosystem-based management tool which aims to develop comprehensive marine spatial plans that are typically implemented by zoning approaches, regulations and "consent" systems (Douvere, 2008). Thus in the future, the implementation and management of MPAs or networks of MPAs might need to be considered in the wider context of other ecosystem-based management measures such as MSP. Within Europe the forthcoming Maritime Strategy Framework Directive (MSFD) will provide guidance on high-level goals and objectives by defining 11 environmental descriptors upon which member states need to assess and ensure "good environmental status" (GES) (European Union, 2008). For instance, some of these descriptors relate to a healthy state of commercially exploited fish and shellfish species or the maintenance of biodiversity. Success can only be achieved if local fisheries management measures become integrated as a component of regional and/or large-scale management systems as well as integrative marine spatial plans. In turn, this would entail that any MPA monitoring should be integrated in larger ecosystem monitoring programs covering ecological, socio-economic, and environmental measurements. We find already a successful example for such an integration of MPAs in wider spatial zoning options in Australia in the Great Barrier Reef marine park (see discussion in Jennings, 2009).

A paradigm shift has occurred in fisheries management in recent years, whereby the emphasis has moved from single-species approaches to a broader ecosystem-based approach as mandated for example, by the US Magnuson–Stevens Fishery Conservation and Management Act, the revised Common Fishery Policy of the European Union, and the Reykjavik Declaration on Responsible Fisheries in the Marine Ecosystem. This has resulted in attempts to evaluate the socio-economic and environmental consequences of fisheries management measures as well as the usual stock-specific parameters. Worldwide a wide range of integrated fisheries assessment systems have been developed which vary in their assumptions and data requirements. For instance, systems have evolved such as the Marine Stewardship Council scheme to assess the merits of a management against a set of externally established criteria. These include the maintenance and/or re-establishment of healthy populations of targeted species; maintenance of the integrity of ecosystems; development and maintenance of effective fisheries management systems, taking into account all relevant biological, technological, economic, social, environmental, and commercial aspects; and compliance with local and national laws and standards (Leadbitter and Ward, 2007). Other integrated fisheries assessment systems include "Rapfish" which was developed by the Food and Agriculture Organization of the United Nations, and which attempts to compare a fishery in relation to other real or hypothetical fisheries to establish relative performance levels and the consequential impacts on ecosystems and society (Pitcher and Preikshot, 2001).

In 2000 the IUCN together with the World Wide Fund for Nature, formed the MPA Management Effectiveness Initiative (MPA–MEI). The MPA–MEI program conducted a survey of MPA goals and objectives from around the world, and categorized these into three broad types: biophysical, socio-economic, and governance. From this 130 "indicators" were investigated and mapped. Operational descriptions and definitions were subsequently provided for 44 indicators as well as a detailed narrative of methods of measurement and guidance on analysis/interpretation of results (Pomeroy *et al.*, 2004). This approach made use of a GOIS (Goal–Objective–Indicator–Success criteria) framework which provides a powerful integrated approach for devising MPA monitoring programs. Although these integrated approaches are promising and can be built up on a case-by-case basis, future work remains on the development of frameworks which enable the implementation of local integrated MPA assessment systems within a regional or large-scale marine planning and fisheries management context. More specifically, the development of MPA monitoring programs that have the capacity to detect local-scale changes and distinguish those from regional and global scale changes remains a future challenge.

7.5 Acknowledgments

The authors would like to thank the UK Department for Environment, Food and Rural Affairs (Defra) and the European Union for financial support, in particular through projects AE1148, EMPAFISH, and PROTECT.

References

Abesamis, R. A., Alcala, A. C., and Russ, G. R. (2006). How much does the fishery at Apo Island benefit from spillover of adult fish from the adjacent marine reserve? *Fishery Bulletin*, **104**, 360–75.

Abesamis, R. A. and Russ, G. R. (2005). Density-dependent spillover from a marine reserve: long-term evidence. *Ecological Applications*, **15**, 1798–812.

Alcala, A. C., Russ, G. R., Maypa, A. P., and Calumpong, H. P. (2005). A long-term, spatially replicated experimental test of the effect of marine reserves on local fish yields. *Canadian Journal of Fisheries and Aquatic Sciences*, **62**, 98–108.

Almany, G. R., Berumen, M. L., Thorrold, S. R., Planes, S., and Jones, G. P. (2007). Local replenishment of coral reef fish populations in a marine reserve. *Science*, **316**, 742–4.

Araujo, M. B. (2004). Matching species with reserves: uncertainties from using data at different resolutions. *Biological Conservation*, **118**, 533–8.

Araujo, M. B. and Guisan, A. (2006). Five (or so) challenges for species distribution modelling. *Journal of Biography*, **33**, 1677–88.

Babcock, E. A., Pikitch, E. K., McAllister, M. K., Apostolaki, P., and Santora, C. (2005). A perspective on the use of spatialized indicators for ecosystem-based fishery management through spatial zoning. *ICES Journal of Marine Science*, **63**, 469–76.

Blanchard, J. L., Maxwell, D. L., and Jennings, S. (2008). Power of monitoring surveys to detect abundance trends in depleted populations: the effects of density-dependent habitat use, patchiness, and climate change. *ICES Journal of Marine Science*, **65**, 111–20.

Claudet, J., Osenberg, C. W., Benedetti-Cecchi, L., *et al.* (2008). Marine reserves: size and age do matter. *Ecology Letters*, **11**, 481–9.

Crec'hriou, R., Bonhomme, P., Criquet, G., *et al.* (2008). Spatial patterns and GIS habitat modelling of fish in two French Mediterranean coastal areas. *Hydrobiologia*, **612**, 135–53.

Cressie, N. A. C. (1991). *Statistics for Spatial Data*. New York: John Wiley.

Dinmore, T. A., Duplisea, D. E., Rackham, B. D., Maxwell, D. L., and Jennings, S. (2003). Impact of a large-scale area closure on patterns of fishing disturbance and the consequences for benthic communities. *ICES Journal of Marine Science*, **60**, 371–80.

Douvere, F. (2008). The importance of marine spatial planning in advancing ecosystem-based sea use management. *Marine Policy*, **32**, 762–71.

Dulvy, N. K., Rogers, S. I., Jennings, S., *et al.* (2008). Climate change and deepening of the North Sea fish assemblage: a biotic indicator of warming seas. *Journal of Applied Ecology*, **45**, 1029–39.

Eastwood, P. D., Mills, C. M., Aldridge, J. N., Houghton, C. A., and Rogers, S. I. (2007). Human activities in UK offshore waters: an assessment of direct, physical pressure on the seabed. *ICES Journal of Marine Science*, **64**, 453–63.

Elliott, M. (2002). The role of the DPSIR approach and conceptual models in marine environmental management: an example for offshore wind power. *Marine Pollution Bulletin*, 44, 3–7.

European Union (1979). *Directive 1979/409/EC* of 2 April 1979 on the Conservation of Wild Birds. *OJ L 103*, 24 March 1979, as amended.

European Union (1992). *Directive 1992/43/EC* of 21 May 1992 on the Conservation of Natural Habitats and of Wild Fauna and Flora. *OJ L 206*, 22 July 1992.

European Union (2008). *Directive 2008/56/EC* of 17 June 2008, establishing a framework for community action in the field of marine environmental policy (Marine Strategy Framework Directive). http://eur-lex.europa.eu/LexUriServ/LexUriServ.do?uri=OJ:L:2008:164:0019:0040:EN:PDF.

Fisher, J. A. D. and Frank, K. T. (2002). Changes in finfish community structure associated with an offshore fishery closed area on the Scotian Shelf. *Marine Ecology Progress Series*, **240**, 249–65

Frank, K. T., Shackell, N. L., and Simon, J. E. (2000). An evaluation of the Emerald/Western Bank juvenile haddock closed area. *ICES Journal of Marine Science*, **57**, 1023–34.

Fraschetti, S., Terlizzi, A., Micheli, F., Benedetti-Cecci, L., and Boreo, F. (2002). Marine protected areas in the Mediterranean Sea: objectives, effectiveness and monitoring. *Marine Ecology*, **23**, 190–200.

Fraser, H. M., Greenstreet, S. P. R., and Piet, G. J. (2007). Taking account of catchability in groundfish survey trawls: implications for estimating demersal fish biomass. *ICES Journal of Marine Science*, **64**, 1800–19.

Fraser, H. M., Greenstreet, S. P. R., and Piet, G. J. (2009). Selecting MPAs to conserve groundfish biodiversity: the consequences of failing to account for catchability in survey trawls. *ICES Journal of Marine Science*, **66**, 82–9.

Galal, N., Ormond, R. F. G., and Hassan, O. (2002). Effect of a network of no-take reserves in increasing catch per unit effort and stocks of exploited reef fish at Nabq, South Sinai, Egypt. *Marine and Freshwater Research*, **53**, 199–205.

García-Charton, J. A. and Pérez-Ruzafa, A. (1999). Ecological heterogeneity and the evaluation of the effects of marine reserves. *Fisheries Research*, **42**, 1–20.

García-Charton, J. A., Pérez-Ruzafa, A., Sanchez-Jerez, P., *et al.* (2004). Multiscale spatial heterogeneity, habitat structure, and the effect of marine reserves on Western Mediterranean rocky reef fish assemblages. *Marine Biology*, **144**, 161–82.

García-Charton, J. A., Pérez-Ruzafa, A., Marcos, C., *et al.* (2008). Effectiveness of European Atlanto-Mediterranean MPAs: do they accomplish the expected effects on populations, communities and ecosystems? *Journal for Nature Conservation*, **16**, 193–221.

Garrabou, J., Sala, E., Arcas, A., and Zabala, M. (1998). The impact of diving on rocky sublittoral communities: a case study of a bryozoan population. *Conservation Biology*, **12**, 302–12.

Gladstone, W. (2007). Requirements for marine protected areas to conserve the biodiversity of rocky reef fishes. *Aquatic Conservation: Marine and Freshwater Ecosystems*, **17**, 71–87.

Goñi, R., Adlerstein, S., Alvarez-Berastegui, D., *et al.* (2008). Spillover from six western Mediterranean marine protected areas: evidence from artisanal fisheries. *Marine Ecology Progress Series*, **366**, 159–74.

Goñi, R., Quetglas, A., and Reñones, O. (2006). Spillover of spiny lobsters *Palinurus elephas* from a marine reserve to an adjoining fishery. *Marine Ecology Progress Series*, **308**, 207–19.

Halpern, B. (2003). The impact of marine reserves: do reserves work and does reserve size matter ? *Ecological Applications*, **13**, 117–37.

Higgins, R. M., Vandeperre, F., Pérez-Ruzafa, A., and Santos, R. S. (2008). Priorities for fisheries in marine protected area design and management: Implications for artisanal-type fisheries as found in southern Europe. *Journal for Nature Conservation*, **16**, 222–33.

Hilborn, R., Stokes, K., Maguire, J. J., *et al.* (2004). When can marine reserves improve fisheries management? *Ocean and Coastal Management*, **47**, 197–205.

Hockings, M., Stolton, S., and Dudley, N. (2000). Evaluating effectiveness: a framework for assessing the management of protected areas. Gland, Switzerland and

Cambridge, UK: IUCN World Commission on Protected Areas Best Practice Protected Area Guidelines.

Horwood, J. W., Nichols, J. H., and Milligan, S. (1998). Evaluation of closed areas for fish stock conservation. *Journal of Applied Ecology*, **35**, 893–903.

Houde, E. (ed.) (2001). *Marine Protected Areas: Tools for Sustaining Ocean Ecosystems.* Washington, DC: National Academy of Sciences.

Hughes, T. P., Baird, A. H., Bellwood, D. R., et al. (2003). Climate change, human impacts, and the resilience of coral reefs. *Science*, **301**, 929–33.

ICES. (2004). *Report of the Study Group on Closed Spawning Areas of Eastern Baltic Cod*, ICES CM 2004/ACFM: 17. Copenhagen: International Council for the Exploration of the Sea.

Jameson, S. C., Tupper, M. H., and Ridley, J. M. (2002). The three screen doors: can marine "protected" areas be effective? *Marine Pollution Bulletin*, **44**, 1177–83.

Jennings, S. (2001). Patterns and prediction of population recovery in marine reserves. *Reviews in Fish Biology and Fisheries*, **10**, 209–31.

Jennings, S. (2009). The role of marine protected areas in environmental management. *ICES Journal of Marine Science*, **66**, 16–21.

Jennings, S., Greenstreet, S. P. R., and Reynolds, J. D. (1999). Structural change in an exploited fish community: a consequence of differential fishing effects on species with contrasting life histories. *Journal of Animal Ecology*, **68**, 617–27.

Kellner, J. B., Tetreault, I., Gaines, S. D., and Nisbet, R. M. (2007). Fishing the line near marine reserves in single and multispecies fisheries. *Ecological Applications*, **17**, 1039–54.

Kjærsgaard, J. and Frost, H. (2008). Effort allocation and marine protected areas: is the North Sea Plaice Box a management compromise? *ICES Journal of Marine Science*, **65**, 1203–15.

Leadbitter, D. and Ward, T. J. (2007). An evaluation of systems for the integrated assessment of capture fisheries. *Marine Policy*, **31**, 458–69.

Legendre, L. and Fortin, M.-J. (1989). Spatial pattern and ecological analysis. *Vegetatio*, **80**, 107–38.

Legendre, P. (1993). Spatial autocorrelation: trouble or new paradigm? *Ecology*, **74**, 1659–1673.

Mangi, S. C., Roberts, C. M., and Rodwell, L. D. (2007). Reef fisheries management in Kenya: preliminary approach using the driver–pressure–state–impacts–response (DPSIR) scheme of indicators. *Ocean and Coastal Management*, **50**, 463–80.

Maxwell, D. and Jennings, S. (2005). Power of monitoring programmes to detect decline and recovery of rare and vulnerable fish. *Journal of Applied Ecology*, **42**, 25–37.

McClanahan, T. R. and Mangi, S. (2000). Spillover of exploitable fishes from a marine park and its effects on the adjacent fishery. *Ecological Applications*, **10**, 1792–805.

Micheli, F., Halpern, B. S., Botsford, L. W., and Warner, R. R. (2004). Trajectories and correlates of community change in no-take marine reserves. *Ecological Applications*, **14**, 1709–23.

Mosquera, I., Cote, I. M., Jennings, S., and Reynolds, J. D. (2000). Conservation benefits of marine reserves for fish populations. *Animal Conservation*, **3**, 321–32.

Murawski, S. A., Rago, P. J., and Fogarty, M. J. (2003). Spillover effects from temperate marine protected areas. In *American Aquatic Protected Areas as Fisheries Management Tools*, ed. J. B.. Shipley. Quebec: American Fisheries Society, pp. 167–84.

Murawski, S. A., Wigley, S. E., Fogarty, M. J., Rago, P. J., and Mountain, D. G. (2005). Effort distribution and catch patterns adjacent to temperate MPAs. *ICES Journal of Marine Science*, **62**, 1150–67.

Newton, A. W., Peach, K. J., Coull, K. A., Gault, M., and Needle, C. L. (2008). Rockall and the Scottish haddock fishery. *Fisheries Research*, **94**, 133–40.

Ojeda-Martínez, C., Giménez Casalduero, F., Bayle-Sempere, J. T., *et al.* (2009). A conceptual framework for the integral management of marine protected areas. *Ocean and Coastal Management*, **52**, 89–101.

Olden, J. D. and Neff, B. D. (2001). Cross-correlation bias in lag analysis of aquatic time series. *Marine Biology*, **138**, 1063–70.

Palumbi, S. R. (2003). Population genetics, demographic connectivity, and the design of marine reserves. *Ecological Applications*, **13**, 146–58.

Panigada, S., Zanardelli, M., MacKenzie, M., *et al.* (2008). Modelling habitat preferences for fin whales and striped dolphins in the Pelagos Sanctuary (Western Mediterranean Sea) with physiographic and remote sensing variables. *Remote Sensing of Environment*, **112**, 3400–12.

Pelletier, D., Claudet, J., Ferraris, J., Benedetti-Cecchi, L., and García-Charton, J. A. (2008). Models and indicators for assessing conservation and fisheries-related effects of marine protected areas. *Canadian Journal of Fisheries and Aquatic Sciences*, **65**, 765–9.

Pérez-Ruzafa, A., González-Wangüemert, M., Lenfant, P., Marcos, C., and García-Charton, J. A. (2006). Effects of fishing protection on the genetic structure of fish populations. *Biological Conservation*, **129**, 244–55.

Pinnegar, J. K., Polunin, N. V. C., Francour, P., *et al.* (2000). Trophic cascades in benthic marine ecosystems: lessons for fisheries and protected-area management. *Environmental Conservation*, **27**, 179–200.

Pitcher, T. J. and Preikshot, D. (2001). RAPFISH: a rapid appraisal technique to evaluate the sustainability status of fisheries. *Fisheries Research*, **49**, 255–70.

Planes, S., Galzin, R., Rubies, A. G., *et al.* (2000). Effects of marine protected areas on recruitment processes with special reference to Mediterranean littoral ecosystems. *Environmental Conservation*, **27**, 126–43.

Pomeroy, R. S., Parks, J. E., and Watson, L. M. (2004). *How Is Your MPA Doing? A Guidebook of Natural and Social Indicators for Evaluating Marine Protected Area Management Effectiveness*. Gland, Switzerland and Cambridge, UK: IUCN.

Rijnsdorp, A. D., Peck, M. A., Engelhard, G. H., Mollmann, C., and Pinnegar, J. K. (2009). Resolving the effect of climate change on fish populations. *ICES Journal of Marine Science*, **66**, 1570–83.

Roberts, C. M., Bohnsack, J. A., Gell, F., Hawkins, J. P., and Goodridge, R. (2001). Effects of marine reserves on adjacent fisheries. *Science*, **294**, 1920–3.

Roberts, C. M., Hawkins, J. P., and Gell, F. R. (2005). The role of marine reserves in achieving sustainable fisheries. *Philosophical Transactions of the Royal Society Series B*, **360**, 123–32.

Russ, G. R. and Alcala, A. C. (1996). Do marine reserves export adult fish biomass? Evidence from Apo Island, central Philippines. *Marine Ecology Progress Series*, **132**, 1–9.

Russ, G. R., Alcala, A. C., Maypa, A. P., Calumpong, H. P., and White, A. T. (2004). Marine reserve benefits local fisheries. *Ecological Applications*, **14**, 597–606.

Sala, E., Boudouresque, C. F., and Harmelin-Vivien, M. (1998a). Fishing, trophic cascades, and the structure of algal assemblages: evaluation of an old but untested paradigm. *Oikos*, **82**, 425–39.

Sala, E., Ribes, M., Hereu, B., *et al.* (1998b). Temporal variability in abundance of the sea urchins *Paracentrotus lividus* and *Arbacia lixula* in the northwestern Mediterranean: comparison between a marine reserve and an unprotected area. *Marine Ecology Progress Series*, **168**, 135–45.

Sale, P. F., Cowen, R. K., Danilowicz, B. S., *et al.* (2005). Critical science gaps impede use of no-take fishery reserves. *Trends in Ecology and Evolution*, **20**, 74–80.

Sánchez Lizaso, J. L., Goñi, R., Reñones, O., *et al.* (2000). Density dependence in marine protected populations: a review. *Environmental Conservation*, **27**, 144–58.

Schroeter, S. C., Reed, D. C., Kushner, D. J., Estes, J. A., and Ono, D. S. (2001). The use of marine reserves in evaluating the dive fishery for the warty sea cucumber (*Parastichopus parvimensis*) in California, U.S.A. *Canadian Journal of Fisheries and Aquatic Sciences*, **58**, 1773–81.

Simard, Y., Legendre, P., Lavoie, G., and Marcotte, D. (1992). Mapping, estimating biomass, and optimizing sampling programs for spatially autocorrelated data: case study of the northern shrimp (*Pandalus borealis*). *Canadian Journal of Fisheries and Aquatic Sciences*, **49**, 32–45.

Scientific, Technical and Economic Committee for Fisheries (2007). *Evaluation of Closed Area Schemes*, SGMOS-07-03. Available online at: http://stefc.jrc.ec.europa.eu.

Stelzenmüller, V., Ehrich, S., and Zauke, G. P. (2006). Analysis of meso-scaled spatial distribution of the dab (*Limanda limanda*) in the German Bight: does the type of fishing gear employed matter? *Fisheries Science*, **72**, 95–104.

Stelzenmüller, V., Maynou, F., and Martín, P. (2007). Spatial assessment of benefits of a coastal Mediterranean Marine Protected Area. *Biological Conservation*, **136**, 571–83.

Stelzenmüller, V., Maynou, F., Bernard, G., *et al.* (2008a). Spatial assessment of fishing effort around European marine reserves: implications for successful fisheries management. *Marine Pollution Bulletin*, **56**, 2018–26.

Stelzenmüller, V., Rogers, S. I., and Mills, C. M. (2008b). Spatiotemporal patterns of fishing pressure on UK marine landscapes, and their implications for spatial planning and management. *ICES Journal of Marine Science*, **65**, 1081–91.

Stelzenmüller, V., Maynou, F., and Martín, P. (2009). Patterns of species and functional diversity around a coastal marine reserve: a fisheries perspective. *Aquatic Conservation: Marine and Freshwater Ecosystems*, **19**, 554–65.

Stokesbury, K. D. E., Harris, B. P., Marino, M. C., and Nogueira, J. I. (2007). Sea scallop mass mortality in a Marine Protected Area. *Marine Ecology Progress Series*, **349**, 151–8.

Syms, C. and Carr, M. H. (2002). *International Clearinghouse for MPA Effectiveness Measures: A Conceptual Design*, prepared for the Commission on Environmental Cooperation as a template for information compilation and dissemination to resource managers. www.piscoweb.org/files/mpa_handouts/MPA_Evaluation_guidelines.pdf.

Tetreault, I. and Ambrose, R. F. (2007). Temperate marine reserves enhance targeted but not untargeted fishes in multiple no-take MPAs. *Ecological Applications*, **17**, 2251–67.

van Keeken, O. A., van Hoppe, M., Grift, R. E., and Rijnsdorp, A. D. (2007). Changes in the spatial distribution of North Sea plaice (*Pleuronectes platessa*) and implications for fisheries management. *Journal of Sea Research*, **57**, 187–97.

Ward, T. J. (2000). Indicators for assessing the sustainability of Australia's marine ecosystems. *Marine and Freshwater Research*, **51**, 435–46.

Ward, T. J. (2004). Marine protected areas in fisheries: design and performance issues. *American Fisheries Society Symposium*, **2004**, 37–61.

Ward, T. J., Heinemann, D., and Evans, N. (2001). *The Role of Marine Reserves as Fisheries Management Tools: A Review of Concepts, Evidence and International Experience*. Canberra, ACT: Bureau of Rural Sciences.

Wilcox, C. and Pomeroy, C. (2003). Do commercial fishers aggregate around marine reserves? Evidence from Big Creek Marine Ecological Reserve, central California. *North American Journal of Fisheries Management*, **23**, 241–50.

8 · BIOECONOMY –
Bioeconomic analysis of marine protected area fisheries effects

JEAN BONCOEUR, FRÉDÉRIQUE ALBAN,
AND OLIVIER THÉBAUD

8.1 Introduction

Bioeconomics may be simply described as economics applied to human activities dealing with biological processes, such as forestry, farming, or fishing. Accordingly, a bioeconomic model is a simplified and formalized representation of interacting biological and economic processes. It is usually made up of three components: a biological component, describing the bioecological processes at work, a technical component, describing the way human activities interact with this processes, and an economic component, describing the results of these activities in terms of (market or non-market) costs and benefits, and the consequences of these results on human behaviors.

Historically, fisheries economics has played a prominent role in the development of bioeconomic modeling (Gordon, 1954; Schaefer, 1957; Clark, 1990). Various topics concerning the fishing industry have been investigated with the help of bioeconomic models and, for the last 15 years, these models have represented a major analytic tool used by economic studies concerning the role of marine protected areas (MPAs) in fisheries management.[1]

In the first part of this chapter, we briefly survey the main types of bioeconomic models that have been applied to the analysis of MPA

---

[1] This situation contrasts with the analysis of other functions of MPAs, where bioeconomic modeling is much less developed. For illustrations of bioeconomic modeling integrating non-consumptive uses of MPA ecosystem services, see Boncoeur *et al.* (2002), and Chapter 4.

Marine Protected Areas: A Multidisciplinary Approach, ed. Joachim Claudet. Published by Cambridge University Press. © Cambridge University Press 2011.

effects on fisheries. Then we illustrate some of the topics concerning the potential role of MPAs in fisheries management with the help of a simple fishery bioeconomic model. After presenting the model and how it works, we compare its results under various scenarios concerning the management of the fishery, some of them including an MPA.

8.2 Bioeconomic modeling of marine protected areas

Bioeconomic models of MPAs may be classified into two major categories. We first characterize each of these categories, and then we consider their outcomes and the issues they raise.

8.2.1 A typology of bioeconomic models of marine protected areas

Models of the first category are directly derived from standard, spatially non-explicit bioeconomic models of marine fisheries. Most of them are equilibrium models dealing with one species and one gear, and relying on the assumption of spatial homogeneity. Their basic purpose is to assess the way fishing is impacted by closing an area representing a given proportion of the former fishing zone.[2] A spillover effect of the reserve is usually assumed with the help of a transfer function, based on the difference between stock density inside and outside the reserve, and on the mobility of fish. Models of this type may vary in terms of complexity. However, their usual emphasis is on the fact that the biological and socio-economic consequences of creating an MPA depend on a range of factors, such as reserve size, fish mobility, and degree of control over fishing effort. For example, Holland and Brazee (1996), making use of a structural model, showed that creating an MPA may help increase the level of sustainable catch in an overfished fishery, provided the spontaneous tendency to increase fishing effort can be controlled. Hannesson (1998) and Anderson (2002) used a global logistic model to address the question of the usefulness of an MPA in a deterministic context, assuming freedom of access to the fishing zone. Sumaila (1998a) and Conrad (1999) depicted the benefits of MPAs for fisheries in a stochastic environment. Grafton et al. (2009) applied a stochastic optimal control model with a jump–diffusion process to the northern cod fishery of Newfoundland and Labrador.

---

[2] Following the terminology used in this book, we will term this area indifferently a reserve or a no-take zone.

In such models, the standard assumptions of a single species fishery and space homogeneity are in many cases oversimplifying; models accounting for the complexity of ecosystem dynamics lead to refine the conclusions concerning the impact of MPAs on fisheries. The multispecies bioeconomic model developed by Holland (2000) showed that the impact of an MPA varies according to species. Boncoeur *et al.* (2002) simulated the introduction of a prey–predator interaction, which may lead to counter-intuitive results, if the predator species is not a commercial species. Introducing space heterogeneity in his bioeconomic model in the form of "hot spots," Schnier (2005) showed that the optimal size of the MPA depends not only on the productive capacity of the reserve and the surrounding fishing grounds, but also on the degree of heterogeneity between the two regions. Armstrong (2007) presented a model incorporating positive habitat effects of area closures.

Spatially explicit models form the second category of bioeconomic models of MPAs.[3] The seminal paper in this category was written by Sanchirico and Wilen (1999).[4] The basic principle of these models is to represent a discrete number of subpopulations distributed in separate zones (patches), but interconnected by biological and economic relations (metapopulations). Spatially explicit models are usually multispecies. Their main focus is on the location of MPAs rather than on their size. Choosing this location needs to integrate the major oceanographic processes in the region, the ecological characteristics of the habitats, and the distance of larval dispersion, but also socio-economic factors. Adopting a patch model instead of a global model for simulating the potential impact of an MPA in a given zone has substantial consequences, e.g., in terms of optimal effort levels, because the two types of models have different qualitative behaviors (Loisel and Cartigny, 2009). For a manager wishing to study the potential role of an MPA in a given zone, it is critical to know if the whole zone has been artificially divided into several areas, or if it has been broken down into entities with their own ecological dynamics (patches).

Developing spatially explicit models requires a realistic description of microeconomic behaviors, not only through time but also through space,

---

[3] In 2004, a special issue of the journal *Marine Resource Economics* (vol. **19**(1), 2004) was devoted to the fast-growing topic of spatial modeling applied to fisheries economics.

[4] Further developments from the same authors may be found in Sanchirico and Wilen (2001) and Sanchirico and Wilen (2002). See also Wilen *et al.* (2002), Smith and Wilen (2003), Holland *et al.* (2004), Smith and Wilen (2004), Sanchirico (2004), Sanchirico (2005), Sanchiro *et al.* (2006), and Smith *et al.* (2009).

in order to explain the mobility of fishing fleets (e.g., Holland, 2000; Chakravorty and Nemoto 2001; Smith and Wilen, 2003; Holland *et al.*, 2004; Valcic, 2009). Several techniques may be used to this end. The most commonly used are the gravity model (Caddy, 1975) and random utility models (Holland and Sutinen, 1999; Wilen *et al.*, 2002; Curtis and McConnell, 2004; Hutton *et al.*, 2004). Other analytic tools, such as game theory (Beattie *et al.*, 2002) or multi-agent modeling (Soulié and Thébaud, 2006) may also be used to simulate fishers' behavior.

8.2.2 Results and issues

Although the bioeconomic literature on MPAs has provided limited empirical evidence concerning their socio-economic benefits for fishers, it has helped to clarify some important issues.

In theory, conservation benefits derived from a well-designed and correctly enforced MPA should increase catches in the fishing zone neighboring the no-take zone,[5] thus overbalancing the negative impact of decreasing the size of the fishing zone. Moreover, they should increase the time-stability of catches, by making fish stocks less vulnerable to overfishing. This "buffer effect" may be considered as a net benefit for fishers provided they are risk-averse (Conrad, 1999; Strand, 2004). However, this might not be the case, according to studies investigating the way fishers choose their fishing place (Holland and Sutinen, 1999; Dalton and Ralston, 2004; Smith and Wilen, 2004). According to these studies, the benefits derived from the buffer effect are not regarded as high enough by fishers to balance the loss of some of their former fishing zones.

As regards landing prices, the implementation of a marine reserve may have different consequences: an impact due to the variation of quantities landed, and a "quality" impact, due to a shift in the size and species composition of landings (Pauly *et al.*, 1998) and to better marketing opportunities. Fishers may also take advantage of the "ecologically correct" image of the fishing zone of the MPA to sell their fish at a higher price (Charles, 2001). However, these price effects of MPAs have been seldom studied, and models usually assume constant ex-vessel prices.

The creation of an MPA is likely to result in a space transfer in fishing effort. In order to maintain their level of catch, fishers are induced to intensify their effort in areas that are left open to fishing. A "fishing the

---

[5] Some models explore the effects of poaching and non-compliance within marine reserve boundaries (e.g., Sethi and Hilborn, 2008; Le Quesne, 2009).

line" effect, i.e., a concentration of fishers close to the limit of the reserve, is likely to outweigh some of the benefits expected from the MPA, like for example in the case of the plaice box in North Sea with concentration of the trawling activity along the borders of the box (Rijnsdorp *et al.*, 1996). In the long run, an MPA may induce a shift of fishing effort towards other fisheries, which may create a variety of negative effects in these fisheries. The effects of reserves on fishing are highly dependent on how fishers spatially reallocate effort (Sanchirico and Wilen, 1999; Soulié and Thébaud, 2006). Fishers have a tendency to reallocate their effort to areas that generate, according to their perception, higher relative rents. Applying this idea to the California sea urchin fishery, Smith and Wilen (2004) showed that accounting for spatial behavior of fishers is likely to produce outcomes that deceive optimistic expectations concerning the positive effect on discounted rents of creating a reserve in a heavily fished area. The perception of expected rent may be influenced by the knowledge about resource location, measured for instance by past catches. It may also be influenced by species prices and harvesting costs (including cost of traveling to fishing grounds). Grafton *et al.* (2005b) concluded that this type of effect generates spatial "economic gradients" that may be quite different from "biological gradients" generated by larval export and adult transfers.

The spatial redistribution of fishing effort induced by the MPA influences directly and indirectly fishing costs. If fishers are compelled to go fishing farther from their home port, this will increase their operating costs. Moreover, if they have to go fishing in places that are unfamiliar to them, this will increase the time they need to look for fish. Another possible consequence of the MPA is to increase the dangerousness of fishing, by inducing under-equipped and under-experienced fishers to go fishing farther offshore (Holland, 2000). The costs resulting from space transfers of effort vary according to the degree of dependency of fishers to a particular fishing zone. Having few alternatives, small boats are usually more concerned by the closure of an area than large boats. Investigating the potential distributional effects of an MPA in the case of the northeast Atlantic cod fishery, Sumaila and Armstrong (2006) concluded that implementing an MPA is likely to be conflictual, which could make this implementation difficult. This analysis contradicts the optimistic view according to which marine reserves reduce conflicts between user groups via physical separation of interests (Bohnsack, 1993).

Not only is spatial distribution of fishing effort likely to be affected by the implementation of an MPA: if this implementation succeeds in increasing the catch per unit of effort (CPUE) in the adjacent fishing zone, and if effort is left uncontrolled in the fishing zone, it is likely to increase the total level of fishing effort, until the additional rent created by the MPA is totally dissipated (Hannesson, 1998).[6] Piet and Rijnsdorp (1996) illustrate this phenomenon with the plaice box in the North Sea: although fishing effort decreased following the exclusion of large trawlers, small boats increased their effort within the box.

Marine protected areas are often presented as an alternative to conventional fisheries management tools. While these tools, e.g., total authorized catches (TACs) and quotas, reflect mainly a monospecific vision, some authors consider that marine reserves favor an ecosystemic approach to fisheries management (Sumaila *et al.*, 2000; Palumbi, 2002). Ludwig *et al.* (1993) argue for the creation of MPAs as an insurance against management failure. In the context of inshore fisheries, generally characterized by a great complexity (multispecific, multi-gear fisheries), conventional tools are often poorly efficient. Moreover, socio-political pressures often make it difficult to reduce fishing effort (Sumaila, 1998b; Roberts, 2000). The choice of a specific fisheries management tool is often more influenced by political considerations than by scientific arguments (Guénette *et al.*, 1998).

When conventional management tools result in a perfect control of fishing mortality, it may be argued that there is no strong case for creating a marine reserve, from a fisheries management point of view. According to Hannesson's model (1998), the first-best optimum (i.e., the maximum rent situation) is reached when the share of the no-take zone in the potential fishing zone is zero.[7] However, in the case where socio-political factors do not make it possible to lower the fishing effort below a given level, creating a marine reserve may correspond to a second-best optimum, because catches and rent, for a given level of effort, may be higher with the reserve than without it (Holland and Brazee, 1996). Such a result requires that fishing mortality is not left fully uncontrolled outside the reserve, i.e., that MPAs are considered as a complement rather than as an alternative to other fisheries management tools (White *et al.*, 2008).

According to several authors, the context of uncertainty characterizing fisheries management is the major factor justifying the use of MPAs

---

[6] A natural (renewable) resource rent is the net income generated, under steady state conditions, by the use of this resource.

[7] By adding a management cost function and increasing the fishing costs to a more realistic level, Armstrong and Reithe (2001) modified some of Hannesson's conclusions.

as fisheries management tools (Ludwig *et al.*, 1993; Clark, 1996; Lauck *et al.*, 1998; Sumaila, 1998a; Conrad, 1999; Mangel, 2000; Grafton *et al.*, 2004; Grafton *et al.*, 2005a; Pitchford *et al.*, 2007; Grafton *et al.*, 2009). Reserves act as a hedge against irreducible uncertainty, especially shocks associated with the harvesting of exploited populations, where harvest rates and fish populations are measured with error and harvests are less than fully controllable. Using a dynamic source–sink model with two forms of uncertainty, Grafton *et al.* (2004) concluded that the key benefit of reserves is that they increase resilience, i.e., the speed it takes a population to return to a former state following a negative shock. Increased resilience due to a reserve can also increase resource rents, even with optimal harvesting. This conclusion contradicts the idea that reserves have no value if harvesting is optimal, as was suggested earlier by deterministic models.

8.3 A simple illustrative model

The model we will now consider has a limited ambition: to introduce the reader, by means of a simplified theoretical example, to the philosophy of bioeconomic modeling applied to fisheries aspects of MPAs, and to illustrate, with a degree of sophistication that does not go beyond elementary algebra, some of the topics that have been identified in the first section of this chapter. This section is dedicated to the description of the model; the following presents its outcomes concerning the management of a fishery under various scenarios.

Considering its limited number of variables and the oversimplifying character of several of its underlying assumptions, our model pertains to the first category described earlier in the chapter. Its framework is basic bioeconomic theory and, for the largest part, its relationships are derived from Hannesson (1998). However, it acknowledges space heterogeneity, which also relates it to the category of metapopulation bioeconomic models initiated by Sanchirico and Wilen (1999). In order to obtain simple graphical solutions, it only considers two zones, but these zones are not arbitrarily defined portions of an assumingly homogeneous territory: (i) their ecological characteristics are not identical, inducing differentiated conditions for fish habitat; (ii) inter-zone fish mobility differs from intra-zone mobility;[8] and (iii) fishing costs may vary from one zone to the

---

[8] Intra-zone mobility is assumed to be infinite, i.e., possible difference between fish densities within a given zone are supposed to be instantaneously corrected by spatial

other, due, e.g., to different distances from harbor. As a result, the relative size of each zone is not a policy variable, unlike what is usually assumed by models of the first category.[9]

After presenting the assumptions underlying the model and their formal transcription, we describe the main processes represented.

8.3.1 Description of the model

The purpose of the model is to simulate, in a highly stylized way, the operation of a fishery. We present here its basic variables and equations. We start with stock dynamics and its components, and then define the conditions of biological equilibrium under which we will run the model. Finally, we characterize the existence of the MPA.

8.3.1.1 Stock dynamics

We consider a single fish stock, with a habitat composed of two distinct zones ($i = 1, 2$). Differences between individual fish are neglected, and the stock is expressed in terms of biomass. Let X_i be the stock biomass inside zone i. Supposing it evolves continuously over time, we may describe its dynamics with the following differential equation:

$$\frac{dX_i}{dt} = N_i - T_{ij} - Y_i \quad \left(\begin{array}{l} i = 1, 2 \\ j = 2, 1 \end{array} \right) \tag{8.1}$$

where N_i is the instantaneous surplus of stock biomass naturally produced per unit of time within zone i, T_{ij} is the net instantaneous transfer of stock biomass per unit of time from zone i to zone j ($T_{ji} = -T_{ij}$), and $Y_i \geq 0$ is the weight of instantaneous catches per unit of time within zone i.

Let us now describe each of these components.

---

redistribution of fish inside the zone. This is not so with fish mobility between the two zones: differences in fish density are not the only factor driving inter-zone transfers, and these transfers are performed at a given finite speed, depending on the characteristics of both fish and zones.

[9] This characteristic may be considered as a weak point of the model, since it makes it unfit for discussing the important issue of the optimal MPA size. In the logic of the model, this difficulty might be overcome by increasing the number of zones considered, which would make it possible to discuss not only the size of the MPA but also its design. This is clearly the field of spatially explicit models.

8.3.1.2 Biomass surplus production within each zone
Let A_i be the surface area of zone i, and D_i be the maximum equilibrium stock density within this zone. Parameter D_i depends on the ecological characteristics of zone i, and may be called the natural productivity of this zone. Multiplying D_i by A_i, we get:

$$K_i = D_i A_i \quad (i = 1, 2) \tag{8.2}$$

which is the carrying capacity of the zone, i.e., the maximum equilibrium stock biomass that the zone's ecosystem can withstand.

Let x_i be the ratio of actual to maximum equilibrium stock biomass in zone i:

$$x_i = \frac{X_i}{K_i} \quad (i = 1, 2). \tag{8.3}$$

This ratio measures the pressure exerted by the fish stock on the local ecosystem. We assume that, within a given zone, the natural dynamics of the stock follows a deterministic logistic law, i.e., that its natural growth rate (N_i/X_i, or $N_i/K_i x_i$) is a linearly decreasing function of its pressure on the local ecosystem:

$$N_i = r K_i x_i (1 - x_i) \quad (i = 1, 2) \tag{8.4}$$

where r is the stock intrinsic growth rate, i.e., the natural growth rate of fish that would be observed if there were no growth limitations due to the ecosystem.

8.3.1.3 Fish mobility between zones
Following Conrad (1999), we suppose that the instantaneous gross flow of fish leaving a given zone is proportional to the pressure exerted by local fish biomass on the ecosystem of this zone, so that inter-zone mobility tends to equalize pressures in both zones:

$$T_{ij} = s(x_i - x_j) \quad (i = 1, 2) \tag{8.5}$$

where s is a positive parameter characterizing the stock mobility between the two zones. In the special case where zones 1 and 2 are equally productive ($D_1 = D_2$), relationship (8.5) implies that net biomass transfer is proportional to the difference between stock densities within each zone (see, e.g., Hannesson, 1998).

8.3.1.4 Catch function and fishing profitability

We assume that the use of the various anthropogenic factors (capital, labor) that fishers mobilize in a given zone may be synthesized into one index of so-called "fishing effort" (E_i),[10] and that CPUE is proportional to stock density (X_i/A_i, or $D_i x_i$):

$$Y_i = q D_i x_i E_i \quad (i = 1, 2) \tag{8.6}$$

where q is a positive parameter reflecting the technical efficiency of fishing effort.[11] Alternatively, the catch function within zone i may be described as:

$$F_i = \frac{q D_i E_i}{K_i} \quad (i = 1, 2) \tag{8.7}$$

where F_i is the instantaneous rate of fishing mortality within zone i:

$$F_i = \frac{Y_i}{K_i x_i} \quad (i = 1, 2). \tag{8.8}$$

The catch function specified by Equation (8.6) or (8.7) implies that, within a given zone, fishing effort (E_i) is proportional to the rate of fishing mortality (F_i). Therefore these two variables may be used as substitutes, provided E_i is multiplied by the proper proportionality constant ($q/A_i = q D_i/K_i$).

The profitability of fishing within a given zone is defined as the difference between the ex-vessel value of catches and the cost of fishing effort:

$$\pi_i = P Y_i - C_i E_i \quad (i = 1, 2) \tag{8.9}$$

where P and C_i are positive parameters representing, respectively, the unit ex-vessel price of catches, and the unit cost of fishing effort in zone i.[12] The exogenous character of P, C_1, and C_2 corresponds to the assumption that the size of the fishery is small compared to the size of the markets.

---

[10] For a discussion of this most usual though far from trivial assumption, see Hannesson (1983).

[11] This parameter is usually named "catchability coefficient." Note that, here, it is defined *per unit of surface*: q is not the ratio of CPUE to stock biomass (X_i), but to stock density (X_i/A_i).

[12] If landing prices also were differentiated according to the catch zone, this would imply replacing P by $P_i(i = 1, 2)$. It would not alter substantially the logic of the model, since what matters is the real cost of fishing in a given zone (C_i/P, or C_i/P_i): whether a difference between real costs in zone 1 and in zone 2 is due to nominal costs (C_i) or to landing prices (P_i) is of little importance for the state of the fishery. We do not address the question of a possible impact of the creation of an MPA on landing prices.

8.3.1.5 Biological equilibrium

A biological equilibrium, or steady state, is reached when stock biomasses in both zones are stabilized, i.e., when:

$$\frac{dX_i}{dt} = 0 \quad (i = 1, 2). \tag{8.10}$$

In such a situation, π_i is called the fishery rent in zone i.[13] Note that the equilibrium value of each local biomass (X_i) cannot be larger than the carrying capacity of the corresponding zone (K_i), so that $x_i \leq 1$.

Putting together Equations (8.1) and (8.9), we get:

$$Y_i = N_i - T_{ij} \quad \begin{pmatrix} i = 1, 2 \\ j = 2, 1 \end{pmatrix}, \tag{8.11}$$

i.e., equilibrium catches within a given zone are equal to the difference between natural surplus production inside this zone and net transfer towards the other zone. In the rest of this chapter, we will only consider biological equilibrium situations (comparative statics analysis).[14] Therefore, when we characterize a variable as "increasing" or "decreasing," this should not be interpreted as expressing a change over time: it is simply a short way for expressing a comparison between different equilibrium values of this variable, meaning that these values are ranked according to an increasing, or a decreasing order.

8.3.1.6 Management

We assume that zone 1 is a no-take zone (NTZ), while zone 2 is a fishing zone (FZ):

$$E_1 = 0 \tag{8.12–1}$$
$$E_2 \geq 0 \tag{8.12–2}$$

As a consequence, equilibrium relationships (8.11) may be reformulated as follows:

$$N_1 = T_{12} \tag{8.13–1}$$
$$Y_2 = N_2 + T_{12}. \tag{8.13–2}$$

Equality (8.13–1) expresses the fact that, under biological equilibrium conditions, net transfer from the NTZ to the FZ balances natural surplus

---

[13] As long as stocks are not stabilized, variables π_i are more properly termed as quasi-rents.

[14] For a dynamic analysis, see Chapter 4.

production within the NTZ. According to (8.13–2), equilibrium catches are equal to natural surplus production within the FZ, plus net transfer from the NTZ (spillover effect). Combining (8.13–1) and (8.13–2) indicates that, under biological equilibrium conditions, catches in the FZ are equal to the total natural surplus production of fish biomass, both in the FZ and in the NTZ.

8.3.2 How it works

We now consider the implications of equilibrium conditions (8.13–1) and (8.13–2) on the state of the fishery, for various levels of fishing effort (or of fishing mortality rate, which is proportional to fishing effort). We first investigate how fishing effort in the FZ impacts fish stock biomasses in each zone. Then we turn to the impact on catches.

8.3.2.1 Impact of fishing effort on equilibrium stock biomasses

For the following analysis, it is convenient to use x_i, the pressure exerted by fish on the ecosystem of zone i, as a proxy for X_i, the local fish biomass (according to (8.3), these two variables are proportional).

Taking into account (8.4), (8.5), and (8.8), we may rewrite (8.13–1) and (8.13–2) respectively as:

$$x_2 = x_1 \left(\frac{x_1 - v_1}{1 - v_1} \right) \qquad (8.14\text{–}1)$$

$$x_1 = x_2 \left(\frac{x_2 - v_2 + F_2/r}{1 - v_2} \right) \qquad (8.14\text{–}2)$$

where:

$$v_i = \frac{rK_i - s}{rK_i} \qquad (i = 1, 2) \qquad (8.15)$$

is an index of the capacity of zone i to retain the surplus of biomass it generates:[15] for this zone, the natural flow of surplus biomass [$N_i = rK_i x_i(1 - x_i)$] is larger than the gross outgoing flow of biomass (sx_i) as long as $x_i < v_i$. Consequently, if $v_i < 0$, the difference between N_i and sx_i is negative for any admissible value of x_i. Conversely, if $v_i > 0$, there is a positive admissible x_i (namely, $x_i = v_i$), such that N_i is just balanced

---

[15] This index is a linear decreasing function of s. It has been standardized so that $\lim v_i = 1$ when $s \to 0$. As a result, $v_i < 1$ for any positive value of s.

by sx_i. This property, as we shall see below, plays a critical role in the functioning of the MPA (note that $sx_i = T_{ij}$ if $x_j = 0$).

When bioecological parameters and the rate of fishing mortality within the FZ are given, Equations (8.14–1) and (8.14–2) form a system determining the equilibrium pressures (and, accordingly, biomasses) in each zone. There is no easy solution to this non-linear system, except for the trivial solution $x_1 = 0$, $x_2 = 0$, which applies for any level of F_2.[16] Fortunately, (8.14–1) and (8.14–2) carry some useful information concerning the influence of F_2 on x_1 and x_2.

Let us first consider Equation (8.14–1). This equation provides an expression of x_2 as a quadratic function of x_1. Let us call this function f_1 (note that f_1 does *not* depend on F_2). The value of $f_1(x_1)$ is zero for $x_1 = 0$ and for $x_1 = v_1$, a root which is positive provided $v_1 > 0$. According to Equation (8.15), this case is more likely to occur when the NTZ is large and highly productive, when the stock has a high intrinsic growth, and when its mobility between NTZ and FZ is limited. Note that, in all cases, $f_1(x_1) = 1$ when $x_1 = 1$, and $f_1(x_1) < x_1$ when $x_1 < 1$.

We now turn to Equation (8.14–2). This relationship expresses x_1 as a quadratic function of x_2, for a given value of F_2. Let us call this function f_2 (unlike f_1, f_2 depends on F_2). The value of $f_2(x_2)$ is zero for $x_2 = 0$ and for $x_2 = v_2 - F_2/r$, a root which is positive only if F_2/r is smaller than v_2 (which obviously requires this index to be positive). Note that $f_2(x_2) = 1$ when, simultaneously, $F_2 = 0$ and $x_2 = 1$.

Let us now plot $f_1(x_1)$ and $f_2(x_2)$ on the same diagram (Figure 8.1). On Figure 8.1, Case A corresponds to the case where $v_1 \leq 0$, and Case B to the alternative case ($v_1 > 0$). On each diagram, only those parts of the f_1 and f_2 curves that are consistent with non-negativity constraints on x_1 and x_2 are visualized. As regards $f_2(x_2)$, several curves, corresponding to different rates of fishing mortality, are represented: the continuous line corresponds to $F_2 = 0$, the dotted lines correspond to positive levels of F_2 (the higher is F_2, the lower is the corresponding curve). For a given value of F_2, the coordinates of the intersection point between the two curves are the equilibrium pressures in each zone.[17] Point G represents

---

[16] However, in a dynamic perspective, if at least one initial biomass is strictly positive, this equilibrium position may be reached only asymptotically, i.e., for $t \to \infty$. Remember that the analysis performed here belongs to comparative statics, i.e., compares various equilibrium positions without investigating transitional processes.

[17] We are referring here to the non-trivial equilibrium (with at least one strictly positive X_i).

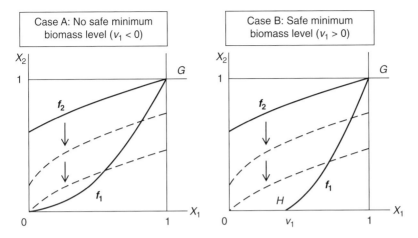

The downward arrows indicate an increasing rate of fishing mortality

Figure 8.1 Determination of the equilibrium biomasses in each zone of the MPA, according to the rate of fishing mortality in the fishing zone. For explanation see text.

this equilibrium when $F_2 = 0$: in this case, the equilibrium biomass in each zone is equal to the corresponding carrying capacity, and the net biomass transfer between zones is equal to zero.

Starting at equilibrium point G, let us progressively increase the rate of fishing mortality in the FZ. The f_2 curve moves downwards, and the equilibrium point slides down along the f_1 curve, as indicated by the arrows on the diagram. This move implies a decrease in both x_1 and x_2, and, hence, in both equilibrium local biomasses (due to the shape of the f_1 curve, $x_2 < x_1$ as soon as $F_2 > 0$). The decrease in the FZ equilibrium biomass (X_2) is a direct consequence of the increase in the rate of fishing mortality in this zone, and the decrease in the NTZ equilibrium biomass (X_1) is a consequence of the decrease in X_2, which generates a net transfer from the NTZ towards the FZ.

How far can we go? This depends on the sign of parameter v_1. Let us first assume that $v_1 < 0$ (Case A in Figure 8.1). In this case, when F_2 becomes positive and increases progressively, the equilibrium point moves from G to the origin of the two coordinate axes, i.e., to a position where both FZ and NTZ biomasses are equal to zero. It reaches this position when F_2 becomes equal to:[18]

$$F_{2\,\mathrm{lim}} = r \left(1 - \frac{1 - v_2}{v_1} \right). \tag{8.16}$$

This result implies that, if v_1 is negative, no positive equilibrium biomass is consistent with a rate of fishing mortality equal to, or higher than $F_{2\mathrm{lim}}$: under such circumstances, an unlimited increase in fishing effort tends to fish down the whole stock, not only in the FZ, but also in the NTZ, due to biomass transfer from the NTZ to the FZ.[19] The explanation of this property lies in the characteristics of index v_1. As noted before, a negative v_1 implies that surplus biomass generated by the NTZ cannot balance the gross outgoing flow towards the FZ. This gross outgoing flow tends to be equal to net biomass transfer T_{12} when local equilibrium biomass within the FZ gets close to zero, i.e., when F_2 gets close to $F_{2\mathrm{lim}}$. As a result, this rate of fishing mortality implies that the equilibrium biomass falls to zero in both zones. Note, however, that $F_{2\mathrm{lim}}$ is larger than r. Under equilibrium conditions, parameter r, the value of the intrinsic growth rate, is the upper limit of F_2 if there is no fish transfer from the NTZ.

Let us now consider the situation when $v_1 > 0$ (see Figure 8.1, Case B). In this case, when F_2 becomes positive and increases progressively, the equilibrium point moves from G to H, a position where FZ biomass is zero, but NTZ biomass is positive, and equal to v_1. Here again, this property may be explained by the characteristics of index v_1. As noted before, if v_1 is positive and x_1 is equal to v_1, the production of biomass surplus within the NTZ is just balanced by the gross outgoing flow of biomass towards the NTZ. Consequently, v_1 may be an equilibrium position for x_1 only if this gross outgoing flow corresponds to net

---

[18] This value may be obtained as follows. Starting from G, progressively increasing F_2 lowers the f_2 curve and brings the equilibrium point closer to the origin of coordinate axes. A necessary condition for the first point to reach the second one is that the upper intersection of the f_2 curve with the x_2–axis is obtained for $x_2 = 0$. This condition, which implies that $F_2/r \geq v_2$, is not sufficient: as long as the f_2 curve has a greater slope than the f_1 curve at the origin of coordinate axes, the two points will remain distinct (see Figure 8.1, Case A). They merge when the two slopes become equal, i.e. when: $f_1'(x_1) = \left[f_2'(x_2) \right]^{-1}$ for $x_1 = 0$ and $x_2 = 0$. Solving this equation in F_2 provides $F_{2\mathrm{lim}}$.

[19] This conclusion also applies if v_1 is just equal to 0, except that, in this case, $F_{2\mathrm{lim}}$ becomes infinite (a difference of little practical impact, since, even with a finite $F_{2\mathrm{lim}}$, the stock can be utterly fished down only when $t \to \infty$).

transfer T_{12}, which requires a zero biomass in the FZ.[20] The equilibrium position represented by point H is asymptotic,[21] i.e., its coordinates are the limits towards which pressures in both zones converge as F_2 grows indefinitely:

$$v_1 > 0 \quad \Rightarrow \quad \begin{cases} \lim_{F_2 \to \infty} x_1 = v_1 \\ \lim_{F_2 \to \infty} x_2 = 0 \end{cases} \tag{8.18}$$

The corresponding asymptotic value of the NTZ equilibrium biomass:

$$X_{1\,\text{lim}} = K_1 v_1 = K_1 - s/r \tag{8.19}$$

is an expression of the concept of "safe minimum biomass level" (SMBL) defined by Anderson (2002): should fishing effort (hence the rate of fishing mortality) be infinitely high in the FZ, there would still remain a positive equilibrium biomass in the NTZ. Remember, however, that a positive $X_{1\text{lim}}$ exists only if $v_1 > 0$.[22]

8.3.2.2 Impact of fishing effort on equilibrium catches

According to Equation (8.13–2), equilibrium catches in the FZ (Y_2) are composed of two elements: biomass surplus production inside the FZ (N_2), and net transfer from the NTZ (T_{12}). In order to characterize the influence of fishing effort on these elements, we write each of them as a function of the equilibrium pressure exerted by fish biomass in the NTZ (x_1), which is a monotonously decreasing function of F_2.[23] If v_1 is negative, x_1 is allowed to vary between 0 and 1. If it is positive, the variation range is more restricted, as the lower bound for x_1 is v_1 (see Figure 8.1).

We will illustrate our analysis with the four diagrams represented on Figure 8.2. On these diagrams, variables T_{12}, N_2, and Y_2 are plotted on

---

[20] This property also helps to understand why x_1 cannot be in equilibrium at a lower level than v_1 when the value of this index is positive: this would imply a gross outgoing flow from the NTZ larger than the net transfer to the FZ, i.e., a negative biomass within the FZ.

[21] This asymptotic character appears when we try to incorporate $x_1 = v_1$ and $x_2 = 0$ into Equation (8.14–2): the equality holds only with an infinite F_2.

[22] If $v_1 = 0$, $X_{1\text{lim}} = 0$, which implies in practice that there is no SMBL.

[23] This function is not easy to express analytically, but doing so with its reciprocal raises no problem, with the help of Equations (8.14–1) and (8.14–2).

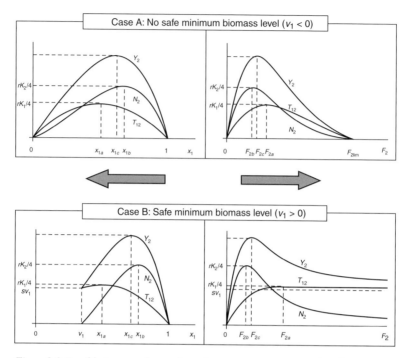

Figure 8.2 Equilibrium catches and catch components expressed as functions of local biomass pressure on the no-take zone (NTZ) ecosystem (left), or of rate of fishing mortality in the fishing zone (FZ) (right).

the vertical axis. The horizontal axis is dedicated to x_1 on the diagrams forming the left side of Figure 8.2, and to F_2 on the diagrams located on the right side. The opposite arrows illustrate the fact that these two variables move in opposite directions: the higher the rate of fishing mortality in the FZ, the lower the equilibrium level of biomass in the NTZ. Just like Figure 8.1, Figure 8.2 distinguishes two cases, according to the sign of parameter v_1: the upper pair of diagrams is dedicated to the case where this parameter is negative, implying that there is no SMBL, and the lower pair considers the case of a positive v_1, implying the existence of a SMBL in the NTZ.

We will successively investigate the influence of fishing effort on variables T_{12} and N_2. Then, adding these two variables, we will characterize the relationship between fishing effort and equilibrium catches.

Expressing T_{12} as a function of x_1 is straightforward, since T_{12} is equal to N_1, a quadratic concave function of x_1, according to the logistic law embodied in Equation (8.4). This function has a zero value for $x_1 = 0$

or $x_1 = 1$, positive values for any x_1 between 0 and 1, and a maximum value, equal to $rK_1/4$, when x_1 reaches:

$$x_{1a} = 0.5. \tag{8.20}$$

If $v_1 > 0$ (see Case A in Figure 8.2), as x_1 gets close to the lower bound of its variation domain (SMBL v_1), T_{12} converges towards sv_1.

Using the properties of the relationship between x_1 and F_2, we may now express T_{12} in terms of F_2. When there is no fishing, x_1 is equal to 1, and T_{12} is equal to zero. When F_2 becomes positive, x_1 gets lower than 1, and T_{12} becomes positive too. If $v_1 < 0$ (Case A), T_{12} reaches it maximum for $F_2 = F_{2a}$ corresponding to $x_1 = x_{1a}$, and converges towards zero as F_2 gets close to $F_{2\lim}$ (corresponding to $x_1 = 0$). If $v_1 > 0$ (Case B), when F_2 grows indefinitely, x_1 and T_{12} converge towards v_1 and sv_1 respectively.[24] In this case, there may be a finite value F_{2a} maximizing T_{12}, just like in the former case (see Case B on Figure 8.2). However, this requires that v_1 is not too large: if it is larger than 0.5 (the value of x_1 maximizing T_{12}), the relationship between F_2 and T_{12} becomes monotonically increasing, making F_{2a} infinitely large.[25]

Let us now turn to N_2. According to the logistic law embodied in Equation (8.4), N_2 is a quadratic concave function of x_2, with a zero value for $x_2 = 0$ or $x_2 = 1$, positive values for any x_2 between 0 and 1, and a maximum value, equal to $rK_2/4$, when x_2 reaches 0.5. To express N_2 in terms of x_1, we substitute $f(x_1)$ for x_2 in Equation (8.4), by combining this relationship with (8.14–1). The resulting function, a fourth-degree polynomial in x_1, is not particularly attractive, but combining the information carried by (8.4) and by (8.14–1) helps to derive its main features. Just like T_{12}, N_2 is equal to zero when $F_2 = 0$ (i.e. when $x_1 = 1$), and starts growing as F_2 becomes positive, making x_1 smaller than 1. It reaches its maximum value when x_1 is equal to:

$$x_{1b} = 0,5 \left[v_1 + \sqrt{1 + (1 - v_1)^2} \right] \tag{8.21}$$

a positive value of NTZ equilibrium pressure (larger than v_1, if $v_1 > 0$), which is obtained for F_{2b}, a positive rate of fishing mortality (smaller than

---

[24] When v_1 is just equal to 0, the asymptotic values of both x_1 and T_{12} are equal to zero.
[25] In this case, which is not represented on Figure 8.2, T_{12} always stays below its asymptotic limit (sv_1).

$F_{2\text{lim}}$, if $v_1 < 0$). Comparing Equations (8.20) and (8.21) shows that x_{1b} is larger than x_{1a}, and, hence, that:[26]

$$F_{2b} < F_{2a}. \tag{8.22}$$

If $v_1 < 0$ (Case A), N_2 tends towards zero as F_2 gets close to $F_{2\text{lim}}$, bringing x_1 close to zero (no SMBL). If $v_1 > 0$ (Case B), N_2 converges towards zero as x_1 gets close to v_1, i.e. as F_2 increases indefinitely.

Recalling that equilibrium catches in the FZ are the sum of biomass surplus production in this zone and of net transfer from the NTZ, we now synthesize the information previously obtained through the survey of these two elements.

If $v_1 < 0$ (Case A), both T_{12} and N_2 converge towards zero as F_2 gets close to $F_{2\text{lim}}$, bringing x_1 close to zero. It follows that Y_2 also converges towards zero in this case. Variables T_{12} and N_2 are maximized for $x_1 = x_{1a}$ and $x_1 = x_{1b}$ respectively, or, in other terms, for $F_2 = F_{2a}$ and $F_2 = F_{2b}$ respectively. As a result, Y_2 is maximized for a value x_{1c} of x_1 which is included between x_{1a} and x_{1b}, and, accordingly, for a value F_{2c} of F_2 which is included between F_{2b} and F_{2a}.

If $v_1 > 0$ (Case B), when F_2 increases indefinitely, x_1 gets close to v_1, N_2 tends towards zero, and T_{12} tends towards a positive sv_1. As a result, Y_2 also tends towards sv_1: when fishing effort is high enough, biomass in the FZ vanishes, biomass in the NTZ gets close to SMBL, and biomass transfer from the NTZ represents the bulk of catches. In the case illustrated by the lower pair of diagrams on Figure 8.2, v_1 is positive but smaller than 0.5. As a result, T_{12} and N_2 are maximized for F_{2a} and F_{2b} respectively, and, accordingly, Y_2 is maximized for a value F_{2c} of F_2 that is included between F_{2b} and F_{2a}. If v_1 is larger than 0.5 (a case not represented on Figure 8.2), T_{12} is a monotonously increasing function of F_2, and this may result in Y_2 also being a monotonously increasing function of F.

8.4 Bioeconomic scenarios of fisheries management

In this section, we make use of the simple model presented above to compare two management systems of the fishery, termed "conventional management" and "MPA-based management" respectively. Under both

---

[26] Strictly speaking, this rule applies when $v_1 < 0.5$, i.e., when there is a finite F_{2a} maximizing T_{12}. In the alternative case, F_{2a} becomes infinite, which makes the inequality trivial.

systems, various regulations may apply, with the following difference: in the case of conventional management, zones 1 and 2 are open to fishing, while under MPA-based management, fishing is authorized in zone 2 only.[27]

The pros and cons of each system will be successively discussed under three different assumptions, concerning the ability of the fishery managers to control fishing mortality in the zone(s) open to fishing: (i) full control; (ii) no control; (iii) limited control. In order to distinguish the values of variables characterizing each management system, we will use the following exponents: *I* for conventional management (or regime *I*), and *II* for MPA-based management (or regime *II*).

8.4.1 Full control of fishing mortality

Various management tools have been designed to help fisheries managers controlling fishing mortality, e.g., fishing time and fishing gear limitations, limited entry license systems, TACs, individual catch quotas. We assume provisionally that at least some items in this toolbox work fine and that fisheries managers may use them, in a discretionary way, to control the dynamics of the harvested stock.[28]

Elaborating a management plan for a fishery requires defining the objective(s) of this management. We will consider two alternative objectives, which are probably the most popular in fisheries literature: maximization of equilibrium catches, and maximization of fishery rent. Despite the fact that it completely neglects the cost of fishing, the maximum volume of catches under biological equilibrium conditions, commonly named "maximum sustainable yield" (MSY) has been internationally acknowledged as a valid target for fisheries management (Caddy and Mahon 1995). Rent maximization is more appealing to economists, because it takes into account not only catches but also fishing costs.[29]

---

[27] For the purpose of this model, we adopt a very simplistic definition of an MPA: we consider an MPA as a permanent fishing ban in part of the area occupied by a fish stock that is targeted by fishers.

[28] This ability does not require only controlling fishing mortality. It also requires stability of bioecological parameters governing stock natural variation, a highly questionable hypothesis.

[29] However, maximizing fishery rent under steady-state conditions is economically justified only if the time discount rate is equal to zero (time discounting allows comparing money flows that pertain to different time periods, with a positive time discount rate reducing the present value of future money flows; the rationale for a positive

If fishery managers perfectly control fishing mortality, obviously MPA-based management cannot do better than conventional management, whether the objective is to maximize sustainable catch or fishery rent. In both cases, from a formal point of view, shifting from conventional to MPA-based management simply consists in adding a constraint to the maximization problem [namely, relationship (8.12–1) stating that fishing effort in the NTZ is zero]: this additional constraint is unable to improve the optimal value of the problem objective-function. Actually, it is most likely to deteriorate it.

The adverse effect of MPAs on the maximum value of the objective-function is easy to establish formally in the case of MSY. Let Y be the symbol representing global equilibrium catches, and $\hat{Y}$ be the maximum value of Y (MSY). Combining (8.11) with (8.4), we may express Y in terms of x_1 and x_2:

$$Y = r \sum_{i=1}^{2} K_i x_i (1 - x_i). \qquad (8.23)$$

Under conventional management, restriction (8.12–1) does not apply. Accordingly, variables x_1 and x_2 are independent as long as fishing efforts in both zones are unsettled. Moreover, according to (8.23), the function relating Y to these variables is strictly concave. Therefore, deriving Y with respect to x_1 and to x_2, and setting the resulting partial derivatives equal to zero, we obtain the levels of these variables that maximize global catches under conventional management:

$$\hat{x}_i^I = 0.5 \quad (i = 1, 2) \qquad (8.24)$$

and the corresponding MSY:

$$\hat{Y}^I = \frac{r(K_1 + K_2)}{4}. \qquad (8.25)$$

This simple calculation cannot be transferred to MPA-based management, because, in this case, x_1 and x_2 cannot be treated as independent

time discount rate lies in (i) capital scarcity, and (ii) preference for the present; under competitive market equilibrium conditions, the time discount rate is equal to the interest rate). When this rate is positive, a time-infinite control program maximizing the inter-temporal flow of discounted quasi-rents may lead the fishery to a bioeconomic equilibrium with characteristics that are intermediate between undiscounted rent maximization and open access. The higher is the time discount rate, the closer to open-access equilibrium is the end state of the optimal control program (see, e.g., Clark, 1990, and Chapter 4) variables: imposing a fishing ban in zone 1 creates a link between x_1 and x_2, as indicated by (8.14–1). In this situation, there is no simple analytic solution to the problem of catch maximization. However, properties that were described in the former section help to characterize MSY under MPA-based management. We have seen that T_{12}, the net transfer from NTZ to FZ, and N_2, the biomass surplus production within the FZ, are maximized for two different levels of F_2, the rate of fishing mortality in the FZ.[30] As a result, Y_2 is maximized for an intermediate level, and its maximum value is inferior to the sum of the maximum values of T_{12} and N_2. Considering these two values, we may write:

$$\hat{Y}^{II} < \frac{rK_1}{4} + \frac{rK_2}{4} \tag{8.26}$$

and, putting together (8.25) and (8.26), we obtain:

$$\hat{Y}^{II} < \hat{Y}^{I} \tag{8.27}$$

which confirms the adverse effect of MPA-based management on catch maximization. As regards rent, the superiority of conventional management is not so easy to establish formally, because, under both management systems, there is no simple analytic solution to the rent maximization problem. However, it is clear that under conventional management, zero effort in one zone will be part of the rent maximizing solution only if special conditions are met, such as a particularly high cost of effort or a particularly low natural productivity in this zone.

8.4.2 No control of fishing mortality in the fishing zone

The above conclusions are not particularly favorable to MPAs, but, considering the restrictive assumptions on which they are based, their practical consequences appear rather limited. Not only have potential non-fisheries benefits of MPAs been neglected in the former analysis, but also the assumption of full control of fishing mortality seems to be unrealistic in many cases. Moreover, even in fisheries where this assumption may be considered as a reasonable approximation of reality, their managers are far from fully controlling the dynamics of harvested stocks, due to the frequent instability of bioecological parameters (part of this instability may

---

[30] If $v_1 > 0.5$, the level of F_2 maximizing T_{12} becomes infinite. This does not affect the conclusion concerning the MSY.

be the consequence of anthropogenic factors other than fishing mortality). Obviously, these neglected considerations might form a strong case for MPAs.

Our model is far too simple to integrate them all. In the following developments, we will restrict ourselves to the question of fishing mortality. Dropping the full-control hypothesis, we now consider the other polar hypothesis, i.e., the case where fishing mortality is unregulated (open access). Even though this assumption seems at odds with the huge mass of regulations that apply to real-world fisheries, it might be less unrealistic than the full-control assumption. Not only because the ability of managers to enforce regulations is often quite limited, but also because the status of fishing effort as a variable controlling fishing mortality is questionable (specially in the long run), a difficulty which is probably a significant cause of failure for many effort-based management policies.

In the case of MPA-based management, we suppose that a fishing ban is enforced in zone 1, and that open access prevails in zone 2. When there is no MPA, we suppose that both fishing zones are under open access (we will avoid using the term "conventional management" in this case, as speaking of the management of a fishery is obviously inappropriate when fishing mortality is totally uncontrolled).

When open access prevails in a fishery, its equilibrium is characterized by zero fishing rent (if it was positive, this would attract new fishers; if it was negative, fishers would leave the fishery). As pointed out by Hannesson (1998), it is not realistic to expect that creating an MPA will durably improve this situation, as long as fishing is left under open access outside the NTZ: if the NTZ generates enough spillover effects to increase the volume of harvestable fish, the resulting quasi-rents will attract more fishers into the FZ, thereby increasing fishing effort. This increase will continue up to the point where quasi-rents initially generated by the MPA have fallen to zero.

Therefore, recalling rent definition (8.9), and using the tilde symbol to characterize equilibrium levels of endogenous variables under open access, we may write:

$$P\tilde{Y}_i^I = C\tilde{E}_i^I \quad (i = 1, 2) \tag{8.28}$$

when there is no MPA, and:

$$P\tilde{Y}_2^{II} = C\tilde{E}_2^{II} \tag{8.29}$$

when a fishing ban is enforced in zone 1.

If creating an MPA is unlikely to generate fishing rent as long as the FZ is left under open access, this configuration does not prevent the MPA from influencing favorably other variables that are usually considered as important for fisheries management. We will consider here the influence of the NTZ on the level of sustainable catches.

Let us first consider the case where fishing is authorized in both zones (regime I). Combining (8.28) with (8.6) provides the equilibrium level of biomass in each zone under open access:

$$\tilde{X}_i^I = \frac{C_i}{D_i qP} \quad (i = 1, 2). \tag{8.30}$$

Alternatively, we may write:

$$\tilde{x}_i^I = c_i \quad (i = 1, 2) \tag{8.31}$$

where c_i is a ratio representing the real cost of harvesting one unit of fish in zone i, assuming a pristine state of the local biomass:[31]

$$c_i = \frac{C_i}{D_i qP} \quad (i = 1, 2). \tag{8.32}$$

Given ex-vessel price, fishing technical efficiency and natural productivity of zone i, c_i is proportional to C_i, and will be used as a proxy for this variable in the following developments.

Combining (8.4), (8.5), and (8.11) with (8.31), we get the values of open-access equilibrium catches in each zone:

$$\tilde{Y}_i^I = rK_i c_i (1 - c_i) - s(c_i - c_j) \quad \binom{i = 1, 2}{j = 2, 1}. \tag{8.33}$$

According to (8.31), local biomass in zone i is proportional to c_i: fishing costs act as a deterrent against fishing, and are therefore favorable to fish in the sea. Obviously, this proportionality relationship is not valid unlimitedly, since equilibrium biomass in a given zone cannot exceed local ecosystem carrying capacity. As a consequence, equality (8.31) may hold only if c_i is not larger than one, and positive catches require c_i to be strictly smaller than 1.[32] However, when fish may move between zones, this condition is not sufficient to make sure that fishing will occur in

---

[31] According to (8.2), D_i represents the local biomass density when $X_i = K_i$. The term "real" indicates that the corresponding cost is not expressed in monetary terms, but in terms of harvested fish.

[32] If $c_i = 1$, open-access equilibrium biomass in zone i is equal to local ecosystem carrying capacity, which implies zero catches.

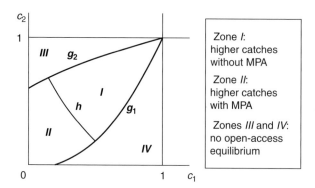

Figure 8.3 Sustainable open-access catches, according to relative fishing costs in each zone.

zone i, because fish mobility creates a link with the situation in zone j. As a result, the upper bounds of c_i and c_j are mutually interdependent. These upper bounds may be derived from non-negativity constraints on catches. According to (8.33):

$$\tilde{Y}_i^I \geq 0 \quad \Leftrightarrow \quad c_j \geq c_i \frac{c_i - v_i}{1 - v_i} \quad \left(\begin{matrix} i = 1, 2 \\ j = 2, 1 \end{matrix} \right). \tag{8.34}$$

This set of constraints defines the domain of admissible costs for simultaneous fishing in both zones under open access conditions. Figure 8.3 visualizes this domain. On this figure, curve g_1, the lower border of the domain, represents equation $g_1(c_1) = c_1(c_1 - v_1)/(1 - v_1)$, and corresponds to the non-negativity constraint on $\tilde{Y}_1^I$. Symmetrically, the upper border (curve g_2) has $g_2(c_2) = c_2(c_2 - v_2)/(1 - v_2)$ for equation, and is associated to the non-negativity constraint on $\tilde{Y}_2^I$. As a result, the area between the two curves represents the cost patterns that are consistent with open-access equilibrium in both fishing zones. In what follows, we will assume that (c_1, c_2) is an interior point of this area, i.e., that conditions (8.34) hold strictly. This assumption implies that, under open-access equilibrium, fishing will occur in both zones simultaneously when no MPA is implemented.

We now turn to the case where fishing is prohibited in zone 1 (regime *II*). The method for obtaining equilibrium biomass in zone 2, where open access prevails, is the same as in the former case, and provides the same result. In terms of pressure exerted by this biomass on the local ecosystem, we may write:

$$\tilde{x}_2^{II} = c_2. \tag{8.35}$$

We then derive the equilibrium pressure in zone 1 by combining (8.35) with (8.14–1), the relationship between equilibrium pressures in the NTZ and in the FZ:

$$\tilde{x}_1^{II} = 0,5 \left[v_1 + \sqrt{v_1^2 + 4(1 - v_1)c_2} \right]. \tag{8.36}$$

Finally, combining (8.4), (8.5), and (8.13–2) with (8.35) and (8.36) provides open-access equilibrium catches in the FZ:

$$\tilde{Y}_2^{II} = s \left[c_2 \frac{c_2 - v_2}{1 - v_2} + 0,5 \left(v_1 + \sqrt{v_1^2 + 4(1 - v_1)c_2} \right) \right]. \tag{8.37}$$

For these catches to be non-negative, it is sufficient that conditions (8.34) hold for both zones: if an open-access equilibrium may exist simultaneously in the two zones, then it may also exist in one of them when fishing is prohibited in the other one.

Having characterized each regime, we may now compare their respective performance. Let us first compare equilibrium biomasses. We have seen that equilibrium biomass in zone 2, which is under open access in both regimes, is the same in regime *I* as in regime *II*. Possible differences are therefore confined to zone 1. Intuitively, local equilibrium biomass should be higher when this zone is closed to fishing than when it is fished. This may be formally confirmed by comparing (8.31) and (8.36). Using these two relationships and rearranging terms, we may write:

$$\tilde{x}_1^{II} > \tilde{x}_1^{I} \quad \Leftrightarrow \quad 2c_1 - v_1 > \sqrt{v_1^2 + 4(1 - v_1)c_2}. \tag{8.38}$$

As open-access equilibrium cannot exist unless $2c_1 - v_1$ is positive,[33] squaring both sides of the inequality and rearranging terms leads to:

$$\tilde{x}_1^{II} > \tilde{x}_1^{I} \quad \Leftrightarrow \quad c_2 > c_1 \frac{c_1 - v_1}{1 - v_1}. \tag{8.39}$$

According to conditions (8.34), the inequality on the right-hand side of (8.39) is equivalent to the existence of positive open-access equilibrium

---

[33] Under open access, $\tilde{x}_1^{I}$ is equal to c_1, and we have seen that equilibrium biomass in zone 1 cannot be lower than v_1. As a result, if open-access equilibrium is possible in zone 1, $c_1 \geq v_1$, which implies $2c_1 > v_1$.

catches in zone 1, when there is no MPA. As a result, we may conclude that, if open access prevails in zones open to fishing, creating a NTZ in one zone will increase total equilibrium biomass $(X_1 + X_2)$. This result would be trivial if the creation of the NTZ resulted in decreasing total catches, but, as we will see now, this is not necessarily the case.

Under both regimes, total equilibrium catches are equal to the sum of natural biomass surplus production in zone 1 (N_1) and in zone 2 (N_2). Equilibrium local biomass in zone 2 is the same under both regimes, and this property extends to natural biomass surplus production in this zone. As a result, possible differences between catches under regime I and under regime II are confined to N_1. In the case of regime I (no MPA), this component of total catches may be obtained by combining (8.31) with (8.4):

$$\tilde{N}_1^I = rK_1 c_1 (1 - c_1). \tag{8.40}$$

When zone 1 is closed to fishing (regime II), N_1 is equal to T_{12}, the net flow of biomass transfer from the NTZ to the FZ. Therefore, combining (8.35) and (8.36) with (8.5), we get:

$$\tilde{N}_1^{II} = s \left[0,5 \left(v_1 + \sqrt{v_1^2 + 4(1 - v_1)c_2} \right) - c_2 \right]. \tag{8.41}$$

In order to compare $\tilde{N}_1^I$ and $\tilde{N}_1^{II}$, let us first have a look at what happens when these terms are equal. If, assuming equality between $\tilde{N}_1^I$ and $\tilde{N}_1^{II}$, we combine (8.40) and (8.41) and solve for c_2, we obtain two real distinct roots. Only the largest one is consistent with non-negativity constraints (8.34). Its value is a function of c_1:

$$\begin{cases} h(c_1) = (1 - c_1) \left(1 - \dfrac{c_1}{1 - v_1} \right) & \text{for } c_1 \leq 0.5 \\[3mm] h(c_1) = c_1 \left(\dfrac{c_1 - v_1}{1 - v_1} \right) & \text{for } c_1 \geq 0.5. \end{cases} \tag{8.42}$$

By construction, if $c_2 = h(c_1)$, $\tilde{N}_1^I = \tilde{N}_1^{II}$, and, accordingly, $\tilde{Y}^I = \tilde{Y}^{II}$. If $c_2 > h(c_1)$, then $\tilde{N}_1^I > \tilde{N}_1^{II}$, and $\tilde{Y}^I > \tilde{Y}^{II}$. Conversely, $c_2 < h(c_1)$ implies that $\tilde{N}_1^I < \tilde{N}_1^{II}$ and $\tilde{Y}^I < \tilde{Y}^{II}$. In this case, turning zone 1 into an NTZ will entail an increase in sustainable catches for the fishery, notwithstanding the reduction of fishing grounds and the increase in equilibrium biomass that it will also generate.

Figure 8.3 helps specify the consistency of this configuration with the constraints delimiting the domain of admissible (c_1, c_2). According to

(8.34) and (8.42), for $c_1 \geq 0.5$, $h(c_1)$ is identical to $g_1(c_1)$, the lower border of the domain, and for $c_1 < 0.5$ it is higher (only the part of curve h that is consistent with non-negativity constraints has been represented on the diagram). As a result, if c_1 falls below 0.5, there is a zone of admissible values of c_2 that make $\tilde{Y}^{II}$ larger than $\tilde{Y}^{I}$ (zone II on Figure 8.3). Note that this zone is located in the south-west corner of the diagram: low fishing costs are a case for MPA-based fisheries management.

8.4.3 Limited control of fishing mortality in the fishing zone

After the polar cases of fully controlled fishing mortality and of open access in the FZ, we now consider an intermediate and possibly more realistic case, where fishery managers have some limited control over fishing mortality in the FZ. More specifically, we suppose that they can set an upper limit $\bar{E}$ to global effort in the fishery, but at a level that is larger than first-best optimum, in terms of catches or rent maximization. This situation is likely to appear, for instance, when a limited-entry license system is introduced, with the aim to prevent additional fishers from entering the fishery. Under such circumstances, it frequently happens that, due to social and political considerations, all fishers with a past record in the fishery automatically receive a license, even if their number is notoriously too high.[34]

As regards MPA-based management, we simply incorporate this limited control assumption in our model by making E_2, the level of effort in the fishing zone, exogenous and equal to $\bar{E}$. Naturally, this makes sense only if $\bar{E}$ is not larger than $\tilde{E}_2^{II}$, the open-access equilibrium level of fishing effort in the FZ.

In the case of conventional management, global fishing effort E is the sum of local fishing efforts E_1 and E_2. Assuming $\bar{E}$ is not larger than $\tilde{E}^{I}$, the open-access equilibrium level of E, we set E at $\bar{E}$. In order to determine the level of effort in each zone, we need to consider fishers' behavior. If fishers are rational (certainly a weaker assumption than the alternative), they will tend to fish where this activity is the most profitable, whenever they are free to do so. As a result, equilibrium fishing effort should be equally profitable in both zones. This condition is the key

---

[34] Obviously, limiting the number of fishers is not enough for limiting fishing effort. We assume here that additional regulations that are usually adopted to this end in limited-entry license systems (e.g., fishing gear and fishing time limitations) work reasonably well.

for distributing $\bar{E}$ between E_1 and E_2. More specifically, we write that the equilibrium value of catches per unit of effort cost (an economic equivalent to the biotechnological concept of CPUE) is the same in each zone:

$$\frac{P Y_i}{C_i E_i} = \alpha \quad (i = 1, 2) \tag{8.43}$$

where α depends on $\bar{E}$. As we shall see later, restrictions apply to this equality. Assuming provisionally it holds, we may use it to express the endogenous variables of our model in terms of α. We start with variables x_i, which represent the pressures exerted by local stock biomasses on the ecosystems of the two zones, and are used as proxies for local biomasses. By combining (8.43) with (8.32) and (8.6), we may write these variables as linear functions of α:

$$x_i = \alpha c_i \quad (i = 1, 2). \tag{8.44}$$

We now turn to equilibrium catches. By combining (8.44) with (8.11), the biological equilibrium condition, and taking into account (8.4), (8.5), and (8.15), we get:

$$Y_i = r K_i \alpha c_i \left[v_i + (1 - v_i) \frac{c_j}{c_i} - \alpha c_i \right] \quad (i = 1, 2). \tag{8.45}$$

Finally, we obtain the expression of local levels of effort in terms of α, by combining (8.45) with (8.2), (8.6), and (8.44):

$$E_i = \frac{r A_i}{q} \left[v_i + (1 - v_i) \frac{c_j}{c_i} - \alpha c_i \right] \quad (i = 1, 2). \tag{8.46}$$

These relationships may be used to clarify the relationship between α and $\bar{E}$. Adding the expressions of effort in each zone given by (8.46) and making the sum equal to $\bar{E}$, we get:

$$\alpha = \frac{1}{\sum_i A_i c_i} \left[\sum_i A_i \left(v_i + (1 - v_i) \frac{c_j}{c_i} \right) - \frac{q \bar{E}}{r} \right] \quad \left(\begin{matrix} i = 1, 2 \\ j = 2, 1 \end{matrix} \right). \tag{8.47}$$

According to (8.47), lowering the global level of effort in the fishery increases the value of catches per unit of cost. However, two restrictions apply.[35] First, as mentioned earlier, $\bar{E}$ should not be larger than $\tilde{E}^I$, the open-access equilibrium level for global effort. This restriction implies that $\alpha \geq 1$: if $\bar{E} = \tilde{E}^I$, rents are equal to zero in the fishery, and, accordingly, $\alpha = 1$; if $\bar{E} < \tilde{E}^I$, positive rents appear in both zones, and, accordingly, $\alpha > 1$. Second, non-negativity constraints on local effort levels imply that α does not exceed an upper bound $\alpha_{\lim}$, which may be obtained through (8.46):

$$\alpha_{\lim} = \min \left[\frac{v_i + (1 - v_i)c_j/c_i}{c_i} \right] \quad \left(\begin{matrix} i = 1, 2 \\ j = 2, 1 \end{matrix} \right). \qquad (8.48)$$

According to (8.47), this limitation to the range of admissible values for α induces a lower bound for $\bar{E}$. Let $\bar{E}_{\lim}$ be the value of $\bar{E}$ generating $\alpha_{\lim}$ through (8.47). Should $\bar{E}$ be set below $\bar{E}_{\lim}$, relationships (8.43) to (8.47) would not hold, since that would imply a negative fishing effort in one zone. In this case, actual effort would be zero in this zone, and the fishery would be run as if an NTZ was enforced: fishers would spontaneously concentrate their effort in the other zone, due to its higher profitability.

If global fishing effort is set between $\bar{E}_{\lim}$ and $\tilde{E}^I$, relationships (8.43) to (8.47) apply. Using (8.47), we may then rewrite the equilibrium values of x_i, Y_i and E_i given by (8.44) to (8.46) in terms of $\bar{E}$. This rewriting is straightforward since, according to (8.48), the relationship between $\bar{E}$ and α is linear. Making use of (8.9), we may also express fishing rents π_i as functions of $\bar{E}$.

All this makes it possible to compare the performance of conventional management and MPA-based management, assuming global effort in the fishery is set at an exogenous level $\bar{E}$. To this end, we will proceed with the help of a diagram. On Figure 8.4, real effort cost and equilibrium catches under each management system have been plotted against E, the global level of effort in the fishery. For the sake of simplicity, the diagram has been built upon the assumption that unit effort costs are equal in both zones ($C_1 = C_2$).[36] As a result, for a given E, real fishing rent under a given management system is the vertical difference between the curve representing catches under this system and the straight dotted line

---

[35] These two restrictions are mutually consistent provided conditions (8.34) hold, i.e., cost pattern allows simultaneous fishing in both zones under open-access equilibrium.

[36] However, we have maintained the assumption of ecological heterogeneity of zones 1 and 2: in the numeric example visualized on Figure 8.4, we have assumed that the FZ is more productive than the NTZ ($D_2 > D_1$). As a result, $c_2 < c_1$, and, for a low level of effort ($E < E_{\lim}$), only zone 2 is fished under conventional management.

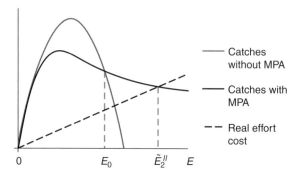

Figure 8.4 Effort–cost and effort–catch relationships.

representing real effort cost. For each management system, the intersection between the catch curve and the real cost dotted line is the open-access equilibrium point.

According to the diagram, MPA-based management will provide higher equilibrium catches than conventional management if $\bar{E}$ is set higher than E_0, the abscissa of the intersection point between catch curves under the two management systems. A sufficient condition for the existence of E_0 is the existence of a SMBL in the NTZ ($v_1 > 0$), which implies that catches converge towards a positive limit when fishing effort increases indefinitely in the FZ. This superiority of MPA-based management extends to the more economic criterion of fishing rent, provided $\bar{E}$ is set at a lower level than $\tilde{E}_2^{II}$, the level of effort corresponding to open-access equilibrium in the FZ of this management system. MPA-based management may therefore correspond to a second-best option in fisheries under heavy fishing pressure, when it is practically impossible, or socially undesirable, to bring fishing effort down to the level corresponding to first-rank optimum. However, at least as regards fishing rent, this possibility is conditioned by the existence of some degree of control over fishing effort in the FZ.

8.5 Conclusion

The model that was presented in this chapter had two purposes: (i) to introduce the reader to the basic concepts and mechanisms of bioeconomic modeling applied to the management of MPAs, and (ii) to illustrate some of the debates that accompanied the development of this technique in recent years. The highly simplifying character of some of its underlying assumptions naturally restricts the interpretative power of this model. These assumptions mainly concern MPA ecosystem (only one stock and two zones were considered), stock dynamics (a simple deterministic law governing the natural dynamics of a homogeneous biomass was assumed), and MPA ecosystem services (only fisheries aspects of MPA were considered). Moreover, the analysis of the model was limited to the comparison of steady-state equilibriums. Nevertheless, the model acknowledges a major feature of MPA management, which is space heterogeneity. This feature relates it to the second family of models that was described in the first section of this chapter (metapopulation models).

Working out the model highlighted some major drivers of the impact of an NTZ on fishing activities. These drivers belong to two categories: i) biophysical factors influencing the capacity of the NTZ to host a minimum safe biomass level (reserve size and productivity, stock intrinsic growth rate, and connectivity between NTZ and FZ); and (ii) technical, economic, and institutional factors influencing the fishing mortality in the FZ (catchability, effort costs, ex-vessel prices, fishing regulations).

The three scenarios that were run with the help of the model illustrated the role played by access regulation mechanisms in the zone that is left open to fishing. If open access prevails in the FZ, implementing an MPA is unlikely to restore fishing rent, but the model suggests that it may, under certain circumstances, improve sustainable catches. Probably the most interesting scenario, from an empirical point of view, is the situation where limited control of fishing mortality prevails in the FZ. According to this scenario, creating an MPA may improve the situation when fishing pressure is high, not only as regards sustainable catches, but also as regards fishing rent.

Bioeconomic modeling of MPAs goes far beyond the simplistic illustration that was provided in this chapter (see Chapter 4 for a more general and more sophisticated model). Nowadays, the major factor limiting the use of bioeconomic modeling in real-world MPA management is not conceptual, but empirical. As regards fishing, a major limit is frequently the poor quantitative knowledge of fish spatial mobility (adult mobility, and, even more, larval dispersal). In the case of non-consumptive use values, we often lack a clear quantitative relationship between conservation measures, the state of ecosystem attributes that are valued by users, and MPA frequentation. Finally, integrating non-use values in bioeconomic modeling is in many cases limited by the absence of realistic valuations of non-use benefits provided by MPAs. A recent panel of experts warned against an uncontrolled use of the so-called "benefit transfer" method as an attempt to fill this gap (US Environmental Protection Agency, 2009).

References

Anderson, L. G. (2002). A bioeconomic analysis of marine reserves. *Natural Resource Modeling*, **15**, 311–34.

Armstrong, C. W. (2007). A note on the ecological–economic modelling of marine reserves in fisheries. *Ecological Economics*, **62**, 242–50.

Armstrong C. W. and Reithe, S. (2001). Comment: Marine reserves, will they accomplish more with management costs? *Marine Resource Economics*, **16**, 165–75.

Beattie, A., Sumaila, U. R., Christensen, N. L., and Pauly, D. (2002). A model for the bioeconomic evaluation of marine protected area size and placement in the North Sea. *Natural Resource Modeling*, **15**, 413–37.

Bohnsack, J. A. (1993). Marine reserves: they enhance fisheries, reduce conflicts and protect resources. *Oceanus*, **36**, 63–71.

Boncoeur, J., Alban, F., Guyader, O., and Thebaud, O. (2002). Fish, fishers, seals and tourists: economic consequences of creating a marine reserve in a multi-species, multi-activity context. *Natural Resource Modeling*, **15**, 387–411.

Caddy, J. F. (1975). Spatial model for an exploited shellfish population, and its application to the Georges Bank scallop fishery. *Journal of the Fisheries Research Board of Canada*, **32**, 1305–28.

Caddy, J. F. and Mahon, R. (1995). *Reference Points for Fisheries Management*, FAO Fisheries Technical Paper No. 347. Rome: Food and Agriculture Organization.

Chakravorty, U. and Nemoto, K. (2001). Modeling the effects of area closure and tax policies: a spatial–temporal model of Hawaii longline fishery. *Marine Resource Economics*, **15**, 179–204.

Charles, A. T. (2001). *Sustainable Fishery Systems*. Madden, MA: Blackwell Science.

Clark, C. W. (1990). *Mathematical Bioeconomics: The Optimal Management of Renewable Resources*, 2nd edn. New York: John Wiley.

Clark, C. W. (1996). Marine reserves and the precautionary management of fisheries. *Ecological Applications*, **6**, 369–70.

Conrad, J. M. (1999). The bioeconomics of marine sanctuaries. *Journal of Bioeconomics*, **1**, 205–17.

Curtis, R. E. and McConnell, K.E. (2004). Incorporating information and expectations in fishermen's spatial decisions. *Marine Resource Economics*, **19**, 131–43.

Dalton, M. G. and Ralston, S. (2004). The California rockfish conservation area and groundfish trawlers at moss landing harbor. *Marine Resource Economics*, **19**, 67–83.

Gordon, H. S. (1954). The economic theory of a common property resource: the fishery. *Journal of Political Economy*, **62**, 124–42.

Grafton, R. Q., Ha, V. P., and Kompas, T. (2004). *Saving the Seas: The Economic Justification for Marine Reserves*. Canberra, ACT: Australian National University.

Grafton R. Q., Kompas, T., and Lindenmayer, D. (2005a). Marine reserves with ecological uncertainty. *Bulletin of Mathematical Biology*, **67**, 957–71.

Grafton, R. Q., Kompas, T., and Schneider, V. (2005b). The bioeconomics of marine reserves: a selected review with policy implications. *Journal of Bioeconomics*, **7**, 161–78.

Grafton, R. Q., Kompas, T., and Ha, V. P. (2009). Cod today and none tomorrow: the economic value of a marine reserve. *Land Economics*, **85**, 454–69.

Guénette, S., Lauck, T., and Clark, C. (1998). Marine reserves: from Beverton and Holt to the present. *Reviews in the Fish Biology and Fisheries*, **8**, 251–72.

Hannesson, R. (1983). Bioeconomic production functions in fisheries: theoretical and empirical analysis. *Canadian Journal of Fisheries and Aquatic Sciences*, **40**, 968–82.

Hannesson, R. (1998). Marine reserves: what would they accomplish? *Marine Resource Economics*, **13**, 159–70.

Holland, D. S. (2000). A bioeconomic model of marine sanctuaries on Georges Bank. *Canadian Journal of Fisheries and Aquatic Sciences*, **57**, 1307–19.

Holland, D. S. and Brazee, R. J. (1996). Marine reserves for fisheries management. *Marine Resource Economics*, **11**, 157–71.

Holland, D. S. and Sutinen, J. G. (1999). An empirical model of fleet dynamics in New England trawl fisheries. *Canadian Journal of Fisheries and Aquatic Sciences*, **56**, 253–64.

Holland, D. S., Sanchirico, J. N., Curtis, R. E., and Hicks, R. L. (2004). An introduction to spatial modeling in fisheries economics. *Marine Resource Economics*, **19**, 1–6.

Hutton, T., Mardle, S., Pascoe, S., and Clark, R. (2004). Modelling fishing location choice within mixed fisheries: English North Sea beam trawlers in 2000 and 2001. *ICES Journal of Marine Science*, **61**, 1443–52.

Lauck, T., Clark, C. W., Mangel, M., and Munro, G. R. (1998). Implementing the precautionary principle in fisheries management through marine reserves. *Ecological Applications*, **8**, S72–S78.

Le Quesne, W. J. F. (2009). Are flawed MPAs any good or just a new way of making old mistakes? *ICES Journal of Marine Science*, **66**, 132–6.

Loisel, P. and Cartigny, P. (2009). How to model marine reserves? *Nonlinear Analysis: Real World Applications*, **10**, 1784–96.

Ludwig D., Hilborn R., and Walters, C. J. (1993). Uncertainty, resource exploitation, and conservation, lessons from history. *Ecological Applications*, **3**, 547–9.

Mangel, M. (2000). Irreducible uncertainties, sustainable fisheries and marine reserves. *Evolutionary Ecology Research*, **2**, 547–57.

Palumbi, S. R. (2002). *Marine Reserves: A Tool for Ecosystem Management and Conservation*. Philadelphia, PA: Pew Oceans Commission.

Pauly, D., Christensen V., Dalsgaard J., Froese R., and Torres, F. (1998). Fishing down the marine food webs. *Science*, **279**, 860–63.

Piet, G. J. and Rijnsdorp, A. D. (1996). Changes in the demersal fish assemblage in the southeastern North Sea following the establishment of a protected area ('plaice box'). In *Ecosystem Effects of Fisheries*, ICES Annual Science Conference, Reykjavik, Iceland.

Pitchford, J. W., Codling, E. A., and Psarra, D. (2007). Uncertainty and sustainability in fisheries and the benefit of marine protected areas. *Ecological Modelling*, **207**, 286–92.

Rijnsdorp, A. D., Buijs, A. M., Storbeck, F., *et al.* (1996). Micro-scale distribution of beam trawl effort in the southern North Sea between 1993 and 1996 in relation to the trawling frequency of the sea bed and the impact on benthic organisms. In *Ecosystem Effects of Fisheries*, ICES Annual Science Conference, Reykjavik, Iceland.

Roberts, C. M. (2000). Why does fishery management so often fail? In *Science and Environmental Decision-Making*, eds. M. Huxham and D. Sumner. New York: Prentice Hall, pp. 170–92.

Sanchirico, J. N. (2004). Designing a cost-effective marine reserve network: a bioeconomic metapopulation analysis. *Marine Resource Economics*, **19**, 41–65.

Sanchirico, J. N. (2005). Additivity properties in metapopulation models: implications for the assessment of marine reserve. *Journal of Environmental Economics and Management*, **49**, 1–25.

Sanchirico, J. N., Malvadkar, U., Hastings, A., and Wilen, J. E. (2006). When are no-take zones an economically optimal fishery management strategy? *Ecological Applications*, **16**, 1643–59.

Sanchirico, J. N. and Wilen, J. E. (1999). Bioeconomics of spatial exploitation in a patchy environment. *Journal of Environmental Economics and Management*, **37**, 129–50.

Sanchirico, J. N. and Wilen, J. E. (2001). A bioeconomic model of marine reserve creation. *Journal of Environmental Economics and Management*, **42**, 257–76.

Sanchirico, J. N. and Wilen, J. E. (2002). The impacts of marine reserves on limited entry fisheries. *Natural Resource Modeling*, **15**, 291–310.

Schaefer, M. B. (1957). Some considerations of population dynamics and economics in relation to the management of marine fisheries. *Journal of the Fisheries Research Board of Canada*, **14**, 669–81.

Schnier, K. E. (2005). Biological "hot spots" and their effect on optimal bioeconomic marine reserve formation. *Ecological Economics*, **52**, 453–68.

Sethi, S. A. and Hilborn, R. (2008). Interactions between poaching and management policy affect marine reserves as conservation tools. *Biological Conservation*, **141**, 506–16.

Smith, M. D. and Wilen, J. E. (2003). Economic impacts of marine reserves: the importance of spatial behavior. *Journal of Environmental Economics and Management*, **46**, 183–206.

Smith, M. D. and Wilen, J. E. (2004). Marine reserves with endogenous ports: empirical bioeconomics of the California sea urchin fishery. *Marine Resource Economics*, **19**, 85–112.

Smith, M. D., Sanchirico, J. N., and Wilen, J. E. (2009). The economics of spatial-dynamic processes: applications to renewable resources. *Journal of Environmental Economics and Management*, **57**, 104–21.

Soulié, J. C. and Thébaud, O. (2006). Modelling fleet response in regulated fisheries: an agent-based approach. *Mathematical and Computer Modelling*, **44**, 553–64.

Strand, I. E. J. (2004). Spatial variation in risk preferences among Atlantic and Gulf of Mexico pelagic longline fishermen. *Marine Resource Economics*, **19**, 145–60.

Sumaila, U. R. (1998a). Protected marine reserve as hedges against uncertainty: an economist's perspective. In *Reinventing Fisheries Management,* eds. T. J. Pitcher, P. J. B. Hart and D. Pauly. Dordrecht, the Netherlands: Kluwer, pp. 303–9.

Sumaila, U. R. (1998b). Protected marine reserves as fisheries management tools: a bioeconomic analysis. *Fisheries Research*, **37**, 287–96.

Sumaila, U. R., Guénette S., Alder J., and Chuenpadgee, R. (2000). Addressing ecosystem effects of fishing using marine protected areas. *ICES Journal of Marine Science*, **57**, 752–60.

Sumaila, U. R. and Armstrong, C. W. (2006). Distributional and efficiency effects of marine protected areas: a study of the northeast Atlantic cod fishery. *Land Economics*, **82**, 321–32.

US Environmental Protection Agency (2009). *Valuing the Protection of Ecological Systems and Services*, Science Advisory Board. Report No. EPA-SAB-09–012. Washington, DC: Environmental Protection Agency.

Valcic, B. (2009). Spatial policy and the behavior of fishermen. *Marine Policy*, **33**, 215–22.

White, C., Kendall, B. E., Gaines, S., Siegel, D. A., and Costello, C. (2008). Marine reserve effects on fishery profit. *Ecology Letters*, **11**, 370–9.

Wilen, J. E., Smith, M. D., Lockwood D., and Botsford, L. W. (2002). Avoiding surprises: incorporating fisherman behavior into management models. *Bulletin of Marine Science*, **70**, 553–75.

9 · SOCIO-ECONOMY – Assessing the impact of marine protected areas on society's well-being: an economic perspective

FRÉDÉRIQUE ALBAN, JEAN BONCOEUR, AND NICOLAS RONCIN

9.1 Introduction

From an economic point of view, marine protected areas (MPAs) may be regarded as public investments in marine ecosystems conservation.[1] As such, the basic question raised by their economic assessment is to determine how they modify society's well-being.

During the twentieth century, two types of methodologies have been developed for assessing the impact of public investments on society's well-being (Bénard, 1985): cost–benefit analysis (CBA) and multicriteria analysis (MCA). The major difference between these methodologies lies in the type of metrics used. While CBA relies on a single metric (money), MCA is multidimensional, taking into account variables that are expressed in various units (monetary, physical, qualitative, . . .). In this respect, MCA belongs to the same paradigm as indicators-based

---

[1] This general assertion is a mere consequence of the widely acknowledged definition of the term "marine protected area": according to IUCN, an MPA is defined as "any area of intertidal or subtidal terrain, together with its overlying water and associated flora, fauna, historical and cultural features, which has been reserved by law or other means to protected part or all of the enclosed environment" (Kelleher and Kenchington, 1992). It does not contradict the fact that various reasons may lead to the creation of an MPA: all social benefits that are expected from an MPA are related, either directly or indirectly, to its allegedly positive impact on marine ecosystem conservation.

Marine Protected Areas: A Multidisciplinary Approach, ed. Joachim Claudet. Published by Cambridge University Press. © Cambridge University Press 2011.

methods that have been recently developed for the monitoring of MPAs (e.g., Hockey and Branch, 1997; Pomeroy et al., 2004; Ojeda-Martinez et al., 2009).[2] But the purpose of MCA, as well as of CBA, is not merely descriptive: these methodologies are intended to help decision-makers in the selection of public investment projects, which requires prioritization.[3] In this respect, MCA is more complex than CBA since it uses variables that are, by nature, incommensurate. Several techniques have been developed to overcome this difficulty (e.g., Keeney and Raiffa, 1976; Roy, 1978; Saaty, 1980), but all of them retain an element of arbitrariness. As a result, CBA is usually considered by economists as the orthodox method for the evaluation of public investment projects.

However, full application of this method to the economic assessment of MPAs raises major theoretical and practical questions, some of which may not be considered as fully settled at the present time. A less ambitious approach consists of assessing the impact of MPAs on the welfare of people living in their neighborhoods. This approach is clearly more restrictive, since it does not address the question of MPA benefits and costs for society as a whole, but focuses on the more limited question of the economic consequences of MPA implementation for local stakeholders. Its relevance is due to the fact that such impacts are critical for the social acceptability of MPAs (Sanchirico, 2000; Carter, 2003; Pomeroy et al., 2004; Charles and Wilson, 2009). The explanation lies in a simple observation: contrasting with the very broad scale of a large class of benefits expected from environment conservation measures (particularly in the case of existence values), most restrictions to human activities imposed by these measures have a local character (Lunney et al., 1997). This discrepancy is likely to undermine the support of local populations, unless they feel that the restrictions they are asked to suffer for the sake of conservation are balanced by some tangible benefits at their own scale. Economic benefits obviously pertain to this category.

In the first section of this chapter, we consider the application of CBA to the economic assessment of MPAs. After recalling the philosophy of CBA, we review the major problems related to its implementation, and

---

[2] Hockey and Branch (1997) implemented a scoring system to measure the effectiveness of MPAs, in terms of scientific, socio-economic, and legal performances. Pomeroy et al. (2004) classified MPA monitoring indicators into three categories: biophysical indicators, socio-economic indicators, and governance indicators. Ojeda-Martinez et al. (2009) developed an assessment of the MPAs functioning and policy decisions based on the driver–pressure–state–impacts–response (DPSIR) framework.

[3] They may also be used for an ex post assessment.

we address more specifically some of the questions raised by its application to the case of MPAs. The second section of the chapter is dedicated to the assessment of the economic impact of MPAs on neighboring populations. In this section, we first deal with the methodological issues raised by this assessment. Then, we provide an illustration concerning 12 MPAs in Southern Europe.

9.2 Cost–benefit analysis and marine protected areas

Various motivations may lead to the creation of an MPA (Hoagland *et al.*, 1995). These may be summarized as (i) ecosystem preservation, (ii) fisheries management, and (iii) development of educational and recreational non-extractive activities. These motivations may overlap, but simultaneously pursuing various objectives implies taking into account the complexity of the consequences induced by the creation of the MPA, and the possible conflicting interests of various stakeholder groups (e.g., Davis, 1981; Davis and Tisdell, 1995; Davis *et al.*, 1995; Polunin *et al.*, 2000; Fabinyi, 2008).

Assessing in economic terms the consequences of a public project, e.g., creating an MPA, requires considering two criteria:

(1) *Efficiency*: what amount of net benefits will the project generate for society?
(2) *Equity*: how will project-related costs and benefits be distributed among society, and what type of measures could compensate those who might suffer from the project?

Assessing the global surplus generated by a project and the way it will be shared among society members falls within the scope of economics. On the other hand, value judgments concerning the fairness of this distribution (and consequently, the relevance of possible compensatory measures) are typically a political topic. In this field, the professional competence of the economist does not go further than characterizing the possible impact of various compensatory measures.

9.2.1. Principles of cost–benefit analysis and problems of implementation

The philosophy of CBA (e.g., Boardman *et al.*, 2006) consists of:

(1) making a census of all stakeholders (individuals or groups affected by the project);

(2) for each stakeholder, valuing all *market and non-market* costs and benefits induced by the project *in monetary terms*, and computing the resulting balance;

(3) aggregating these balances in order to calculate the global surplus of the project.

As an aid to decision-making, the method is generally used for calculating several alternative scenarios. The scenario that is normally selected is the one with the highest global surplus, provided that it respects a set of constraints that should be specified ex ante (one of these scenarios may be the status quo).

Many problems may arise when implementing CBA, with an intensity varying according to the nature of the considered project. Part of these problems falls within the general scope of project analysis, whether these projects are private or public (Squire and Van der Tak, 1975; Kendrick and Stoutjesdijk, 1979). In this field, difficulties may concern the determination of the variables and relations that are liable to influence the yield of the project (production functions, costs, demand), and, a fortiori, the anticipation of their evolution. Other problems are specific to the public character of the projects that are assessed through CBA. Three questions belonging to this category are presented hereafter.

The first difficulty consists of accurately characterizing the complete set of stakeholders. Not only direct stakeholders (producers, financing bodies, direct users) should be considered. It is necessary to determine the consequences of the project for the whole society, which implies, for instance, taking into account upstream producers, consequences on the balance of external trade, or on the state budget. The so-called "effects method," which makes use of such tools as input–output tables, is applied to calculate chain perturbations generated by a public project throughout the economy of the country (Chervel and Le Gall, 1981). However, the theoretical foundation of this method is questionable. If opportunity costs are correctly expressed in market prices,[4] and if the project is marginal compared to the size of the markets directly related to it, then equilibrium prices on these markets convey all the necessary economic information for the assessment of the project, which leaves no ground for calculating the chain perturbations characterizing the "effects

---

[4] The opportunity cost of a scarce resource that is allocated to a given activity is equal to the maximum value of net benefits an alternative allocation of this resource would have generated.

method."[5] How far does this theoretical view represent an acceptable simplification of real-world economy is an unsettled question. From a more practical point of view, the data it requires are not always available, and their accuracy or reliability may be questionable. Moreover, in some cases, the very nature of stakeholders may be hard to define precisely. For instance, in the case of a project aiming at protecting a site with a heritage character, the whole set of beneficiaries may be much larger than the population of the visitors of the site.

A second difficulty stems from the need to express non–market costs and benefits in monetary terms. Non–market costs and benefits may be related to two kinds of values: (i) non–market use values, which are related to non–market human activities (e.g., value of fish caught by a recreational fisherman, or opportunity cost of time that he devotes to this activity); (ii) non-use values, which are essentially non–market: existence, bequest, and option value (e.g., value of biodiversity). Non–market costs and benefits are often critical to the evaluation of a public project. However, the underlying values, unlike market values, are not naturally expressed in monetary terms. Several techniques have been developed to address this problem. These include: (i) revealed preferences methods, such as hedonic pricing and travel costs, which consist of measuring indirectly the value that is attributed to a non–market benefit on the basis of the price that the beneficiaries actually accept to pay for an associated market benefit (Palmquist, 2005; Phaneuf and Smith, 2005; Bockstael and McConnel, 2007);[6] and (ii) stated preference methods, such as contingent valuation, which aims at directly measuring the value attributed to a non–market benefit by asking concerned people what would be their willingness to pay for it, or what would be their willingness to receive in exchange of being deprived of it (Carson and Hanemann, 2005).[7]

---

[5] If the marginality condition is not satisfied, it is necessary to make use of a general equilibrium model (i.e., a model where all prices are set simultaneously), in order to compute the changes in equilibrium prices due to the project.

[6] These methodologies may be illustrated by the following examples: (i) assessing the value attributed to a landscape on the basis of the higher price people accept to pay for a house with a view on this landscape (hedonic pricing); (ii) assessing the value attributed to the visit of a natural site on the basis of the time and money people accept to spend for traveling to this site (travel cost – in this methodology, traveling time is itself converted into money, on the basis of incomes people could have earned during the time they spend traveling).

[7] For example, estimating the value attributed to an endangered historical monument by asking people how much would they accept to pay (by means of a tax, for instance) for its conservation.

These techniques should not be regarded as panaceas. Their scope is not general (non-use values are out of the scope of revealed preference methods), their methodology may be difficult to implement, and the reliability of their results is often controversial (see Arrow *et al.* [1993] for a definition of the conditions that should be satisfied for a good use of contingent valuation). A problem frequently met when stated preference methods are applied to environmental questions is the fact that persons who are asked to state their preferences do not necessarily have a clear view of what is at stake, which may generate instability in their willingness to pay and other biases. As a result, some authors propose to use a deliberative process (e.g., mediated modeling) to help respondents to construct their preferences (Lichtenstein and Slovic, 2006). Some valuation studies try to overcome the difficulty by using the benefits transfer method (Hoagland *et al.*, 1995), which consists of making use of information about benefits derived from a previous study, concerning a different site (e.g., transferring the value of 1 square mile of protected mangrove that was estimated in one case study to another case study). This method is popular among government and consultancy agencies because it saves time and money, but obviously it raises questions due to the specificity of each site, both from an ecological and from a social point of view (Wilson and Hoehn, 2006). As a result, a recent panel of experts recommended to be very cautious with the use of benefit transfer in the valuation of environmental services (US Environmental Protection Agency, 2009).

A third difficulty is due to the necessity of correctly expressing market values. If market values, unlike non-market values, may be directly observed in monetary terms, the results of these observations do not necessarily provide results that can be considered as relevant for CBA. This problem is twofold: (i) at a given date, observed market prices may not represent correctly the social costs and benefits of scarce resources that are used and of commodities that are produced, because of various distortions on markets (non-neutral taxes, subsidies, monopolistic positions, custom rights, politically determined exchange rates, externalities, . . .);[8] (ii) costs and benefits generated by the project at various time periods may be compared only through the time-discounting technique.

---

[8] This difficulty may theoretically be overcome by computing a set of shadow-prices on the basis of an optimization program representing the objective-function and the constraints of the project (Squire and Van der Tak, 1975). However, this type of artefact may prove difficult to implement in practice.

The level of the adopted discount rate may influence heavily the results of the analysis, especially if the project is to have important long-term consequences. The choice of the discount rate to use for public projects is difficult and controversial. The scarcer is the saving available for funding the project, the higher the discount rate should be. A high discount rate, however, mechanically induces disregarding long-term effects of the project, which may create a "short-sight" bias in the assessment of the project, but also a problem of intergenerational equity.[9]

In order to mitigate some of the difficulties encountered by CBA, a less ambitious method, called "cost–efficiency analysis," is sometimes used (e.g., Bénard, 1985). According to this method, the objective to reach is exogenous, and the various scenarios are ranked according to their social cost.

9.2.2 Application of cost–benefit analysis to marine protected areas

There is a wide scope for the use of CBA in the field of environmental economics (Hanley and Spash, 1993) and especially in the case of economic assessment of MPAs (Hoagland *et al.*, 1995; Sanchirico, 2000; Carter, 2003). However, few studies have estimated the global economic surplus generated by MPAs. These estimates would imply that the whole array of economic values provided by the ecosystem is covered. But few studies take account of non-use values (Dharmaratne *et al.*, 2000; Bhat, 2003; Togridou *et al.*, 2006; Subade, 2007), which results in underrating the economic value of MPAs, and may create a bias in favor of the development of commercial activities inside MPAs (Salm and Clark, 1984).

Considering use-values, until the 2000s, the bulk of the economic literature dedicated to MPAs was focused on fisheries management, though with few empirical applications. During the same period, the topic of recreational benefits of MPAs was addressed only by a small number of studies, mainly related to the tourist potential of MPAs in tropical areas. However, this topic has attracted an increasing number of studies during the 2000s, focusing on two majors issues: (i) feasibility analysis of a self-financing mechanism based on users' fees (e.g., Depondt and Green, 2006; Asafu-Adjaye and Tapsuwan, 2008; Peters and Hawkins, 2009; Reid-Grant and Bhat, 2009); and (ii) assessment of compensation mechanisms between users (e.g., Wielgus *et al.*, 2008).

---

[9] For a discussion of the role of the time-discount rate in the context of fisheries management, see Hannesson (1993).

As regards fishing, a valuation problem may arise where a significant part of catches is not marketed. In the case of subsistence fishing, landings should be valued by using ex-vessel market prices for similar products landed by commercial fishing boats – which, in practice, may raise some problems. In the case of recreational fishing, this solution does not apply, because recreational fishers do not value their activity on the basis of the fish consumption it provides, but merely for the leisure it represents. When recreational fishing takes the form of charter fishing, its economic value is normally represented in the price paid by customers to chartering companies. In the frequent case where recreational fishing is a non-market activity, it is necessary to value the willingness to pay of fishers by appropriate methods, such as the contingent valuation method, the travel cost method, or a combination of both methods (Layman *et al.*, 1996). Assuming fishing-related values are properly estimated, the assessment of costs and benefits of the MPA for fishers mainly relies on the following considerations:

- The prohibition of fishing in the no-take zone (NTZ) of the MPA reduces catch, ceteris paribus. This is the negative effect of the MPA for fishers. The economic importance of this drawback varies according to the degree of dependency of fishers on the zone affected by the prohibition, and to the cost of going elsewhere for fishing.
- On the other hand, by protecting a part of fish populations against fishing mortality, the fishing ban favors an increase in biomass in the no-take part of the MPA, which is likely to induce a net transfer from the NTZ to the fishing zone (spillover effect), thereby increasing catches in this zone.[10] This favorable effect of the MPA depends on two types of factors: biological parameters of the targeted stocks (recruitment, natural mortality, space mobility), and the level of fishing mortality (hence of fishing effort) in the zone left open to fishing. This factor is critical when assessing the economic performance of the MPA: if the fishing zone is under open access, the increase in catch will be followed by an increase in effort, and this process will normally go on until the rent resulting from the spillover effect is totally dissipated (Hannesson, 1998). But if the increase in fishing effort may be prevented (e.g., by a system of limited entry licenses in the fishing zone), the rent dissipation will not happen, and the MPA may improve the situation of the fishery, both in economic and in biological terms, even though

---

[10] The protected spawning stock biomass inside the NTZ may also generate increased larval dispersal outside. However, the effect of this dispersal on fish stocks is usually more difficult to ascertain than adult biomass transfer.

this fishery suffers from some overcapacity (Holland and Brazee, 1996; Sanchirico and Wilen, 2002).

- The existence of a zone where fish resources are protected from fishing mortality may also be considered as an application of the precautionary principle to fisheries management (Clark, 1996; Lauck *et al.*, 1998; Sumaïla, 1998), limiting the risk of accidental collapse of the fishery by the constitution of a buffer stock.
- Benefits of the MPA for fishers will be maximized if the location of the NTZ is such that it protects a critical zone for the stock renewal. On the other hand, these benefits may be jeopardized by the opportunistic development of predators (Boncoeur *et al.*, 2002).

Concerning tourism, assessing costs and benefits generated by an MPA relies on the assumption that protecting the marine ecosystem inside the MPA is likely to attract visitors. This assessment raises several types of questions. First, it is necessary to work out a statistically significant quantitative relationship between some attributes of the ecosystem that are favorably influenced by conservation measures and the number of visitors of the MPA (Dixon *et al.*, 1993; Rudd and Tupper, 2002). A reasonable assumption is that such a relationship is positive but non-linear, due to congestion phenomena that appear once a certain level of frequentation is reached. Second, it is necessary to take account of the negative consequences tourist flows may have on the ecosystem, especially when their increase is left uncontrolled (Lindberg, 1990). Finally, it is necessary to establish a relevant valuation system for the net benefits generated by visits to the MPA. This generally involves both market values (e.g., fees paid by visitors) and non-market use values (consumer's surplus).

9.3 Assessing the local economic impact of marine protected areas

In this section, we discuss the methodological issues related to the assessment of the local economic impact of MPAs, and provide an illustration concerning 12 Southern European MPAs.

9.3.1 Methodological issues

Anthropogenic uses of the services provided by the ecosystem of the MPA have a local economic impact so far as they generate incomes in the neighboring coastal zone.

The category of "neighboring zone" cannot be defined generically because it depends on the size and frequentation of the considered MPA. For instance, in the case of the Great Barrier Reef Marine Park (GBRMP) in Australia, economic impacts were assessed at the scale of the whole State of Queensland (Driml, 1987), a choice that is consistent with the characteristics of the GBRMP (350 000 km^2; 3.8 million visitors in 1990). In other areas like Europe, MPAs are generally much smaller, and the most appropriate definition of "neighboring zone" probably corresponds to the concept of "employment zone," i.e., a zone encompassing the majority of everyday commuting trips between home and workplace.

Incomes that are locally generated by the uses of MPA ecosystem services may be of two types: cash or non-cash. Non-cash incomes correspond to the non-market benefits that the ecosystem of the MPA provides to the local population, and cash incomes are generated by the market-oriented private activities induced by the MPA ecosystem uses.

In the case of market-oriented productive activities, the only incomes that should be taken into account, from a theoretical point of view, are the net resource rents generated by these activities (e.g., fishery rent), since other incomes are supposed to be the opportunity costs of scarce production factors that could have been employed in other activities, or in other places. However, this view implies that markets are fully competitive and full employment prevails, an assumption that is frequently at odds with real-world circumstances. As a result, it is usually considered more appropriate to assume that by providing jobs, wages, and other activities that generate incomes to coastal populations, neighboring MPAs have a positive contribution to human well-being. Figure 9.1 describes in short terms the process of estimating incomes and jobs locally generated by uses of services provided by the marine ecosystem of an MPA. These jobs and incomes pertain to three categories (Lindberg, 2001): (i) direct incomes and jobs, generated by MPA ecosystem service users themselves (e.g., fishers); (ii) indirect incomes and jobs, generated by industries technically related to direct users (e.g., industries providing inputs to fishers); (iii) induced incomes and jobs, generated by the expenditure of direct and indirect incomes (final consumption).[11] At each stage of the process, it is necessary to make a distinction between

---

[11] On Figure 9.1, the generation of indirect and induced incomes is represented under the form of two feedback loops, named "Leontief" and "Keynesian," from the input–output matrix and the investment multiplier developed by Leontief and Keynes, respectively.

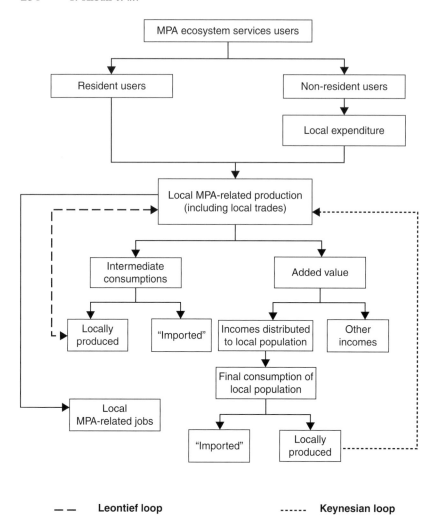

Figure 9.1 Assessing the local economic impact of MPA ecosystem services uses: theoretical scheme.

local economic flows (e.g., consumption of goods produced locally) and flows linking the local economic system to the external world (e.g., consumption of "imported" goods). In practice, estimates are often limited to the calculation of direct incomes and jobs: taking into account indirect and induced effects requires information on the structure of the local economy (input–output matrix and income-elasticity coefficients of final consumption, with a distinction between "imported" and locally produced goods and services), which is frequently unavailable at the scale adopted for the analysis.[12]

A major problem encountered when attempting to estimate incomes and jobs generated by the MPA is the necessity to sort out the "site effect" from the "reserve effect," in order to capture the real economic consequences of protecting a marine area (Pendleton, 1995). In many cases, the lack of baseline and the difficulty to define a control zone make it impossible to estimate directly the reserve effect on the basis of observed behaviors. An alternative is to ask users how they would behave if the area were not protected. Carlsen and Wood (2004) used this type of contingent approach in their assessment of the economic impact of recreation and tourism in Western Australia's national parks, marine parks, and forests. These authors estimated a "substitution factor" which they defined as "the amount of retained tourist expenditure attributable to national parks, marine parks and forests that would otherwise not have occurred." Their estimate is based on answers to a field survey, where park visitors were asked what would have been their holidaying behavior if the natural environments of the national park and forests in the region did not exist (Carlsen and Wood, 2004). However, answers to this question are not easy to interpret, because it does not clearly separate what is due to the site from what is due to its protection. Moreover, in various cases, the population under survey is not composed only of holidaying visitors. For instance, in the case of local commercial fishers, the question is not simply whether they would still fish in the area or not, but rather, how much money they would still make if the area was not protected. Generally speaking, the obvious problem raised by the contingent approach to the reserve effect is that respondents do not necessarily have a clear vision of the implications of protection on the ecosystem services they use. In the survey presented hereafter, 18% of recreational fishers and 30% of scuba-divers in the sample did not even know that they were operating in an MPA (from which it would be imprudent to conclude that there is no reserve effect in their case).

---

[12] The assessment of the economic impact of the GBRMP in 2000 made use of an input–output table to estimate indirect effects of park-related economic activities, but these effects were estimated for the whole State of Queensland (KPMG Consulting, 2000). Coffman and Kim (2009) examined the economic impacts of banning commercial bottomfish fishing in the north-western Hawaiian Islands, based on input–output framework.

9.3.2 Assessing the local economic impact of 12 marine protected areas in southern Europe

A majority of studies assessing the local economic impact of nature reserves, including MPAs, are concentrated in North America and Australia, and mainly deal with recreational uses of these reserves. Alongside with various monographic surveys, efforts have been made to develop generic methodologies (Stynes and Propst, 1993). In southern Europe, an important number of MPAs have been created, particularly in the Mediterranean (IUCN, 2007; Abdulla *et al.*, 2008). Compared to the Australian or North American context, these MPAs share two distinctive figures: (i) their size is relatively small (112 km^2 on average, according to IUCN, 2007); (ii) they are usually located in or close to highly urbanized zones, with a considerable flow of tourists driven there by various factors of attractiveness, including an important cultural and historic heritage. Some information concerning their economic impact is provided by monographic studies, but no attempt had been made, up to a recent date, to assess this impact on the basis of a standardized methodology. This was the purpose of a socio-economic survey of 12 southern European MPAs by Roncin *et al.* (2008). As an illustration of some of the questions raised in the former subsection, we sum up hereafter the methodology and results of this survey.

The assessment was performed within the framework of an EU-funded multidisciplinary research project, devoted to the use of European MPAs as tools for fisheries management and conservation (EMPAFISH). This project covered 20 MPAs in southern Europe (western Mediterranean and Atlantic Ocean), among which 12 were used as case studies for the socio-economic assessment. Generally composed of a NTZ and a buffer zone where fishing is allowed with restrictions, these case studies are located in four different countries (Spain, Portugal, France, and Italy), and their sizes are very heterogeneous, from 4 km^2 to 800 km^2. The same remark applies to the NTZ of these MPAs, which represents 5% of their total surface on the average, with a minimum of 2% and a maximum of 43%.

In each case study, MPA managers provided information concerning the yearly number of visits to their MPA, and the number of people or firms making use of the services provided by its ecosystem, for recreational or commercial purposes. The accuracy of this information varies according to case studies and uses. This caveat applies particularly to recreational fishing, which is informal in most cases (no operators, no permits). Nevertheless, in accordance with facts observed at a broader scale (Abdulla *et al.*, 2008), estimates provided by MPA managers suggest that, in most case studies under review, recreational uses play a major role in the pattern of MPA ecosystem services uses. According to these estimations, the yearly number of people paying a recreational visit to each MPA is approximately 110 000 on average, including 7000 scuba-divers and 2000 recreational fishers (likely an underestimate). In the same time, an average 50 commercial fishing boats, all of them less than 12 m long (except in one case study), were recorded as operating the fishing zone of each MPA.[13]

The socio-economic survey of the 12 MPAs was performed in 2005 and 2006. It covered a range of MPA ecosystem uses, with a main focus on fishing and scuba-diving, which were considered as the two major uses of the ecosystem services provided by the MPAs under survey. Its first purpose was to provide information on the identity of users, on their MPA-related activity, and on their attitude towards the MPA. The scope of the survey was limited to persons with an activity inside the MPA. With regards to fishing, this limitation implied that only fishers operating (at least part-time) inside the fishing zone of the MPA were interviewed. This approach may be considered as excessively conservative, since the NTZ is liable to generate spillover effects beyond the administrative limits of the MPA. However, little information concerning the range of these effects was available, and it was decided to take the fishing zone of the MPA as a proxy for the zone impacted by significant spillover effects. On the whole, a total of 1836 questionnaires concerning fishing or scuba-diving were filled within the 12 case studies (Roncin *et al.*, 2008).

Concerning the neighboring zone where economic impacts were to be assessed, no standardized definition was available at the scale of the four countries covered by the survey, and the following approximations were adopted:

(1) All commercial fishers were considered as "local" (an assumption based on consideration of the home port and size of commercial fishing boats operating within the fishing zone or the vicinity of the MPA).

(2) Recreational users were considered as "local," or "resident," if the distance between the MPA and their permanent home was within

---

[13] In one case an ad hoc zone had to be defined, because the MPA did not include formally a fishing zone.

50 km (according to survey results, most people living beyond this limit have to spend at least one night out of their home to perform the considered activity in the MPA).

The assessment of incomes generated by the use of MPA ecosystem services was limited to cash incomes. This restrictive choice certainly resulted in underscoring the local benefits generated by MPA ecosystem services, since it amounted to excluding the consumer's surplus of local recreational users from the assessment. The degree of underestimation of benefits may vary according to the type of activity and case study considered: if, in all case studies, a large majority of divers are non-resident (88% for the whole survey sample), in some MPAs the majority of recreational fishers are resident. Two indicators of economic impact were computed: (i) added value (i.e., value of production minus consumption of intermediate goods and external services), which represents the direct contribution of the considered activity to the local GDP; (ii) local jobs that are required to run this activity. Indirect and induced incomes and jobs were not considered, another restrictive choice due to the lack of reliable data at the local scale.

The methodology that was used for assessing money incomes and related jobs was based on a distinction between users transforming ecosystem services into commodities (commercial fishers), and users consuming ecosystem services for recreational purposes (recreational fishers and scuba-divers). In the first case, incomes and jobs derived from the activity within the fishing zone of the MPA were estimated assuming proportionality between these variables and time spent fishing within the zone. In the case of recreational fishing and scuba-diving, incomes and jobs that were taken into account were the ones that various local businesses (e.g., hotels, restaurants, diving or charter-fishing operators) derive from the expenditures of non-resident recreational users of the MPA during their stay. The amount of local added value and the number of local jobs generated by these expenditures were estimated on the basis of standard ratios derived from statistical data concerning the seaside tourism industry. In order to avoid overrating the impact of the MPA, a filter ("attribution factor") based on the motivation of these non-resident users was implemented (Johnson and Moore, 1993): only those whose stay in the area was motivated mainly by diving or fishing in the MPA were retained.

The whole set of data required by the estimation process was not available for every case study. Moreover, in some cases, the actual sampling rate was too low for drawing significant conclusions. As a consequence, the estimation could be carried out in 11 cases concerning scuba-diving, but only in five cases for professional fishing, and in four cases for recreational fishing. According to these estimations, the average yearly money incomes locally generated by MPA ecosystem services uses amounted to €710 000 per MPA in the case of professional fishing, €551 000 per MPA in the case of scuba diving, and €88 000 in the case of recreational fishing.[14] In order to provide an order of magnitude, these figures may be compared to the yearly MPA management costs, which amounted to €588 000 per year on the average, according to data provided by MPA managers.

Due to available information, the relative importance of commercial fishing and recreational activities could be compared only in a few case studies. The Mediterranean cases of Columbretes and Medes Islands, both located in Spain, provided illustrations of two opposite situations. In the case of Columbretes Islands, commercial fishing is dominant in terms of economic impact: according to the estimation, this activity generates nearly 90% of all money incomes provided by the MPA ecosystem uses. The situation is completely opposite in the case of Medes Islands, where incomes generated by commercial fishing amount to only 5% of those generated by scuba-diving. The number and size of commercial fishing boats operating in the various MPAs surveyed suggest that most of them are closer to the Medes model than to the Columbretes model. At a much smaller scale, the pattern of uses exhibited by Medes Islands MPA is similar to the one characterizing the GBRMP in Australia, where the estimated distribution of economic weights between recreational uses and commercial fishing is approximately 4 : 1 (KPMG Consulting, 2000).

As noted earlier, such results cannot be attributed unambiguously to the protection of marine areas, because they are the joint product of both "site" and "reserve" effects. Due to the age of the surveyed MPAs (more than 15 years on the average when the field survey started), it was impossible to ask questions concerning the changes produced by their implementation. However, answers concerning perceptions and opinions of MPA ecosystem services users provided some qualitative information about the relative importance of these two effects.

---

[14] These mean values conceal a great diversity of local situations. For instance, the estimation of value locally added by scuba-diving (the activity with the most exhaustive coverage in the survey) ranged from €16 000 per year in the case of Sinis (Italy) to €1.1 million per year in the case of Medes Islands (Spain).

A first type of information was provided by answers of recreational users concerning the influence of the MPA status on their decision to fish or dive in the area: on the whole, divers were more disposed to acknowledge the influence of this status on their decision than recreational fishers.[15] Questioning commercial operators provided a similar result: managers of recreational diving businesses were more positive than commercial fishers concerning the influence of the MPA on their business.[16]

Considering the major criteria mentioned by fishers and divers for choosing a site of activity may help to explain these differences. Answers to the field survey pinpoint the major role played by fish abundance as a site selection criteria, for both fishers and divers (in the case of scuba-diving, the quality of the underwater scenery and the presence of some spectacular, or "emblematic" species, such as groupers, were also declared of high importance). In the case of diving, several regulations taken by MPA authorities directly influence the variables that are regarded as major decision criteria: for instance, banning spearfishing in a given place is likely to influence directly the abundance, average size and behavior of fish in this place. This circumstance may account for the positive perception of MPAs by divers and diving operators. On the other hand, the expected positive influence of MPAs on fishing mainly relies on their alleged spillover effects, which are less conspicuous, and partly balanced by the restrictive impact of MPA regulations on fishing activities. Opinions of fishers reflect this ambivalence.

9.4 Conclusion

Assessing the consequences of MPAs on society's welfare clearly falls within the scope of cost–benefit analysis. However, several problems frequently limit the application of this standard economic methodology to the assessment of net benefits provided to society by MPAs. The most common ones are related to the measurement of non-market

---

[15] More than half of interviewed scuba-divers acknowledged this influence, while three recreational fishers out of four denied it.

[16] While 71% of interviewed scuba-diving operators acknowledged a positive influence of the MPA on their business, the figure was only 25% with commercial fishers. Negative opinions and positive opinions were balanced among interviewed commercial fishers (half of them considering that the MPA had no influence on their activity), while negative opinions were shared by only 2% of interviewed diving operators.

values, including non-use values such as the value of marine biodiversity. Assessing the impact of an MPA on some market values (e.g., fishery rent) may also be problematic, due to limited quantitative information on underlying ecological processes (spillover effects of no-take zones). As a result, applications of cost–benefits analysis to MPAs are generally incomplete, providing an assessment of only a part of the net benefits they generate.

Surveys assessing the economic impact of MPAs on local populations pertain to this category. Despite its more restricted ambition, this type of assessment may also face substantial difficulties. Two of them have been underlined in this chapter. First, the limited availability of economic data at the relevant scale frequently hinders a complete assessment of the influence exerted by uses of MPA ecosystem services on the economy of the neighboring zone. Second, the frequent lack of reference points makes it difficult to sort out the "site" effect from the "reserve" effect. As a result, it is necessary to address this question on the basis of qualitative and subjective information provided by MPA ecosystem services users. This approach highlights the importance of perception indicators, which are widely used by social scientists analyzing the governance and effectiveness of MPAs (see Chapter 5).

References

Abdulla, A., Gomei, M., Maison, E., and Piante, C. (2008). *Status of Marine Protected Areas in the Mediterranean Sea*. Malaga, Spain: IUCN.

Arrow, K., Solow, R., Portney, P. R., *et al.* (1993). Report of the NOAA Panel on contingent valuation. *Federal Register*, **58**, 4601–14.

Asafu-Adjaye, J. and Tapsuwan, S. (2008). A contingent valuation study of scuba diving benefits: case study in Mu Ko Similan Marine National Park, Thailand. *Tourism Management*, **29**, 1122–30.

Bénard, J. (1985). *Economie publique*. Paris: Economica.

Bhat, M. G. (2003). Application of non-market valuation to the Florida Keys marine reserve management. *Journal of Environmental Management*, **67**, 315–25.

Boardman, A. E., Greenberg, D. H., Vining, A. R., and Weimer, D. L. (2006). *Cost–Benefit Analysis: Concept and Practice*, 3rd edn. Upper Saddle River, NJ: Prentice Hall.

Bockstael, N. B. and McConnell, K. E. (2007). *Environmental and Resource Valuation with Revealed Preferences: A Theoretical Guide to Empirical Models*. New York: Springer.

Boncoeur J., Alban, F., Guyader, O., and Thébaud, O. (2002). Fish, fishers, seals and tourists: economic consequences of creating a marine reserve in a multi-species, multi-activity context. *Natural Resource Modeling*, **15**, 387–411.

Carlsen, J. and Wood, D. (2004). *Assessment of the Economic Value of Recreation and Tourism in Western Australia's National Parks, Marine Parks and Forests*. Townsville, QLD: Sustainable Tourism CRC.

Carson, R. T. and Hanemann, W. M. (2005). Contingent valuation. In *Handbook of Environmental Economics*, vol. 2, ed. K. Mäler and J. Vincent. Amsterdam, the Netherlands: North-Holland, pp. 821–936.

Carter, D. W. (2003). Protected areas in marine resource management: another look at the economics and research issues. *Ocean and Coastal Management*, **46**, 439–56.

Charles, A. and Wilson, L. (2009). Human dimensions of Marine Protected Areas. *ICES Journal of Marine Science*, **66**, 6–15.

Chervel, M. and Le Gall, M. (1981). *Manuel d'évaluation économique des projets: la méthode des effets*. Paris: SEDES/Ministère de la Coopération.

Clark, C. W. (1996). Marine reserves and the precautionary management of fisheries. *Ecological Applications*, **6**, 369–70.

Coffman, M. and Kim, K. (2009). The economic impacts of banning commercial bottomfish fishing in the Northwestern Hawaiian Islands. *Ocean and Coastal Management*, **52**, 166–72.

Davis, G. E. (1981). On the role of underwater parks and sanctuaries in the management of coastal resources in the Southeastern United States. *Environmental Conservation*, **8**, 67–70.

Davis, D. and Tisdell, C. (1995). Recreational scuba-diving and carrying capacity in marine protected areas. *Ocean and Coastal Management*, **26**, 19–40.

Davis, D., Harriott, V., Macnamara, C., Roberts, L., and Austin, S. (1995). Conflicts in a marine protected area: scuba divers, economics, ecology and management in Julian Rocks Aquatic Reserve. *Australian Parks and Recreation*, **31**, 29–35.

Depondt, F. and Green, E. (2006). Diving user fees and the financial sustainability of marine protected areas: opportunities and impediments. *Ocean and Coastal Management*, **49**, 188–202.

Dharmaratne, G. S., Sang, F. Y., and Walling, L. J. (2000). Tourism potentials for financing protected areas. *Annals of Tourism Research*, **27**, 590–610.

Dixon, J. A., Scura, L. F., and Van't Hof, T. (1993). Meeting ecological and economic goals: marine park in the Caribbean. *Ambio*, **22**, 117–25.

Driml, S. (1987). *Economic Impacts of Activities on the Great Barrier Reef*. Townsville, QLD: Great Barrier Reef Marine Park Authority.

Fabinyi, M. (2008). Dive tourism, fishing and marine protected areas in the Calamianes Islands, Philippines. *Marine Policy*, **32**, 898–904.

Hanley, N. and Spash, C. (1993). *Cost–Benefit Analysis and the Environment*. Cheltenham, UK: Edward Elgar.

Hannesson, R. (1993). *Bioeconomic Analysis of Fisheries*. Oxford, UK: Fishing News Books.

Hannesson, R. (1998). Marine reserves: what would they accomplish? *Marine Resource Economics*, **13**, 159–70.

Hoagland, P., Kaoru, Y., and Broadus, J. M. (1995). *A Methodological Review of Net Benefit Evaluation for Marine Reserves*. New York: The World Bank.

Hockey, P. A. R. and Branch, G. M. (1997). Criteria, objectives and methodology for evaluating marine protected areas in South Africa. *South African Journal of Marine Sciences*, **18**, 369–83.

Holland, D. S. and Brazee, R. J. (1996). Marine reserves for fisheries management. *Marine Resource Economics*, **11**, 157–71.

IUCN (2007). *Use of the IUCN Protected Areas Management Categories in the Mediterranean Region*. Sevilla, Spain: Consejeria de Medio Ambiente de la Junta de Andalucia, and Gland, Switzerland: IUCN.

Johnson, R. L. and Moore, E. (1993). Tourism impact estimation. *Annals of Tourism Research*, **20**, 279–88.

Keeney, R. L. and Raiffa, H. (1976). *Decisions with Multiple Objectives: Preferences and Value Trade-Offs*. New York: John Wiley.

Kelleher, G. and Kenchington, R. (1992). *Guidelines for Establishing Marine Protected Areas: A Marine Conservation Development Report*. Gland, Switzerland: IUCN.

Kendrick, D. A. and Stoutjesdijk, A. J. (1979). *The Planning of Industrial Investment Programs: A Methodology*. Baltimore, MD: Johns Hopkins University Press.

KPMG Consulting (2000). *Economic and Financial Values of the Great Barrier Reef Marine Park*. Townsville, QLD: Great Barrier Reef Marine Park Authority.

Layman, R. C., Boyce, J. R., and Criddle, K. R. (1996). Chinook salmon sport fishery. *Land Economics*, **72**, 113–28.

Lauck, T., Clark, C. W., Mangel, M., and Munro, G. R. (1998). Implementing the precautionary principle in fisheries management through marine reserves. *Ecological Applications*, **8**, S72–S78.

Lichteinstein, S. and Slovic, P. (2006). *The Construction of Preference*. Cambridge, UK: Cambridge University Press.

Lindberg, K. (1990). *Economic Policies for Maximizing Nature: Tourism's Contribution to Sustainable Development*. Washington, DC: World Resources Institute.

Lindberg, K. (2001). Economic impacts. In *Encyclopaedia of Ecotourism*, ed. D. Weaver. Wallingford, UK: CAB International, pp. 363–77.

Lunney, D., Pressey, B., Archer, M., Hand, S., Godthelp, H., and Curtin, A. (1997). Integrating ecology and economics: illustrating the need to resolve the conflicts of space and time. *Ecological Economics*, **23**, 135–43.

Ojeda-Martínez, C., Giménez Casalduero, F., Bayle-Sempere, J. T., *et al.* (2009). A conceptual framework for the integral management of marine protected areas. *Ocean and Coastal Management*, **52**, 89–101.

Palmquist, R. B. (2005). Property value models. In *Handbook of Environmental Economics*, vol. 2, eds. K. Mäler and J. Vincent. Amsterdam, the Netherlands: North-Holland, pp. 763–819.

Pendleton, L. (1995). Valuing coral reef protection. *Ocean and Coastal Management*, **26**, 119–31.

Peters, H. and Hawkins, J. P. (2009). Access to marine parks: a comparative study in willingness to pay. *Ocean and Coastal Management*, **52**, 219–28.

Phaneuf, D. J. and Smith, V. K. (2005). Recreation demand models. In *Handbook of Environmental Economics*, vol. 2, eds. K. Mäler and J. Vincent. Amsterdam, the Netherlands: North-Holland, pp. 671–761.

Polunin, N. V. C., Williams, I., Carrier, J., and Robertson, L. (2000). *Ecological and Social Impacts in Planning Caribbean Marine Reserves: Strategy for Research on Renewable Natural Resources, Natural Resources Systems Programme*, Final Technical Report R6783. Newcastle, UK: University of Newcastle for DFID.

Pomeroy, R. S., Parks, J. E., and Watson, L. M. (2004). *How Is Your MPA Doing? A Guidebook of Natural and Social Indicators for Evaluating Marine Protected Area Management Effectiveness.* Gland, Switzerland: IUCN.

Reid-Grant, K. and Bhat, M. G. (2009). Financing marine protected areas in Jamaica: an exploratory study. *Marine Policy*, **33**, 128–36.

Roy, B. (1978). ELECTRE III: algorithme de classement basé sur une représentation floue des préférences en présence de critères multiples. *Cahiers du CERO*, **20**, 3–24.

Roncin, N., Alban, F., Charbonnel, E., *et al* (2008). Uses of ecosystem services provided by MPAs: how much do they impact the local economy? A southern Europe perspective. *Journal for Nature Conservation*, **16**, 256–70.

Rudd, M. A. and Tupper, M. H. (2002). The impact of Nassau grouper size and abundance on scuba diver site selection and MPA economics. *Coastal Management*, **30**, 133–51.

Saaty, T. L. (1980). *The Analytic Hierarchy Process.* New York: McGraw Hill.

Salm, R. V. and Clark, J. R. (1984). *Marine and Coastal Protected Areas: A Guide for Planners and Managers.* Gland, Switzerland: IUCN.

Sanchirico, J. N. (2000). *Marine Protected Areas as Fishery Policy: A Discussion of Potential Costs and Benefits.* Discussion Paper No. 00–23. Washington, DC: Resources for the Future.

Sanchirico, J. N. and Wilen, J. E. (2002). The impacts of marine reserves on limited entry fisheries. *Natural Resource Modeling*, **15**, 291–310.

Squire, L. and Van Der Tak, H. G. (1975). *Economic Analysis of Projects.* Baltimore, MD: Johns Hopkins University Press.

Stynes, D. J. and Propst, D. B. (1993). *Micro-Implan Recreation Economic Impact Estimation System: MI-REC User's Manual*, Version 3. East Lansing, MI: Department of Park and Recreation Resources, Michigan State University.

Subade, R. F. (2007). Mechanisms to capture economic values of marine biodiversity: the case of Tubbataha Reefs UNESCO World Heritage Site, Philippines. *Marine Policy*, **31**, 135–42.

Sumaila, U. R. (1998). Protected marine reserve as hedges against uncertainty: an economist's perspective. In *Reinventing Fisheries Management*, eds. T. J. Pitcher, P. J. B. Hart, and D. Pauly. Dordrecht, the Netherlands: Kluwer, pp. 303–9.

Togridou, A., Hovardas, T., and Pantis, J. D. (2006). Determinants of visitors' willingness to pay for the National Marine Park of Zakynthos, Greece. *Ecological Economics*, **60**, 308–19.

US Environmental Protection Agency (2009). *Valuing the Protection of Ecological Systems and Services*, Science Advisory Board Report No. 09–012. Washington, DC: Environmental Protection Agency.

Wielgus, J., Sala, E., and Gerber, L. R. (2008). Assessing the ecological and economic benefits of a no-take marine reserve. *Ecological Economics*, **67**, 32–40.

Wilson, M. and Hoehn, J. (2006). Valuing environmental goods and services using benefit-transfer: the state-of-the-art and science. *Ecological Economics*, **60**, 335–42.

10 · INDICATORS – Constructing and validating indicators of the effectiveness of marine protected areas

DOMINIQUE PELLETIER

10.1 Introduction

Marine protected area (MPA) effectiveness is also termed MPA *management* effectiveness to emphasize that it relates to how well the protected area is being managed, and primarily the extent to which it is protecting values and achieving the various goals and objectives for which it was created (IUCN–WCPA Guidelines: Hockings *et al.*, 2006). Values include ecosystem services and functions, biodiversity, landscape and geomorphological features, as well as cultural, socio-economic, and research- and education-related aspects. Assessing MPA effectiveness has become a crucial issue as many MPAs are designed all over the world in response to international commitments regarding biodiversity conservation and resource management. Such strong commitments cannot be achieved through ineffective MPAs, either because they are poorly enforced ("paper parks") or poorly designed. Pressure to evaluate management effectiveness is also increasing in a world where accountability and performance evaluation is more and more compelling.

While several previous chapters have focused on the assessment of MPA effects, I here consider the issues of assessment in the light of decision support for MPA management. Rather than assessing MPA effects, the focus is thus on assessing MPA effectiveness with respect to intended management objectives.

Management of MPAs can be envisaged at several scales. Locally, it relates to the aim of complying with the objectives for which the MPA

Marine Protected Areas: A Multidisciplinary Approach, ed. Joachim Claudet. Published by Cambridge University Press. © Cambridge University Press 2011.

was designed. At an intermediate scale, there exist more and more government agencies that are in charge of managing the national network of MPAs (although this might not be a network of MPAs *sensu stricto*; see Chapter 11), e.g., the National Marine Sanctuary Program (NMSP) in the USA (http://sanctuaries.noaa.gov/science/welcome.html) and the French Agency for Marine Protected Areas in France (http://www.aires-marines.fr), and might require some evaluations at the network scale. Finally, at both national and international levels, global assessments may be needed for tracking progress toward agenda objectives (see Chapter 13). This chapter will mainly address the local scale, which forms the basis for the assessments at other scales.

Assessing MPA effectiveness here consists in providing reliable, and if possible quantitative, science-based advice for supporting management and decision-making. According to the IUCN World Commission on Protected Areas Guidelines, management effectiveness evaluation is defined as "the assessment of how well the protected area is being managed" (see above). A way to assess effectiveness lies in the provision and documentation of indicators able to track progress toward this achievement of MPA management objectives.

An indicator is commonly defined as a function of observations or of the outputs of a model, which value indicates the present state and/or dynamics of the system of interest (FAO, 1999). Over the last decade, the term "indicator" has become very popular. A bibliographic search carried out in October 2009 on the key words indicator, and marine environment or fish, showed that between 1980 and 2000, 751 peer-reviewed scientific papers referred directly to indicators of either marine environment or fish, whereas this number rose to 1331 papers between 2000 and October 2009. This increasing scientific production is obviously related to the growing social and institutional demand for environmental monitoring and assessment. Yet, there should be a distinction between indicators used mainly for scientific purposes, and indicators aimed at assisting and guiding management actions. As mentioned above, this chapter focuses on management-oriented indicators.

Constructing and validating indicators of MPA effectiveness implies considering a range of candidate indicators, and evaluating and comparing their performance with respect to assessing MPA effectiveness. Indicator performance mainly lies in its sensitivity to the question addressed and in its statistical properties. In order to stress the importance of validating candidate indicators through performance criteria, I distinguish: (i) *metrics*, values of variables observed or calculated at given spatial, temporal, and socio-ecosystem scales, from a specific observation system or model; from (ii) *indicators*, metrics displaying desirable performances for testing MPA effects. Therefore, not all metrics can lead to indicators.

This chapter will deal with the selection, test and validation of indicators of MPA effectiveness. Indicators will refer to all MPA management objectives encompassing biodiversity conservation, management of fisheries and other MPA-related uses, and other social and economic aspects including governance. In the first section, I will present a methodology for selecting and validating indicators. This methodology is currently being implemented in the research project PAMPA (http://www.ifremer.fr/pampa). In the following sections, each step of the approach will be discussed and illustrated through a number of case studies pertaining to French and European MPAs.

10.2 State of the art on the evaluation of effectiveness of marine protected areas

Guidelines were produced quite early as to the design of MPAs (Kelleher and Kenchington, 1992; Kelleher, 1999), as much effort was dedicated to the designation of new MPAs in the last decades. Today, thousands of MPAs exist across the world and this trend is still ongoing due to the commitments of many countries to reach the objective of establishing a consistent and comprehensive global network of MPAs by 2012 (2002 World Summit: http://www.earthsummit2002.org).

Although the need for developing operational tools and guidance "to evaluate the ecological and management quality of existing Protected Areas (PA)" has long been acknowledged by conservation organizations such as the World Conservation Union (IUCN) (for instance at the 3rd World Parks Congress in Bali, Indonesia in 1982), the issue of management effectiveness appeared much later in the work of the IUCN World Commission on PA. More recently, the Programme of Work for PA of the Convention on Biological Diversity (CBD: http://www.biodiv.org) called on parties to "develop and adopt appropriate methods and standards, criteria and indicators for evaluating management effectiveness and governance by 2008, and to assess at least 30% of their protected areas by 2010."

In the marine environment, the question of MPA effectiveness has become stringent these last years not only due to the multiplication of MPAs. At the World Park Congress in 2003, there was a paradigm shift for protected areas when it was recognized that these are a crucial element of sustainable development and as such should contribute to globally agreed goals (IUCN, 2003), making PA effectiveness a larger and even more compelling issue than it used to be. Also, in a number of cases, MPAs are poorly accepted by local populations (see, e.g., Christie, 2004) or suffer from a lack of human and financial resources for management. These conditions compromise the success of the MPA in terms of both conservation and management of uses and governance. Such examples are also detrimental to the concept of MPAs as a management tool for coastal ecosystems (Agardy *et al.*, 2003). In this respect, management effectiveness evaluations provide a mechanism to encourage accountability of MPA management and foster its acceptance by stakeholders and the public. According to Hockings *et al.* (2006), PA evaluation results are usually used for several purposes: (i) to improve PA management performance through adaptive management; (ii) to promote accountability and transparency; and (iii) to assist effective funds and resource allocation within the protected area system.

10.2.1 Scales, scopes, and existing frameworks

There are many frameworks for evaluating progress toward management objectives where management is taken in the wider sense, e.g., project management or environmental management. The well-known Pressure–State–Response (PSR) framework often referred to in sustainable development and in environmental assessment has initially been developed by the OECD to structure its work on environmental policies and reporting (OECD, 2003). This conceptual framework is related with other frameworks such as DSR (Driver–State–Response), DPSR (Driver–Pressure–State–Response) and DPSIR (Driver–Pressure–State–Impact–Response) (e.g., Garcia *et al.*, 2000). Pressure stands here for anthropogenic pressures upon the environment. State is reflected by indicator values. Response corresponds to the measures undertaken by society to reduce impacts revealed by State, and caused by Pressure. The advantage of this framework is to make anthropogenic pressures explicit, to link them with their environmental consequences reflected by State, and to consider remediation actions through Response. The DPSIR framework generalizes the PSR by considering in addition Driving forces which operate at larger scales and cause Pressures. The DPSIR framework is retained as a reference by the CBD and by related initiatives concerning biodiversity conservation.

Table 10.1 *Components of the IUCN–WCPA framework for evaluating management effectiveness. Outputs refer to the achievement of identified activities or work program whereas outcomes reflect whether the long-term objectives are met*

Context	Understanding the context of the protected areas, including its values, the threats that it faces, available opportunities, and stakeholders, management, and political environment
Planning	Progress towards planning: establishing vision, goals, objectives, and strategies to conserve values and reduce threats
Inputs	Allocating resources of staff, money, and equipment to work toward the objectives
Processes	Implementing management actions according to accepted processes
Outputs	Goods and services, which should usually be outlined in management plans and workplans
Outcomes	Achieving defined goals and objectives

Source: After Hockings (2006).

Numerous management questions can be addressed within these general conceptual frameworks, which were designed to organize and categorize indicators and facilitate their use. Many indicator systems, i.e., sets of indicators, focusing on the environmental dimension of sustainable development use frameworks based on variations of the PSR model (UN Commission on Sustainable Development, 2006).

In the more specific field of PA, the IUCN overarching framework for assessing management effectiveness (Hockings *et al.*, 2006) relies on the principle that management follows a cyclical process with six important components that should, ideally, all be assessed for effectiveness (Table 10.1). In 2006, the IUCN–WCPA listed numerous mechanisms for evaluating the effectiveness of PA management (*MPA News*, vol. **7**, no. 10), among which Wells and Dahl-Tacconi (2006) described six mechanisms dedicated to MPAs. These authors identified three kinds of approaches: broad-scale, fine-scale, and scorecard-based. Broad-scale approaches are derived from the World Heritage Management Effectiveness Workbook (http://www.enhancingheritage.net) and encompass a wide range of issues from planning to outcomes. Fine-scale approaches include the IUCN "How is your MPA doing?" (Pomeroy *et al.*, 2004) and the Nature Conservancy 5-S framework (http://www.nature.org/files/five_s_eng.pdf), the latter being more focused on conservation issues, while the former addresses biophysical, socio-economic, and governance issues. Finally, the approaches based on scorecards are quicker, more qualitative and may allow comparisons between sites; but they are rather intended for general reporting purpose for funding bodies (http://www.icriforum.org/mpa/mpaeffectiveness.html). The evaluation system to be selected depends on: (i) the scope of the evaluation, system-wide vs. site-specific, but also themes addressed; and (ii) on the recipient of the report, e.g., funding bodies, policy-makers, or stakeholders.

As mentioned in the introduction, the kind of assessment needed depends on both the spatial scale considered and the scope and motivation of the evaluation process. On the one hand, funding bodies, policy-makers, and conservation lobbyists are more interested in highlighting problems, setting priorities, and promoting better management practices (Hockings, 2006). Many countries and organizations are increasingly applying so-called headline indicators, i.e., a short set of indicators providing easily understandable signals to high-level policy-makers and to the general public (UN Commission on Sustainable Development, 2006). The World Bank–WWF Management Effectiveness Tracking Tool (Stolton *et al.*, 2002) was developed to help monitoring progress in the achievement of their worldwide PA management effectiveness targets. As stressed in the cited reference, "it should not replace more thorough methods of assessment for the purpose of adaptive management."

On the other hand, managers may wish to build on evaluation results to improve MPA performance and report to senior managers, the government, or other stakeholders, either locally or at the national scale. Such evaluations focus on outcomes. For instance, each US National Marine Sanctuary documents so-called condition reports in order to serve as a tool to determine if it is achieving resource protection and improvement goals as reflected in NMSP performance measures (http://sanctuaries.noaa.gov/science/condition/faq.html). The reports are supporting documents during the Management Plan Review Process, but are also used for: (i) reporting by policy-makers, particularly within the National Oceanic and Atmospheric Administration (NOAA) and the Department of Commerce; and (ii) education and outreach. Condition reports follow the same approach and format; they are based on a set of 17 questions which is common to all MPAs and depict the status and trends of sanctuary resources. These questions relate to water, habitat, living resources, and maritime archeological resources. Each question is answered using a qualitative "status and trends" reporting system. Additional text, tables, and figures are provided to explain the basis for the judgment determining the status and trends. More specific questions are not discussed in these reports but rather used to document the answer to the set of general questions.

To date, the most complete contribution in terms of tools and guidance for the assessment of management effectiveness for existing MPAs was provided under IUCN auspices (Pomeroy et al., 2004; Pomeroy et al., 2005). The MPA Management Effectiveness Initiative (MEI) was formed in 2000 by IUCN–WCPA and by World Wide Fund for Nature with the main objective "to develop a set of marine-specific natural and social indicators to evaluate MPA management effectiveness," based on both scientific and practitioner expertise. Results are presented in a guidebook aimed at helping managers and practitioners to better achieve the goals and objectives for which their MPA was created (Pomeroy et al., 2004). The approach relies on a four-step process: (i) select the appropriate indicators; (ii) plan and prepare for the evaluation; (iii) collect and analyze data for the selected indicators; and (iv) communicate and use evaluation results to adapt the MPA's management (Pomeroy et al., 2005). According to the IUCN–WCPA framework (see above), indicators to be considered pertain to context (where are we now?), planning (where do we want to be?), inputs (what do we need?), processes (how do we go about it?), outputs (what were the results?) and outcomes (what did we achieve?) (Table 10.1). The MPA MEI effort deliberately focused on output and outcome indicators. A survey of goals and objectives from MPAs around the world was first conducted. Goals and objectives are related to governance, biophysical, and socio-economic aspects. A review of the indicators used for the marine environment and for coastal communities led to identify over 130 indicators out of which 42 were retained and subsequently linked to one or several objectives (Table 10.2). For each indicator, a profile was defined in terms of measurability, resource needs, protocols, analysis, and communication, and in a summary of strengths and limitations. Finally, 18 pilot sites volunteered to test the methodology over a period of 8 months, enabling a revision of the guidebook. At the end of the project, the guide was deemed to be a useful instrument. It provides clear and easily understandable insight into the meaning and construction of indicators. Yet, as clearly stated by the authors, it is not prescriptive, nor is it an exhaustive state of the art on monitoring and assessment methods. Indicator performance, in particular in relation with design recommendations and data analysis, is not addressed, as it might be too technical. Likewise, it provides little guidance on indicator interpretation, with respect to resulting management actions.

Table 10.2 *Common MPA themes, goals, and associated indicators*

Themes	Goals (number of objectives)	Indicators
Biophysical	Marine resources sustained or protected (6)	Focal species abundance
	Biological diversity protected (7)	Focal species population structure
	Individual species protected (4)	Habitat distribution and complexity
	Habitat protected (4)	Composition and structure of the community
	Degraded habitat restored (5)	Recruitment success within the community
		Food web integrity
		Type, level, and return on fishing effort
		Water quality
		Area showing signs of recovery
		Area under no or reduced impact
Socio-economic	Food security enhanced or maintained (6)	Local marine resource use patterns
	Livelihoods enhanced or maintained (4)	Local values and beliefs regarding the marine resources
	Non-monetary benefits to society enhanced or maintained (6)	Level of understanding of human impacts on resources
	Benefits from the MPA equitably distributed (3)	Perceptions of seafood availability
	Compatibility between management and local culture maximized (2)	Perceptions of local resource harvest
	Environmental awareness and knowledge enhanced (4)	Perceptions of non-market and non-use value
		Material style of life
		Quality of human health
		Household income distribution by source
		Household occupational structure
		Community infrastructure and business
		Number and nature of markets
		Stakeholder knowledge of natural history
		Distribution of formal knowledge to community
		Percent of stakeholder group in leadership positions
		Changes in conditions of ancestral and historical sites, features, and/or monuments

Table 10.2 (*cont.*)

Themes	Goals (number of objectives)	Indicators
Governance	Effective management structures and strategies maintained (6)	Level of resource conflict
		Existence of a decision-making and management body
	Effective legal structures and strategies for management maintained (5)	Existence and adoption of a management plan
		Local understanding of MPA rules and regulations
	Effective stakeholder participation and representation ensured (3)	Existence and adequacy of enabling legislation
		Availability and allocation of MPA administrative resources
	Management plan compliance by resource users enhanced (6)	Existence and application of scientific research/input
		Existence and activity level of community organization(s)
	Resource use conflicts managed and reduced (1)	Degree of interaction between managers and stakeholders
		Proportion of stakeholders trained in sustainable use
		Level of training provided to stakeholders in participation
		Level of stakeholder participation and satisfaction in management process and activities
		Level of stakeholder involvement in surveillance, monitoring, and enforcement
		Clearly defined enforcement procedures
		Enforcement coverage
		Degree of information dissemination to encourage stakeholder compliance

Source: After Pomeroy *et al.* (2005).

The framework developed in the guidebook was implemented in a number of regions, e.g., in Central America (Corrales, 2005), and in the Mediterranean (Port-Cros National Park, 2007). The IUCN methodology is also recommended by the Western Indian Ocean Marine

Science Association (WIOMSA) MPA Toolkit (http://www.wiomsa. org/mpatoolkit), a series of handsheets that was designed to support MPA managers in the Western Indian Ocean by providing them with a hands-on guide to a diverse array of topics, including among others the assessment of management success.

10.2.2 Scientific contributions to assessing management effectiveness and constructing indicators

Over the last two decades, there has been a wealth of papers dealing with the assessment of MPA effects, in particular for biodiversity conservation (Pelletier *et al.*, 2005a; see also Chapters 2 and 6), whereas fisheries-related effects have been documented more recently (Pelletier *et al.*, 2008: see also Chapter 3 and 7). In searching the scientific literature for both MPA assessment and indicators, I found that between January 2000 and October 2009, 84 peer-reviewed papers and communications addressing MPA assessment were listed, whereas over the same period, only 15 papers mentioning indicators and MPA were listed. Out of these, very few addressed the definition of operational indicators for decision support systems. Pelletier *et al.* (2005b) reviewed a number of metrics used for the assessment of ecological, economic, and social effects of MPAs, and examined their performance as potential indicators (see Sections 10.3.2 and 10.3.3). Pelletier *et al.* (2008) reviewed and compared MPA assessment methods for conservation and fisheries-related effects and confronted their ability to provide indicators for informing the decision process. The authors highlighted the gaps and challenges in this respect. Muthiga (2009) recently presented an application of Pomeroy *et al.* (2004) framework to Kenya's oldest MPA taking into account ecological, socio-economic, and governance aspects of MPA effectiveness. Interestingly, results are presented under a conventional graphical display for each theme and summarized in a table that does not show management objectives. Biodiversity conservation objectives appeared to be generally met, but the objective of sustaining livelihood was not fully reached, and governance indicators showed the weakest scores.

In contrast, there are more papers proposing and discussing indicators of fishing effects (among others Trenkel and Rochet, 2003; Daan *et al.*, 2005; Jennings, 2005).

In the fisheries management context, there are few descriptions of frameworks that involve scientists, the fishing industry, and managers, and that can be used as a decision support system. This may probably be explained by the fact that many fisheries operate in international settings, where this kind of collaboration may be difficult to implement. For instance, in the north-east Atlantic, scientific advice is still transferred to decision-makers via a number of complex stages involving a suite of expert groups and commissions. Trenkel *et al.* (2007) attribute this prescriptive approach to the fact that scientific advice is based on models and propose an indicator-based approach instead. It seems however that the assessment tool, although imperfect, is less to be blamed than the complexity and lack of flexibility implied by the process producing the advice and the lack of interaction between managers and scientists, including, e.g., failure to clearly formulate management targets. Issues in developing appropriate frames for decision support systems for fisheries management have been discussed in Smith and Link (2005). The Australian Fisheries Management Authority (AFMA) is responsible for ensuring the sustainable and efficient use of federal fishery resources. The AFMA partnership model involves scientists, managers and the fishing industry (Smith *et al.*, 1999). At a more general level, and in order to facilitate the implementation of the FAO Code of Conduct for Responsible Fisheries, the FAO proposed the Sustainable Development Reference System, a framework to develop a set of indicators for the management of capture fisheries with a tentative application to an Australian fishery (Garcia *et al.*, 2000).

In summary, there exists substantial published guidance for MPA practitioners and managers to devise indicators of MPA effectiveness. The existing documents are remarkably easy to understand, and they deliberately exclude too technical issues from their scope of interest. Thus, there is a lack of guidance about efficient indicator estimation, sampling protocols, data analysis, indicator validation, and statistical issues of monitoring and assessment in general. On the other hand, there are a lot of contributions to the assessment of MPA effects in the peer-reviewed literature. Some of these contributions specifically address monitoring and assessment issues and provide some general recommendations for a correct assessment of MPA ecological effects, e.g., proper design, or importance of habitat considerations (Chapter 6). However, it is difficult to derive concrete recommendations for the assessment of MPA effectiveness, in particular concerning monitoring protocols that are cost-effective and suited to MPA managers' constraints. Also, there is no published study dealing with the methodological issues of constructing indicators of MPA effectiveness. In this respect, there is thus room for further collaborative approaches involving managers and scientists. This is essential to properly address managers' needs, while sorting out questions that require scientific input. It is also needed to integrate managers' constraints in terms of funding and human resources, capacity, and communication. In the next section, I present a framework that enables such an approach. According to Section 10.2.1, it is thus a fine-scale approach to MPA evaluations for tracking achievements and progress toward management objectives (outcomes according to the IUCN framework). Objectives pertain to biodiversity conservation, management of fisheries and other uses, and governance. Hence the scope is close to that of Pomeroy *et al.* (2004).

10.3 A collaborative approach between scientists and managers for selecting and validating indicators of marine protected area management effectiveness

10.3.1 Metrics, indicators, and performance criteria

A metric is defined as a function of experimental observations or model outputs; it is calculated at given spatial and temporal scales and at a given level of the socio-ecosystem of interest. The observation system or alternatively the model must be specified, as it determines distinct statistical properties and sampling costs. Examples are the percent coverage of seagrass observed at a given transect by underwater visual censuses (UVC), the number of boats observed over a given period of time in a given area, or the abundance of a fish species at the beginning of the year as calculated from a dynamic model.

An indicator is a metric displaying desirable properties for assessing management effectiveness. In practice it is deemed to perform well if it points toward the appropriate decision while minimizing risks of error.

Performance criteria for indicators have been listed and discussed in a number of papers, both in environmental assessment (Hilty and Merenlender, 2000; Kurz *et al.*, 2001) and in fish stock assessment (Garcia *et al.*, 2000; Rochet and Trenkel, 2003; Trenkel and Rochet, 2003). Rice and Rochet (2005) consider nine criteria for selecting indicators: concreteness, theoretical basis, public awareness, cost, measurement, historic data, sensitivity, responsiveness, and specificity. Garcia *et al.* (2000) list 13 criteria: policy priorities, practicality/feasibility, data availability, cost-effectiveness, understandability, accuracy and precision, robustness to uncertainty, scientific validity, acceptability to users/stakeholders (consensus among parties), and ability to communicate information, timeliness, formal (legal) foundation, and adequate documentation. Numerous criteria raise the problem of weighing and prioritization. In addition,

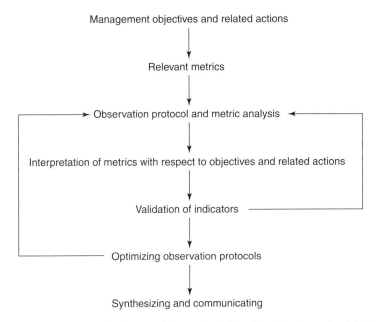

Management objectives and related actions

Relevant metrics

Observation protocol and metric analysis

Interpretation of metrics with respect to objectives and related actions

Validation of indicators

Optimizing observation protocols

Synthesizing and communicating

Figure 10.1 Overall scheme of the methodology for selecting and validating indicators of marine protected areas effectiveness. Most steps involve collaboration with marine protected area managers.

there should be some chronology in considering performance criteria. For instance, it is useless to consider communication issues, if the indicator is poorly linked with the question at stake.

Here, I will thus only consider two criteria that are determining for indicator performance, relevance and effectiveness (Nicholson and Fryer, 2002). A metric is relevant when there is an unambiguous link between the metric and the effect it is supposed to indicate, and (if possible) when there are reference points for interpreting metrics values. A relevant metric is efficient if its statistical properties, and more generally its reliability, enable a diagnostic to be reached about the effect of interest while minimizing associated errors.

10.3.2 Formulation of management objectives and management actions

The first step in the process (Figure 10.1) is to formulate management objectives in an unequivocal and sufficiently precise manner, so that there is a common understanding of these objectives by managers and scientists. This enables to evaluate whether the evaluation of the degree of achievement of the objective calls for a scientific contribution, which is not always the case. For instance, reporting about the MPA budget, enforcement means, or other input indicators does not need scientific input or expertise. In contrast, reporting short-term outputs, results, or long-term impact implies collecting data and analyzing and interpreting them, which may benefit from scientific contribution.

Marine protected area management goals and objectives are in general described in a management plan, although this document does not always exist, or may be under construction. Guidelines for the desirable content of an MPA management plan may be found in Kelleher (1999); they include the clear specification of objectives and sub-objectives for each zone of the managed area. Yet, it happens that management plans are still missing or in construction, as its definition and writing is a comprehensive time-consuming process. In some cases, management plans may even be considered by managers as a tedious and mostly administrative task (Pelletier *et al.*, 2005a). This formulation is essential to define targets against which progress can be assessed (see also Claudet and Pelletier, 2004). As stated by Dale and Beyeler (2001), the choice of ecological indicators is often confounded in management programs that have vague long-term goals and objectives.

A second important aspect to be specified relates to the management actions that can be undertaken by MPA managers. When dealing with indicators for guiding management decisions, potential management actions must be listed for each objective. If progress toward a given objective is not linked with a potential action, then reaching this objective is out of the manager's prerogatives. To mitigate this limitation, reporting by the manager to a higher authority may be considered as a management action.

It is essential that this first step stems from discussions and workshops involving both managers and scientists, because it will determine the orientation of the work to be achieved for designing indicators that match objectives and actions. It is also important as it forms the basis for collaborative work. This non-technical step thus enables to set up a common understanding of MPA management issues for both managers and scientists, including the setting up of a common semantic.

10.3.3 Identification of relevant metrics

In a second step, it is necessary to identify a number of relevant metrics for each objective and related management action. The main constraint here lies in the means that are available to collect the information needed for calculating the metrics. When there were few MPAs, most data were collected by scientists directly or indirectly involved in the MPA. The number of MPAs has dramatically increased and often MPAs touch on various management objectives ranging from biodiversity conservation to coastal management in general, so that it is difficult to expect continuing supervision of MPA monitoring by scientists. In contrast, it is the scientists' duty to provide assessment tools that can be implemented with the existing staff capacities and financial resources. Therefore, the selection of relevant metrics must start from the data that can be collected at the MPA level, or that are available to the MPA manager, a high-level MPA agency, or through other – public or not – information systems.

As in the first step, this constraint is best accounted for through discussions with MPA manager or super-managers. Once the potential data collection systems are identified, relevant metrics are selected for each objective. In general, a large number of metrics can be calculated from a given data set, at no extra cost once the data are collected. But many of them are redundant, and scale issues are important. Conditioning the selection of most relevant metrics on management objective is important as conveying many results is not efficient for decision support. Estimating the a priori relevance of metrics should be done by scientists. This is generally based on expert's opinion but Pelletier *et al.* (2005a) provided a literature-based score of relevance for metrics aimed at assessing MPA ecological effects. Yet, this was only possible because the metrics had been used in many different situations, and between-case variability could be averaged out.

10.3.4 Observation protocols and analysis of metrics

At this stage, an observation protocol that is a priori appropriate for estimating the selected metrics must be devised. Recall that the definition of the metric includes that of the observation system, therefore the challenge is to design a protocol that enables the estimation of a set of values of the metrics from which the assessment of MPA performance can be achieved. There is a wealth of literature on appropriate designs for the assessment of direct MPA effects on biodiversity (Chapters 6 and 7). Still, there is much less literature on how best to assess MPA effects on uses or the effects of uses on MPA effectiveness, although such approaches are developing since the human component is more and more taken into account in MPA management (and in coastal management in general).

Scientific papers often rely on the analysis of a number of metrics per taxa or species group, in which variability is assessed in relation to protection status. More rarely, there is an attempt to provide a synthetic answer to questions such as: is biodiversity maintained in the MPA? Are fish species sustainably exploited (but see Guidetti and Claudet, 2010), and if not how can the MPA contribute to this objective? More generally, there is a lack of overall diagnostic at the MPA level, although scientific studies are more logically oriented toward analytical approaches.

Most assessments of MPA effects have been carried out from the statistical analysis and modeling of field data. Yet, dynamic models are also used to quantify the consequences of MPAs on the dynamics of populations, communities, and fisheries (Pelletier et al., 2008). They enable exploring management scenarios involving alternative MPA designs and other management policies. In its construction such a model must embrace the whole dynamic of the entity modeled, whether it is a species, a fish community, an ecosystem or a fishery. This concerns the spatial extent, the main drivers of the dynamics, and the interacting components. The direction and magnitude of changes in indicators may then be used to provide a system-wide assessment of MPA, the system involving the fishery or ecosystem where the MPA is located, which generally extends beyond its boundaries. Conversely, in such models, the link with observation protocols is less direct, as model parameterization and calibration generally depends on a large amount of information and data.

10.3.5 Interpretation of indicators

Assuming that metrics have been analyzed, interpreting indicators consists in gauging the value taken by the metrics with respect to the management objective at stake, if possible against a reference value. A reference point is a desired target or limit for an indicator (Sainsbury and Sumaila, 2003). It may be expressed as the trend or value of the indicator associated with meeting the management objective (Jennings, 2005). This trend or value may be a limit (threshold), a target, a direction, and/or a time horizon to reach a given status. But a limit reference point can also be regarded in terms of risk and thus associated with an unacceptable outcome. The issue of reference points for MPA indicators was discussed in Pelletier et al. (2008). In the context of fisheries science, reference points have been used and discussed for a number of years (Caddy, 1998; Collie and Gislason, 2001; Hilborn, 2002; Koeller, 2003) and are commonly used in stock assessments and for scientific advice (e.g. ICES, 2001; http://www.ices.dk/products/icesadvice).

In another context, for the assessment of water quality, the European Water Framework Directive (WFD) requires the definition of reference conditions with respect to the objective of a good status (including both good ecological status [GES] and good chemical status) to be reached by 2015 (http://ec.europa.eu/environment/water/water-framework/objectives/index_en.htm). From an ecological point of view, these reference conditions correspond to reference values of various biological indicators observed *in situ*. Being based on monitoring data, water quality assessment does not differ from empirical assessments of MPA effects from a methodological standpoint.

Establishing reference points or values for indicators related to GES raises the same challenge for the WFD and for MPA. It is a largely multidimensional issue, subject in addition to possible irreversibility and shifting baselines problems (Knowlton and Jackson, 2009). In this respect, considering trends and directions rather than distance to absolute values is likely to foster the achievement of targets by managers, because it is intuitive and less questionable. It also makes the assessment easier. There are however some advantages to defining references for MPA indicators. First, the trivial fact that MPAs have an inside and an outside facilitates the assessment of effects and the establishment of references for objectives linked to preservation within the MPA, particularly for no-take zones. Second, in the long term, such areas may themselves become reference as control areas for the assessment of anthropogenic stressor effects, particularly fishing; although the restored ecosystem may be different from the pristine ecosystem due to irreversibility. Historical data coupled to monitoring before and after MPA establishment may then help to understand the causes of ecological changes at several scales, both retrospectively and within the MPA.

Beyond gauging values or trends, the interpretation of indicators must lead to a management or a set of management actions. This is made possible because the potential management actions attached to a given objective have been previously listed (see Section 10.3.1). Yet, further discussion is needed here to select the appropriate actions depending on indicator values, and this may require more than a single indicator (see Section 10.4 for illustrations). Interpreting indicators thus requires that scientists assess values and trends with respect to reference points, and that managers link this assessment to management actions as a function of management priorities. Desirable targets, but also undesirable outcomes and corresponding management time-frames must obviously be accounted for in this process.

10.3.6 Validation of metrics as indicators

Validation is the process of checking whether something satisfies a certain criterion. It implies one can document that the metrics is suited for its intended use, i.e., it is able to track progress toward the achievement of the corresponding management objective. In quality management systems, validation amounts to confirming that stakeholders' or users' needs are satisfied.

Validating metrics as indicators of MPA performance has been overlooked in the past, in relation to a lack of interest for the use of indicators for decision support. It can be achieved in various ways. On the one hand, one might apply the metric in a variety of contexts and case studies, and check how well it performs, to ensure that the metric is not too specific and relatively robust in coping well with variations (sometimes unpredictable ones). On the other hand, one could imagine resorting to more formal validation methods. For a statistical model, validation means that model assumptions are met. If the model is used to analyze a metric, it means that variations of the metrics can be analyzed and interpreted from the model. In addition it is necessary to ensure that the metric would lead to the same response if it were calculated from an independent data set drawn from the same population. In the case of quantitative metrics and when a sufficient number of observations is available, this can be achieved by computational methods such as cross-validation (Everitt, 2006). To my knowledge, it has not yet been applied for validating MPA-related indicators (see Pont *et al.* [2006] for an application to fish assemblages in continental waters). Lastly, for indicators obtained from complex models, model calibration with respect to real data ensures that the model is a reasonable representation of the system modeled (see Section 10.4.2).

10.3.7 Increasing indicator efficiency through improved and cost-effective observation protocols

At this stage, once the way the indicator is used in the decision support process is fully specified, it is possible to optimize or, at least, to improve the observation protocol in order to increase the indicator's efficiency. Based on the outputs of the a priori protocol already experienced, it is often possible to adjust the observation protocol. This may relate to the spatial extent, the level of detail of the information, or the statistical population sampled. Besides, the scientist can suggest a distinct observation system that better matches the manager's needs, e.g., in relation to new technological developments.

In the case of quantitative metrics, a more formal optimization may be done through simulation and resampling aimed at precisely allocating sampling effort among the stages of the observation protocol.

10.3.8 Synthesizing and communicating indicators

In the context of MPAs, this step is still little advanced and structured. At this point, it is useful to emphasize that the indicator used to establish a diagnostic may not be the same as the one conveyed to the manager or stakeholder. To some extent, this simplifies the challenge, as it is difficult to have an indicator that is at the same time relevant, efficient, and easily understandable by non-experts. But it is crucial to make explicit how to proceed from relevant and efficient indicators to simpler indicators for decision support.

This raises several issues: (i) synthesis – how to present results pertaining to a set of indicators that is always deemed too large by managers? (ii) uncertainty – how to convey uncertainties about indicators without weakening the information communicated? (iii) simplification – how to communicate simply a complex result?

Synthesis is inevitable as most of the time a single indicator cannot reflect complex, multiple linkages and feedbacks, e.g., within the ecosystem (Chapter 1). Similarly, multiple standpoints on a question cannot be easily accommodated from a single indicator. In such situations, multiple indicators can mirror inputs from several stakeholders. Brown *et al.* (2001) considered this use of indicators for trade-offs in MPA planning, but it might also be interesting to account for various or even conflicting management objectives. The synthesis issue encompasses also several questions. Are the indicators to be presented individually, e.g., by using a performance chart approach? Or is it necessary to combine indicators into synthetic indices that are meaningful to the manager? Combining indicators implies to assign weights to individual indicators. This is never insignificant as it relates to the priorities given to indicators, and thus to underlying objectives and standpoints. Yet, there are some methods like multicriteria analysis that evaluate the outcomes of several management actions while making explicit the priorities of a range of criteria (Brown *et al.*, 2001). On the other hand, a dashboard nicely summarizes an assessment, particularly in the case of a single question. For instance, Koeller *et al.* (2000) presented a performance report for the assessment of a shrimp stock. But in the case of several questions, and this is definitely the case of MPA assessment, the interpretation may become more difficult as the number of entries increases. Thus, considering performance charts per management goal is a reasonable option.

Simplification is often addressed through color rating, each color corresponding to a range of values of the indicator. For instance, NMSP condition reports use six colors rating the status of a given response from "poor" to "good," with an additional "undetermined" category (http://sanctuaries.noaa.gov/science/condition/welcome.html). Status rating is completed by an evaluation of indicator trend under the form of a symbol comprising five categories: "improving," "not changing," "getting worse," "undetermined trend," and "question not applicable." A simplified use of color rating is provided by the traffic-light approach to fisheries management (Koeller *et al.*, 2000; Caddy, 2002). Color rating raises the problem of defining thresholds between distinct colors, particularly in the presence of uncertainty. Colors are also perceived differently depending on cultural settings, a well-known issue in marketing, design, and psychology (see, e.g., http://en.wikipedia.org/wiki/Color_symbolism_and_psychology). As an alternative to colors, one may choose to transform indicators to dimensionless values, sometimes called indices. Such values, preferably ranging between 0 (or -1) and 1, are easier to interpret, see, e.g., the conservation of biological originality index in Mouillot *et al.* (2008) and Chapter 2, or the social acceptability indicator of Thomassin *et al.* (2009).

10.4 Illustration of the approach

The approach is illustrated through experiences from Liteau II-AMP (Pelletier, 2007) and PAMPA (http://www.ifremer.fr/pampa), two multidisciplinary research projects involving scientists and managers of French MPAs. The objective of Liteau II-AMP (2004–2007) was to develop diagnostic and exploratory decision support tools for assessing MPA performance. Diagnostic tools enable one to evaluate whether management objectives are reached in existing MPA. Exploratory tools yield more prospective insights about possible scenarios regarding zoning of uses in existing or projected MPAs. They also permit one to assess the potential consequences of changes in anthropogenic pressure on ecosystem uses, goods, and services, and the relevance of MPA management facing such changes. In this project, the issue of communicating indicators toward the public or more general stakeholders was not addressed, but the project focused on indicators that guide MPA managers toward management actions. Biodiversity conservation and fisheries management were the main themes addressed by Liteau II-AMP. The ongoing PAMPA project (2008–2011) has a larger scope as it addresses all uses linked to the existence of MPA, mostly recreational ones, as well as governance issues. Scientists belong to a panel of disciplines including law studies, geography, economy, ecology, fisheries science, and biostatistics.

In the next section, I will illustrate several steps of the framework described in Section 10.3. First I will address management objectives and actions. Second, indicators pertaining to biodiversity and resources will be discussed. The third step will relate to management of uses and governance. Interpretation of indicators will be discussed in the last subsection. I do not intend to be exhaustive, but rather to illustrate in a concrete manner the questions linked with these indicators. Validation and communication of indicators will not be dealt with here, as some previous steps need be handled first that are currently not yet advanced in the project.

10.4.1 Formulation of management objectives and management actions

Workshops were organized to establish a list of goals with corresponding detailed objectives, which was suited to the MPA partners of the projects. Goals and objectives from Pomeroy et al. (2004) were discussed and reformulated when managers felt it was needed, some objectives were merged, and some were not considered because they were not relevant to the MPA concerned. As also underlined by Pomeroy et al. (2005), listing and, more importantly, clearly formulating goals and objectives was deemed very useful by all participants of the workshop.

Managers of MPAs had then to list the management actions they could undertake to reach a given objective (Tables 10.3 and 10.4). Actions could be regarded as (i) regulatory (e.g., restricted access, fishing controls), (ii) aimed at establishing good practices through mutual agreements with user groups (e.g., divers or fishers), or (iii) relating to information and education of stakeholders and the general public. The two latter favor the participation of stakeholders to management and the social acceptance

Table 10.3 *Management objectives and actions identified under the goal of sustainable uses linked to marine protected areas*

Objectives	Questions	Actions
Sustainable exploitation of resources	Restoring and maintaining invertebrate and fish stocks	Regulatory actions: Regulation of commercial and recreational fishing in the MPA (e.g., size limits, licenses, zoning, time closures, gear restrictions) Enforcement of regulation (both general and MPA-specific) Artificial reefs Establishment of agreements with users, e.g., code of conduct (fishers, divers) Information and education, e.g., training in professional schools for sea-related jobs, leaflets
Sustainable fisheries	Viability of artisanal fisheries, both as an economic activity and because of its patrimonial value leading to indirect local benefits	Regulatory actions: Regulation of commercial and recreational fishing in the MPA Favor the coexistence of fishing activities through appropriate space occupation Control of illegal activities, e.g., trawling within the 3 nautical miles zone Installing anti-trawling devices (e.g., artificial reefs) Establishment of agreements with users Contribute to added value for sea products (labels, direct sales) Promote polyvalence (fishing and tourism-related activities) Promote the use of repulsive devices for marine mammals Information and education
Management of multiple uses	Reduce conflicts between uses and between users	Regulating frequentation and nuisances Promote adequate zoning in space and time between uses Foster consultation between uses

of the MPA (governance objectives: Table 10.2). Finally, a number of monitoring actions have been listed as being in the range of manager actions. Indeed, a number of management plans listed monitoring as being an objective of the MPA.

Table 10.4 *Management objectives and actions identified under the goal of conservation of biodiversity and habitats*

Objective	Actions
Maintaining or restoring endangered or protected species	Enforcement and control of regulations Monitoring species abundance Protect essential habitat for these species (see below)
Maintaining or restoring biodiversity	Enforcement and control of regulations Monitoring invasive species and species indicating global trends and biogeographical changes Interventions to reduce identified nuisances Reintroduction of species

Maintaining or restoring habitats and associated biodiversity	Monitoring important habitats and water quality
	Identifying perturbations and evaluating impacts, e.g., for seagrass
	Preventing risks of chronic and accidental pollution
	Regulatory actions:
	  Enforcement and control of regulations
	  Limit the impact of fishing gears on habitats (anti-trawling devices, gear-specific closures)
	  Control boat anchoring, e.g., through permanent moorings
	  Limit frequentation of sensitive areas, e.g., number of boats or diving trips
	  Redirect or limit tourist frequentation via access to sea (boat ramps) or via underwater pathway
	  Control underwater pathway frequentation
	  Control and exclude illegal moorings
	  Establishment of agreements with users, e.g., code of conduct (fishers, divers)
	  Information and education, e.g., training of concerned operators and staff, leaflets, communication with tourists and local people
	  Installation of devices, works: permanent moorings, maintenance or enhancement of degraded habitats (artificial reefs, wrecks)

10.4.2 Indicators related to biodiversity and resources

10.4.2.1 Identification and estimation of relevant metrics

Biodiversity is here restricted to underwater flora and fauna, while resource is to be understood here as fishing resources. Biodiversity and resources rely on similar types of observations. Underwater visual censuses (UVC) have been successfully used for years to estimate fish abundance or biomass in studies of population dynamics, ecology and management. Advantages and disadvantages of this method have been discussed in several papers (e.g., Harmelin-Vivien et al., 1985; Cappo and Brown, 1996; Samoilys, 1997; Willis et al., 2000; Watson et al., 2005). These UVC are widely used for fish, benthic macrofauna, including invertebrates and fixed fauna, and for flora in tropical and subtropical coastal waters, but also in temperate waters. They are for instance recommended for monitoring by Reef Check (http://www.reefcheck.org/). The second most frequently used data for biodiversity and resources are catch and effort data, either experimental catch carried out from scientific protocols, or sampling of fishing activities at sea or at landing sites. A third technique that has been more recently developed relies on the use of underwater video (Cappo and Brown, 1996; Willis et al., 2000; Tessier et al., 2008), and particularly baited remote underwater video (BRUV) (Watson et al., 2005; Langlois et al., 2006; Stobart et al., 2007), although unbaited techniques are developing. Likewise, photo-based techniques have been recently tested for monitoring benthic invertebrates and habitat in MPAs (Dumas et al., 2009).

In terms of relevance for indicators of biodiversity and resources, UVC and image-based techniques provide direct observations of macrofauna and habitat, although they depend on underwater visibility. They yield presence/absence data, abundance indices for density and biomass, and coverage of sea bottom by fixed benthic fauna and flora (e.g., coral, seagrass) and by abiotic components of habitat. Catch-based observations only reflect the fraction of macrofauna that is catchable by the gear used, in general mostly carnivorous species, but catchable species may include species that are not commonly observed underwater, either because they are cryptic or night-dwelling. Catch and effort data yield catch per unit effort (CPUE) which can be considered as an abundance index under certain assumptions that have long been discussed in fisheries science (Richards and Schnute, 1986; Pelletier, 2003). The surface observed and thus densities can be estimated in the case of UVC, photo and unbaited video, but not for catch nor for BRUV where bait plume is difficult to evaluate.

Willis et al. (2000) examined the relative merits of UVC, BRUV, and experimental catch for detecting spatial variations of fish density. These techniques provide complementary information. For techniques requiring underwater divers, human presence must be regarded as a potential source of bias for estimating the abundance of mobile species in MPAs. Species behavior may differ in protected areas, as they become less afraid of human presence underwater and might affect observed differences in abundance between the no-take area and unprotected areas. To some extent, this can be circumvented in the observation protocol, e.g., by counting the species concerned first. But techniques not requiring human presence underwater bear an advantage in this respect. With regard to resources, it might also appear logical to resort to catch data to assess an objective like sustainable exploitation of resources (Table 10.3). There is however a drawback to catch data, since they are destructive. This does not matter in the case of sampling of fishing activities, but poses a problem for conducting observations within no-take areas. More generally, tracking the achievement of progress toward conservation and restoration objectives by using extractive observation means is questionable and may in some cases be detrimental to the acceptability of the MPA, e.g., by fishers.

In a second step, collected data are combined using, e.g., information on species to compute more sophisticated metrics, such as biodiversity indices and metrics per species groups. Pelletier *et al.* (2005b) investigated the relevance of the metrics used for assessing MPA effects, on the basis of a bibliographic review of empirical studies. The relevance of the metrics was scored using the number of times the metrics had been used for assessing a given effect. Results show that some metrics are consistently more often used for MPA assessment than others (Table 10.5). Candidate indicators for conservation and fisheries-related effects of MPAs have also been listed by Pelletier *et al.* (2008). In addition to empirical metrics directly computed from field data, these authors considered model-based metrics. Such metrics include abundance, catch and biomass per population and time step, and possibly per area obtained from spatially explicit models. They can be combined into ratios or dimensionless indices that are suitable for comparisons and interpretation (see Section 10.4.3.2). Depending on the model, more sophisticated metrics may be calculated such as size or biomass spectra, risk of collapse, or population growth rate. By construction, model-based metrics integrate the information and knowledge that was required to build the model (see Pelletier and Mahévas [2005] for an example of model).

The existence of reference points is linked with the relevance issue (Section 10.3.2). No such references exist for empirical metrics, while for model-based metrics, in most instances, reference points can be determined by exploring through simulations other domains of the dynamic modeled.

Table 10.5 *Relevance and effectiveness of metrics related to biodiversity and resources. Relevance was scored from the number of times the metric has been used in the literature; effectiveness was scored from the proportion of papers where its use led to a statistically significant marine protected area effect in the reviewed studies (★ ≤ 33%, ★★33–66%, ★★★ ≥ 66%). All metrics refer to underwater visual census data, except two from catch per unit of effort*

Metric	Maintaining or restoring biodiversity and habitat		Sustainable exploitation of resources	
	Relevance	Effectiveness	Relevance	Effectiveness
Density per species or genus	★★★	★★	★★★	★★
Density per species per stage	★		★★	★★★
Size distribution per species	★		★★	★★★
Biomass per species or genus	★	ns	★★	★★
Mean size per species or genus	★★	★★	★★★	★★
CPUE per species or genus			★★	★★
Density per family	★★	ns	★★★	★★
Biomass per family	★		★	★★★
Species richness per family	★★	★★	★	★
Density per trophic group			★★	★★★
Density of fishable species			★	★★
Biomass per trophic group			★	★★★
Overall density	★	★★	★★★	★★
Overall biomass	★	★★★	★★	★★★
Overall species richness	★★★	★★	★	★
Overall CPUE	★		★★	★★
Benthic cover	★★★	★★★		

Source: After Pelletier *et al.* (2005a).

Last, a few remarks may be drawn regarding the relevance of existing metrics. Biodiversity and fisheries-related management objectives are highly integrated; they quote biodiversity conservation or sustainable exploitation of resources as a whole, not species per species. Regulatory measures are consistent with this holistic standpoint. Yet, in many assessments, effects are evaluated per species or species group. Producing overall insight on biodiversity or resource status is difficult in these conditions. A few papers have handled this through multivariate statistical modeling (Amand *et al.*, 2004; Langlois *et al.*, 2005; Ceccherelli *et al.*, 2006; Claudet *et al.*, 2006), but results are not easily interpreted to guide management actions, primarily due to a lack of references for setting targets. Alternatively, integrated indices can be investigated to reflect the whole species assemblage concerned and possibly account for species function in the ecosystem (Mistri and Munari, 2007). Such approaches are still rare (Mouillot *et al.*, 2008) and need be developed. Several common biodiversity indices exhibit shortcomings limiting their relevance as an indicator for biodiversity conservation. For instance, species richness is known to depend on the surface area observed, or variations of the Shannon index may be difficult to interpret.

10.4.2.2 Analysis of metrics

There has been a substantial literature about the assessment of ecological and fisheries-related effects of MPAs (see Chapter 2, 3, 6, and 7). Here I will rather focus on a few points that can give insight into the construction of indicators. Additional details may be found in Pelletier *et al.* (2008).

The first point deals with including context information when analyzing the spatiotemporal variations of metrics. Habitat is obviously a very important variable to account for as underlined by many authors (e.g., Garcia-Charton *et al.*, 2004; Chapter 6). Ferraris *et al.* (2005) provided a clear-cut illustration of the interest of controlling for habitat to assess MPAs. By considering habitat at two different scales, they showed that MPA effects were more significantly detected when more precise information was included in the analysis. Alternatively, the observation design can a priori cross protection and habitat factors, particularly when habitat can be described through a single proxy and at a scale compatible with the design. Another context variable is the pressure endured by biodiversity and resources. Procedures to integrate explicitly this information in the assessment of MPA effects have not yet been developed. A first step in this direction is to consider resources depending on their interest for fishers. In an analysis of UVC data, Preuss *et al.* (2009) distinguished species according to (i) the fishing gear that targets them, and (ii) the magnitude of this interest, e.g., incidental catch, which led to more discrimination of MPA effects. Claudet *et al.* (2006) and Rocklin *et al.* (unpublished data) also considered groups of distinct fishing interests.

The second point relates to the usefulness of model-based metrics. These are indispensable to address some questions, notably temporal issues or scenario evaluation. Many models published in the past are theoretical contributions and sometimes simple heuristic models have been used to justify simplistic one-size-fits-all prescriptions, e.g., about the desirable size of no-take zones (Pelletier and Mahévas, 2005). Dynamic models are nevertheless indispensable to tackle certain issues raised by managers, such as evaluating the impact of current fishing activities and the consequences of alternative fishing regulations (Table 10.3). In order to design regulations that appropriately target the fishing activities that have the most detrimental impact on resources, it is necessary to quantify these impacts and to anticipate the outcomes of changes in regulation or other scenarios, e.g., an increase in demographic pressure. More generally, models are needed to project the consequences of scenarios at the scale of fisheries and ecosystems. A major perspective is to implement models that achieve a trade-off between parsimony and complexity, and are parameterized and calibrated against real data. In the MPA context, such models must describe the spatiotemporal dynamics of population and exploitation at the scale of MPA design, and they must account for several species and several fishing activities. These issues have been discussed elsewhere in detail (Pelletier and Mahévas, 2005; Pelletier *et al.*, 2008). The ISIS–Fish model provides a generic framework for applications to actual fisheries on the basis of all available knowledge (http://isis-fish.labs.libre-entreprise.org). There are to date a number of applications that have been successfully used to assess fisheries-related effects of MPAs (Drouineau *et al.*, 2006; Kraus *et al.*, 2009; Lehuta *et al.*, 2010) and a number of applications are in progress. Many resource indicators can be calculated from such models. Pelletier and Mahévas (2005) proposed two ratios that enable the comparison the outcomes of alternative fishing regulations over a simulation: (i) for a given scenario, value at the end of the simulation versus initial value; and (ii) value at the end of the simulation for a scenario versus value at the end of the simulation under a statu quo scenario. These values are calculated for biomass and catch (examples in Table 10.6). The first metric measures the consequences of the regulation scenario, while the second metric gauges this scenario with respect to the current situation. Sensitivity analysis may be used to further evaluate the relevance and efficiency of a given metric.

A real challenge for both empirical and model-based metrics is the provision of uncertainties associated with metric estimation and analysis. In the case of model-based metrics, simulation experiments enable to estimate the sensitivity of model outcomes to uncertainties (Drouineau *et al.*, 2006). For empirical metrics, statistical models should provide confidence bounds for metrics and for resulting analyses. This issue is somehow linked with that of formal indicator validation discussed in Section 10.3.5.

Table 10.6 *Interpretation of indicator values in relation to management objectives and actions under the goals of sustainable exploitation of resources and biodiversity conservation and restoration*

Goal	Objective	Management actions	Indicator(s)	Interpretation of indicator values
Sustainable exploitation of resources	Restoring and maintaining target species	No action Fishing regulation Fishing regulation and restricted MPA access	D = inside–outside difference Tr = outside trend over time (both density of target species calculated from UVC data)	D ↑ and (Tr ↑ or →) no action required (D ↑ or →) and Tr ↓ action required outside D ↓ and Tr ↓ action required inside and outside
		A range of regulatory actions regarding fishing	B = final biomass / initial biomass C = final catch / initial catch (both predicted by model)	Ratio B > 1 population is restored via measure Ratio C > 1 catch increases via measure Ratio B < 1 disregard measure where population is not restored Maximum ratio C among measures that restore population, prefer those that yield the highest catch
Biodiversity conservation	Maintaining or restoring habitats	No action Install permanent moorings in MPA Restrict boat access to MPA	SC = seagrass cover in MPA (calculated from UVC data) NM = number of boats anchored in MPA (from frequentation survey)	SC ↑ and (NM → or ↓) no action required SC → and NM ↑ anticipate further frequentation increase with permanent moorings SC ↓ and NM ↑ restrict access to MPA

10.4.2.3 Increasing indicator efficiency through improved and cost-effective observation protocols

Beyond the relevance of a metric that depends on the observation system (see Section 10.4.2.1), indicator efficiency must be increased through the design of cost-effective protocols. Costs depend on requirements in both staff capacity and time spent at sea and at the office. Observation techniques that can be implemented by the MPA staff should be preferred. Many UVC protocols require expert divers who are able to identify species, but after fieldwork, UVC only requires data input. Photo and video transects require divers who are not necessarily experts (Francour *et al.*, 1999; Dumas *et al.*, 2009; Pelletier *et al.*, 2011). Most video-based techniques are operated from autonomous systems and require no diver (Cappo and Brown, 1996; Pelletier *et al.*, 2007), but they need the assistance of experts at the office for detailed image analysis at species level. Pelletier *et al.* (2011) found out that overall time at sea and at the office was similar for UVC and video transects.

When the observation system is operated by a diver, the number of feasible observations per day and the maximum depth at which they are conducted are limited. Autonomous systems are less restricted in this respect. Baited systems take in general more time per station, while there are unbaited systems that enable a large number of observations to be conducted in a single day (Pelletier *et al.*, 2007b). It should also be noted that local habitat and macrofauna can be evaluated from the same images, whereas UVC require additional stations or longer time underwater for observing both. In general, image-based techniques reduce the time spent at sea, thus implying less field costs, which are always greater than office costs.

These considerations are important for MPA monitoring, as for a given precision/accuracy of the assessment, there is a trade-off between the number of observations that can be realized at a given time period and the spatial extent or the density of the observations, leading to different spatial coverage and replication levels.

Note that the level of expertise required does not depend only on the technique but also on the protocol. Hence, some simplified UVC monitoring programs, e.g., the protocols recommended by the Global Coral Reef Monitoring Network (Hill and Wilkinson, 2004) also resort to volunteers that must observe a limited number of species and species groups. There are still very few studies evaluating the relevance of simplified protocols for deriving biodiversity and resource indicators able to track MPA effectiveness (Edgar and Stuart-Smith, 2009).

Finally, image-based techniques provide information that can be archived, for other analyses, but also, and this is important in environmental assessment, for accountability of the information, thereby avoiding any doubt raised about the potential lack of reproducibility of the observation process, e.g., an observer effect.

10.4.3 Indicators related to uses and governance

Although objectives linked to management of uses and to governance are clearly distinct (Tables 10.2 and 10.3), both relate to human activities and behavior, and the ways they can be investigated bear some similarities, particularly in contrast to highly quantitative approaches of biodiversity and resources. With regard to MPA effectiveness, there has been in the past a much larger emphasis on ecological aspects than on social and economic aspects (but see Chapters 4 and 5).

As stated in Chapter 9, socio-economic effects of MPA can be regarded as the consequences of a public investment on the society's well-being, and in a more practical way, MPA managers have to face the question of assessing how the MPA impacts the welfare of neighboring local communities, which in turn determines their acceptance of the MPA. Social and economic effects are thus linked. This subsection will focus on uses, users, and governance, which are only a subset of socio-economic aspects (see Chapter 9), but represent the main questions that MPA managers can face through the range of actions they can undertake (see, e.g., Table 10.3 for management of uses).

The term "use" is here restricted to those uses that rely on the ecosystem in which the MPA is located, mostly fishing, recreational, and tourist uses. Consistently with the objectives in Tables 10.2 and 10.3, the questions addressed encompass assessing: (i) the pressure of uses on the ecosystem and resources; (ii) the role of MPAs in promoting or mitigating the impact resulting from this pressure; (iii) the local economic benefits linked to these uses; and (iv) the contribution of MPAs to local governance, including reduction of conflicts between uses and social acceptance of MPAs.

10.4.3.1 Identification and estimation of relevant metrics

Pelletier *et al.* (2005a) attempted to evaluate the relevance of metrics used to assess economic and social effects of MPAs but they found few empirical studies in comparison to ecological studies. Yet, there are several types of data that can document these issues. Regarding the pressure of uses on the ecosystem, frequentation studies in and around the MPA can be conducted from direct observations, such as aerial surveys, or observations from boats or particular observation points on the coast. Pressure is then quantified by the number of boats or users in and around the MPA, and must be estimated for each activity practiced and depending on boat characteristics when the activity requires embarking. Direct observations yield snapshot maps where frequentation is georeferenced or indicated per small area. Indirect estimates of frequentation can also be obtained from user interviews. Users' location is then not georeferenced, but can be subjectively located on a map displaying the MPA. In reverse, interviews may provide information about the location and intensity of frequentation at other time periods than the date of the interview. Embarked frequentation studies may be carried out in collaboration with the MPA staff; collecting such information may even be done by MPA staff during the patrols (see, e.g., Gamp et al., 2009).

Studying the role of MPAs in promoting or mitigating the impact resulting from use pressure has rarely been investigated. It first requires to estimate the impacts of uses on the ecosystem: biodiversity (including habitat) and resources. Then it is necessary to relate pressure and impact, which has mainly been done up to now for fishing activities and resources. In the absence of an established link between pressure and impact, it is difficult to guide management toward the appropriate actions to remediate impacts (see Tables 10.3 and 10.4 for possible actions), although precautionary measures can be implemented. One might also qualify activities by interviewing users about the way they practice, their motivations, and the way the MPA influences their practice (Gamp et al., 2009).

Local economic benefits linked to MPA uses are investigated through interviews of users and operators. Market data are needed to quantify benefits, but proxies can also be found, as economic data may sometimes be difficult to obtain. An illustration is provided in Chapter 9 (see also Roncin et al., 2008) in which benefits are evaluated through the numbers of visits to the MPA, and the number of persons or firms using the services provided by the MPA. Methodological caveats were also discussed in Chapter 9.

The contribution of the MPA to local governance can be studied from interviews of local populations and MPA managers, and from administration data. The latter inform about the management process (resources, procedures, etc.) and its integration in the regional coastal management. Interviews with MPA managers further document these issues, but they also provide integrated perceptions of MPA governance. User interviews are needed to appraise individual perceptions regarding conflicts between users, MPA effectiveness, MPA benefits for local populations, and information and participation processes around the MPA. Interviews may be realized with different methodologies either on site or during individual appointments with users (Gamp et al., 2009; Thomassin et al., 2009). Other techniques were also described in Bunce et al. (2000) for coral reef management.

A main challenge for designing appropriate protocols for investigating uses and users in and around MPA lies in the definition and estimation of the reference population. Many uses related to MPA are informal so that this population is not a priori known. Similarly, it is necessary to define the geographical range of influence of the MPA. Information can be obtained from pilot studies, e.g., through the origin of interviewed persons, but will be conditioned on the scope of the studies. Ideally, a large-scale survey, e.g., a phone or mail survey, should be undertaken for an independent estimation.

10.4.3.2 Analysis of metrics

Compared to ecological aspects of MPA, there is generally a lack of knowledge and information on uses and governance. Therefore, a first question often expressed by MPA managers is that of characterizing existing uses and appraising the present governance of the MPA (Pelletier et al., 2005a). Monitoring comes in a subsequent step. This underpins the analysis of the metrics, as temporal aspects are generally not developed (with the exception of commercial fishing pressure which has a longer history of monitoring and assessment). Depending on the protocol and on sample size, a formal statistical analysis may or may not be possible. Besides, some metrics are qualitative or semi-quantitative. Yet, their information is very valuable and should not be discarded. Most of the time, metrics are used in a descriptive way and presented in tables or figures.

10.4.3.3 Designing cost-effective observation protocols

As the efficiency of the metrics is generally not estimated for the reasons explained in Section 10.3.3.2, the question of cost-effective protocols first amounts to choosing a relevant observation system, obtaining a representative sample from the population of interest, and selecting the appropriate spatial and temporal frame for monitoring. The observation system is preferably to be operated by MPA staff. Furthermore monitoring can be coupled with patrolling in the MPA, although it might not always be desirable. It is possible to determine an appropriate sample size for frequentation studies and semi-directed interviews and to structure the protocol to avoid biased results by accounting properly for the different sources of variations in the data. A major issue in interviews lies in the formulation of questionnaires so as to minimize equivocal answers, lies, and interview refusals.

10.4.4 Interpretation of indicators

Let us illustrate this issue through a brief example with two objectives relating respectively to the goals of sustainable use of marine resources and biodiversity conservation (Table 10.6). Under the first goal, the objective of maintaining and restoring target species is assessed through three indicators, two directly calculated from monitoring data, and one model-based. There are no reference points for any of these indicators, thus interpretation must proceed from their spatial and temporal variations. For the empirical indicators, the statistical significance and direction of the inside–outside difference in abundance (D) and of the outside temporal trend in abundance (Tr) may be used to evaluate whether restoration occurs in the MPA with respect to outside. Such information results for instance from a BACI (or BACIPS) design (see Chapter 6). Analyses may be more sophisticated if observations are replicated across several sites and at several dates. The aim is to be able to decide upon management actions on the basis of reliable significant changes in indicator values. These may help to discern between problems requiring action inside or outside the MPA, but they do not demonstrate whether or not protection is restoring the target species, and they do not show what might be the appropriate fishing regulation to achieve this restoration, which is a highly relevant question in the case of multiple use MPAs. The model-based indicator provides more insight into this question by investigating the consequences of several candidate fishing regulations. Population is restored when the final/initial biomass ratio (B) is greater than 1. The final/initial catch ratio (C) enables in addition selection from among the regulations that restore the population, the ones that are not detrimental to catch.

Under the goal of biodiversity conservation, the objective of restoring or maintaining habitats is assessed through the seagrass cover (SC) indicator. It may evolve over time as a result of changes in water quality or detrimental effects of anchoring. A decreasing SC indicates a problem, but does not point to its cause. If estimates of the pressure due to anchoring are available, changes in seagrass cover within the MPA may be interpreted in relation with frequentation. Again, there are no reference points for these indicators. The number of boats moored in the MPA (NM), particular nearby or in the seagrass area, yields additional clues as to the cause of changes in SC. In the absence of reference values, it is difficult to demonstrate that decreases in SC are due to large NM. This implies the need to compare seagrass areas with different boat pressures and to find a correlation that is independent of other sources of variation for SC. When trends are available, it is possible to derive management actions from the joint trends of SC and NM. Hence, even in the absence of reference points that would provide thresholds, the statistical significance, magnitude, and direction of the variations of the indicators considered are helpful for establishing the diagnostic and targeting management actions. Determining the appropriate significance level, magnitude, and direction stems from scientific knowledge about ecological dynamics, but also from the time-frame required for restoration which in turn depends on the initial ecological status. Note that as years of data accumulate, the interpretation of indicator values may become more sophisticated by accounting for values taken over successive years. Hopefully, the information collected may eventually provide evidence for establishing a relationship between the pressure (NM) and the impact (SC).

These illustrations show that it is often necessary to consider several indicators to decide upon actions linked to a given objective.

10.5 Conclusions

Similarly to other domains of environmental management, there is a growing demand for the provision of rigorously established indicators of MPA effectiveness that can be used to assist decision-making. A review of the literature showed a gap between on the one hand, institutional frameworks and methodologies designed at international levels, which exhibit a lack of formalization but are aimed at management issues, and on the other hand scientific contributions, which do not account for management constraints but are better formalized.

The proposed framework appears to be applicable to the three major MPA goals: biodiversity conservation, sustainable exploitation of resources, and management and governance of multiple uses. The way it should be applied differs according to management objectives, as for biodiversity and resources, data and knowledge are commonly available, including temporal series of data, whereas they are scarcer for social and economic aspects.

It favors the construction of relevant and efficient indicators. Grounding the approach in collaborations with managers guarantees that indicators satisfy managers' needs and constraints. The framework is currently being implemented in a variety of contexts (including Mediterranean and tropical ecosystems) by a multidisciplinary team within the PAMPA project. It might also be applied to other domains of coastal management, as long as managers are a well-identified group for collaboration. Indeed, MPAs are a favorable case in this respect, as they are limited in space. In addition, many MPA managers, at least in developed countries, have a scientific background which facilitates progress during discussions. The process relies on a sustained collaboration between scientists and managers but it is not a participatory approach as not all stakeholders are associated. Note that they might be represented for discussing communication and monitoring if they are to be involved in management. For pragmatic reasons, it is nevertheless necessary that there are not too many persons for discussions. Managers of the MPA are key to the process as they know the context, the issues, and the stakeholders, and they are the ones who are going to use the indicators.

In terms of perspectives, issues of validation and communication still need to be documented and tested. Also, synthesizing and communicating results for management purpose is often quoted in the literature, but there are few concrete contributions (e.g., Section 10.3.7), particularly with regard to uncertainty. But this does not preclude the construction and validation of indicators, and can be considered separately. As explained in Section 10.3.7, synthesis and aggregation, and to a lesser extent presenting indicators, is never insignificant. Combining scores or color codes from different goals may exceed the scope of the scientists' work, as it pertains to management priorities in which scientists should not interfere.

Regarding evaluation of relevance and effectiveness, scientists should provide more guidance and communicate on the usefulness and relevance of candidate approaches for monitoring, indicator selection and implementation, sampling design improvement, and indicator interpretation. In addition, managers often appreciate updates on scientific progress (Pelletier *et al.*, 2007a). Scientists are also expected to convey insight from systemic perspective to help managers to stand back from day-to-day problems that might distract discussions on MPA management. Last, they should also indicate and explain when some questions raised by managers cannot be addressed by simple and cheap monitoring methods and simplified indicators. In this case, managers may need scientific expertise, e.g., for prospective questions about ecosystem and resource dynamics. In contrast, part of the monitoring might be achieved by non-expert (although trained) persons, such as MPA staff, but also volunteers, such as divers or fishers, which will contribute to MPA social acceptance.

The methods used at each step of the framework can be tailored to the MPA context and logistics, because collaboration with managers is central here. But it can only be applied if there are issues acknowledged by managers as requiring scientific input to MPA management, and if some scientific experts are willing and available to work with MPA managers.

10.6 Acknowledgments

Many ideas expressed in this chapter stem from the experiences benefitted from the Liteau II-AMP and PAMPA projects. Partners of these projects are gratefully acknowledged, in particular MPA managers.

References

Agardy, T., Bridgewater, P., Crosby, M. P., *et al.* (2003). Dangerous targets? Unresolved issues and ideological clashes around marine protected areas. *Aquatic Conservation : Marine and Freshwater Ecosystems*, **13**, 353–67.

Amand, M., Pelletier, D., Ferraris, J., and Kulbicki, M. (2004). A step toward the definition of ecological indicators of the impact of fishing on the fish assemblage of the Abore Reef Reserve (New Caledonia). *Aquatic Living Resources*, **17**, 139–49.

Brown, K., Adger, W. N., Tompkins, E., *et al.* (2001). Trade-off analysis for marine protected area management. *Ecological Economics*, **37**, 417–34.

Bunce, L., Townsley, P., Pomeroy, R., and Pollnac, R. (2000). *Socioeconomic Manual for Coral Reef Management*. Gland, Switzerland: Global Coral Reef Monitoring Network, IUCN.

Caddy, J. (1998). *A Short Review of Precautionary Reference Points and Some Proposals for Their Use in Data-Poor Situations*. Rome: Food and Agriculture Organisation.

Caddy, J. (2002). Limit reference points, traffic lights, and holistic approaches to fisheries management with minimal stock assessment input. *Fisheries Research*, **56**, 133–7.

Cappo, M. and Brown, I. (1996). *Evaluation of Sampling Methods for Reef Fish Populations of Commercial and Recreational Interest.* Townsville, QLD: CRC Reef Research Centre.

Ceccherelli, G., Casu, D., Pala, D., Pinna, S., and Sechi, N. (2006). Evaluating the effects of protection on two benthic habitats at Tavolara-Punta Coda Cavallo MPA (North-East Sardinia, Italy). *Marine Environmental Research*, **61**, 171–85.

Christie, P. (2004). Marine protected areas as biological successes and social failures in Southeast Asia. *American Fisheries Society Symposium*, **42**, 155–64.

Claudet, J. and Pelletier, D. (2004). Marine protected areas and artificial reefs: a review of the interactions between management and scientific studies. *Aquatic Living Resources*, **17**, 129–38.

Claudet, J., Pelletier, D., Jouvenel, J. Y., Bachet, F., and Galzin, R. (2006). Assessing the effects of Marine Protected Area (MPA) on a reef fish assemblage in a northwestern Mediterranean marine reserve: identifying community-based indicators. *Biological Conservation*, **130**, 349–69.

Collie, J. S. and Gislason, H. (2001). Biological reference points for fish stocks in a multispecies context. *Canadian Journal of Fisheries and Aquatic Sciences*, **58**, 2167–76.

Cook, R. M. (1998). A sustainability criterion fro the exploitation of North Sea cod. *ICES Journal of Marine Science*, **55**, 1061–70.

Corrales, L. (2005). *Manual for the Rapid Evaluation of Management Effectiveness in Marine Protected Areas of Mesoamérica.* Belize City: Mesoamerican Barrier Reef System Project.

Daan, N., Christensen, V., and Cury, P. (2005). Quantitative ecosystem indicators for fisheries management. *ICES Journal of Marine Science*, **62**, 307–14.

Dale, V. H. and Beyeler, S. C. (2001). Challenges in the development and use of ecological indicators. *Ecological Indicators*, **1**, 3–10.

Drouineau, H., Mahévas, S., Pelletier, D., and Beliaeff, B. (2006). Assessing the impact of different management options using ISIS–Fish, and sensitivity analysis of the model: application to the Hake-Nephrops mixed fishery of the Bay of Biscay. *Aquatic Living Resources*, **19**, 15–29.

Dumas, P., Bertaud, A., Peignon, C., Léopold, M., and Pelletier, D. (2009). A "quick and clean" photographic method for the description of coral reef habitats. *Journal of Experimental Biology and Ecology*, **368**, 161–8.

Edgar, G. J. and Stuart-Smith, R. D. (2009). Ecological effects of marine protected areas on rocky reef communities: a continental-scale analysis. *Marine Ecology Progress Series*, **388**, 51–62.

Everitt, B. S. (2006). *The Cambridge Dictionary of Statistics*, 3rd edn. Cambridge, UK: Cambridge University Press.

FAO (1999). *Indicators for Sustainable Development of Marine Capture Fisheries.* Rome: Food and Agriculture Organization.

Ferraris, J., Pelletier, D., Kulbicki, M., and Chauvet, C. (2005). Assessing the impact of removing reserve status on the Abore Reef fish assemblage, New Caledonia. *Marine Ecology Progress Series*, **292**, 271–86.

Francour, P., Liret, C., and Harvey, E. (1999). Comparison of fish abundance estimates made by remote underwater video and visual census. *Naturalista siciliana*, **23**, 155–68.

Gamp, E., Pelletier, D., Jumel, M.-C., and Coutures, E. (2009). Distribution, motivations and perceptions of informal users in a coral reef Marine Protected Areas (MPA): Survey methodology and analysis. In *Pacific Science Inter-Congress*. Tahiti, French Polynesia, March 2–6.

Garcia, S. M., Staples, D. J., and Chesson, J. (2000). The FAO guidelines for the development and use of indicators for sustainable development of marine capture fisheries and an Australian example of their application. *Ocean and Coastal Management*, **43**, 537–56.

Garcia-Charton, J. A., Pérez-Ruzafa, A., Sànchez-Jerez, P., *et al.* (2004). Multi-scale spatial heterogeneity, habitat structure, and the effect of marine reserves on Western Mediterranean rocky reef fish assemblages. *Marine Biology*, **144**, 161–82.

Guidetti, P. and Claudet, J. (2010). Co-management practices enhance fisheries in marine protected areas. *Conservation Biology*, **24**, 312–18.

Halpern, B. (2003). The impact of marine reserves: do reserves work and does reserve size matter? *Ecological Applications*, **13**, S117–S137.

Harmelin-Vivien, M. L., Harmelin, J. G., Chauvet, C., *et al.* (1985). Evaluation visuelle des peuplements et populations de poissons: méthodes et problèmes. *Revue d'Ecologie (Terre et Vie)*, **40**, 467–539.

Hilborn, R. (2002). The dark side of reference points. *Bulletin of Marine Science*, **70**, 403–8.

Hill, J. and Wilkinson, C. (2004). *Methods for Ecological Monitoring of Coral Reefs.* Townsville, QLD: Australian Institute of Marine Science.

Hilty, J. and Merenlender, A. (2000). Faunal indicator taxa selection for monitoring ecosystem health. *Biological Conservation*, **92**, 185–97.

Hockings, M. (2006). On defining MPA "success" and choosing an evaluation method. *MPA News*, **7**, 4.

Hockings, M., Stolton, S., Leverington, F., Dudley, N., and Courrau, J. (2006). *Evaluating Effectiveness: A Framework for Assessing Management Effectiveness of Protected Areas,* 2nd edn. Gland, Switzerland: IUCN – World Commission on Protected Areas.

ICES (2001). *Report of the ICES Advisory Committee on Fishery Management*. Copenhagen: International Council for the Exploration of the Sea.

IUCN (2003). Vth IUCN World Park Congress: Benefits beyond boundaries. *World Conservation*, **2**, 3.

Jennings, S. (2005). Indicators to support an ecosystem approach to fisheries. *Fish and Fisheries*, **6**, 212–32.

Kelleher, G. (ed.) (1999). *Guidelines for Marine Protected areas*. Gland, Switzerland: IUCN.

Kelleher, G. and Kenchington, R. (1992). *Guidelines for Establishing Marine Protected Areas*. Gland, Switzerland: IUCN.

Knowlton, N. and Jackson, J. B. C. (2009). Shifting baselines, local impacts, and global change on coral reefs. *PLoS Biology*, **6**, 215–20.

Koeller, P. (2003). The lighter side of references points. *Fisheries Research*, **62**, 1–6.

Koeller, P., Savard, L., Parsons, D. G., and Fu, C. (2000). A precautionary approach to assessment and management of shrimp stocks in the Northwest Atlantic. *Journal of Northwest Atlantic Fishery Science.*, **27**, 235–46.

Kraus, G., Pelletier, D., Dubreuil, J., *et al.* (2009). A model-based evaluation of Marine Protected Areas for fishery management in the case of strong environmental forcing: the example of Eastern Baltic cod (*Gadus morhua callarias*). *ICES Journal of Marine Science*, **66**, 109–21.

Kurtz, J. C., Jackson, L. E., and Fisher, W. S. (2001). Strategies for evaluating indicators based on guidelines from the Environmental Protection Agency's Office of Research and Development. *Ecological Indicators*, **1**, 49–60.

Langlois, T. J., Anderson, M. J., and Babcock, R. C. (2005). Reef-associated predators influence adjacent soft-sediment communities. *Ecology*, **86**, 1508–19.

Langlois, T. J., Chabanet, P., Pelletier, D., and Harvey, E. (2006). Baited underwater video for assessing reef fish populations in marine reserves. *Secretariat of the South Pacific Community Fisheries Newsletter*, **118**, 53–6.

Lehuta, S., Mahévas, S., Petitgas, P., and Pelletier, D., (2010). Combining sensitivity and uncertainty analysis to evaluate the impact of management measures with ISIS–Fish: Marine Protected Areas for the Anchovy (*Engraulis encrasicolus L.*) fishery in the Bay of Biscay. *ICES Journal of Marine Science*, **67**, 1063–75.

Micheli, F., Halpern, B., Botsford, L. W., and Warner, R. R. (2004). Trajectories and correlates of community change in no-take reserves. *Ecological Applications*, **14**, 1709–23.

Mistri, M. and Munari, C. (2007). BITS, a smart indicator for soft-bottom, non-tidal lagoons. *Marine Pollution Bulletin*, **56**, 587–99.

Mouillot, D., Culioli, J. M., Pelletier, D., and Tomasini, J. A. (2008). Do we protect biological originality in protected areas? A new index and an application to the Bonifacio Strait Natural Reserve. *Biological Conservation*, **141**, 1569–80.

Muthiga, N. A. (2009). Evaluating the effectiveness of management of the Malindi-Watamu marine protected area complex in Kenya. *Ocean and Coastal Management*, **52**, 417–23.

Nicholson, M. D. and Fryer, R. (2002). Developing effective environmental indicators: does a new dog need old tricks? *Marine Pollution Bulletin*, **45**, 53–61.

OECD (2003). *OECD Environmental Indicators: Development, Measurement and Use.* Paris: Organization for Economic Co-operation and Development.

Office of National Marine Sanctuaries (2004). *A Monitoring Framework for the National Marine Sanctuary System.* National Oceanic and Atmospheric Administration. Available at httpp://sanctuaries.noaa.gov/

Pelletier, D. (2003). *Dynamique spatiale et saisonnière de pêcheries démersales et benthiques: caractérisation, modélisation, et conséquences pour la gestion par Zones Marines Protégées.* Montpellier, France: Université de Montpellier II.

Pelletier, D. (2005). Designing operational quantitative tools and indicators for the assessment of Marine Protected Area Performance : a multidisciplinary project between scientists and managers. In *First International Marine Protected Areas Congress (IMPAC1)*, eds. J. C. Day, J. Senior, S. Monk, and W. Neal, Geelong, Victoria, Australia, p. 635.

Pelletier, D. (2007). *Développement d'outils diagnostics et exploratoires d'aide à la décision pour évaluer la performance d'Aires Marines Protégées*, Rapport final de contrat Liteau II, Ministère de l'Ecologie et du Développement Durable. Plouzané, France: Institut français de recherche pour l'exploitation de la mer (IFREMER).

Pelletier, D. and Mahévas, S. (2005). Spatially explicit fisheries simulation models for policy evaluation. *Fish and Fisheries*, **6**, 1–43.

Pelletier, D., Charbonnel, E., Licari, M.-L., *et al.* (2005a). Synthesis of the workshop on interactions between managers and scientists. In *Report of the LiteauII-AMP Project: Development of Diagnostic and Exploratory Decision-Support Tools for Assessing MPA Performance*. Available at www.ifremer.fr/docelec/doc/2005/rapport-6797.pdf

Pelletier, D., Garcia-Charton, J. A., Ferraris, J., *et al.* (2005b). Designing indicators for evaluating the impact of Marine Protected Areas on coral reef ecosystems: a multidisciplinary standpoint. *Aquatic Living Resources*, **18**, 15–33.

Pelletier, D., Ferraris, J., Alban, F., *et al.* (2007a). Involving scientists and managers for designing operational tools and indicators for assessing the performance of coastal MPAs. In *European Symposium on Marine Protected Areas as a Tool for Fisheries Management and Ecosystem Conservation*, Murcia, Spain, September 25–28.

Pelletier, D., Leleu, K., Mou-Tham, G., *et al.* (2007b). Video-based observation techniques for monitoring fish assemblages in coral reef MPAs. In *European Symposium on Marine Protected Areas as a Tool for Fisheries Management and Ecosystem Conservation*, Murcia, Spain, September 25–28.

Pelletier, D., Claudet, J., Ferraris, J., Benedetti-Cecchi, L., and García-Charton, J. A. (2008). Models and indicators for assessing conservation and fisheries-related effects of marine protected areas. *Canadian Journal of Fisheries and Aquatic Sciences*, **65**, 1–15.

Pelletier, D., Leleu, K., Mou-Tham, G., Chabanet, P. ,and Guillemot, N. (2011). Comparision of visual census and high-definition video transects for monitoring coral reef fish assemblages. *Fisheries Research*, **107** 84–93.

Pomeroy, R. S., Parks, J. E., and Watson, L. M. (2004). *How is Your MPA Doing? A Guidebook of Natural and Social Indicators for Evaluating Marine Protected Area Management Effectiveness*. Gland, Switerzerland: IUCN.

Pomeroy, R. S., Watson, L. M., Parks, J. E., and Cid, G. A. (2005). How is your MPA doing? A methodology for evaluating the management effectiveness of marine protected areas. *Ocean and Coastal Management*, **48**, 485–502.

Pont, D., Hugueny, B., Beier, U., *et al.* (2006). Assessing river biotic condition at a continental scale: a European appraoch using functional metrics and fish assemblages. *Journal of Applied Ecology*, **43**, 70–80.

Port-Cros National Park (2007). *Guide d'aide à la gestion des Aires Marines Protégées: évaluation de la pertinence et de la performance de la gestion marine*. MedPAN Interreg Project IIIC. Available at www.medpan.org

Preuss, B., Pelletier, D., Wantiez, L., *et al.* (2009). Considering multiple-species attributes to understand better the effects of successive changes in protection status on a coral reef first assemblage. *ICES Journal of Marine Science*, **66**, 170–9.

Rice, J. C. and Rochet, M. J. (2005). A framework for selecting a suite of indicators for fisheries management. *ICES Journal of Marine Science*, **62**, 580–92.

Richards, L. J. and Schnute, J. T. (1986). An experimental and statistical approach to the question: is CPUE an index of abundance? *Canadian Journal of Fisheries and Aquatic Sciences*, **43**, 1214–27.

Rochet, M. J. and Trenkel, V. (2003). Which community indicators can measure the impact of fishing? A review and proposals. *Canadian Journal of Fisheries and Aquatic Sciences*, **60**, 86–99.

Roncin, N., Alban, F., Charbonnel, E., *et al.* (2008). Uses of ecosystem services provided by MPAs: how much do they impact the local economy? A southern Europe perspective. *Journal for Nature Conservation*, **16**, 256–70.

Sainsbury, K. and Sumaila, U. R. (2003). Incorporating ecosystem objectives into management of sustainable marine fisheries, including "best practice" reference point and use of marine protected areas. In *Responsible Fisheries in the Marine Ecosystem*, eds. M. Sinclair and G. Valdimarsson. Rome: Food and Agriculture Organization, pp. 343–61.

Samoilys, M. (1997). Underwater visual census surveys. In *Manual for Assessing Fish Stocks on Pacific Coral Reefs*, ed. M. Samoilys. Townsville, QLD: Department of Primary Industries, pp. 16–29.

Smith, A. D. M., Sainsbury, K. J., and Stevens, R. A. (1999). Implementing effective fisheries-management systems and management strategy evaluation and the Australian partnership approach. *ICES Journal of Marine Science*, **56**, 967–79.

Smith, T. D. and Link, J. S. (2005). Autopsy your dead... and living: a proposal for fisheries science, fisheries management and fisheries. *Fish and Fisheries*, **6**, 73–87.

Stobart, B., Garcia-Charton, J. A., Espejo, C., *et al.* (2007). A baited underwater video technique to assess shallow-water Mediterranean fish assemblages: methodological evaluation. *Journal of Experimental Marine Biology and Ecology*, **345**, 158–74.

Stolton, S., Hockings, M., and Dudley, N. (2002). *Reporting Progress on Management Effectiveness in Marine Protected Areas*. New York: The World Bank.

Tessier, E., Chabanet, P., Pothin, K., Soria, M., and Lasserre, G. (2008). Visual census of tropical fish assemblages on artificial reef: slate versus video recording techniques. *Journal of Experimental Biology and Ecology*, **315**, 17–30.

Thomassin, A., David, G., Guennégan, Y., and Messaci, Y. (2009). Building social acceptability indicators to assist Marine Protected Area governance: the case of professional fishermen in Reunion Island. In *International Marine Conservation Congress*, George Madison University, Fairfax, VA, May 20.

Trenkel, V. and Rochet, M. J. (2003). Performance of indicators derived from abundance estimates for detecting the impact of fishing on a fish community. *Canadian Journal of Fisheries and Aquatic Sciences*, **60**, 67–85.

Trenkel, V., Rochet, M.-J., and Mesnil, B. (2007). From model-based prescriptive advice to indicator-based interactive advice. *ICES Journal of Marine Science*, **64**, 768–74.

UN Commission on Sustainable Development (2006). *Global Trends and Status of Indicators of Sustainable Development*. New York: United Nations.

Watson, D. L., Harvey, E. S., Anderson, M. J., and Kendrick, G. A. (2005). A comparison of temperate reef fish assemblages recorded by three underwater stereo-video techniques. *Marine Biology*, **148**, 415–25.

Wells, S. and Dahl-Tacconi, N. (2006). Why should we evaluate the management effectiveness of a MPA? *MPA News*, **7**, 2–3.

Willis, T. J., Millar, R. B., and Babcock, R. C. (2000). Detection of spatial variability in relative density of fishes: comparison of visual census, angling, and baited underwater video. *Marine Ecology Progress Series*, **198**, 249–60.

Part IV

Scale-up of marine protected area systems

11 · NETWORKS – The assessment of marine reserve networks: guidelines for ecological evaluation

KIRSTEN GRORUD-COLVERT, JOACHIM CLAUDET, MARK CARR, JENNIFER CASELLE, JON DAY, ALAN FRIEDLANDER, SARAH E. LESTER, THIERRY LISON DE LOMA, BRIAN TISSOT, AND DAN MALONE

11.1 Introduction

As marine ecosystems are plagued by an ever-increasing suite of threats including climate change, pollution, habitat degradation, and fisheries impacts (Roessig *et al.*, 2004; Lotze *et al.*, 2006; Jackson, 2008), there are now no ocean areas that are exempt from anthropogenic impacts (Halpern *et al.*, 2008). In order to preserve marine biodiversity, ecosystem function, and the goods and services provided by resistant and/or resilient systems, marine reserves have been increasingly recommended as part of an ecosystem-based approach to management (Browman and Stergiou, 2004; Levin *et al.*, 2009). Marine reserves are defined as "areas of the ocean completely protected from all extractive and destructive activities" (Lubchenco *et al.*, 2003) and can be experimental controls for evaluating the impact of these activities on marine ecosystems. Growing scientific information has shown consistent increases in species density, biomass, size, and diversity in response to full protection inside reserves of varying sizes and ages located in diverse regions (Claudet *et al.*, 2008; Lester *et al.*, 2009; Molloy *et al.*, 2009). However, most of these data are from individual marine reserves and therefore have inherently limited transferability to networks of marine reserves, which when properly designed

Marine Protected Areas: A Multidisciplinary Approach, ed. Joachim Claudet. Published by Cambridge University Press. © Cambridge University Press 2011.

can outperform single marine reserves for a variety of ecological, economic, and social management goals (Roberts *et al.*, 2003; Almany *et al.*,
2009; Gaines *et al.*, 2010).

The concept of marine reserve networks grew out of a desire to
achieve both conservation and fishery management goals by minimizing
the potential negative economic, social, and cultural impacts of a single
large reserve while still producing similar or even greater ecological
and economic returns (Murray *et al.*, 1999; Gaines *et al.*, 2010). In
addition, reserves networks can provide insurance by protecting areas
across a region and spreading the risk that these sites may be impacted by
localized catastrophes such as hurricanes or oil spills (Allison *et al.*, 2003).
The World Conservation Union's Marine Programme defines a network
as "a collection of individual marine protected areas (MPAs) or reserves
operating co-operatively and synergistically, at various spatial scales and
with a range of protection levels that are designed to meet objectives that a
single reserve cannot achieve" (IUCN–WCPA, 2008). However, general
terms such as "co-operatively" and "synergistically" can have myriad
meanings. Without a clear definition of a network, it becomes difficult to
identify attainable management goals and design a process for evaluating
whether the network achieves those goals. Besides, different management
goals may in turn result in the need for different types of networks.
The use of MPAs with varying protection levels together with no–take
zones in multiple-zoning schemes adds another layer of complexity to
network design and evaluation; however, partially protected areas are
generally used to manage coastal uses and avoid conflicts (rather than
for strict ecological purposes) and are therefore a function of the local
social, economic, and cultural context. As we are here interested in the
ecological effects of networks, for the purposes of this chapter, we focus
on marine reserves because these areas are no-take and therefore offer
greater ecological benefits than other types of MPAs that allow some
forms of extraction (Lester and Halpern, 2008).

Despite commitments made to establish a network of MPAs by 2012
with 20–30% of marine habitats in strictly protected zones (Vth World
Parks Congress 2003) and to protect 10% of the world's coastal and
marine Exclusive Economic Zones (EEZ) by 2010 (CBD, 2006), current
rates of MPA establishment indicate goals for EEZ protection will not be
met until 2047, and 20% of marine habitats will not be protected until
2083 (Wood *et al.*, 2008). In 2006 only 0.2% of the total marine area
under national jurisdictions was protected in no-take zones (Wood *et al.*,

2008) and in 2008, the approximately 5000 MPAs located around the world represented less than 1% of the world's oceans (UNEP–WCMC, 2008). The total area protected in marine reserves and other MPAs is a distant value from the 10–30% targets set for the next 3–5 years, and the number of marine reserves is thus destined to grow, albeit at a much slower rate than the targets require (Wood *et al.*, 2008).

Although there is an abundance of theoretical insight into the design of marine reserve networks (e.g., Allison *et al.*, 2003; Baskett *et al.*, 2007; Beech *et al.*, 2008; Kaplan *et al.*, 2009), much of which addresses optimal size and spacing of marine reserves via population connectivity (Shanks *et al.*, 2003; Palumbi, 2004; Almany *et al.*, 2009), there is no empirical evidence for the predicted outcomes. Likewise there is no established framework for assessing whether ecological effects across the network as a whole are greater than the sum of the effects within the individual reserves in the network. Practical advice about setting management goals and evaluating and monitoring effects of marine reserve networks is critical for identifying the key elements (such as data and budgetary requirements) of a successful management plan, both for networks that already exist and those in current or future planning discussions. In this chapter we provide: (1) definitions of different network types to clarify their realistic outcomes; (2) the conceptual requirements for evaluating whether a group of marine reserves is functioning as a network; and (3) an analytical framework for evaluating the success of a marine reserve network.

11.2 Defining networks: different types, different outcomes

Whether a single large marine reserve or several smaller ones would be more effective at achieving management goals is a central question as old as the science of marine reserves (e.g. Simberloff, 2003). The SLOSS (Single Large or Several Small) debate has led to many theoretical works (Gerber *et al.*, 2003; Hastings and Botsford, 2003) and has been considered when siting and designing marine reserves, but the theory has never been assessed empirically for marine systems. As for any evaluation of management measures, empirical evaluation of a network should test whether the objectives of the marine reserve network are being met (Claudet and Pelletier, 2004). Situation-dependent criteria, such as marine habitat distribution, the life history traits of species

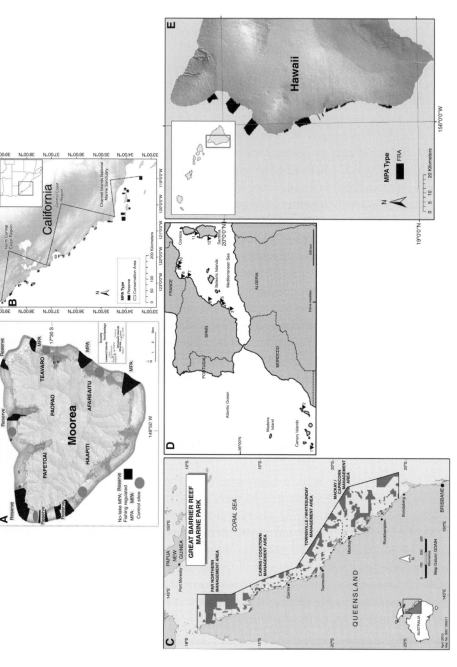

Figure 11.1 Maps of existing networks in (A) Moorea, French Polynesia (management network), (B) California, USA (connectivity network), (C) the Great Barrier Reef, Australia (conservation network), (D) the north-western Mediterranean (regional network), and (E) West Hawaii, USA (management network).

targeted by management, and the socio-economic and cultural context in which the network is established, can lead to networks with different goals and outcomes, preventing the development of a single, one-size-fits-all assessment. How can we appropriately assess the effectiveness of a marine reserve network to achieve a set of specific objectives? First, we must understand the different types of networks (Figure 11.1) and the potential outcomes and limitations of each type.

For example, marine reserves in a given area that were established independently of each other may be considered an *ad hoc* or *regional network* (Table 11.1). It can be tempting to consider these sites a cohesive network that will produce synergistic effects across the single reserves, but this broad assumption should be tested. For instance, a regional network in the Mediterranean Sea is an existing collection of marine reserves that is considered to be an integral part of marine policy goals to meet international conservation targets. However, recent work demonstrates that the ecological effectiveness of well-enforced, individual marine reserves in the north-western Mediterranean (Figure 11.1D) is not increased by the proximity of other marine reserves (Claudet *et al.*, 2008). According to the IUCN–Marine MPA network definition, such an ad hoc network could not therefore be considered an ecologically effective network of marine reserves since this collection of reserves does not exceed the ecological outcomes of multiple, unconnected marine reserves. Further, we do not necessarily consider the no-take zones in a multiple-use MPA, and the partially protected buffer zones surrounding them, to be part of a regional network if they are unconnected. Large buffer zones, if not managed properly, can have detrimental effects on the ecological effectiveness of no-take zones (Claudet *et al.*, 2008; but see Guidetti and Claudet, 2010), although they may be required for management of coastal uses.

A marine reserve network can also be designed to have strict conservation goals (Table 11.1). The underlying objective of a *conservation network* is to conserve the representative ecological characteristics of an area or ecosystem by protecting replicated sites that encompass habitats or species of interest. The replication of marine reserves acts as a buffer against potential threats that could impact a portion of the protected sites. Connectivity among protected components may be assumed but it is not planned for or assessed (Roberts *et al.*, 2003). If network sites are not connected, conservation goals may be undermined by a lack of protection afforded to upstream sources (e.g., if larval supply is from an unprotected area).

Table 11.1 *Definitions, goals, potential limitations, and examples for each type of marine reserve network*

Marine reserve network type	Definition	General network goals	Potential limitations	Example network(s)
Ad hoc or regional	An unplanned collection of reserves in a given area not established with an overall aim	To meet international conservation targets, serve as potential foundation for a planned network	Sites are protected but without advance planning may not achieve synergistic effects across the network	North-western Mediterreanean, Hawaii, Caribbean
Conservation	A collection of reserves in a given area aimed at protecting conservation priority sites	To protect replicates of representative ecosystems, critical areas, damaged habitats	Connectivity among protected components may be assumed but it is not planned for, conservation goals may be undermined if sites are not connected	Great Barrier Reef, Chile, Australian Commonwealth MPA networks, Florida Keys, Moorea
Management	A collection of reserves in a given area established to manage a marine resource and multiple human uses	To protect targeted species, increase reproductive capacity, increase yield, optimize coastal uses while meeting conservation targets, avoid conflicts	Focus on target species may lead to ineffective design for other species, connectivity among protected components may be assumed but it is not planned for, management goals may be undermined if sites are not connected, reallocation of coastal uses may lead to increased attendance and unplanned impacts	West Hawaii
Social	A collection of reserves whose managers, practitioners, stakeholders, decision-makers, scientists, and others interact and transfer knowledge	To promote interaction among participants to effectively plan, manage, implement, or monitor area-based management of marine resources and associated uses	Often lack scientific input	Mediterreanean Protected Areas Network (MedPAN), Caribbean Marine Protected Area Managers (CaMPAM)
Connectivity	A set of multiple reserves connected by the movement and dispersal of larvae, juveniles, or adults	To maximize conservation benefits but minimize no-take area by establishing multiple, interconnected reserves	Complex to design and monitor for connectivity, appropriate design only based on ecological inputs and may therefore conflict with user interests	Papua New Guinea, Gulf of California, California coast

Marine reserve networks can also be *management networks* (Table 11.1). Their aim is to manage and facilitate the economic uses of a marine resource (e.g., fisheries management) at a broader scale than a single marine reserve approach would have afforded (Eisma-Osorio *et al.*, 2009). These differ from conservation networks in their focus on overall benefits via fisheries yields, or other economic benefits such as eco-tourism, as opposed to the preservation of biodiversity. For example, the West Hawaii network of marine reserves (Figure 11.1E) was initially established to manage species that were highly targeted for aquarium trade (Tissot *et al.*, 2004).

A marine reserve network can be a *social network* (Table 11.1). The aim of a social network is to involve different marine reserve managers, stakeholders, decision-makers, and scientists to transfer knowledge, share best practices, and build capacity. For instance, MedPAN South, a social network directed towards non-European Mediterranean countries, is dedicated to improving the management plans of existing MPAs, to provide support when little information is available, to help fundraise and train field staff, and to integrate marine reserves into broader development plans.

Finally, marine reserve networks can be *connectivity networks* (Table 11.1), defined as a set of multiple marine reserves connected by the dispersal of larvae and/or movement of juveniles and adults (Planes *et al.*, 2009). The general objective of such networks is to maximize conservation and/or fisheries benefits from no-take areas, which are designed to be of optimal size and spacing to achieve productive populations inside reserves and connectivity among reserves, while devoting the remaining space to fisheries or other coastal uses.

The definitions of these five network types raise a new question: can a single network achieve all of the above objectives? For example, combining social networks with any of the other four management types may achieve better regional governance. If the reserves in an ad hoc regional network, conservation network, or management network are serendipitously established in sites that are connected, they can serve as de facto connectivity networks. In fact, to effectively achieve the goals of protecting an adequate portion of a region (regional network), a particular species, set of taxa, or habitat (conservation network), and a set of fished species that are targeted in areas outside the network (management network), all network types will need to consider connectivity in order to better achieve their goals. A properly designed connectivity network should achieve the goals of regional, conservation, and management networks by ensuring that these network types are protecting a connected set of sites and species beyond just a collection of single reserves, covering an appropriate geographical gradient, and considering the needs of managed fisheries in the surrounding waters. Although multiple types of potentially non-connected reserve networks may exist, we assert that connectivity should be a driving goal of network establishment. Thus, the remainder of the chapter focuses solely on the establishment and monitoring of connectivity networks.

11.3 Network evaluation: is a group of reserves functioning as a network?

How do we measure whether an existing network meets its objectives? What framework should be used to assess the success of a network? Here we concentrate on evaluating the effectiveness of connectivity networks using both empirical and modeling approaches to assess network success.

11.3.1 General criteria and challenges

Although there is a large literature on marine reserve design and evaluation (NRC, 2001; Pomeroy *et al.*, 2004), there are relatively few papers on the evaluation of a marine reserve network. Given the large scale of reserve networks, effectively monitoring them is a challenging and potentially expensive proposition that requires attention to several unique issues related to experimental design. Field *et al.* (2007) noted that monitoring programs often fail to detect effects unless there is: (1) a clearly defined target of what constitutes "success" with regard to a specific objective; (2) well-coupled sampling and analytical designs capable of detecting and interpreting real change; and (3) adequate funding and infrastructure to support the long time period needed to detect effects. It is important to establish suitable controls and identify appropriate sampling power to detect local vs. regional effects. However, as individual marine reserves are hierarchically nested within a network, all the tools used to evaluate marine reserve effects are also applicable to evaluating a network. One key consideration that is unique to networks is how to measure the "network effect." In other words, does a network provide benefits that are greater than the sum of the individual marine reserves within it?

11.3.2 Cumulative versus synergistic responses

The network effect can be addressed by focusing on three variables of success – replenishment within reserves, spillover to adjacent open areas, and connectivity between and among marine reserves and open areas. While marine reserves can be evaluated by comparing a particular reserve to its reference site(s), a network evaluation requires an analysis involving reserves and paired reference sites in an unprotected area, both inside and outside the network, where some paired sites may display positive or negative effects. The key question is whether there is a significant overall network effect greater than the sum of individual reserve effects. Thus, we must test if the magnitude of a response (e.g., greater biomass of a target species inside reserves relative to outside the reserves) at the scale of the network ($M_{network}$, i.e., both inside and outside marine reserves) is greater than the sum of the magnitudes of change occurring in individual reserves ($M_{reserve}$). In other words, there is a synergistic interaction occurring among marine reserves, such that:

$$M_{network} = \sum M_{reserve} + M_{interaction}$$

where $M_{interaction}$ is the magnitude of the interaction effect for the reserves within a network, and the hypothesis to be tested is:

$$H : M_{interaction} > 0.$$

For example, comparing a well-enforced connectivity network to a well-enforced regional network where connectivity is assumed to be zero would demonstrate the added ecological value of a connectivity network. The evaluation of this effect would require both consideration of the overall goals of the network, which vary with the type of network (see Table 11.1), and data from a rigorously designed monitoring program at the appropriate scale with suitable controls at both local and regional levels. Below we discuss the challenges associated with meeting this often-unrealistic set of requirements.

11.4 Empirically assessing marine reserve networks

11.4.1 Experimental designs for network assessments

Ideally, quantitative monitoring of densities and sizes for algae, fish, and invertebrates (inside marine reserves and in unprotected areas inside and outside the network), catch (in unprotected areas inside and outside the network), and socio-economic indicators will be used to assess whether networks are achieving their goals. In addition, measuring the extent of connectivity among marine reserves and between reserves and open areas is a key consideration for evaluating network effects and distinguishing between local self-recruitment and long-distance dispersal (Jones *et al.*, 2009). The major challenges of selecting an optimal monitoring design for networks are: (1) sufficient sample replication; (2) avoidance of spatial confounding; and (3) appropriate temporal replication (Willis *et al.*, 2003). Beyond these, the essentially non-random placement of reserves (which can largely result from selecting sites to include unique features, facilitate ease of enforcement, or protect the most productive habitats) presents another challenge for analysis. The limited resources available for monitoring in many management contexts make it prohibitive to collect every type of data, requiring prioritization of the extensive data wish-list (Costello *et al.*, 2010).

The range of sampling designs for assessing ecological effects in an area includes Control–Impact (CI), Before–After (BA), Before–After–Control–Impact (BACI), and BACI–Paired Series (BACIPS). Applied to a single marine reserve assessment, CI designs sample multiple sites at the impact location (marine reserve) and at an adjacent unprotected location as the control site. The sampling scheme may include repeated comparisons over time, but this design does not include data collected before reserve establishment. Such CI designs are limited because spatial variation between control and impact sites are confounded with the reserve effect unless multiple control locations are used (Glasby, 1997). The underlying, untested assumption is that control and impact sites were similar *before* the marine reserve was established. Although several reviews have indicated that these designs can show significant reserve effects (e.g., Halpern, 2003), the interpretation of these studies is still somewhat ambiguous and they are insufficient in distinguishing between local and regional effects (Osenberg *et al.*, 2006) unless compiled within a regional meta-analysis and weighted by the among-controls component of variation (Claudet *et al.*, 2008). Similarly, BA designs with no controls are limited because reserve effects are confounded with temporal variation; BACI designs require simultaneously sampling an impact and control site both before and after reserve establishment, and BACIPS designs control for both spatial and temporal variation when multiple paired control and impacts locations are sampled simultaneously several times before and after marine reserves are established (Figure 11.2A and B) (Underwood, 1991; Osenberg *et al.*, 2006). As conservation targets change over time in response to protection within a marine reserve

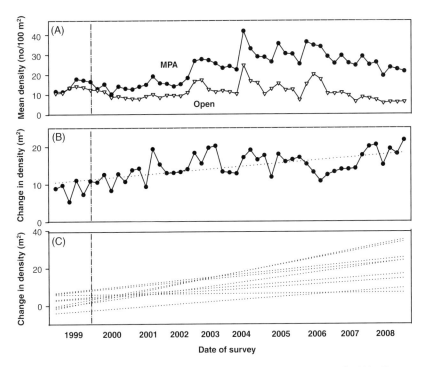

Figure 11.2 Illustration of reserve network effects and suitable controls. (A) The mean density of fish (*Zebrasoma flavescens*) in nine reserves and five controls sites in Hawaii, (B) mean change in density between reserves and control sites, and (C) changes in density in nine reserves relative to pooled control sites. (T. Tissot, W. Walsh, and I. Williams, unpublished data.)

network, each reserve might have a different trajectory relative to controls (Figure 11.2C). Few marine reserve studies to date have used BACI (9%) and even fewer have used the most statistically powerful BACIPS design (Lison de Loma *et al.*, 2008), while 70% of marine reserve studies have used a CI design (Osenberg *et al.*, 2006). In reality, few marine reserve studies have biological data taken before implementation because MPA design is usually ad hoc and driven by a number of agendas, with science just one of many. In addition, the strongest BA designs require a time series of monitoring before the enforcement of reserves. This means that monitoring has to be planned well in advance of reserve establishment, a decision or opportunity rarely available in reality.

Unless a BA analysis is used, the selection of appropriate control locations is a critical component of a sound monitoring scheme. A good control location should have similar habitat and community structure

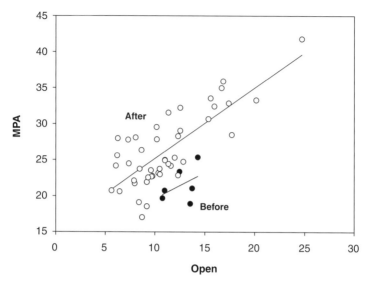

Figure 11.3 A response variable shows temporal covariation between reserves and control sites before and after reserve establishment, demonstrating that sites with high temporal concordance minimize non-treatment effects and provide more power to detect a reserve effect. (Tissot, Walsh, and Williams, unpublished data.)

(Friedlander *et al.*, 2007a) and display temporal variation similar to the marine reserve (temporal tracking: Osenberg *et al.*, 2006; Lison de Loma *et al.*, 2008) with respect to the response variable(s) measured, also called temporal concordance (Figure 11.3). Sites that have high temporal concordance minimize non-treatment effects and provide more power to detect a reserve effect (Osenberg *et al.*, 2006; Lison de Loma *et al.*, 2008). Thus, both temporal concordance and site similarity are important for control locations. To be effective, reserve network monitoring schemes should include a sufficient number of control sites located within the network (which should be adjacent to and dispersed among marine reserves with spacing distances in proportion to the dispersal distances of target species) and control locations outside the network. In addition, if fishing effort varies among control sites, monitored locations should be situated and replicated adequately to capture this variability.

Power analyses are essential to marine reserve network evaluations in order to ensure that sufficient sampling is occurring relative to expected reserve effect sizes (Lison de Loma *et al.*, 2008). Power analyses should address both type I and type II statistical errors relative to the costs of their consequences (Mapstone, 1996), the length of time required to detect an effect (Field *et al.*, 2007), financial costs (Field *et al.*, 2004), and logistical constraints relative to experimental design (Tissot *et al.*, 2004). Since resources often limit the frequency and extent of sampling efforts after reserve designation, important choices need to be made regarding the timing and allocation of sampling efforts. Stratification of sampling effort by habitat and other variables can help to homogenize variance within strata and reduce overall variability, therefore reducing the overall sampling effort. If data are only available from inside and outside paired areas without an adequate time span, a space-for-time substitution may be used (e.g., Friedlander *et al.*, 2007b), but a large sample size is often required to achieve sufficient statistical power (Pickett, 1989).

Importantly, although very difficult to achieve, the monitoring program must separate local from regional marine reserve effects to evaluate the regional effects of a network (Hamilton *et al.*, 2010). Controls adjacent to reserves will be influenced by both local marine reserve effects and regional variation influencing both control and protected sites. Ideally the system of controls must operate at the same scale as the network in order to control for regional variability as well as assess the contribution of the network at the regional scale. The control system should be close enough to the network to be similarly affected by oceanographic and weather conditions and experience similar levels of fishing effort outside reserves. The prediction is that fishing yields outside a marine reserve near the network will be higher than those of a control system without a network (Osenberg *et al.*, 2006). An ideal situation might be two adjacent islands, one with and one without a reserve network, or an island near a mainland. However, the criteria listed above are rarely met, and even then may only be possible for the smallest reserve networks with nearby locations that are amenable to control comparisons. Further, given the time and energy required to monitor a marine reserve, let alone even a small marine reserve network, the logistical and financial considerations associated with such an endeavor would be high.

From a practical point of view, when the ideal criteria cannot be met (e.g., Before data, paired sample series, appropriate controls), there are still ways to assess the ecological effectiveness of a network, although with less power than the ideal framework outlined above. The main question addressed by a reserve network assessment is whether the network effect as a whole is greater than the sum of its individual reserve effects (see equation above). Thus a weighted meta-analytical approach to Beyond-CI designs could help to address this issue while minimizing the inherent loss of power from foregoing the ideal monitoring design. The reserves within the network would act as the impacted locations (with adequate nested spatial factors to assess not only the among-reserves variability but also the within-reserve variability of the response analyzed, e.g., fish density), and reserves outside the network would act as multiple controls. To cope with the among-controls variability that could potentially mask the overall network effect, the reserves acting as controls should either be set in areas similar to the network area or they should be numerous enough to capture the majority of the underlying spatial variability. The choice of reserves as control locations is similar to the choice of control locations in Beyond-CI or Beyond-BACI designs. A weighting scheme should be built to incorporate the within-reserves variability and obtain an overall weighted effect size of the response to protection. If the effect size is positive and the confidence interval does not overlap the null effect, the response variable is significantly higher in the network than in the control locations, and we can indirectly conclude that the whole is greater than the sum of its parts.

If it is impossible to adequately assess the ecological effectiveness of a given network (e.g., for the myriad reasons outlined above), monitoring programs should meanwhile focus on connectivity. Measuring and optimizing connectivity among the components of a given network should be part of the main monitoring goals, as connectivity among reserves within a network is the only underlying factor that could make, from an ecological point of view, the whole greater than the sum of its parts. Connectivity among the reserves within a network could therefore be an indirect indicator of network performance. Below we address the inclusion of connectivity data in monitoring programs for reserve network assessments.

11.4.2 Practical considerations for assessing connectivity in a network

Connectivity within a network can occur when juveniles and adults move across boundaries of marine reserves to and from outside areas and/or when larvae are transported away from marine reserves to other reserves in the network or fished areas outside the reserves. Thus, an understanding of habitat connectivity is critical in the assessment (and design) of marine reserve networks. If reserves are to maintain ecosystem integrity and structure, all necessary components for ensuring ecosystem function must be included within the network. A seascape approach may be used to characterize ecosystem patterns within and outside a network at scales appropriate to the resources and their users (Pittman *et al.*, 2007; Wedding *et al.*, 2008). Digital benthic habitat maps can provide valuable and spatially discrete ecological criteria that can be integrated in GIS and used to help define spatial and temporal distributions by life stage of fishes and invertebrates, determine species habitat affinities, and understand ecological connections among habitats (Monaco *et al.*, 1998; Friedlander *et al.*, 2007b; Purkis *et al.*, 2008). This integrated approach aids in defining large-scale community structure and in addressing specific questions about particular families of economically and ecologically important species at appropriate scales for management within a network (Pittman *et al.*, 2007).

In order to sample organisms across the seascape more effectively and examine habitat utilization patterns of juveniles and adults, complementary methods that incorporate movement patterns need to be employed (Chapman *et al.*, 2005). The rate at which fish disperse from marine reserves can be determined using active "tag and release" methodologies, with fish being "recaptured" either through fishing activity or underwater visual surveys. Acoustic telemetry, especially the use of automated tracking via listening stations (e.g., passive acoustic monitoring), is an alternative and effective way to track the movement patterns of individual fish, allowing for direct measurement of adult movement within and among reserves and outside areas. This passive approach can be accomplished over much longer time periods and greater spatial scales (Heupel *et al.*, 2006; Nielsen *et al.*, 2009). Information gained from tracking or monitoring tagged fishes can help to explain immigration/emigration, residence time, habitat preference, site fidelity, and many other key life history traits, all of which have important implications for the effectiveness of marine reserves (Meyer *et al.*, 2000; Lowe *et al.*, 2003). Further, traditional knowledge of the timing and location of fish movement patterns and spawning is highly relevant to network design and helps to engage local communities in network design and evaluation (Johannes, 1981).

Larval dispersal and recruitment also play an important role in marine reserve network effectiveness (Planes *et al.*, 2009). An effective reserve network design will protect populations and enhance both protected and non-protected populations through larval dispersal. Because the great majority of marine organisms have planktonic larvae that are exposed to varying oceanographic regimes during their larval phase, current profilers and other measures of ocean circulation patterns are helpful in determining dispersal potential and retention capability of larvae (Cowen, 2002;

Cudney-Bueno *et al.*, 2009). To identify whether some sites within the network are receiving greater numbers of dispersing larvae and settling juveniles, larval supply and early juvenile recruitment can be monitored by *in situ* surveys (Tissot *et al.*, 2004) and standardized collecting devices such as tows, light traps, channel nets, and other collectors (Dufour *et al.*, 1996; Fisher and Bellwood, 2002; Sponaugle *et al.*, 2003; Ammann, 2004). However, measurements of realized connectivity remain challenging to obtain (Pelc *et al.*, 2010). Larval behavior coupled with physical oceanographic models can predict potential sources and sinks of larvae across a network, leading to a greater understanding of potential patterns of connectivity among sites (Cowen *et al.*, 2006; Paris *et al.*, 2007). Because productivity and trace-element concentrations differ between coastal and oceanic water masses, otoliths can be used to reconstruct the dispersal history of larvae (Swearer *et al.*, 1999; Thorrold *et al.*, 2007) and examine population connectivity, spawning behavior, and stock associations in a number of fish species (Thorrold *et al.*, 2001). Transgenerational tagging of larvae using enriched stable isotopes allows for the transmission of markers from spawning females to the otoliths of embryos, who then retain the tags that are detectable upon capture as recruits (Thorrold *et al.*, 2006). Recent developments in genetics are also essential for demonstrating connectivity via genetic markers (Planes *et al.*, 2009) and for determining the proportion of self-recruitment and dispersal for target species, a fundamental issue in network assessment and design (see Chapter 12). Although data for larval connectivity are still lacking for most systems, patterns of dispersal based on pelagic larval duration, estimated larval dispersal kernels, and/or the predictions of coupled biophysical models are currently used to design connectivity networks in some contexts (Palumbi, 2004; Kaplan *et al.*, 2009; Costello *et al.*, 2010).

11.5 The need for interactive empirical modeling approaches

In the vast majority of cases, full monitoring with a balanced BACIPS design will be impossible to achieve empirically, and spatial predictions generated from coupled ocean circulation–metapopulation models can serve as model experiments to examine the expected benefits from the implemented marine reserve network. For example, one can ask how the ecosystem and fisheries responses would change if each reserve existed in isolation and compare the individual reserve responses to how ecosystems and fisheries respond to the fully implemented spatial network. A spatially explicit model can be run with each marine reserve in isolation and with the entire network as a whole. Differences in spatially explicit population changes (e.g., abundance, size structures, recruitment) are a measure of the hypothesized network benefits. These forecasts can be compared to empirical monitoring results to see if locations projected to receive large network benefits actually perform better than other areas along the coastline.

For example, three-dimensional ocean circulation models coupled with spatially explicit models of the dynamics of fished species and fishermen have been used to evaluate the projected impact on abundance and fishery yield of all MPA designs submitted in California's Marine Life Protection Act (MLPA), which mandates the design and management of a network of marine protected areas (CDFG, 2008). These spatially explicit metapopulation models predict spatial and temporal patterns of larval production and replenishment, which in turn predict resulting geographic patterns of adult abundance, size structure, biomass and spawning potential, and levels of population sustainability (White *et al.*, 2008; Kaplan *et al.*, 2009). These models use estimated larval dispersal kernels, habitat distribution, and fishing mortality (inside and outside reserves) to generate predictions of current and future population distributions. Empirical estimates of abundance, size structure, and recruitment rates derived from monitoring studies are used both to parameterize these population models and to evaluate model predictions. These predictions include both the spatial patterns of network performance (i.e., which reserve and non-reserve populations are likely to respond to reserve establishment) and sustainable population levels arising at equilibrium under a given set of management conditions. Integrating key components of these models with other process models can enhance their predictive capabilities. For example, coupled biophysical–oceanographic models combined with larval traits (e.g., pelagic duration, depth distribution, behavior) (Cowen *et al.*, 2000; Cowen *et al.*, 2006; Mitarai *et al.*, 2009; Berkley *et al.*, 2010; Watson *et al.*, 2010) can refine estimates of connectivity among populations inside and outside reserves. Similarly, ecosystem models that incorporate multiple species within a network based on functional roles or trophic interactions can extend these metapopulation models to metacommunity–ecosystem models (e.g., Guichard *et al.*, 2004; Baskett *et al.*, 2007) and can further predict how entire ecosystems will respond to network-wide patterns of population connectivity generated by marine reserves. Ecosystem models can also identify responses such as trophic cascades that would not be detected based on single species responses.

Therefore, by comparing model predictions (e.g., region-wide state of populations and ecosystems) made using assumptions of network connectivity and larval subsidies to predictions made under the assumption of no reserve interaction or no reserve establishment (e.g., removing certain reserves one at a time from the network to assess their contribution to overall network performance), it is possible to estimate the magnitude and geographical scale of network interaction effects. Thus, the monitoring–modeling approach provides a robust framework for predicting short- and long-term regional responses of populations and ecosystems to the establishment of reserve networks as well as testable predictions.

Model predictions can also inform the design of monitoring programs. For example, models can predict not only the magnitude of change in response variables but also the likely degree of associated spatial and temporal variability (Joseph *et al.*, 2009). This allows monitoring to be streamlined, with effort optimally allocated to sampling designs that increase the likelihood of detecting responses (i.e., the number and distribution of spatial and temporal replicates). Thus an iterative approach in which empirical data from monitoring informs models, and models, in turn, refine monitoring designs, can enhance the responsive management of monitoring programs.

11.6 Specific challenges at varying spatial and temporal scales

Each of the above approaches for assessing network effects, whether empirical or model-based, shares common implications for the design of evaluation programs. To be most informative, monitoring that is sufficiently intensive at the scale of individual reserves (inside and outside) but also comprehensive across all reserves of a particular ecosystem type will enable scientists, managers, stakeholders, and policy-makers to assess reserve performance at varying spatial scales. Because each reserve in a network may have been designed with specific and different objectives, assessment of individual reserves allows managers to determine if each is achieving its particular goals. By comparing subsets of reserves that include similar habitats yet vary in design criteria (e.g., spacing, size, habitat area, depth range, or permitted activities), decision-makers can assess the effects of these design differences and make their decisions accordingly. Sampling and assessment across spatial scales also provide managers and policy-makers with a foundation for adaptively managing networks of reserves.

Given the likely financial and logistic limitations to implementing "perfect" monitoring programs, a key objective of a network evaluation program will require identifying sets of representative reserves that can support network-wide inferences of system response. Subsampling representative reserves across the network will reduce the overall number of reserves sampled yet can still allow inferences at larger scales. At the scale of the entire network, inferences about the general response of a species or ecosystem to protection by a particular reserve designation (i.e., partial vs. complete protection, buffer zone vs. reserve) can be drawn and used to predict the effects of new or unsampled MPAs in similar environments and study regions. Central to this goal is characterizing geographic patterns of environmental variation and ecosystem structure to assure a representative sample of that variation (Hamilton *et al.*, 2010). For example, in 2003, a network of reserves and other types of MPAs was implemented in the northern Channel Islands, California, USA. The network of reserves spans a major environmental and biogeographic gradient, making it a challenge to assess network-wide responses of many species. In order to deal with large environmental variation over relatively small geographic distances, geographic patterns in community structure of kelp forest communities were first delineated to determine the scale at which sites could be grouped for analysis (Hamilton *et al.*, 2010).

Protection within reserves can lead to a variety of direct and indirect effects occurring at different times after network establishment (Chapter 2). Due to the wide diversity of life history traits and demographic rates (e.g., generation times, recruitment episodes) of protected species, an optimal sampling frequency will involve a balance between sufficient temporal resolution to capture rapidly responding species and lower frequency and longer-term sampling appropriate for characterizing species that respond slowly.

11.7 Humans as key players in the success of marine reserve networks

Effective marine reserve networks cannot occur without explicitly considering the role of humans in marine ecosystems, both as impacting and protecting forces (Shackeroff *et al.*, 2009). Marine reserves are in essence a human construct and cannot succeed without the cooperation of local resource users, whose compliance can be critical for overall reserve success (Guidetti and Claudet, 2010; Pollnac *et al.*, 2010). Monitoring of the human dimension of marine reserves should encompass detailed information about changes in local uses including fisheries, public feedback and impact assessments for coastal populations, and other anthropological data sets illustrating the interplay between the public and the marine resources protected via reserve networks. However, these data are largely lacking for the great majority of single reserves and networks, and their integration into monitoring programs needs to increase in order to fully understand how coupled social–natural systems respond to establishment of marine reserves. Indeed, information about how human communities have responded to single reserves can contribute to effective implementation when scaling up from single reserves to regional networks, such as in the Philippines (Lowry *et al.*, 2009).

The human dimension should also be included in the planning, design, and assessment phases of a reserve network. Support from politicians, decision-makers, and stakeholders throughout the process of planning, implementing, and evaluating a reserve network is critical. In West Hawaii, success was largely driven by synergy among key individuals with diverse skills from different worldviews and institutions (legislature, state resource agency, state extension agent, university researchers, non-governmental organizations) that came together to build a holistic, integrative solution to marine resource issues (Tissot *et al.*, 2009). Community support was derived from a long history (several decades) of forming working groups, advisory groups, and both formal and informal education activities (Capitini *et al.*, 2004). A key factor was the presence of both top–down and bottom–up support. The local communities need to "buy in" and support the idea, but there also needs to be governmental support via legislation, administrative rule-making, management, and enforcement.

Past experiences have shown that many management networks succeed primarily because stakeholders were involved in these processes, usually from the beginning. Recent adaptive management of the Great Barrier Reef Marine Park, which resulted in the increase of total no-take area in the park from 4.5% to 33%, involved extensive stakeholder input via 31 000 public comments and public forums facilitated by a staff trained to garner the input of the general populace (Fernandes *et al.*, 2005). Stakeholders in West Hawaii were organized into the West Hawaii Fishery Council, which made recommendations about the size, shape, and location of the MPA network to the state resource agency (Tissot,

2005; Tissot *et al.*, 2009). The Fishery Council, which involved both regional and stakeholder representation, provided not only a process to generate the location of the reserves and other MPAs, but also a means to resolve conflicts among the diverse members of the community. California's Initiative to implement the MLPA (CDFG, 2008) has worked to build bottom–up support by heavily involving stakeholders at all levels of the MPA planning process (Klein *et al.*, 2008). Stakeholders representing major interests (e.g., recreational fishing, commercial fishing, tribal or environmental groups) have contributed input throughout the process via several mechanisms including educational workshops held in local communities as well as the participation in regional stakeholder groups (RSGs). The RSGs from each region develop MPA proposals which are reviewed and evaluated by a Science Advisory Team (SAT), the California Department of Fish and Game, MLPA Initiative staff, the public and a policy-level Blue Ribbon Task Force (BRTF). The MPA proposals are then refined by the RSGs in an iterative process and eventually presented to the BRTF, who makes a recommendation to the California Fish and Game Commission. Stakeholders' involvement has been critical for generating acceptance of what will be the largest network of reserves in the continental USA. Levels of community involvement such as these have also been key to the ecological success of single reserves in areas such as the West Indian Ocean, South Pacific, and Caribbean (Pollnac *et al.*, 2010).

The perception of a reserve network's success is integrally linked to stakeholders' expectations of network effects and timelines. Scientific education can help communicate information that promotes a more realistic awareness of the potential benefits and limitations of reserve networks. Conversely, failure to demonstrate beneficial effects to the stakeholders usually translates into failure to establish a persistent management network. In Moorea, French Polynesia, where support from politicians and decision-makers has been strong, fishermen in general have not been informed of the real impacts of protection on commercial fish populations, such as the time lag necessary to document actual reserve effects on biological communities. As a result, poaching has been a standard observation inside the networked reserves, particularly where enforcement is poor (Gaspar and Bambridge, 2008).

Finally, jurisdictional differences at regional scales can represent a major pitfall to the establishment and assessment of reserve networks at the regional scale. Habitat and species distribution at sea do not necessarily correspond to political and jurisdictional boundaries, yet most conservation programs are applied at national or subnational levels (Kark *et al.*, 2009). Effective conservation and resources management therefore require cooperation among administrative and political entities. Transboundary networks are a way to cope with issues of fisheries operating across political boundaries (Sandwith *et al.*, 2001), although these networks are very difficult to put into practice because administrative sovereignty is at stake. Very few examples of transboundary marine parks (and not marine reserve networks) exist worldwide, occurring primarily in coastal areas with many bordering nations such as the Mediterranean Sea, where the Pelagos Sanctuary spans France, Monaco, and Italy (Notarbartolo-DiSciara *et al.*, 2008) and the Marine Park of the Strait of Bonifacio is located between Corsica (France) and Sardinia (Italy). In the Mediterranean, a region with 23 coastal countries whose scientists and managers are usually willing to collaborate, past experience illustrates the extreme difficulty in establishing transborder reserve networks from an administrative point of view. Conversely, in some places like the South Pacific, where traditional practices are still strong and shared by many countries, there may be opportunities to use these traditional common grounds and transcend jurisdictional differences. In the Polynesian/Melanesian societies, coral reefs are traditionally perceived as a village's territory extension and are often still managed accordingly. The "Rahui" system (which involves closing some reef areas for a varying amount of time) was shared by many societies, from French Polynesia to New Zealand, and is still officially occurring in countries such as the Cook Islands and New Zealand (Johannes, 1982).

11.8 Conclusion

As reserve networks are implemented more and more frequently, it becomes ever more necessary to adequately define these management tools and implement thoughtful and rigorous monitoring plans to assess their effectiveness. While connectivity remains a driving goal when establishing a network, the other types of networks defined here can accomplish their own set of protective objectives, and thus it is essential to carefully consider which network type is most in line with the stated goals. Prior to network establishment, thorough monitoring designs should account for outside, inside, control, and experimental reserve sampling across an appropriate spatial and temporal scale, prioritizing the data types most critical for assessing network effects. The reality of logistical constraints necessitates the coupling of models with empirical data to test network hypotheses as well as the integration of public support for ensuring network compliance. We assert that a thorough discussion of all these key components should become a regular part of the network planning process and that regional management bodies, scientists, and stakeholders should interact to develop optimal monitoring strategies given the resources at hand.

11.9 Acknowledgments

We thank M. Gomei for useful discussions about social networks. This paper is an outcome of a symposium organized by the Communication Partnership for Science and the Sea (COMPASS) and the Partnership for Interdisciplinary Studies of Coastal Oceans (PISCO) and held at the 2009 International Marine Conservation Congress in Washington, DC. TLDL would like to thank the French Agency for MPAs for their financial support during the symposium. This is contribution 392 from PISCO, the Partnership for Interdisciplinary Studies of Coastal Oceans, funded primarily by the Gordon and Betty Moore Foundation and David and Lucile Packard Foundation.

References

Allison, G. W., Gaines, S. D., Lubchenco, J., and Possingham, H. P. (2003). Ensuring persistence of marine reserves: catastrophes require adopting an insurance factor. *Ecological Applications*, **13**, S8–S24.

Almany, G. R., Connolly, S. R., Heath, D. D., *et al.* (2009). Connectivity, biodiversity conservation and the design of marine reserve networks for coral reefs. *Coral Reefs*, **28**, 339–51.

Ammann, A. J. (2004). SMURFs: standard monitoring units for the recruitment of temperate reef fishes. *Journal of Experimental Marine Biology and Ecology*, **299**, 135–54.

Baskett, M. L., Micheli, F., and Levin, S. A. (2007). Designing marine reserves for interacting species: insights from theory. *Biological Conservation*, **137**, 163–79.

Beech, T., Dowd, M., Field, C., Hatcher, B., and Andrefouet, S. (2008). A stochastic approach to marine reserve design: incorporating data uncertainty. *Ecological Informatics*, **3**, 321–33.

Berkley, H. A., Kendall, B. E., Mitarai, S., and Siegel, D. A. (2010). Turbulent dispersal promotes species coexistence. *Ecology Letters*, **13**, 360–71.

Browman, H. I. and Stergiou, K. I. (2004). Marine protected areas as a central element of ecosystem-based management: defining their location, size and number. *Marine Ecology Progress Series*, **274**, 271–2.

Capitini, C. A., Tissot, B. N., Carroll, M. S., Walsh, W. J., and Peck, S. (2004). Competing perspectives in resource protection: the case of marine protected areas in west Hawai'i. *Society and Natural Resources*, **17**, 763–78.

CBD (2006). *Decisions Adopted by the Conference of the Parties to the Convention on Biological Diversity at its Eighth Meeting* (Decision VIII/15, Annex IV). Curitiba, Brazil: Convention on Biological Diversity.

CDFG (2008). *California Marine Life Protection Act: Master Plan for Marine Protected Areas*, revised draft January 2008. Sacramento, CA: California Department of Fish and Game.

Chapman, D. D., Pikitch, E. K., Babcock, E. A., and Shivji, M. S. (2005). Marine reserve design and evaluation using automated acoustic telemetry: a case-study involving coral reef-associated sharks in the Mesoamerican Caribbean. *Marine Technology Society Journal*, **39**, 42–55.

Claudet, J. and Pelletier, D. (2004). Marine protected areas and artificial reefs: A review of the interactions between management and scientific studies. *Aquatic Living Resources*, **17**, 129–38.

Claudet, J., Osenberg, C. W., Benedetti-Cecchi, L., *et al.* (2008). Marine reserves: size and age do matter. *Ecology Letters*, **11**, 481–9.

Costello, C., Rassweiler, A., Siegel, D., *et al.* (2010). The value of spatial information in MPA network design. *Proceedings of the National Academy of Sciences of the United States of America*, **107**, 18 294–9.

Cowen, R. K. (2002). Oceanographic influences on larval dispersal and retention and their consequences for population connectivity. In *Coral Reef Fishes*, ed. P. F. Sale. York: Academic Press, pp. 149–70.

Cowen, R. K., Lwiza, K. M. M., Sponaugle, S., Paris, C. B., and Olson, D. B. (2000). Connectivity of marine populations: open or closed? *Science*, **287**, 857–9.

Cowen, R. K., Paris, C. B., and Srinivasan, A. (2006). Scaling of connectivity in marine populations. *Science*, **311**, 522–7.

Cudney-Bueno, R., Lavin, M. F., Marinone, S. G., Raimondi, P. T., and Shaw, W. W. (2009). Rapid effects of marine reserves via larval dispersal. *PLoS One*, **4**.

Dufour, V., Ricklet, E., and Lo-Yat, A. (1996). Colonization of reef fishes at Moorea Island, French Polynesia: temporal and spatial variation of the larval flux. *Marine and Freshwater Research*, **47**, 413–22.

Eisma-Osorio, R. L., Amolo, R. C., Maypa, A. P., White, A. T., and Christie, P. (2009). Scaling up local government initiatives toward ecosystem-based fisheries management in southeast Cebu Island, Philippines. *Coastal Management*, **37**, 291–307.

Fernandes, L., Day, J., Lewis, A., *et al.* (2005). Establishing representative no-take areas in the Great Barrier Reef: large-scale implementation of theory on marine protected areas. *Conservation Biology*, **19**, 1733–44.

Field, S. A., Tyre, A. J., Jonzen, N., Rhodes, J. R., and Possingham, H. P. (2004). Minimizing the cost of environmental management decisions by optimizing thresholds. *Ecology Letters*, **7**, 669–75.

Field, S. A., O'Connor, D. J., Tyre, A. J., and Possingham, H. P. (2007). Making monitoring meaningful. *Austral Ecology*, **32**, 485–91.

Fisher, R. and Bellwood, D. R. (2002). The influence of swimming speed on sustained swimming performance of late-stage reef fish larvae. *Marine Biology*, **140**, 801–7.

Friedlander, A. M., Brown, E., and Monaco, M. E. (2007a). Defining reef fish habitat utilization patterns in Hawaii: comparisons between marine protected areas and areas open to fishing. *Marine Ecology Progress Series*, **351**, 221–33.

Friedlander, A. M., Brown, E. K., and Monaco, M. E. (2007b). Coupling ecology and GIS to evaluate efficacy of marine protected areas in Hawaii. *Ecological Applications*, **17**, 715–30.

Gaines, S. D., White, C., Carr, M. H., and Palumbi, S. (2010). Designing marine reserve networks for both conservation and fisheries management. *Proceedings of the National Academy of Sciences of the United States of America*, **107**, 18 286–93.

Gaspar, C. and Bambridge, T. (2008). Territorialités et aires marines protégées à Moorea (Polynésie française). *Journal de la Société des Océanistes*, 2008, 126–7.

Gerber, L. R., Botsford, L. W., Hastings, A., *et al.* (2003). Population models for marine reserve design: a retrospective and prospective synthesis. *Ecological Applications*, **13**, S47–S64.

Glasby, T. M. (1997). Analysing data from post-impact studies using asymmetrical analysis of variance: a case study of epibiota on marinas. *Australian Journal of Ecology*, **22**, 448–59.

Guichard, F., Levin, S. A., Hastings, A., and Siegel, D. (2004). Toward a dynamic metacommunity approach to marine reserve theory. *BioScience*, **54**, 1003–11.

Guidetti, P. and Claudet, J. (2010). Comanagement practices enhance fisheries in marine protected areas. *Conservation Biology*, **24**, 312–18.

Halpern, B. S. (2003). The impact of marine reserves: do reserves work and does reserve size matter? *Ecological Applications*, **13**, S117–S137.

Halpern, B. S., Walbridge, S., Selkoe, K. A., *et al.* (2008). A global map of human impact on marine ecosystems. *Science*, **319**, 948–52.

Hamilton, S. L., Caselle, J. E., Malone, D., and Carr, M. H. (2010). Incorporating biogeography into evaluations of the Channel Islands marine reserve network. *Proceedings of the National Academy of Sciences of the United States of America*, **107**, 18 272–7.

Hastings, A. and Botsford, L. W. (2003). Comparing designs of marine reserves for fisheries and for biodiversity. *Ecological Applications*, **13**, S65–S70.

Heupel, M. R., Semmons, J. M., and Hobday, A. J. (2006). Automated acoustic tracking of aquatic animals: scales, design and deployment of listening station arrays. *Marine and Freshwater Research*, **57**, 1–13.

IUCN-WCPA (2008). *Establishing Marine Protected Area Networks: Making It happen.* Washington, DC: IUCN World Commission on Protected Areas, National Oceanic and Atmospheric Administration, and The Nature Conservancy.

Jackson, J. B. C. (2008). Ecological extinction and evolution in the brave new ocean. *Proceedings of the National Academy of Sciences of the United States of America*, **105**, 11 458–65.

Johannes, R. E. (1981). Working with fishermen to improve coastal tropical fisheries and resource management. *Bulletin of Marine Science*, **31**, 673–80.

Johannes, R. E. (1982). Traditional conservation methods and protected marine areas in Oceania. *Ambio*, **11**, 258–61.

Jones, G. P., Almany, G. R., Russ, G. R., *et al.* (2009). Larval retention and connectivity among populations of corals and reef fishes: history, advances and challenges. *Coral Reefs*, **28**, 307–25.

Joseph, L. N., Elkin, C., Martin, T. G., and Possingham, H. P. (2009). Modeling abundance using N-mixture models: the importance of considering ecological mechanisms. *Ecological Applications*, **19**, 631–42.

Kaplan, D. M., Botsford, L. W., O'Farrell, M. R., Gaines, S. D., and Jorgensen, S. (2009). Model-based assessment of persistence in proposed marine protected area designs. *Ecological Applications*, **19**, 433–48.

Kark, S., Levin, N., Grantham, H. S., and Possingham, H. P. (2009). Between-country collaboration and consideration of costs increase conservation planning efficiency in the Mediterranean Basin. *Proceedings of the National Academy of Sciences of the United States of America*, **106**, 15 368–73.

Klein, C. J., Chan, A., Kircher, L., *et al.* (2008). Striking a balance between biodiversity conservation and socioeconomic viability in the design of marine protected areas. *Conservation Biology*, **22**, 691–700.

Lester, S. E. and Halpern, B. S. (2008). Biological responses in marine no-take reserves versus partially protected areas. *Marine Ecology Progress Series*, **367**, 49–56.

Lester, S. E., Halpern, B. S., Grorud-Colvert, K., *et al.* (2009). Biological effects within no-take marine reserves: a global synthesis. *Marine Ecology Progress Series*, **384**, 33–46.

Levin, P. S., Kaplan, I., Grober-Dunsmore, R., *et al.* (2009). A framework for assessing the biodiversity and fishery aspects of marine reserves. *Journal of Applied Ecology*, **46**, 735–42.

Lison de Loma, T., Osenberg, C. W., Shima, J. S., *et al.* (2008). A framework for assessing impacts of marine protected areas in Moorea (French Polynesia). *Pacific Science*, **62**, 431–41.

Lotze, H. K., Lenihan, H. S., Bourque, B. J., *et al.* (2006). Depletion, degradation, and recovery potential of estuaries and coastal seas. *Science*, **312**, 1806–9.

Lowe, C. G., Topping, D. T., Cartamil, D. P., and Papastamatiou, Y. P. (2003). Movement patterns, home range, and habitat utilization of adult kelp bass *Paralabrax clathratus* in a temperate no-take marine reserve. *Marine Ecology Progress Series*, **256**, 205–16.

Lowry, G. K., White, A. T., and Christie, P. (2009). Scaling up to networks of marine protected areas in the Philippines: biophysical, legal, institutional, and social considerations. *Coastal Management*, **37**, 274–90.

Lubchenco, J., Palumbi, S. R., Gaines, S. D., and Andelman, S. (2003). Plugging a hole in the ocean: the emerging science of marine reserves. *Ecological Applications*, **13**, S3–S7.

Mapstone, B. (1996). Scalable decision criteria for environmental impact assessment: effect size, Type I, and Type II errors. In *Detecting Ecological Impacts: Concepts and Applications in Coastal Habitats*, eds. R. J. Schmitt and C. W. Osenberg. San Diego, CA: Academic Press, pp. 67–79.

Meyer, C. G., Holland, K. N., Wetherbee, B. M., and Lowe, C. G. (2000). Movement patterns, habitat utilization, home range size and site fidelity of whitesaddle goatfish, *Parupeneus porphyreus*, in a marine reserve. *Environmental Biology of Fishes*, **59**, 235–42.

Mitarai, S., Siegel, D. A., Watson, J. R., Dong, C., and McWilliams, J. C. (2009). Quantifying connectivity in the coastal ocean with application to the Southern California Bight. *Journal of Geophysical Research – Oceans*, **114**. doi: 10.1029/2008JC005166.

Molloy, P. P., McLean, I. B., and Cote, I. M. (2009). Effects of marine reserve age on fish populations: a global meta-analysis. *Journal of Applied Ecology*, **46**, 743–51.

Monaco, M. E., Weisberg, S. B., and Lowery, T. A. (1998). Summer habitat affinities of estuarine fish in US mid-Atlantic coastal systems. *Fisheries Management and Ecology*, **5**, 161–71.

Murray, S. N., Ambrose, R. F., Bohnsack, J. A., *et al.* (1999). No-take reserve networks: sustaining fishery populations and marine ecosystems. *Fisheries*, **24**, 11–25.

Nielsen, J., Sibert, J., Hobday, A. J., *et al.* (eds.) (2009). *Tagging and Tracking of Marine Animals with Electronic Devices*. New York: Springer.

Notarbartolo-DiSciara, G., Agardy, T., Hyrenbach, D., Scovazzi, T., and Van Klaveren, P. (2008). The Pelagos Sanctuary for Mediterranean marine mammals. *Aquatic Conservation: Marine and Freshwater Ecosystems*, **18**, 367–91.

NRC (2001). *Marine Protected Areas: Tools for Sustaining Ocean Ecosystems*. Washington, DC: National Academy Press.

Osenberg, C. W., Bolker, B. M., White, J. S., St. Mary, C., and Shima, J. S. (2006). Statistical issues and study design in ecological restorations: lessons learned from marine reserves. In *Foundations of Restoration Ecology*, eds. D. A. Falk, M. A. Palmer, and J. B. Zedler. Washington, DC: Island Press, pp. 280–302.

Palumbi, S. R. (2004). Marine reserves and ocean neighborhoods: the spatial scale of marine populations and their management. *Annual Review of Environment and Resources*, **29**, 31–68.

Paris, C. B., Cherubin, L. M., and Cowen, R. K. (2007). Surfing, spinning, or diving from reef to reef: effects on population connectivity. *Marine Ecology Progress Series*, **347**, 285–300.

Pelc, R., Gaines, S. D., Warner, R. R., and Paris, C. B. (2010). Detecting larval export from marine reserves. *Proceedings of the National Academy of Sciences of the United States of America*, **107**, 18 266–71.

Pickett, S. T. A. (1989). Space-for-time substitution as an alternative to long-term studies. In *Long-Term Studies in Ecology: Approaches and Alternatives*, ed. G. E. Likens. New York: Springer, pp. 110–35.

Pittman, S. J., Christensen, J. D., Caldow, C., Menza, C., and Monaco, M. E. (2007). Predictive mapping of fish species richness across shallow-water seascapes in the Caribbean. *Ecological Modelling*, **204**, 9–21.

Planes, S., Jones, G. P., and Thorrold, S. R. (2009). Larval dispersal connects fish populations in a network of marine protected areas. *Proceedings of the National Academy of Sciences of the United States of America*, **106**, 5693–7.

Pollnac, R. B., Christie, P., Cinner, J. E., *et al.* (2010). Marine reserves as linked social-ecological systems. *Proceedings of the National Academy of Sciences of the United States of America*, **107**, 18 262–5.

Pomeroy, R., Parks, J., and Watson, L. (eds.) (2004.) *How Is Your MPA Doing? A Guidebook of Natural and Social Indicators for Evaluation of Marine Protected Areas Management and Effectiveness.* Gland, Switzerland: IUCN.

Purkis, S. J., Graham, N. A. J., and Reigl, B. M. (2008). Predictability of reef fish diversity and abundance using remote sensing data in Diego Garcia (Chagos Archipelago). *Journal of Animal Ecology*, **77**, 220–8.

Roberts, C. M., Branch, G., Bustamante, R. H., *et al.* (2003). Application of ecological criteria in selecting marine reserves and developing reserve networks. *Ecological Applications*, **13**, S215–S228.

Roessig, J. M., Woodley, C. M., Cech, J. J., and Hansen, L. J. (2004). Effects of global climate change on marine and estuarine fishes and fisheries. *Reviews in Fish Biology and Fisheries*, **14**, 251–75.

Sandwith, T., Shine, C., Hamilton, L., and Sheppard, D. (2001). *Transboundary Protected Areas for Peace and Co-operation.* Gland, Switzerland: IUCN.

Shackeroff, J. M., Hazen, E. L., and Crowder, L. B. (2009). The oceans as peopled seascapes. In *Ecosystem-Based Management for the Oceans*, eds. K. L. McLeod and H. Leslie. Washington, DC: Island Press, pp. 33–54.

Shanks, A. L., Grantham, B. A., and Carr, M. H. (2003). Propagule dispersal distance and the size and spacing of marine reserves. *Ecological Applications*, **13**, S159–S169.

Simberloff, D. (2003). The contribution of population and community biology to conservation science. *Annual Review of Ecology and Systematics*, **19**, 473–511.

Sponaugle, S., Fortuna, J., Grorud, K., and Lee, T. (2003). Dynamics of larval fish assemblages over a shallow coral reef in the Florida Keys. *Marine Biology*, **143**, 175–89.

Swearer, S. E., Caselle, J. E., Lea, D. W., and Warner, R. R. (1999). Larval retention and recruitment in an island population of a coral-reef fish. *Nature*, **402**, 799–802.

Thorrold, S. R., Jones, G. P., Planes, S., and Hare, J. A. (2006). Transgenerational marking of embryonic otoliths in marine fishes using barium stable isotopes. *Canadian Journal of Fisheries and Aquatic Sciences*, **63**, 1193–7.

Thorrold, S. R., Latkoczy, C., Swart, P. K., and Jones, C. M. (2001). Natal homing in a marine fish metapopulation. *Science*, **291**, 297–9.

Thorrold, S. R., Zacherl, D. C., and Levin, L. A. (2007). Population connectivity and larval dispersal using geochemical signatures in calcified structures. *Oceanography*, **20**, 32–41.

Tissot, B. N. (2005). Integral marine ecology: community-based fishery management in Hawaii. *World Futures*, **61**, 79–95.

Tissot, B., Walsh, W., and Hallacher, L. (2004). Evaluating effectiveness of a marine protected area network in west Hawai'i to increase productivity of an aquarium fishery. *Pacific Science*, **58**, 175–88.

Tissot, B. N., Walsh, W. J., and Hixon, M. A. (2009). Hawaiian islands marine ecosystem case study: ecosystem and community-based management in West Hawaii. *Coastal Management*, **37**, 255–73.

Underwood, A. J. (1991). Beyond BACI: experimental designs for detecting human environmental impacts on temporal variations in natural populations. *Australian Journal of Marine and Freshwater Research*, **42**, 569–87.

UNEP–WCMC (2008). *National and Regional Networks of Marine Protected Areas: A Review of Progress.* Cambridge, UK: UNEP World Conservation Monitoring Centre.

Watson, J. R., Mitarai, S., Siegel, D. A., *et al.* (2010). Realized and potential larval connectivity in the Southern California Bight. *Marine Ecology Progress Series*, **401**, 31–48.

Wedding, L., Friedlander, A., McGranaghan, M., Yost, R., and Monaco, M. (2008). Using bathymetric LIDAR data to measure benthic habitat complexity associated with coral reef fishes. *Remote Sensing of the Environment*, **112**, 4159–65.

White, C., Kendall, B. E., Gaines, S., Siegel, D. A., and Costello, C. (2008). Marine reserve effects on fishery profit. *Ecology Letters*, **11**, 370–9.

Willis, T. J., Millar, R. B., Babcock, R. C., and Tolimieri, N. (2003). Burdens of evidence and the benefits of marine reserves: putting Descartes before des horse? *Environmental Conservation*, **30**, 97–103.

Wood, L. J., Fish, L., Laughren, J., and Pauly, D. (2008). Assessing progress towards global marine protection targets: shortfalls in information and action. *Oryx*, **42**, 340–51.

12 · CONNECTIVITY –
Spacing a network of marine protected areas based on connectivity data

SERGE PLANES

12.1 Introduction

Networks of marine protected areas (MPAs) have been widely advocated for the conservation of marine biodiversity (see Figure 12.1). Such a conceptual framework assumes marine species as capable of dispersal that will interconnect patches of protected marine habitat. However, in order for MPA networks to be successful in protecting marine populations, individual MPAs must be self-sustaining or adequately connected to other MPAs via dispersal.

There are different views on the connectivity of marine fish populations. The distinction may partially be due to the different spatial and temporal scales being considered, as well as related to expectations of managers and stakeholders (Hilborn *et al.*, 2004; Ojeda-Martinez *et al.*, 2009). For example, managers of MPAs, when referring to connectivity, may be most interested in movement of juveniles and adults at small spatial scales (leading to spillover: Roberts *et al.*, 2001; Stobart *et al.*, 2009), while fisheries scientists may be most interested in the dispersal potential of eggs and larvae produced within the MPA at much larger spatial scales. Some biological oceanographers may refer to connectivity in the context of retention by physical processes near a reef, while others may explore physical processes that lead to dispersal events through geological time among many reefs. Ecologists may be interested in changes in biodiversity arising from range extensions, while this type of connectivity may simply be viewed by an evolutionary biologist as a small part

Marine Protected Areas: A Multidisciplinary Approach, ed. Joachim Claudet. Published by Cambridge University Press. © Cambridge University Press 2011.

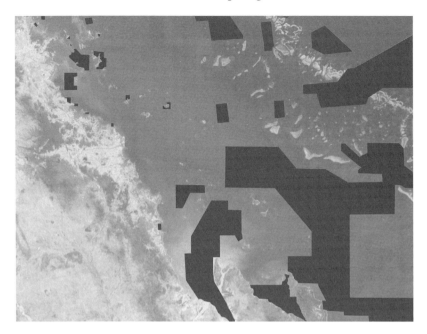

Figure 12.1 Example of an MPA zoning in the Great Barrier Reef (GBR), Australia. Black zones superimposed to the structured habitat are fully protected areas, where only a few traditional uses are allowed. Within this layer of patchiness, management units come in different sizes and configurations. For effective conservation strategies, the importance of connectivity appears through the following questions: are the populations in fully protected areas isolated from one another? Do fish freely move from these zones to outside of them? And to what degree are distant fully protected areas in the management network connected?

of a cycle of range extension and extirpation on the margins of species' ranges.

Even from these few examples, it should be clear that connectivity among fish populations encompasses different processes, each of which is neither completely discrete nor redundant in space and time. Considering the wide processes behind the concept of connectivity, we restricted the further synthesis to the aspect of connectivity related to larval dispersal. Such a choice was driven by the fact that connectivity through adult movement has been largely documented and approaches through tagging or acoustic tracking provide clear understanding of home ranges and migrations (Kerwath *et al.*, 2009; March *et al.*, 2010). These approaches have been already implemented in MPA management plans through analysis of the border effect and led to the establishment of buffer zones with some partial restrictions around borders (Stezenmüller *et al.*, 2008). Conversely, connectivity through the larval stage and during the pelagic period remains obscure to date.

Here, we first review actual knowledge on connectivity in marine species and its inherent spatial and temporal scales. Then, we show how this knowledge can be incorporated into the context of MPA planning and design and discuss the implications of connectivity for future conservation strategies.

12.2 Update status of connectivity in the sea: from open to semi-closed populations

Not long ago, there was a widely accepted paradigm that assumed that fish populations were open and driven by widely dispersing propagules of their early life history stages (Sale, 1991). Matching the metapopulation theories of the early 1990s, local populations could frequently become extinct, and be quickly reintroduced by dispersed larvae from other populations, allowing regional, long-term biodiversity to be decoupled from local exclusion by predators or competitors (Levin, 1976; Bohonak, 1999). Yet population dispersal was considered unbounded, even if species composition was not identical everywhere and often species-specific, or if assemblage-wide geographic boundaries could be observed in several different biogeographic areas (Briggs, 1999; Galarza *et al.*, 2009). In the context of coral reefs this paradigm culminated in the paper by Roberts (1997) that suggested that oceanic current patterns and larval duration would dictate the exchange rate of larval from a specific "upstream" reef to a specific "downstream" reef throughout biogeographic scales. Therefore, propagules mixed openly, and reefs could be linkened to rock outcrops in a stream, with river speed and direction dictating the movement of individuals, hence gene flow, among these isolated reefs.

More recently, scientists have started to question expectations of high dispersal rates among marine populations, integrating new evidence of unexpected local genetic differentiation and new results of modeling approaches including larval behavior. Genetic studies have begun to suggest unexpectedly low levels of exchange among neighboring reefs (Planes, 1993; Barber *et al.*, 2000; Taylor and Helberg, 2003; Carreras-Carbonell *et al.*, 2006). Fish larvae exhibit a surprisingly high capacity to swim long distances or alternatively to counteract movements of water masses, and are also able to orientate to coastal-derived environmental signals (Stobutski and Bellwood, 1997; Dixson *et al.*, 2008). The inclusion of such behaviors into fine scale individual-based modeling showed that local retention may contribute significantly to local recruitment (Irisson *et al.*, 2004; Cowen *et al.*, 2006). While some fish have long been known to home to natal populations (e.g., salmon) and other estuarine species have been found to do so recently (Thorrold *et al.*, 2001), there is now new evidence on the capability of larvae to return or not to move so much from the reefs or/and coastal zones where they originated (Jones *et al.*, 2005; Planes *et al.*, 2009; Saenz-Agudelo *et al.*, 2009). Evidence has mostly appeared in the last few years and is now fundamentally redrawing views and perspectives regarding dispersal of larval pelagic stages.

This capability of larvae to return to the reefs and/or coastal zones where they originated, or local retention, has been termed "self-recruitment" in most empirical studies. Self-recruitment was initially calculated as the proportion of settlers at a location that were spawned locally (e.g., Jones *et al.*, 1999; Swearer *et al.*, 1999). This measure is now widely used. This quantity is, in some way, a measure of how isolated a focal population is. The first direct evidence about the capability of larvae to return to their original reef arose in 1999 when Jones *et al.* (1999) demonstrated from otolith tagging that at least 15% of the larvae of a Pomacentridae species settling within an island originated from the reef at which they spawned. Since that study, several works have gone further and have demonstrated direct evidence of significant level of self-recruitment that can reach 50% of the local recruitment and therefore the renewal of the local population (Jones *et al.*, 2005; Alemany *et al.*, 2007; Planes *et al.*, 2009). Jones *et al.* (2005) directly estimated levels of self-recruitment in a clownfish population by combining parentage analysis and chemical tagging and found similar results with the two methods. More interestingly, they highlighted the fact that parentage analysis can provide high-resolution connectivity information and direct estimates of dispersal distances at the individual level. These parentage analyses were based on individual-based genetic analysis looking for the parent of the new recruits (Saenz-Agudelo *et al.*, 2009; Christie *et al.*, 2010). These works corroborate in some way some of the modeling studies coupling physics and biology that also suggested significant self-recruitment (Paris *et al.*, 2002; Cowen *et al.*, 2006; Irisson *et al.*, 2004). Overall, there is now a consensus on the existence of local retention which emphasizes the necessity to consider it in conservation planning.

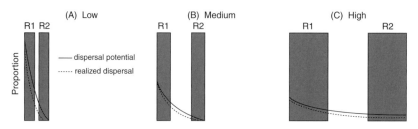

Figure 12.2 Theoretical size and spacing of marine reserves based on dispersal and connectivity among two reserves (R1 and R2).

12.3 Implications for design and assessment of marine protected area networks

Marine protected areas have been suggested as a mean of maintaining high resilience in metapopulations (e.g., Lubchenco *et al.*, 2003; Mumby *et al.*, 2006; Worm *et al.*, 2006). Planning of MPAs' often focuses on simply protecting a target fraction of key habitats (review: Sale *et al.*, 2005) and assumes the ecological processes naturally occurring in those habitats will persist in the MPAs and contribute to unprotected habitats outside of the MPAs (see Chapters 3 and 4). Then, networks of MPAs have been widely advocated (Palumbi, 2004). A network of MPAs is a group of protected sites that are linked in some ecologically meaningful way (Chapter 11). Networks of MPAs can address the problem of how to protect important and/or representative areas without limiting human uses on vast areas of coast and ocean. They share and enhance many of the benefits of individual MPAs, providing opportunities to preserve marine biodiversity, resolve user conflicts, and restore degraded or overexploited areas (Agardy, 1999).

Optimal MPA network designs have been largely investigated through modeling approaches so far (Figure 12.2). Modeling studies have indicated how characteristics of larval dispersal and the spatial configurations of MPAs interact to promote population persistence (Crowder *et al.*, 2000; Stockhausen *et al.*, 2000; Botsford *et al.*, 2001; Morgan and Botsford, 2001; Kaplan *et al.*, 2006). However, while these interactions are clear in modeling results, efforts to apply conclusions from these modeling studies to the design of effective MPAs and assess their benefits are hindered by uncertainty concerning larval dispersal (Stockhausen *et al.*, 2000; Gaines *et al.*, 2003; Kaplan and Botsford, 2005).

Recently, a meta-analysis of Mediterranean and Atlantic no-take zones (i.e., marine reserves) looked at the influence of distance to the nearest neighboring reserve on the effectiveness of single reserves (Claudet *et al.*, 2008). There was no effect of distance to neighboring reserves on the response of commercial fish mean densities or species richness, suggesting that the distance per se to the nearest neighboring marine reserve did not play any significant role.

However, results from the previous model-based and experimental studies have to be appreciated in the light of the current knowledge on connectivity. As we described earlier, there has been complete shift regarding connectivity through larval dispersal. The high levels of percent self-recruitment reported recently have drawn attention to how small the scale of dispersal can be (Jones *et al.*, 1999; Swearer *et al.*, 1999; Jones *et al.*, 2005). Such a new vision of connectivity, which appears much restricted than thought previously, needs to be integrated in the context of network of MPAs.

12.4 Integrating connectivity into the design of marine protected area networks

In the late 1990s a magic number came out of some modeling studies suggesting that 30% of the coastlines should be included in MPAs in order to ensure maintenance of the overall ecosystem functioning (Murray *et al.*, 1999; Botsford *et al.*, 2001). Meanwhile, networks of MPAs were viewed in the perspective of spreading local communities. Since these studies, the spacing of MPAs within a network has been largely questioned. Dispersal scale parameters, including the scales of diffusion and advection, are difficult to estimate in the field (see Section 12.3), and these parameters remain poorly understood for most species, which may present an obstacle to determining optimal MPA design. In some cases, diffusion and advection parameters may be directly estimated using oceanographic flow field models and/or drifter or dye studies. More often, basic knowledge of oceanographic conditions (e.g., the presence of advection currents, retention features such as eddies, etc.) and planktonic larval duration are used to estimate first-order approximations of mean larval dispersal scales, including diffusion and advection parameters (Cowen *et al.*, 2006). However, a high uncertainty that is difficult to address remains within these approaches.

Recent results emphasized the original idea that no-take reserves should be no larger than about twice the target species' dispersal scale to ensure that enough larvae are exported to surrounding areas open to fisheries (Halpern *et al.*, 2004). Clearly, there are trade-offs between sustainability within reserves and export of production to areas outside reserves, but networks of variably spaced reserves on the scales of 10–100 km^2 can meet both conservation and fisheries enhancement goals (Halpern, 2003). Recent modeling studies including new larval dispersal tracking have also come out with similar results, showing that the optimal fraction of coastline protected by reserves should be about 35–40% (Pelc *et al.*, 2010), which is in agreement with many previous theoretical MPA studies (Murray *et al.*, 1999; Botsford *et al.*, 2001; Botsford *et al.*, 2009). Moreover, with typical larval neighborhood sizes on scales of tens to hundreds of kilometers for most marine fish and invertebrates, and a median size of only 3.3 km^2 for existing reserves (Mora and Sale, 2002), net benefits from the export of larvae outside reserves is assumed to be the rule rather than the exception.

However, recent evidence of high local self-recruitment showed that most extra larval production for short-distance dispersers is retained within MPAs (Crec'hriou *et al.*, 2010). Therefore, a strong advection is required to export those extra larvae with very short larval diffusion scales. In the context of small marine reserves, a large part of the larvae produced within the reserves are exported (Roussel *et al.*, 2010), so that the benefits of export of larvae increase with increasing fractions of coastline placed in reserves. A greater proportion of coastline in reserves leads to more enhanced larval production, and enough of the extra production is exported due to advection to offset the additional fishery squeeze effect. Mathematical models of marine reserve networks demonstrate the importance of proximity, although the optimal distance between reserves depends on management goals, the input data considered, and the assumptions made (Sala *et al.*, 2002; Hastings and Botsford, 2003). Overall, there is logic behind the idea of increasing the number of MPA networks, as all modeling approaches so far, as well as few field studies, have argued for significant advection and dispersal of larvae from MPAs and the connectivity among MPAs units.

Recent modeling studies also demonstrated the need of MPA networks in order to maintain populations in each MPA (Botsford *et al.*, 2009). Similarly to the metapopulation concept, each MPA will be seen as a unit that may be affected by local anthropogenic impact and there is a need to establish an overall system with migration among units maintaining its overall stability. While this view is logical it is also associated with uncertainty due to an overall lack of field evidence and model validations.

Uncertainty is an inherent characteristic of biological systems. However, the actual collapse of fisheries requires urgent decisions and any additional protection will be useful. Therefore establishment of new MPAs must continue whatever the remaining uncertainty surrounding ecological processes in general and connectivity in particular. Reconciling the two conflicting pressures of management certainty and ecological uncertainty is the main challenge facing the social science of MPAs. Planning for uncertainty has a tradition in management risk analysis, but has only recently been explicitly incorporated into conservation and resource management science (e.g., Pascual and Hilborn, 1995; Flather *et al.*, 1997). Uncertainties must be considered when selecting management measures, and incorporated into the setting of conservation targets and limits.

12.5 Conclusion

Here we have shown the importance of the larval dispersal component of connectivity in designing MPAs. Despite recent advances in dispersal models coupling oceanographic simulations with larval physical and behavioral information, some uncertainty remains. Validation of these models via comparisons with direct measures of larval dispersal patterns (such as those described above) and integration of improved data on larval behavior and mortality (also potentially from the techniques described above) remain major areas of future research.

References

Agardy, T. (1999). Creating havens for marine life. *Issues in Science and Technology*, **16**, 37–44.

Almany, G. R., Berumen, M. L., Thorrold, S. R., Planes, S., and Jones, G. P. (2007). Local replenishment of coral reef fish populations in a marine reserve. *Science*, **316**, 742–4.

Ballantine, W. (1991). Marine reserves: the need for networks. *New Zealand Journal of Marine and Freshwater Research*, **25**, 115–16.

Barber, P. H., Palumbi, S. R., Erdmann, M. V., and Moosa, M. K. (2000). A marine Wallace's line? *Nature*, **406**, 692–3.

Bohonak, A. J. (1999). Dispersal, gene flow, and population structure. *Quaterly Review of Biology*, **74**, 21–45.

Botsford, L. W., Hastings, A., and Gaines, S. G. (2001). Dependence of sustainability on the configuration of marine reserves and larval dispersal distance. *Ecology Letters*, **4**, 144–50.

Botsford, L. W., White, J. W., Coffroth, M.-A., *et al.* (2009). Connectivity and resilience of coral reef metapopulations in MPAs: matching empirical efforts to predictive needs. *Coral Reefs*, **28**, 327–37.

Briggs, J. C. (1999). Coincident biogeographic patterns: Indo-west Pacific Ocean. *Evolution*, **53**, 326–35.

Carreras-Carbonell, J., Macpherson, E., and Pascual, M. (2006). Population structure within and between subspecies of the Mediterranean triplefin fish *Tripterygion delaisi* revealed by highly polymorphic microsatellite loci. *Molecular Ecology*, **15**, 3527–39.

Christie, M. R., Johnson, D. W., Stallings, C. D., and Hixon, M. A. (2010). Self-recruitment and sweepstakes reproduction amid extensive gene flow in a coral-reef fish. *Molecular Ecology*, **19**, 1042–57.

Claudet, J., Osenberg, C. W., Benedetti-Cecchi, L., et al. (2008). Marine reserves: size and age do matter. *Ecology Letters*, **11**, 481–9.

Cowen, R. K., Paris, C. B., and Srinivasan, A. (2006). Scaling of connectivity in marine populations. *Science*, **311**, 522–7.

Crec'Hriou, R., Alemany, F., Roussel, E., et al. (2010). Early life stage of fisheries targeted taxa: evidence of larval export in Cabrera Archipelago National Park (Balearic Islands, Western Mediterranean Sea). *Fisheries Oceanography*, **19**, 135–50.

Crowder, L. B., Lyman, S. J., Figueira, W. F., and Priddy, J. (2000). Source–sink population dynamics and the problem of siting marine reserves. *Bulletin of Marine Science*, **66**, 799–820.

Dixson, D. L., Jones, G. P., Munday, P. L., et al. (2008). Coral reef fish smell leaves to find island homes. *Proceedings of the Royal Society Series B*, **275**, 2831–9.

Flather, C. H., Wilson, K. R., Dean, D. J., and McComb, W. C. (1997). Identifying gaps in conservation networks: of indicators and uncertainty in geographic-based analyses. *Ecological Applications*, **7**, 531–42.

Gaines, S. D., Gaylord, B. and Largier, J. L. (2003). Avoiding current oversights in marine reserve design. *Ecological Applications*, **13**, S32–S46.

Galarza, J. A., Carreras-Carbonell, J., Macpherson, E., et al. (2009). The influence of oceanographic fronts and early-life-history traits on connectivity among littoral fish species. *Proceedings of the National Academy of Sciences of the United States of America*, **106**, 1473–8.

Halpern, B. S. (2003). The impact of marine reserves: do reserves work and does reserve size matter? *Ecological Applications*, **13**, S117–S137.

Halpern, B. S., Gaines, S. D., and Warner, R. R. (2004). Confounding effects of the export of production and the displacement of fishing effort from marine reserves. *Ecological Applications*, **14**, 1248–56.

Hastings, A. and Botsford, L. W. (2003). Comparing designs of marine reserves for fisheries and for biodiversity. *Ecological Applications*, **13**, S65–S70.

Hastings, A. and Botsford, L. W. (2006). Persistence of spatial populations depends on returning home. *Proceedings of the National Academy of Sciences of the United States of America*, **103**, 6067–72.

Hilborn, R., Stokes, K., Maguire, J.-J., et al. (2004). When can marine reserves improve fisheries management? *Ocean and Coastal Management*, **47**, 197–205.

Irisson, J.-O., Le Van, A., De Lara, M., and Planes, S. (2004). Strategies and trajectories of coral reef fish larvae optimizing self-recruitment. *Journal of Theoretical Biology*, **225**, 205–18.

Jones, G. P., Milicich, M. J., Emslie, M. J., and Lunow, C. (1999). Self-recruitment in a coral reef fish population. *Nature*, **402**, 802–4.

Jones, G. P., Planes, S., and Thorrold, S. R. (2005). Coral reef fish larvae settle close to home. *Current Biology*, **15**, 1314–18.

Kaplan, D. M. and Botsford, L. W. (2005). Effects of variability in spacing of marine reserve on fisheries yield and sustainability. *Canadian Journal of Fisheries and Aquatic Sciences*, **62**, 905–12.

Kaplan, D. M., Botsford, L. W., and Jorgensen, S. (2006). Dispersal-per-recruit: an efficient method for assessing sustainability in networks of marine reserves. *Ecological Applications*, **16**, 2248–63.

Kerwath, S. E., Thorstad, E. B., Naesje, T. F., *et al.* (2009). Crossing invisible boundaries: the effectiveness of the Langebaan Lagoon Marine Protected Area as a harvest refuge for a migratory fish species in South Africa. *Conservation Biology*, **23**, 653–61.

Levin, S. A. (1976). Population dynamic models in heterogeneous environments. *Annual Review of Ecology and Systematic*, **7**, 287–310.

Lubchenco, J., Palumbi, S. R., Gaines, S. D., and Andelman, S. (2003). Plugging a hole in the ocean: the emerging science of marine reserves. *Ecological Applications*, **13**, S3–S7.

March, D., Palmer, M., Alos, J., Grau, A., and Cardona, F. (2010). Short-term residence, home range size and diel patterns of the painted comber *Serranus scriba* in a temperate marine reserve. *Marine Ecology Progress Series*, **400**, 195–206.

Mora, C. and Sale, P. F. (2002). Are populations of coral reef fish open or closed? *Trends in Ecology and Evolution*, **17**, 422–8.

Morgan, L. E. and Botsford, L. W. (2001). Managing with reserves: modeling uncertainty in larval dispersal for a sea urchin fishery. *In Spatial Processes and Management of Marine Populations.* Fairbanks, AK: Alaska Sea Grant College, pp. 667–84.

Mumby, P. J., Dahlgren, C. P., Harbone, A. R., *et al.* (2006). Fishing, trophic cascades, and the process of grazing on coral reefs. *Science*, **311**, 98–101.

Murray, S. N., Ambrose, R. F., Bohnsack, J. A., *et al.* (1999). No-take reserve networks: sustaining fishery populations and marine ecosystems. *Fisheries*, **24**, 11–25.

Ojeda-Martinez, C., Gimenez Casalduero, F., Bayle-Sempere, J. T., *et al.* (2009). A conceptual framework for the integral management of marine protected areas. *Ocean and Coastal Management*, **52**, 89–101.

Palumbi, S. R. (2004). Marine reserves and ocean neighborhoods: the spatial scale of marine populations and their management. *Annual Review of Environmental Resources*, **29**, 31–68.

Paris, C. B., Cowen, R. K., Lwiza, K. M. M., Wang, D.-P., and Olson, D. B. (2002) Multivariate objective analysis of the coastal circulation of Barbados, West Indies: implications for larval transport. *Deep-Sea Research*, **49**, 1363–86.

Pascual, M. A. and Hilborn, R. (1995). Conservation of harvested populations in fluctuating environments: the case of the Serengeti wildebeest. *Journal of Applied Ecology*, **32**, 468–80.

Pelc, R. A., Baskett, M. L., Tanci, T., Gaines, S., and Warner, R. R. (2009). Quantifying larval export from South African marine reserves. *Marine Ecology Progress Series*, **394**, 65–78.

Pelc, R. A., Warner, R. R., Gaines, S. D., and Paris, C. (2010). Detecting larval export from marine reserves. *Proceedings of the National Academy of Sciences of the United States of America*, **107**, 18 266–71.

Planes, S. (1993). Genetic differentiation in realtion to restricted larval dispersal of the convict surgeonfish, *Acanthurus triostegus*, in French Polynesia. *Marine Ecology Progress Series*, **98**, 237–46.

Planes, S., Jones, G. P., and Thorrold, S. R. (2009) Larval dispersal connects fish populations in a network of marine protected areas. *Proceedings of the National Academy of Sciences of the United States of America*, **106**, 5693–7.

Roberts, C. M. (1997). Connectivity and management of Caribbean coral reefs. *Science*, **248**, 1454–7.

Roberts, C. M., Bohnsack, J. A., Gell, F., Hawkins, J. P., and Goodridge, R. (2001). Effects of marine reserves on adjacent fisheries. *Science*, **294**, 1920–3.

Roussel, E., Crec'Hriou, R., Lenfant, P., Mader, J., and Planes, S. (2010). Relative influences of space, time and environment on coastal ichthyoplankton assemblages along a temperate rocky shore. *Journal of Plankton Research*, **32**, 1443–57.

Saenz-Agudelo, P., Jones, G. P., Thorrold, S. R., and Planes, S. (2009). Estimating connectivity in marine populations: an empirical evaluation of assignment tests and parentage analysis at different spatial scales. *Molecular Ecology*, **18**, 1765–76.

Sala, E., Aburto-Oropeza, O., Paredes, G., *et al.* (2002). A general model for designing networks of marine reserves. *Science*, **298**, 1991–3.

Sale, P. F. (1991). *The Ecology of Fishes on Coral Reefs*. San Diego, CA: Academic Press.

Sale, P. F., Cowen, R. K., Danilowicz, B. S., *et al.* (2005). Critical science gaps impede use of no-take fishery reserves. *Trends in Ecology and Evolution*, **20**, 74–80.

Stezenmüller, V., Maynou, F., Bernard, E., *et al.* (2008). Spatial assessment of fishing effort around European marine reserves: implications for successful fisheries management. *Marine Pollution Bulletin*, **56**, 2018–26.

Stobart, B., Warwick, R., González, C., *et al.* (2009). Long-term and spillover effects of a marine protected area on an exploited fish community. *Marine Ecology Progress Series*, **384**, 47–60.

Stobutzki, I. C. and Bellwood, D. R. (1997). Sustained swimming abilities of the late pelagic stages of coral reef fishes. *Marine Ecology Progress Series*, **149**, 35–41.

Stockhausen, W. T., Lipcius, R. N., and Hickey, B. M. (2000). Joint effects of larval dispersal, population regulation, marine reserve design, and exploitation on production and recruitment in the Caribbean spiny lobster. *Bulletin of Marine Science*, **66**, 957–90.

Swearer, S. E., Caselle, J. E., Lea, D. W., and Warner, R. R. (1999). Larval retention and recruitment in an island population of a coral-reef fish. *Nature*, **402**, 799–802.

Taylor, M. S. and Hellberg, M. E. (2003). Larvae retention: genes or oceanography? *Science*, **300**, 1657–8.

Thorrold, S. R., Latkoczy, C., Swart, P. K., and Jones, C. M. (2001). Natal homing in a marine fish metapopulation. *Science*, **291**, 297–9.

Worm, B., Barbier, E. B., Beaumont, N., *et al.* (2006). Impacts of biodiversity loss on ocean ecosystem services. *Science*, **314**, 787–90.

13 · REPRESENTATIVENESS – *Effectiveness of the global network of marine protected areas*

CAMILO MORA

13.1 Introduction

Marine biodiversity is increasingly being lost due to human-related activities. Several marine ecosystems such as estuaries (Lotze *et al.*, 2006), mangroves (Valiela *et al.*, 2001), seagrasses (Waycott *et al.*, 2009), coral reefs (Gardner *et al.*, 2003; Pandolfi *et al.*, 2003; Bruno and Selig, 2007), and coastal and oceanic fish communities (Jackson *et al.*, 2001; Worm *et al.*, 2005) are rapidly losing populations, species, or entire functional groups due to threats such as exploitation, habitat loss, and climate change, among others (Jackson *et al.*, 2001; Hoegh-Guldberg *et al.*, 2007; Mora *et al.*, 2007; Mora, 2008). The rate of these losses and extent of these threats are expected to drive many marine species to collapse and possible extinction before the middle of this century (Worm *et al.*, 2006; Hoegh-Guldberg *et al.*, 2007; Donner, 2009). These losses, in turn, may impair the capability of ecosystems to cope with natural and anthropogenic impacts and harm the services that biodiversity provides to a growing human population that increasingly uses coastal habitats and marine resources (Worm *et al.*, 2006; Donner and Potere, 2007).

The accelerated decay of ecosystems is a modern concern to humankind and has motivated concerted global efforts such as the Convention on Biological Diversity, which was endorsed by more than 190 countries and aimed to reduce the rate of biodiversity loss by 2010 (Balmford *et al.*, 2005). In practical terms, one of the solutions that

Marine Protected Areas: A Multidisciplinary Approach, ed. Joachim Claudet. Published by Cambridge University Press. © Cambridge University Press 2011.

was proposed and that has received significant support to reverse the loss of biodiversity is the establishment of protected areas (Lubchenco *et al.*, 2003; Balmford *et al.*, 2005; Chape *et al.*, 2005; Lubchenco *et al.*, 2007; Wood *et al.*, 2008). The expected effect of protected areas is that by reducing pressures from harvesting and habitat loss, wild populations will recover if they have been impacted or will maintain natural levels of resilience to cope with natural and other human-related disturbances (Lubchenco *et al.*, 2003; Palumbi, 2003; Micheli *et al.*, 2004; Palumbi, 2004). The fact that such an expected effect has been documented (Halpern and Warner, 2002; Micheli *et al.*, 2004; Worm *et al.*, 2006) and that governments need to fulfill international agreements (Balmford *et al.*, 2005; Wood *et al.*, 2008), has resulted in a proliferation of marine protected areas (MPAs). Today, 4435 MPAs exist worldwide (Wood *et al.*, 2008) covering 0.65% of the world's oceans, although only 0.08% is inside no-take MPAs (Wood *et al.*, 2008). It may be understood, however, that the number and coverage of MPAs are the simplest proxies for biodiversity conservation and that "coverage effectiveness" is what ultimately will determine the real conservation of biodiversity (Chape *et al.*, 2005; Mora *et al.*, 2006). Unfortunately, global assessments on the effectiveness of MPAs are still limited, given the difficulties in collecting data that are patchy and changing rapidly (Mora *et al.*, 2006). Here I analyze a combination of databases to assess the effectiveness of the current global network of protected areas in ensuring the maintenance of populations and the likely constraints that humans pose to the effective management of MPAs.

13.2 World Database on Protected Areas

I used the most recent data on global MPAs, as provided in the 2009 release of the World Database on Protected Areas. That database contained the corrections done by Wood *et al.* (2008) and included polygons for 4705 MPAs and the geographical coordinates for the center points of 1796 other MPAs. Center points were converted to polygons by creating a buffer of the same size of the reported MPA. Most of the point MPAs are very small (Wood *et al.*, 2008) and creating such a buffer around them is known to introduce only small errors (Mora *et al.*, 2006). Using GIS, I removed the spatial overlap among MPAs. The final database contained 4363 independent MPAs (Figure 13.1). This reduction in the number of MPAs occurs because a substantial number of MPAs were duplicated in the original database and because the polygons of several MPAs overlap

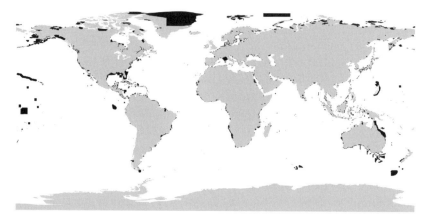

Figure 13.1 Global distribution of marine protected areas. Data from the 2009 release of the World Database on Protected Areas. Map not to scale; I have bolded the borders of MPAs so that they would be visible at this global scale.

each other. These two problems in the World Database of Protected Areas have been documented before (Chape *et al.*, 2005; Wood *et al.*, 2008) but are easily resolved by dissolving the overlap among polygons, which maintains the same area of coverage which is the main purpose of conservation.

13.3 Maintenance of populations in the global network of marine protected areas

The stability of most marine populations is determined by metapopulation dynamics, in which local populations are seeded by a combination of locally and distantly produced propagules (Kritzer and Sale, 2006). These types of systems require a precise understanding of the home ranges where benthic individuals live and the spatial scales over which their propagules disperse (Mora and Sale, 2002; Palumbi, 2003; Palumbi, 2004; Sale *et al.*, 2005). In other words, extensive movement can expose benthic individuals to harvesting outside the boundaries of the MPAs (Kramer and Chapman, 1999; Palumbi, 2004; Sale *et al.*, 2005), whereas the arrival of new recruits can be favored if source populations are protected (Shanks *et al.*, 2003; Sale *et al.*, 2005). Additionally, it is expected that protected habitats are suitable for the maintenance of local populations (Jameson *et al.*, 2002). In other words, local habitats are not polluted, environmentally stressful, or dominated by exotic species

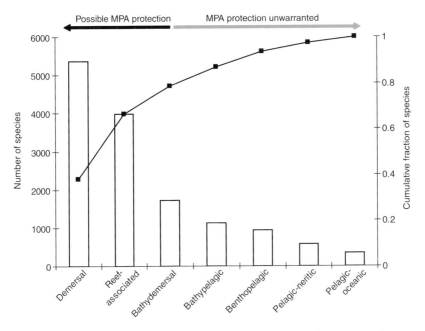

Figure 13.2 Frequency distribution of marine fish species by habitat types. The figure is intended to provide a rough quantification of the groups of species that may and may not be protected by MPAs. This quantification is based on the habitats of residence of marine fish species. If habitats of residence are too large, protected individuals may face mortality outside the boundaries of MPAs, such as for instance pelagic residing species. Data from FishBase (www.fishbase.org).

(Jameson *et al.*, 2002). The extent to which these attributes are met in the global network of MPAs is poorly known and is the main objective of this chapter.

13.3.1 Protection of benthic neighborhoods

One fact that needs to be understood about the use of MPAs is that they warrant the protection of species whose home ranges, at some point during their life history, are restricted to areas that could be reasonably protected as part of an MPA (Palumbi, 2004; Sale *et al.*, 2005). That excludes a large fraction of biodiversity, such as those species whose life cycles occur entirely in open water and large pelagic and benthic fishes whose home ranges are too large to be covered within the area of common MPAs. For marine fishes alone that may represent up to 22% of their global diversity (Figure 13.2).

For species that have benthic habits at some point during their life cycle, MPAs provide protection depending on the ratio between the size of the species' home range and the size of the MPA (Kramer and Chapman, 1999; Palumbi, 2003; Palumbi, 2004; Sale et al., 2005). This occurs because individuals can trespass the boundaries of the MPA and become vulnerable to mortality outside the MPA even if MPA enforcement is successful. This effect is known to create gradients in abundance around the borders of MPAs (Kramer and Chapman, 1999) and possibly cause extinction if the protected area is small and mortality outside the protected area is severe (Woodroffe and Ginsberg, 1998). Kramer and Chapman (1999) illustrate, for instance, that to reduce fishing mortality of a particular species inside an MPA to 2% of the mortality outside the MPA, the MPA has to be 12.5 times larger than the home range of the species. By using the previous calculation in combination with the home ranges of marine fishes (as scaled from their body size: Kramer and Chapman [1999]), I calculated that complete protection of fish assemblages is warranted in only 14.4% of the MPAs in the world (see Figure 13.3 for details). This suggests that at the global scale a significant fraction of the MPAs are too small to protect the large variety of species that may occur at any particular assemblage.

13.3.2 Ensuring propagule connectivity

The scale of propagule dispersal (I refer to propagules because the vectors of dispersal can be eggs, larvae, juveniles, and even adults in some species) is a critical, yet poorly known, characteristic for the effective design of MPAs, or, in other words, for ensuring that populations will remain viably interconnected within the network of MPAs (Shanks et al., 2003; Palumbi, 2004; Sale et al., 2005). Although data about the relative role of long-distance dispersal versus local retention remain limited (Mora and Sale, 2002), recommendations about the spacing between MPAs to ensure connectivity ranges from 10 to 20 km (Shanks et al., 2003) and 20 to 150 km (Palumbi, 2003). In the global network of MPAs, the average distance from any MPA to its nearest MPA is 42 km (Figure 13.4A), with that distance increasing rapidly as more than one MPA is considered. For instance, the average distance from any MPA to the nearest 20 MPAs is 430 km (Figure 13.4B). If exploitation or habitat loss outside MPAs is severe, these results indicate that the life cycle of many marine populations can be truncated during the dispersal stage because viable or protected reproductive benthic populations are separated by distances larger than

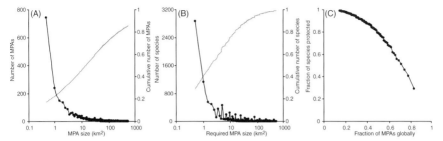

Figure 13.3 Protection of fish neighborhoods in the global network of marine protected areas. Plot (A) depicts the frequency distribution of MPA sizes globally. Plot (B) depicts the required MPA size to protect the described marine fishes of the world. The required MPA size was calculated based on the calculations of Kramer and Chapman (1999). In their analysis, for a particular species, reducing fishing mortality inside a MPA to 2% of the fishing mortality outside the MPA requires MPAs 12.5 times larger than the home range of the species. The home ranges of the species were calculated from the escalation of home range with body size (Kramer and Chapman, 1999). In this analysis, I included only the subset of species with discrete habitats of residence that can be protected by MPAs (i.e., the groups of species outlined in Figure 13.2). In total 9830 fish species were considered and data on their body size were obtained from FishBase (www.fishbase.org). Given that local pools of species are random subsets of the species seen at regional scales (Karlson *et al.*, 2004), Plot (B) is intended to provide a relative view of the frequency distribution of the MPA sizes required to protect particular fractions of species at local communities. Plot (C) depicts the fraction of species protected, according to the criteria of reducing fishing mortality to 2%, by the different MPAs in the world. To exemplify how to read the figure, note the dotted lines in the plot. According to that example protecting 99.9% of the species in a given community is warranted in only 14.4% of the MPAs in the world.

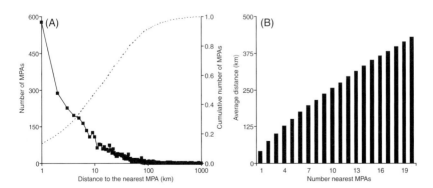

Figure 13.4 Protection of connectivity in the global network of marine protected areas. Plot (A) depicts the distance between any MPA and its nearest MPA in the global network of MPAs. Plot (B) depicts the global average distance from any MPA to increasingly higher numbers of nearby MPAs.

the ones at which their propagules can connect them. In other words, the entire metapopulation dynamics expected from MPAs alone may be endangered due to low connectivity resulting from distant MPAs (Kritzer and Sale, 2006).

13.3.3 Habitat suitability inside the network of marine protected areas

There are a large number of human threats such as pollution, invasive species, ocean warming, acidification, and many others that are hard to regulate as part of the management plan of an MPA (Aronson *et al.*, 2003; Birkeland, 2004; Jameson, 2006). Unfortunately, many of these threats can have deleterious effects on the viability of populations, including extinction (Myers, 1995; Walther *et al.*, 2002; Aronson *et al.*, 2003; Parmesan and Yohe, 2003; Perry *et al.*, 2005; Halpern *et al.*, 2007; Hoegh-Guldberg *et al.*, 2007; Mora *et al.*, 2007; Portner and Knust, 2007; Caitlin Mullan *et al.*, 2008). Consequently, populations can still be vulnerable and possibly at high risk of extinction inside even well-managed MPAs or where threats of fishing and habitat loss are minimum (Jones *et al.*, 2004; Graham *et al.*, 2006; Coelho and Manfrino, 2007; Monaco *et al.*, 2007; Graham *et al.*, 2008; Russ *et al.*, 2008). To provide a global overview of this problem, I overlapped the MPAs of the world with the recent Ocean Human Footprint developed by Halpern *et al.* (2008), which combined a variety of human threats into a single score. According to this analysis, over 70% of the MPAs in the world are in areas of high human impact (i.e., over areas with human footprint scores larger than 12: see Halpern *et al.* [2008])(Figure 13.5). Clearly, the possible imperilment of populations inside MPAs due to threats other than fishing and habitat loss are significant worldwide. Unfortunately, the extent of human threats, other than fishing, is very pervasive in the oceans worldwide, which certainly reduces the areas of the ocean where MPAs can be minimally affected by such threats (Halpern *et al.*, 2008).

13.4 Human imperilment of marine protected areas

Humans play a critical role in the biological success and management viability of MPAs. Human populations on the edges of MPAs can increase the chances of conscious (i.e., poaching) and unconscious intrusions inside MPAs, which cause mortality of populations inside MPAs (Kritzer, 2004). Even if MPAs are strongly enforced, fishing pressure

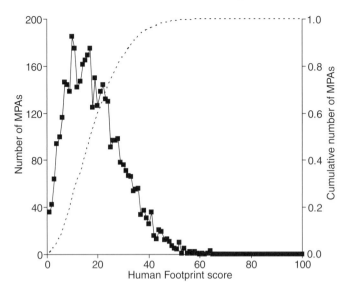

Figure 13.5 Suitability of habitats inside the global network of marine protected areas. Here I show the frequency distribution of MPAs along the gradient of combined human stressors. As measure of combined human stressors, I used the original data of the Ocean Human Footprint score developed by Halpern *et al.* (2008). The human footprint inside each MPA was determined by overlapping the MPAs of the world with the human footprint and calculating the mode score inside each MPA. Some of the threats considered in the Halpern *et al.* (2008) footprint include climate change, ocean acidification, invasive species, pollution, and overfishing.

outside MPAs can create density gradients inside MPAs (Kramer and Chapman, 1999) and possibly cause extinction due to edge effects (Woodroffe and Ginsberg, 1998). Conflicts between MPA objectives and local residents can reduce compliance with MPA regulations, which can increase poaching (Kramer and Chapman, 1999; Christie *et al.*, 2003; Christie, 2004), or alternatively increase the operation cost of surveillance of the MPA (Balmford *et al.*, 2004). As indicated, there are different effects on MPAs that can be triggered by the effects of human settlements inside or around the borders of MPAs. Although we lack a direct quantification of these issues for each MPA globally, the number of people inside or around MPAs provides a suitable proxy for their likely effect on MPAs. To provide a global overview of the likely difficulty of managing MPAs due to human settlements, I overlapped the global network of MPAs with the gridded Human Population of the

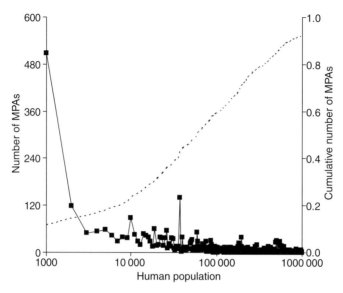

Figure 13.6 Likely imperilment of marine protected areas by humans. Here I show the frequency distribution of MPAs by the number of people in or around their borders. As mentioned in text the number of people was used as proxy for the different effects that humans can have on the biological and management effectiveness of MPAs. Some of these effects may include poaching, increases in the surveillance cost of the MPAs, and/or harvesting outside the borders of MPAs, which could create density gradients in protected populations inside MPAs. For this analysis I created a 50-km buffer around each MPA and then calculated the maximum number of people found inside the MPA as well as its buffer. Data on human population were obtained from Gridded Population of the World, version 3 (http://sedac.ciesin.columbia.edu/gpw/).

World (http://sedac.ciesin.columbia.edu/gpw/) to quantify the number of people living inside or around each MPA. Caution: it is certainly possible that the mechanistic effects of the number of people on MPAs may vary due to different social and economical backgrounds, but the net results may be very similar. For instance, in poor communities, fishing can be used as a source of food and income, in which often labeled as "artisanal fishing." In richer communities, the same fishing can be used as a source of recreation, in which is named "recreational fishing." Interestingly, the extent of these two types of fishing almost balance each other out when comparing fishing in poor and rich countries (Mora *et al.*, 2009). Worldwide there are only 136 MPAs located in areas where no humans are located within a 50-km radius of their borders. For the rest of the MPAs, human population density averages 308 940 people per cell of 25 × 25 km, although they are almost evenly distributed along the entire gradient of human density (Figure 13.6). Clearly, humans pose a significant challenge to the management of MPAs worldwide and this is only likely to worsen given the expected major increase in the world's human population in the coming few decades (e.g., the United Nations Global Human Population Prospects: http://esa.un.org/unpp/).

13.5 Concluding remarks

Marine protected areas are created for different purposes, including the protection of species under imminent risk of extinction, protection of unique habitats, and enhancement of local fisheries. Under many of these circumstances, MPAs are an immediate and practical solution and although they may provide an umbrella effect for the protection of overall biodiversity, it is clear that the escalation of this strategy with the aim of protecting global marine biodiversity is unrealistic. The results presented in this chapter reveal the still limited coverage of the world's oceans by MPAs, the failure to warrant the viability of most metapopulations, and the increasing challenge of MPA success given the pervasive distribution of the human population on coastal areas. While increasing funding for the deployment of new MPAs and improvement of existing ones remains a possibility, the reality is that MPAs have been largely operating at a loss (e.g., the deficit for the adequate operation of existing MPAs is calculated at 44.8%: Balmford *et al.*, 2004) and this situation is only likely to get worse given the current global economic crisis. At the global scale, a concerted effort to reduce the extent of human impacts, which are likely to be related to the increasing size of the human population and its excessive use of natural resources (Wackernagel *et al.*, 2002; Kitzes *et al.*, 2008), is likely to provide a more ultimate solution to a variety of human stressors including those not controlled by MPAs. Achieving this will require ecologists to re-evaluate our view of the role of MPAs in protecting global marine biodiversity and our recommendations when it comes to protecting the world's ocean biodiversity.

References

Aronson, R. B., Bruno, J. F., *et al.* (2003). Causes of coral reef degradation. *Science*, **302**, 1502–2.

Balmford, A., Gravestock, P., Hockley, N., McClean, C. J., and Roberts, C. M. (2004). The worldwide costs of marine protected areas. *Proceedings of the National Academy of Sciences fot the United States of America*, **101**, 9694–7.

Balmford, A., Bennun, L., ten Brink, B., *et al.* (2005). The Convention on Biological Diversity's 2010 target. *Science*, **307**, 212–13.

Birkeland, C. (2004). Ratcheting down the coral reefs. *BioScience*, **54**, 1021–7.

Bruno, J. F. and Selig, E. R. (2007). Regional decline of coral cover in the Indo-Pacific: timing, extent, and subregional comparisons. *PLoS One*, **2**, e711, 1–8.

Caitlin Mullan, C., Kristy, K., and Benjamin, S. H. (2008). Interactive and cumulative effects of multiple human stressors in marine systems. *Ecology Letters*, **11**, 1304–15.

Chape, S., Harrison, J., Spalding, M., and Lysenko, I. (2005). Measuring the extent and effectiveness of protected areas as an indicator for meeting global biodiversity targets. *Philosophical Transactions of the Royal Society Series B*, **360**, 443–55.

Christie, P. (2004). Marine protected areas as biological successes and social failures in Southeast Asia. *American Fisheries Society Symposium*, **42**, 155–64.

Christie, P., McCay, B. J., Miller, M. L., *et al.* (2003). Toward developing a complete understanding: a social science research agenda for marine protected areas. *Fisheries*, **28**, 22–6.

Coelho, V. R. and Manfrino, C. (2007). Coral community decline at a remote Caribbean island: marine no-take reserves are not enough. *Aquatic Conservation: Marine and Freshwater Ecosystems*, **17**, 666–85.

Donner, S. D. (2009). Coping with the commitment: projected thermal stress on coral reefs under different future scenarios. *PLoS One*, 4, e5712.

Donner, S. D. and Potere, D. (2007). The inequity of the global threat to coral reefs. *BioScience*, **57**, 214–15.

Gardner, T. A., Cote, I. M., Gill, J. A., Grant, A., and Watkinson, A. R. (2003). Long-term region-wide declines in Caribbean corals. *Science*, **301**, 958–60.

Graham, N. A. J., Wilson, S. K., Jennings, S., *et al.* (2006). Dynamic fragility of oceanic coral reef ecosystems. *Proceedings of the National Academy of Sciences of the United States of America*, **103**, 8425–9.

Graham, N. A. J., McClanahan, T. R., MacNeil, M. A., *et al.* (2008). Climate warming, marine protected areas and the ocean-scale integrity of coral reef ecosystems. *PLoS One*, **3**, e3039, 1–9.

Halpern, B. S. and Warner, R. R. (2002). Marine reserves have rapid and lasting effects. *Ecology Letters*, **5**, 361–6.

Halpern, B. S., Selkoe, K. A., Micheli, F., and Kappel, C. V. (2007). Evaluating and ranking the vulnerability of marine ecosystems to anthropogenic threats. *Conservation Biology*, **21**, 1301–15.

Halpern, B. S., Walbridge, S., Selkoe, K. A., *et al.* (2008). A global map of human impact on marine ecosystems. *Science*, **319**, 948–52.

Hoegh-Guldberg, O., Mumby, P. J., Hooten, A. J., *et al.* (2007). Coral reefs under rapid climate change and ocean acidification. *Science*, **318**, 1737–42.

Jackson, J. B. C., Kirby, M. X., Berger, W. H., *et al.* (2001). Historical overfishing and the recent collapse of coastal ecosystems. *Science*, **293**, 629–38.

Jameson, S. C. (2006). How protected are coral reefs? *Science*, **314**, 757–8.

Jameson, S. C., Tupper, M. H., and Ridley, J. M. (2002). The three screen doors: can marine "protected" areas be effective? *Marine Pollution Bulletin*, **44**, 1177–83.

Jones, G. P., McCormick, M. I., Srinivasan, M., and Eagle, J. V. (2004). Coral decline threatens fish biodiversity in marine reserves. *Proceedings of the National Academy of Sciences of the United States of America*, **101**, 8251–3.

Karlson, R. H., Cornell, H. V., and Hughes, T. P. (2004). Coral communities area generally enriched along an ocean biodiversity gradient. *Nature*, **429**, 867–70.

Kitzes, J., Wackernagel, M., Loh, J., *et al.* (2008). Shrink and share: humanity's present and future Ecological Footprint. *Philosophical Transactions of the Royal Society Series B*, **363**, 467–75.

Kramer, D. L. and Chapman, M. R. (1999). Implications of fish home range size and relocation for marine reserve function. *Environmental Biology of Fishes*, **55**, 65–79.

Kritzer, J. P. (2004). Effects of noncompliance on the success of alternative designs of marine protected-area networks for conservation and fisheries management. *Conservation Biology*, **18**, 1021–31.

Kritzer, J. P. and Sale, P. F. (2006). *Marine Metapopulations*. San Diego, CA: Academic Press.

Lotze, H. K., Lenihan, H. S., Bourque, B. J., *et al.* (2006). Depletion, degradation, and recovery potential of estuaries and coastal seas. *Science*, **312**, 1806–9.

Lubchenco, J., Palumbi, S. R., Gaines, S. D., and Andelman, S. (2003). Plugging a hole in the ocean: the emerging science of marine reserves. *Ecological Applications*, **13**, S3–S7.

Lubchenco, J., Gaines, S., Grorud-Colvert, K., *et al.* (2007). *The Science of Marine Reserves*, 2nd edn. Available at www.piscoweb.org.

Micheli, F., Halpern, B. S., Botsford, L. W., and Warner, R. R. (2004). Trajectories and correlates of community change in no-take marine reserves. *Ecological Applications*, **14**, 1709–23.

Monaco, M. E., Friedlander, A. M., Caldow, C., *et al.* (2007). Characterizing reef fish populations and habitats within and outside the US Virgin Islands Coral Reef National Monument: a lesson in marine protected area design. *Fisheries Management and Ecology*, **14**, 33–40.

Mora, C. (2008). A clear human footprint in the coral reefs of the Caribbean. *Proceedings of the Royal Society Series B*, **275**, 767–73.

Mora, C. and Sale, P. F. (2002). Are populations of coral reef fish open or closed? *Trends in Ecology and Evolution*, **17**, 422–8.

Mora, C., Andrefouet, S., Costello, M. J., *et al.* (2006). Coral reefs and the global network of marine protected areas. *Science*, **312**, 1750–1.

Mora, C., Metzger, R., Rollo, A., and Myers, R. A. (2007). Experimental simulations about the effects of overexploitation and habitat fragmentation on populations facing environmental warming. *Proceedings of the Royal Society Series B*, **274**, 1023–8.

Mora, C., Myers, R. A., Coll, M., *et al.* (2009). Management effectiveness of the world's marine fisheries. *PLoS Biology*, **7**, e1000131.

Myers, N. (1995). Environmental unknowns. *Science*, **269**, 358–60.

Palumbi, S. R. (2003). Population genetics, demographic connectivity, and the design of marine reserves. *Ecological Applications*, **13**, S146–S158.

Palumbi, S. R. (2004). Marine reserves and ocean neighborhoods: the spatial scale of marine populations and their management. *Annual Review of Environment and Resources*, **29**, 31–68.

Pandolfi, J. M., Bradbury, R. H., Sala, E., *et al.* (2003). Global trajectories of the long-term decline of coral reef ecosystems. *Science*, **301**, 955–8.

Parmesan, C. and Yohe, G. (2003). A globally coherent fingerprint of climate change impacts across natural systems. *Nature*, **421**, 37–42.

Perry, A. L., Low, P. J., Ellis, J. R., and Reynolds, J. D. (2005). Climate change and distribution shifts in marine fishes. *Science*, **308**, 1912–15.

Portner, H. O. and Knust, R. (2007). Climate change affects marine fishes through the oxygen limitation of thermal tolerance. *Science*, **315**, 95–7.

Russ, G. R., Cheal, A. J., Dolman, A. M., *et al.* (2008). Rapid increase in fish numbers follows creation of world's largest marine reserve network. *Current Biology*, **18**, R514–R515.

Sale, P. F., Cowen, R. K., Danilowicz, B. S., *et al.* (2005). Critical science gaps impede use of no-take fishery reserves. *Trends in Ecology and Evolution*, **20**, 74–80.

Shanks, A. L., Grantham, B. A., and Carr, M. H. (2003). Propagule dispersal distance and the size and spacing of marine reserves. *Ecological Applications*, **13**, 159–69.

Valiela, I., Bowen, J. L., and York, J. K. (2001). Mangrove forests: one of the world's threatened major tropical environments. *BioScience*, **51**, 807–15.

Wackernagel, M., Schulz, N. B., Deumling, D., *et al.* (2002). Tracking the ecological overshoot of the human economy. *Proceedings of the National Academy of Sciences of the United States of America*, **99**, 9266–71.

Walther, G. R., Post, E., Convey, P., *et al.* (2002). Ecological responses to recent climate change. *Nature*, **416**, 389–95.

Waycott, M., Duarte, C., Carruthers, T., *et al.* (2009). Accelerating loss of seagrasses across the globe threatens coastal ecosystems. *Proceedings of the National Academy of Sciences of the United States of America*, **106**, 12377–81.

Wood, L. J., Fish, L., Laughren, J., and Pauly, D. (2008). Assessing progress towards global marine protection targets: shortfalls in information and action. *Oryx*, **42**, 340–51.

Woodroffe, R. and Ginsberg, J. R. (1998). Edge effects and the extinction of populations inside protected areas. *Science*, **280**, 2126–8.

Worm, B., Sandow, M., Oschlies, A., Lotze, H. K., and Myers, R. A. (2005). Global patterns of predator diversity in the open oceans. *Science*, **309**, 1365–9.

Worm, B., Barbier, E. B., Beaumont, N., *et al.* (2006). Impacts of biodiversity loss on ocean ecosystem services. *Science*, **314**, 787–90.

14 · *MISSING DIMENSION – Conserving the largest habitat on Earth: protected areas in the pelagic ocean*

ALISTAIR J. HOBDAY, EDWARD T. GAME,
HEDLEY S. GRANTHAM, AND ANTHONY
J. RICHARDSON

14.1 So far from the coast: is protection needed for pelagic habitats and species?

The pelagic environment is the area of the ocean from the surface to just above the sea floor and includes all the physical and chemical conditions and biology in the water column. This environment forms the largest habitat on Earth, constituting 99% of the biosphere volume (Angel, 1993). Pelagic ecosystems account for nearly half of the photosynthesis on Earth through phytoplankton (Field *et al.*, 1998) and supply >80% of the fish consumed by humans (Pauly *et al.*, 2002). These ecosystems also play a major role in the pace and extent of climate change via the uptake of carbon dioxide and its removal to the deep ocean through the biological pump, and via the dynamics of the overturning circulation within the solubility pump (Hays *et al.*, 2005).

While the open ocean can be divided into a number of vertical zones (Figure 14.1), here we collectively refer to these zones as the pelagic environment, and focus on the upper 200 m of the water column where the majority of the life in the pelagic zone resides and where most human activities occur. Note that the benthopelagic region includes the sea floor, and is not a focus of this chapter, as benthic protected areas typically encompass only the immediate overlying water, or are located in shallow coastal regions where ocean processes do not occur.

Marine Protected Areas: A Multidisciplinary Approach, ed. Joachim Claudet. Published by Cambridge University Press. © Cambridge University Press 2011.

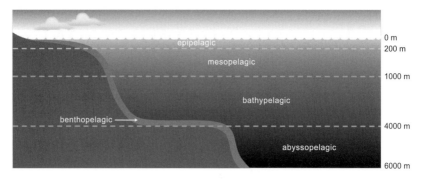

Figure 14.1 Division of the open ocean into vertical layers on the basis of light penetration (epipelagic) and depth zones. The benthopelagic zone connects the water column and the benthos.

In shallow or coastal regions, the whole water column may be considered benthopelagic.

Spatial protection, through instruments such as marine protected areas (MPAs), has typically been applied to coastal, nearshore, or benthic environments (e.g., Halpern 2003). These regions are conceptually similar to terrestrial environments in that their habitats tend to be relatively fixed in space and time. By contrast, the physical, chemical, and biological features that comprise habitats in pelagic systems are spatially and temporally more variable. Perhaps as a result, the pelagic ocean is the least protected of all Earth's major habitats, although as we show in subsequent sections, jurisdictional issues are also a major challenge. Depending on the exact definition used for a protected area, the total percentage of the world's oceans in MPAs is between 0.08% (no-take) and 0.65% (all MPA categories) (Wood *et al.*, 2008). The proportion of pelagic systems in protected areas does not even register in a recent review of the global MPA network (Wood *et al.*, 2008). Given that the vast majority of MPAs are biased towards benthic features, both in territorial waters and the high seas, it is likely that <0.1% of pelagic habitat is currently adequately protected within MPAs. There are several ways in which pelagic MPAs have been defined in the literature; here we define a pelagic MPA as one encompassing the upper portion of the water column, in either territorial waters (inside a country's Exclusive Economic Zone, EEZ) or on the high seas (outside the EEZ of any country). Some pelagic MPAs may extend to the sea floor, but we focus here on those MPAs for which protection of the water column is a key establishment goal.

Despite being far from land, out of sight, and rarely visited by most people, pelagic regions still face a variety of threats including climate change, eutrophication, mining, ocean acidification, overfishing, pollution, and species introductions (Figure 14.2A) (Halpern *et al.*, 2008; Game *et al.*, 2009; Halpern *et al.*, 2009). These threats, while of lower impact in pelagic than in many coastal waters (Halpern *et al.*, 2008), are still having substantial effects. Heavy exploitation has resulted in the declining abundance of fish stocks globally (Pauly and Watson, 2003), a decline in the size of many commercially harvested species (Ward and Myers, 2005), a replacement of larger slower-growing species by smaller faster-growing ones (Pauly and Watson, 2003; Essington *et al.*, 2006), and a shift in dominance in some systems from fish to "weedy" species such as jellyfish (Richardson *et al.*, 2009). Declining abundances of higher trophic levels has also cascaded down to lower trophic levels (Frank *et al.*, 2005). Global warming is shifting the distribution of marine organisms toward the poles (Beaugrand *et al.*, 2002; Perry *et al.*, 2005), causing earlier timing of annual plankton blooms and migrations (Sims *et al.*, 2001; Edwards and Richardson, 2004), and is shifting the spatial pattern of ocean productivity (Martinez *et al.*, 2009; Richardson and Schoeman, 2004). Ocean acidification is also having an impact on key primary calcifiers in pelagic ecosystems (Riebesell *et al.*, 2000; Orr *et al.*, 2005). Species introductions have changed the dominant species in some pelagic communities (e.g., Edwards *et al.*, 2001). Not all vertical layers in the pelagic environment are equally affected by these threats, which are concentrated in surface layers or at the sea floor (Figure 14.2B).

The focus of this chapter is to explore the existing use and future potential of pelagic MPAs. The use of protected areas in managing the threats to pelagic ecosystems is not widely accepted due to a number of perceived barriers, which is a major theme explored in this chapter. A small number of pelagic protected areas have already been implemented around the world, and we will draw on these, together with a growing literature, to illustrate the potential for protected areas as a conservation instrument in the pelagic realm. We note that protected areas are only one option for threat management in pelagic ecosystems, and as for protecting biodiversity on land, a range of solutions is likely to be needed for threat management and mitigation in the open ocean. The threatening process that many pelagic MPAs, and MPA advocates, seek to eliminate is fishing and fishing-related activities, and consequently, many examples we present are fishing-related. This is partly because fisheries represent the largest anthropogenic threat, but also because in

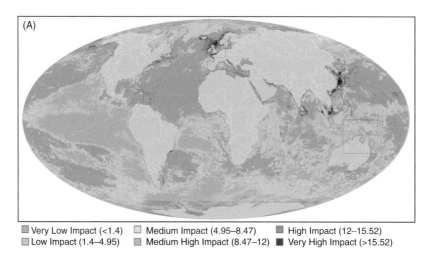

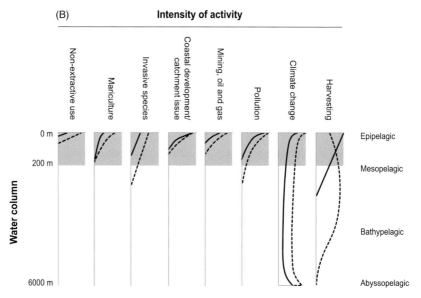

Figure 14.2 Threats in the ocean. (A) Global map of cumulative human impact across 20 ocean ecosystem types. Note that this includes both pelagic and benthic threats. *Source:* Halpern *et al.* (2008). (B) A stylized vertical distribution of threats in pelagic ecosystems. The shaded areas represent the depths to which light penetrates, and the lines indicate the current (solid) and future (dashed) distribution of threats. The *y*-axis represents low to high distribution. *Source:* Game *et al.* (2009).

many regions, fisheries are the sole industry exploiting pelagic resources (Game *et al.*, 2009).

14.2 Existing pelagic protected areas

As for coastal and terrestrial protected areas, a range of levels of protection are possible in pelagic MPAs, from single-use exclusion areas (i.e., no fishing but other uses and extractive activities are allowed) through to fully protected no-take no-access areas (i.e., no mining, transit, fishing, or recreation). While more limited in protection than year-round no-take MPAs, temporary spatial closures are used to protect a variety of pelagic species exposed to threatening processes such as fishing, boat strikes of marine mammals and sea turtles, and mining. Seasonal fisheries closures of specific areas are used to limit incidental capture of non-target species in pelagic longline fisheries. For instance, seasonal closures limit pelagic fishing around a number of fixed areas in the Gulf of California (NOAA, 2000) and within the core habitat of southern bluefin tuna off the east coast of Australia (Hobday and Hartmann, 2006; Hobday *et al.*, 2009b). In the latter case, the location of southern bluefin tuna habitat is predicted in real time, and fishery managers regulate access to this habitat (Hobday *et al.*, 2009b). The goal is not to eliminate capture of this species but to limit its capture to those fishers holding quota-rights. The closed area is dynamic in space and time, and compliance is monitored through observers and with electronic vessel monitoring systems (VMS). This style of MPA represents only a partial conservation approach, as fishing still occurs for some of the species in the area.

Marine protected areas also exist for the specific protection of marine mammals in both territorial and high seas waters. These MPAs focus on areas of key habitat for marine mammals such as frontal systems (e.g., the Mediterranean Pelagos marine sanctuary: Notarbatolo di Sciara *et al.*, 2008; Figure 14.3A) or calving areas (e.g., the Great Australian Bight Marine Park in southern Australia), and their primary purpose is for the protection of pelagic marine mammals. While aiming to limit threats to marine mammals, these MPAs remain essentially multiple-use zones. They do, however, clearly demonstrate that closed area management of pelagic features are logistically feasible.

In November 2009, the first high seas MPA in the Southern Ocean was declared in an area south of the South Orkney Islands under the management of the Commission for the Conservation of Antarctic Marine Living Resources. The South Orkneys MPA ($\sim$94 000 km^2) situated in

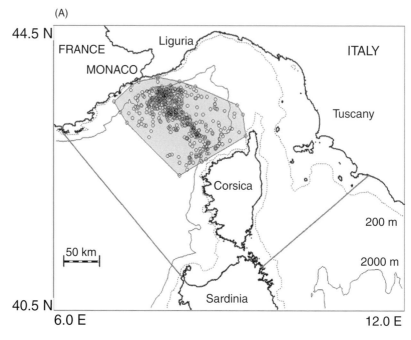

(A)

44.5 N

FRANCE

Liguria

MONACO

ITALY

Tuscany

Corsica

200 m

50 km

2000 m

Sardinia

40.5 N

6.0 E

12.0 E

Figure 14.3 Example pelagic marine protected areas. (A) Location of the Pelagos Sanctuary in the Mediterranean Sea showing the extent of the shelf (200 m depth contour) and the slope (2000 m depth contour). The gray shaded region represents the area of fin whale concentration, with individual sightings indicated by dots. *Source:* Notarbartolo di Sciara *et al.* (2007). (B) The first high seas MPA in the Southern Ocean, located south of the South Orkney Islands, became effective in May 2010. *Source:* www.wdcs.org/news.php?select=497.

the northern Weddell Sea, east of the tip of the Antarctic Peninsula, was identified as a critical foraging area for pelagic predators such as penguins, and contains important examples of both pelagic and benthic bioregions (Figure 14.3B). No commercial fishing activities and no discharge or refuse disposal from fishing vessels will be allowed in the area (http://www.ccamlr.org/pu/e/e_pubs/cm/09–10/91–03.pdf).

Weaker and less formal pelagic protection measures also exist. In Hawaii, "Turtle Watch" was developed to provide daily information predicting loggerhead turtle habitat based on oceanographic characteristics for the region of the Pacific Ocean north of the Hawaiian Islands (Figure 14.4) (Howell *et al.*, 2008). This information is provided to longline fishers so they can voluntarily avoid fishing those areas to reduce

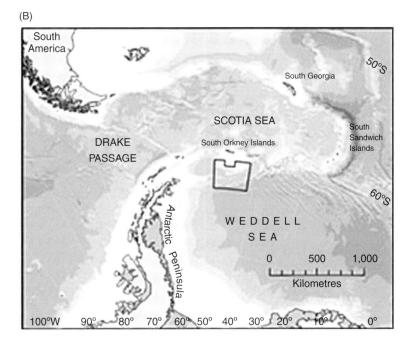

Figure 14.3 (cont.)

EXPERIMENTAL PRODUCT
avoid fishing between solid black 63.5°F and 65.5°F lines
to reduce turtle interactions

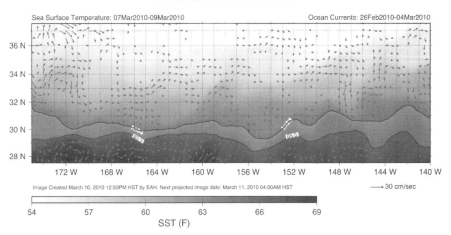

Figure 14.4 An example of a voluntary pelagic spatial management strategy to reduce interactions between fishers and turtles in the North Pacific based on sea surface temperatures. Fishers can reduce interactions with turtles by not fishing within the solid gray band, defined by two temperature isotherms. *Source:* www.pifsc.noaa.gov/eod/turtlewatch.php and Evan Howell (NMFS).

bycatch of these turtles. While focused on reducing a single-threat (fishing) to a single species (loggerhead turtle), this is an example of high seas spatial management that could be formalized within an MPA network.

14.3 Perceived barriers to pelagic protection

Perceived barriers to implementation of pelagic MPAs fall into four major categories: (1) physical and biological complexity; (2) design challenges; (3) enforcement challenges; and (4) governance challenges (Game *et al.*, 2009). As these barriers are seen by many to limit the application of a protected area strategy for pelagic environments (Kaplan *et al.*, 2010), it is worthwhile to explore each of these challenges to assess whether they invalidate management of the pelagic realm using pelagic MPAs.

14.3.1 Physical and biological complexity

Environments are often characterized by their key habitat, for example seagrass beds or sand flats in shallow waters. Identification of these habitats serves as a basis and focus for conservation efforts – consider the wide appeal of coral reefs and rainforests and the management strategies in these environments. Just as on land, benthic MPAs in both coastal and deep waters tend to be designed around recognizable habitats or species that are persistently found within the protected area. By contrast, the pelagic environment is characterized by complex and dynamic physical processes that can cause marine organisms to be more variable in space and time. However, the physical processes in the pelagic ocean lead to a suite of features with distinct properties, which make them analogous to "habitat types" on land and in marine benthic systems. Examples of distinct pelagic habitats include ocean currents, thermal fronts, upwelling and downwelling regions, and ocean eddies and gyres. These habitats influence the abundance, distribution, and composition of biological life in the pelagic realm (Palacios *et al.*, 2006). Thus, physical features serve as important surrogates for much pelagic biodiversity.

This dynamism has been thought to limit the utility of spatial management as a tool for protecting pelagic biodiversity (Martell *et al.*, 2005), but there are three key points that make pelagic MPAs viable. First, virtually all important physical process in the pelagic environment exhibit some spatial or temporal predictability (Etnoyer *et al.*, 2004; Belkin *et al.*, 2009). Second, despite many marine animals having wide ranges, they show site fidelity or have relatively small and defined areas of critical habitat because of the influence of the temporal and spatial predictability of the physical habitat, such as seasonal aggregation of birds and mammals (e.g., Weimerskirch, 2007), that can assist in the design of MPAs (Hyrenbach *et al.*, 2000). Last, pelagic MPAs, like seasonal species-specific fishery closures, need not be fixed, as for terrestrial protected environments, but rather can track dynamic pelagic features or habitats that serve as important surrogates for pelagic species or biodiversity (e.g., Hobday and Hartmann, 2006).

The spatial and temporal predictability of pelagic features can help dictate the design of pelagic protected areas. Some pelagic habitats are in fact predictable in space and/or time, as the processes that generate them are related to fixed bathymetric features such as seamounts, the edge of the continental shelf, or relatively consistent oceanographic features such as major currents. For example, elevated productivity resulting from localized upwelling at seamounts (Boehlert, 1987) and thermal fronts along the shelf edge aggregate prey species (Young *et al.*, 2001), thereby attracting top predators (Bost *et al.*, 2009). Other pelagic habitats that are spatially predictable but temporally variable include areas of wind-driven coastal upwelling (Bakun, 1973; Nieblas *et al.*, 2009). Such features can be protected by seasonal or permanent spatially fixed MPAs, depending on the time of year that the feature is present. If the protection is directed at a particular species that uses this habitat only at certain times of the year, such as seasonal migration to a breeding or feeding ground, static seasonal MPAs can be applied (Lombard *et al.*, 2007).

Alternatively, pelagic habitats and species that are temporally predictable but spatially variable, such as major currents and some fronts, can be represented either within a series of fixed MPAs designed to capture the feature at different times through the year or inter-annually for longer cycles (Alpine and Hobday, 2007; Grantham *et al.*, 2011). An alternative approach is to implement a larger single MPA aligned along the likely axis of habitat movement (Shillinger *et al.*, 2008; Lombard *et al.*, 2007). For example, Grantham *et al.* (2011) showed that pelagic MPAs designed by setting targets for the distribution or abundance of conservation features at different time periods (e.g., annual sardine abundance) captured the dynamics of the ecosystem better than setting targets based on the average distribution or abundance over all time periods (Figure 14.5). This approach assumes that past trends in the distribution or abundance of a conservation feature will also occur in the future. Developing predictive models of ecosystem dynamics to inform MPA design is an area of current

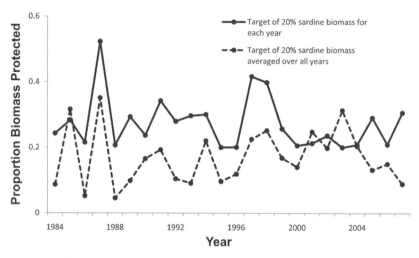

Figure 14.5 Two hypothetical pelagic MPA networks were developed based on the representation of various oceanographic features and pelagic species in the Southern Benguela and Agulhas Bank ecosystems in South Africa (Grantham *et al.*, 2011). As many of the features had time-series data characterizing their spatiotemporal distribution, the first network was designed based on averaging time-series data, the second by representing different time periods. For example, for sardines biomass (measured from biannual acoustic surveys between 1984 and 2007) the first MPA network captured 20% of the average biomass of sardines over all years while the second MPA network captured 20% of annual sardine biomass in each year (1984–2007). When retrospectively measuring the proportion of sardine biomass captured in the two MPA networks, targeting the average biomass over all years results in some years not achieving the 20% target.

research effort, and such predictions could also be included in the design process.

A more sophisticated approach to the dynamism of the pelagic ocean is to implement spatial management that reflects this complexity, with closures that are truly mobile and change with time. This logical solution has typically been considered infeasible because of enforcement difficulties and cost. However, just as the pelagic environment is more dynamic than terrestrial or coastal areas, so are the fishers who exploit it (e.g., Healey *et al.*, 1990; Waluda *et al.*, 2006). As most of the pelagic ocean lacks place-based property rights, resource users are highly mobile and accurate navigators. Knowing exactly where you are is as critical for fishers as it is for oil and gas companies. Advances in satellite positioning and communications mean that information can be conveyed to remote vessels in near real-time (Hobday *et al.*, 2009b). Thus, dynamic protected areas

(A)

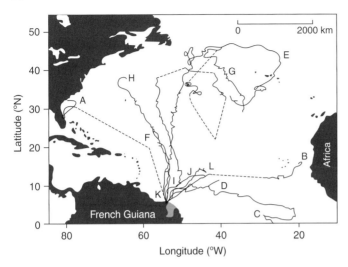

Figure 14.6 Wide ranging pelagic species in two example ocean basins.
(A) Reconstructed movements of 12 leatherback turtles nesting in French Guiana
and Suriname in 1999–2002 showing wide range of movements and temporal
variability. Source: Ferraroli *et al.* (2004). (B) Tracks of several pelagic species
tagged as part of the Tagging of Pacific Pelagics program. *Source:* www.topp.org/
topp_census.

are easier to implement in pelagic ecosystems than elsewhere, as most
users are already equipped with the necessary navigation tools. In addition, the total area required for effective protection and probable impact
on stakeholders (e.g., due to displacement costs) in the case of dynamic
design is likely to be reduced compared to static closed areas (Hobday
et al., 2009b). As an example of dynamic pelagic MPAs, mobile fisheries
closures for southern bluefin tuna have been effectively implemented off
eastern Australia since 2003 based on near real-time predictions of the
species' preferred pelagic habitat (Hobday and Hartmann, 2006; Hobday
et al., 2009b). Finally, acquisition of pelagic habitat to create an MPA in
the open ocean may be easier and cheaper than on land or in coastal areas
(Sumaila *et al.*, 2007), as there are no property rights or "ownership" in
the ocean beyond national claims to EEZs; however, jurisdictional issues
and international agreements still represent major hurdles.

The pelagic ocean is highly dynamic, and as a result, so are the species
that live there. Many pelagic species are highly mobile, with some species
covering thousands of kilometers annually (Figure 14.6) (Luschi *et al.*,

(B)

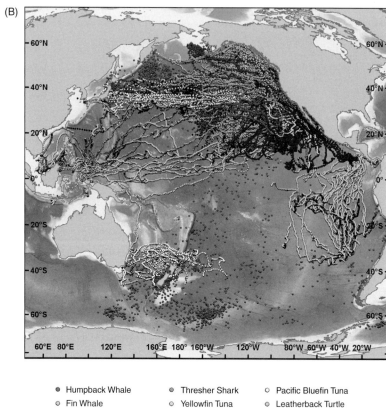

● Humpback Whale	◉ Thresher Shark	○ Pacific Bluefin Tuna
◎ Fin Whale	◎ Yellowfin Tuna	◎ Leatherback Turtle
● Sperm Whale	● Albacore Tuna	◎ Salmon Shark
● Sooty Shearwater	● Blue Shark	● Laysan Albatross
● California Sea Lion	● Mako Shark	● Black-footed Albatross
● Northern Fur Seal	◎ White Shark	◎ Humboldt Squid
● Blue Whale	◎ Loggerhead Turtle	
◎ Northern Elephant Seal	◎ *Mola mola*	

Figure 14.6 (cont.)

2003; Ferraroli *et al.*, 2004; Block *et al.*, 2005; Bonfil *et al.*, 2005; Sibert *et al.*, 2006; Bestley *et al.*, 2008). Short of protecting entire ocean basins, it is clearly impossible to encompass the full distribution of individuals of such species within an MPA. Establishing an MPA over just a small portion of a species annual distribution might be of limited value if individuals remain exposed to significant threats outside the protected area. This represents a significant criticism of pelagic MPAs because charismatic and commercially valuable species, such as tunas, cetaceans, sea turtles, and seabirds, are important targets for conservation action but are amongst the most mobile of all marine organisms.

Despite the mobility of many organisms, MPAs can still be effective tools for the conservation of many pelagic species. Species are not equally vulnerable over their entire range, and show site fidelity or have relatively small and defined areas of critical habitat within their range or life histories. For example, many species exhibit increased vulnerability in a small number of demographically critical areas, such as breeding or foraging areas (Louzao et al., 2006) or migration routes (Shillinger et al., 2008). In other cases, there is only limited overlap between the range of a species and the key threatening processes; for example, fishing may only occur in a small fraction of a species range (Ferraroli et al., 2004; Weimerskirch et al., 2006). In the same way that small protected areas help conserve migratory bird species on land (Martin et al., 2007), pelagic MPAs encompassing critical habitat, or in places that will minimize area-specific threats, have the potential to dramatically reduce overall mortality even though they might protect only a tiny proportion of a species range. Hyrenbach et al. (2005) reported that relatively small MPAs off the coast of California could effectively protect the foraging grounds, and substantially reduce overall mortality of the black-footed albatross, a species that breeds 4500 km away. Rapid advances in satellite tagging technology have detailed the location of these critical areas (Ferraroli et al., 2004; Louzao et al., 2006; Sydeman et al., 2006; Hobday et al., 2009a). Improvements in our ability to model and map the distribution of threats in the open ocean, including global warming, ocean acidification, various forms of fishing, species introductions, eutrophication, and pollution, are valuable for designing pelagic MPAs (Halpern et al., 2008). A cumulative global map of 17 threats, at 1-km^2 resolution, is now available for the global ocean (Figure 14.2A) as well as for individual threats, and can be used as a basis for spatial conservation planning. While some threats such as non-point-source pollution cannot be directly mitigated by protected areas, the presence of MPAs might influence the management of adjacent areas that produce these threats.

Even where pelagic MPAs are recognized as a potentially useful tool, the high mobility of pelagic species leads to the common perception that the area required for adequate protection is so large that socio-economic costs (e.g., from compensating displaced fisheres) of closure would be prohibitive (Angel, 1993; Boersma and Parrish, 1999). However, protection can still be directed to a few critical locations, such that the area required to adequately protect many pelagic species and processes represents only a small proportion of the total seascape and is comparable with the proportion of area required in nearshore or terrestrial systems (Sumaila *et al.*, 2007). For example, Alpine and Hobday (2007) showed that 13% of the key pelagic area off eastern Australia including major physical features such as frontal systems and upwelling areas could protect 20% of the annual distribution of 40 important pelagic species.

14.3.2 Design challenges

Even if we accept that well-designed and located MPAs would be a valuable tool for pelagic management, there are still concerns over a lack of data, methods, and tools to enable defensible identification of the areas for protection that best meet design objectives. The pelagic ocean is generally data-poor compared with terrestrial or coastal systems. Additionally, the selection of terrestrial and coastal protected areas has typically been based on broad, static biodiversity surrogates such as habitats, which are more difficult to identify in the pelagic ocean. From these realities has come the criticism that the complexities of pelagic systems are not well characterized and it is therefore difficult to make informed decisions on the placement of MPAs (e.g., Sale *et al.*, 2005). These perceived limitations, however, may actually favor the use of MPAs. The selection of protected areas on land or in the sea does not rely on a full understanding of ecosystem components, dynamics, and functioning to have broad benefits. This is in contrast to other forms of marine management such as conventional fisheries regulations, which to be effective as conservation tools, require detailed information at the species level. For example, high seas longline fisheries catch as many as 100 species as bycatch, and the expectation that appropriate catch limits, or gear modifications, can be applied and monitored for all of these species and their complex interaction with abiotic changes is unrealistic (Hobday *et al.*, 2007). In this regard, MPAs represent a more precautionary and complementary approach to pelagic conservation than just relying on management controls over a few species to provide protection for entire ecosystems.

Although often considered devoid of data relative to coastal areas, the pelagic ocean is in fact covered by extensive data sets useful for designing protected areas. Rapid advances in remote data collection mean that broad surrogates for biodiversity and its dynamics are now arguably easier to obtain for the pelagic ocean than for coastal benthic systems. The elevated primary productivity that is closely linked to the occurrence of many pelagic species (e.g. Etnoyer *et al.*, 2004; but see Grémillet *et al.*, 2008) can be inferred from remotely sensed surrogates such as sea surface chlorophyll, sea surface temperature, or sea surface height, and even from ecosystem models running in real time (Cury *et al.*, 2008). Remotely sensed data can also be usefully applied in combination with *in situ* observations and fisheries data to differentiate distinct and temporally variable pelagic habitats (Devred *et al.*, 2007; Oliver and Irwin, 2008). As a basis for identifying potential MPA sites, remotely sensed data have two strong advantages: they are relatively cheap (or free) for conservation planners to acquire and they generally have extensive and consistent spatial coverage. Satellite sea surface temperatures, for example, have been consistently measured since the mid-1980s, while ocean color, a proxy for chlorophyll, in turn a proxy for phytoplankton, has been observed since 1997. A number of such products have been processed and used in MPA design in eastern Australia (Figure 14.7) (A. J. Hobday, unpublished data).

Over the past decade the design of protected areas has developed into a rigorous science (Lubchenco *et al.*, 2003; Parnell *et al.*, 2006; Possingham *et al.*, 2006; Pressey *et al.*, 2007). As in other habitats, pelagic MPAs will have greatest likelihood of achieving multiple objectives if their design and assessment is the outcome of a formal spatial prioritization, including stakeholder participation. A formal framework should address quantitative conservation objectives (e.g., percentage representation of habitats and species and protection of threatened species), qualitative design criteria (e.g., size or orientation), patterns of threat and likely impact on species or habitats, competing demands for resource use and legal, social, and economic constraints to implementation (Possingham *et al.*, 2006). Formal protected area decision frameworks often emphasize the importance of estimating the costs and benefits of alternative scenarios for MPA placement and the need for a monitoring program for adaptive management and learning (Nichols and Williams, 2006; Lyons *et al.*, 2008). Although there is a well-developed theory to support the planning of coastal and benthic-based MPAs (Lubchenco *et al.*, 2003), the absence of structured planning approaches in the pelagic ocean means that conservation management is seen as inferior to directed fisheries

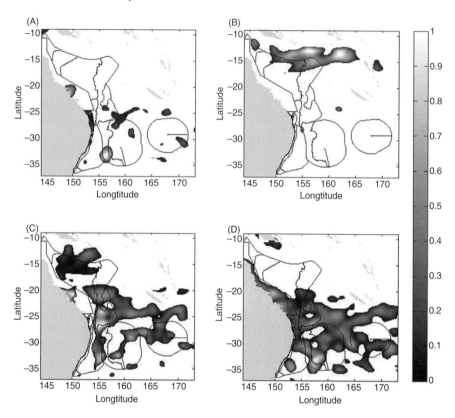

Figure 14.7 Seasonal distribution of pelagic habitat type (upwelling eddies) used to represent pelagic features in a MPA selection algorithm. This example shows the probability (color bar) of the presence of upwelling features during each of four seasons over 10 years (1998–2007). (A) Summer (Dec, Jan, Feb). (B) Autumn (Mar, Apr, May). (C) Winter (Jun, Jul, Aug). (D) Spring (Sep, Oct, Nov). Polygons represent different MPA planning regions in eastern Australia. *Source:* A. J. Hobday (unpublished data).

management (e.g., Hilborn *et al.*, 2005). Exacerbating this problem is the fact that systematic conservation planning approaches, now the standard for identifying both terrestrial and coastal protected areas (Possingham *et al.*, 2006), have generally failed to deal adequately with dynamic systems (Pressey *et al.*, 2007).

Despite the limited theory for selecting pelagic MPAs, systematic frameworks are being developed. Hyrenbach *et al.* (2000) identified important features of the pelagic ocean that are suitable targets for spatial protection, categorizing them as static bathymetric, persistent hydrographic, or ephemeral hydrographic, and suggested a series of MPA design considerations for each category. These considerations included flexible boundaries, buffer zones, and seasonal application. Alpine and Hobday (2007) extended these ideas by showing how quantitative targets can be applied to pelagic features mobile in space and time, as well as to selected individual species. Their study also demonstrated how freely available protected areas selection software can be used to design an efficient network of pelagic MPAs that minimizes the impact on existing fisheries. Similarly, Lombard *et al.* (2007) provided an example of how the boundaries of MPAs can be defined to adequately capture important pelagic processes around islands in the Southern Ocean and are likely to aid compliance.

Criteria for MPA design have been developed under the Convention on Biological Diversity (CBD). One collaborative program working to implement MPAs in the high seas using the seven criteria is the Global Ocean Biodiversity Initiative (GOBI: http://openoceansdeepseas.org/). The GOBI partners have begun to use a range of data sets and tools to identify ecologically significant areas in the deep sea and high seas to advance the CBD goals in these regions. These criteria are relevant to the selection of pelagic MPAs and could be used in reserve design processes, using a range of the data we have discussed above.

14.3.3 Enforcement challenges

Regardless of the legal support for protected areas, the pernicious influence of illegal, unreported, and unregulated (IUU) fishing in the high seas and national waters of both developing and developed countries remains a major challenge for pelagic MPAs (Kaplan *et al.*, 2010). In national waters, the problem hinges on a lack of technical capacity to monitor remote vessel activities and enforce MPA violations. New information sharing networks such as the voluntary International Monitoring, Surveillance and Control Network of enforcement professionals (www.imcsnet.org) and improved technical tools (e.g., remote sensing, synthetic-aperture radar [SAR], and VMS) suggest these challenges will soon be overcome (see Game *et al.*, 2010; Kaplan *et al.*, 2010). As well as assisting enforcement, VMS can aid compliance by including boundaries of pelagic MPAs and issuing automatic warnings to vessels when these boundaries are approached. Currently VMS technology is being used successfully in many pelagic fisheries in the Southern Ocean (see Game *et al.*, 2010). Because of the real potential to detect violations remotely, ensuring widespread compliance with spatial restrictions might be easier than using catch or gear restrictions (Sumaila *et al.*, 2007).

14.3.4 Governance challenges

By far the greatest part of the pelagic ocean is beyond the sight of land, distant from ports, and not owned by individuals, companies, or countries. Management of pelagic threats via restricting access to some areas presents a substantial governance challenge due to the fragmented and sectoral management framework common for most offshore regions, particularly in countries with limited resources and on the high seas (Hyrenbach *et al.*, 2000; Kaplan *et al.*, 2010). Within the 200 nautical mile EEZ, coastal states have the legal ability to establish and enforce laws to protect their marine resources. States can thus establish pelagic protected areas out to 200 nautical miles and develop management regimes, assuming the appropriate national legislation exists and the applicable international rules, such as the right to safe passage, are complied with. On the high seas, there is no single body with the authority to establish protected areas or to regulate access to and use of an area for more than one purpose. This has been seen as a major obstacle to the establishment of MPAs to protect valuable pelagic resources (Kaplan *et al.*, 2010). Coordination between nations will likely be required, as pelagic processes will likely cross EEZ boundaries in some areas.

With respect to fishing activities, progress can nevertheless be made through regional fisheries management organizations. The 1995 UN Fish Stocks Agreement specifically calls on its state parties to "protect biodiversity in the marine environment." Though many regional fisheries management organizations have not yet used their authority to protect biodiversity, increased international scrutiny is prompting action, at least with respect to deep sea biodiversity. In particular, the UN General Assembly adopted a resolution in 2006 specifically calling for regional fisheries management organizations to manage deep-sea bottom fisheries on the high seas to protect biodiversity. As a result, a number of large areas have been closed to benthic fishing (Gjerde *et al.*, 2008). Such powers could equally be used to protect pelagic biodiversity. High seas shipping activities that contribute to pollution and refuse dumping could also be regulated through measures adopted by the International

Maritime Organization. However, this would still not address other high seas activities such as potential carbon dioxide sequestration activities via ocean fertilization, or of course military activities subject to sovereign immunity. While some suggest that a new international agreement is an essential next step to enable coordinated management of high seas pelagic MPAs, ad hoc agreements among states, such as that for the Mediterranean Pelagos Sanctuary (Notarbartolo di Sciara *et al.*, 2007), can also be usefully employed, at least as an interim step.

14.4 Prospects for the future

The limited implementation of pelagic MPAs currently implies that their effectiveness as tools for the conservation of pelagic biodiversity remains largely unproven. Similarly, the complex and dynamic nature of ocean ecosystems are such that even comprehensive modelling studies can be limited in their ability to provide robust conclusions about the efficacy of pelagic protected areas (Martell *et al.*, 2005). Further, there are relatively few coupled hydrodynamic and ecosystem models, with most including only the lower trophic levels and not extending to fish, marine mammals, sea turtles, or seabirds. However, failing to implement pelagic protected areas for want of robust analysis or more evidence will make it substantially more difficult to ever acquire this evidence.

The creation of pelagic MPAs could be treated as large-scale adaptive management experiments (Game *et al.*, 2009). With low investment in immovable infrastructure and the high adaptive capacity of most stakeholders, pelagic protected areas lend themselves to adaptive adjustment of designations. The experimental establishment of pelagic protected areas, however, needs to be accompanied by a clear framework for monitoring and learning about the response of the system. At present, few fisheries independent measures of pelagic ecosystem and biodiversity health exist, with a key exception being the condition and fecundity of shore-breeding fauna such as birds and seals, satellite estimation of chlorophyll, and some large-scale plankton surveys. Not only will new metrics, other than commercial catch records, need to be developed, but additional ways to obtain the necessary data are also required. Extensive data on physical, biological, and socio-economic factors can be used in concert with new conservation planning techniques to guide the defensible selection and design of pelagic MPAs. Advances in satellite technology can facilitate compliance and enable dynamic pelagic MPAs in space and time. However, it is important not to understate remaining challenges.

Effective collection and interpretation of data needed to adaptively manage MPAs requires continued and improved engagement among marine conservation planners, fisheries managers, and the oceanographic community. Although new and tractable approaches to MPA selection in dynamic environments are emerging, such as using probabilities in place of static habitat and species occurrence data (Pressey *et al.*, 2007; Game *et al.*, 2008), their application in pelagic systems will require extending classical conservation planning from two to four dimensions, with the inclusion of both depth and time components. There remains an urgent need for a more integrated approach to management of non-fisheries threats (e.g., pollution) and IUU activities (e.g., ship discharges, dumping) on the high seas (Gjerde *et al.*, 2008). Similarly, the cost of remote monitoring and surveillance technologies is a significant obstacle to its use in developing nations. Universal mandate of such technologies, combined with expansion of the existing program of subsidies that operate in many developing nations, is an important governance step for pelagic MPAs.

Here we have argued that there are enormous opportunities for implementing MPAs in the pelagic ocean. Several conditions found in the pelagic ocean make this possible; weak private property rights allowing top–down government decision-making, limited habitat transformation, and potentially lower costs of protected area management. Overall, the costs of closures on the high seas have been estimated to result in relatively little global annual profit loss, with 20% closure estimated to lead to the loss of only 1.8% of the current global reported marine fisheries catch, and a decrease in profits to the high seas fleet of about US$270 million per year (Sumaila *et al.*, 2007). Thus, it may even be that solutions to the broad challenge of conservation planning and management of dynamic systems can be best demonstrated in the pelagic ocean. Indeed, given the new challenges presented by a rapidly changing climate, the future of MPAs more generally might lie in creative solutions developed in the pelagic ocean, where dynamic approaches are now being considered. With shifts in climate moving habitat zones and species in many environments, both in the ocean and on land (Parmesan and Yohe, 2003; Poloczanska *et al.*, 2007; Rosenzweig *et al.*, 2008; Nye *et al.*, 2009; Hobday, 2010), dynamic spatial protection may be the way of the future.

14.5 Acknowledgments

Ideas presented here were generated in part through a workshop held in 2007 and in subsequent discussions; we thank Bob Pressey, Lynnath Beckley, Kristina Gjerde, Rodrigo Bustamante, and Hugh Possingham. The clarity of the manuscript was improved by the comments of an anonymous reviewer and the editor, Joachim Claudet.

References

Alpine, J. E. and Hobday, A. J. (2007). Area requirements and pelagic protected areas: is size an impediment to implementation? *Marine and Freshwater Research*, **58**, 558–69.

Angel, M. V. (1993). Biodiversity of the pelagic ocean. *Conservation Biology*, **7**, 760–72.

Bakun, A. (1973). *Coastal upwelling indices, west coast of North America, 1946–71*, NOAA Technical Report NMFS SSRF 671. Silver Spring, MD: National Marine Fisheries Service, National Oceanic and Atmospheric Administration.

Beaugrand, G., Reid, P. C., Ibanez, F., Lindley, J. A., and Edwards, M. (2002). Reorganization of North Atlantic marine copepod biodiversity and climate. *Science*, **296**, 1692–4.

Belkin, I. M., Cornillon, P. C., and Sherman, K. (2009). Fronts in large marine ecosystems. *Progress in Oceanography*, **81**, 223–36.

Bestley, S., Patterson, T. A., Hindell, M. A., and Gunn, J. S. (2008). Feeding ecology of wild migratory tunas revealed by archival tag records of visceral warming. *Journal of Animal Ecology*, **77**, 1223–33

Block, B. A., Teo, S. L. H., Walli, A., *et al.* (2005). Electronic tagging and population structure of Atlantic bluefin tuna. *Nature*, **434**, 1121–7.

Boehlert, G. W. (1987). A review of the effects of seamounts on biological processes. In *Seamounts, Islands and Atolls*, eds. B. H. Keating, P. Fryer, R. Batiza, and G. W. Boehlert. Washington, DC: American Geophysical Union, pp. 319–34.

Boersma, P. D. and Parrish, J. K. (1999). Limiting abuse: marine protected areas, a limited solution. *Ecological Economics*, **31**, 287–304.

Bonfil, R., Meyer, M., Scholl, M. C., *et al.* (2005). Transoceanic migration, spatial dynamics, and population linkages of white sharks. *Science*, **310**, 100–3.

Bost, C.-A., Cotte, C., Baileul, F., *et al.* (2009). The importance of oceanographic fronts to marine birds and mammals of the southern oceans. *Journal of Marine Systems*, **78**, 363–76.

Cury, P. M., Shin, Y.-J., Planque, B., *et al.* (2008). Ecosystem oceanography for global change in fisheries. *Trends in Ecology and Evolution*, **23**, 338–46.

Devred, E., Sathyendranath, S., and Platt, T. (2007). Delineation of ecological provinces using ocean colour radiometry. *Marine Ecology Progress Series*, **346**, 1–13.

Edwards, M., John, A. W. G., Johns, D. G., and Reid, P. C. (2001). Case history and persistence of the non-indigenous diatom *Coscinodiscus wailesii* in the north-east Atlantic. *Journal of the Marine Biology Association of the UK*, **81**, 207–11.

Edwards, M. and Richardson, A. J. (2004). Impact of climate change on marine pelagic phenology and trophic mismatch. *Nature*, **430**, 881–4.

Essington, T. E., Beaudreau, A. H., and Wiedenmann, J. (2006). Fishing through marine food webs. *Proceedings of the National Academy of Sciences of the United States of America*, **103**, 3171–5.

Etnoyer, P., Canny, D., Mate, B., and Morgan, L. (2004). Persistent pelagic habitats in the Baja California to Bering Sea (B2B) ecoregion. *Oceanography*, **17**, 90–101.

Ferraroli, S., Georges, J.-Y., Gaspar, P., and Le Maho, Y. (2004). Where leatherback turtles meet fisheries. *Nature*, **429**, 521–2.

Field, C. B., Behrenfeld, M. J., Randerson, J. T., and Falkowski, P. (1998). Primary production of the biosphere: integrating terrestrial and oceanic components. *Science*, **281**, 237–40.

Frank, K. T., Petrie, B., Choi, J. S., and Leggett, W. C. (2005). Trophic cascades in a formerly cod-dominated ecosystem. *Science*, **308**, 1621–3.

Game, E. T., Watts, M. E., Wooldridge, S., and Possingham, H. P. (2008). Planning for persistence in marine reserves: a question of catastrophic importance. *Ecological Applications*, **18**, 670–80.

Game, E. T., Grantham, H. S., Hobday, A. J., *et al.* (2009). Pelagic protected areas: the missing dimension in ocean conservation. *Trends in Ecology and Evolution*, **24**, 360–9.

Game, E. T., Grantham, H. S., Hobday, A. J., *et al.* (2010). Pelagic protected areas: the devil you know. *Trends in Ecology and Evolution*, **25**, 63–4.

Gjerde, K. M., Dotinga, H., Hart, S., *et al.* (2008). *Options for Addressing Regulatory and Governance Gaps in the International Regime for the Conservation and Sustainable Use of Marine Biodiversity in Areas beyond National Jurisdiction*. Gland, Switzerland: IUCN.

Grantham, H. S., Game, E. T., Hobday, A. J., *et al.* (2011). Accommodating dynamic oceanographic processes and pelagic biodiversity in marine conservation planning. *PLoS ONE*, **6**, e16522.

Grémillet, D., Lewis, S., Drapeau, L., *et al.* (2008). Spatial match–mismatch in the Benguela upwelling zone: should we expect chlorophyll and sea-surface temperature to predict marine predator distributions? *Journal of Animal Ecology*, **45**, 610–21.

Halpern, B. S. (2003). The impact of marine reserves: do reserves work and does reserve size matter? *Ecological Applications*, **13**, S117–S137.

Halpern, B. S., Kappel, C. V., Selkoe, K. A., *et al.* (2009). Mapping cumulative human impacts to California Current marine ecosystems. *Conservation Letters*, **2**, 138–48.

Halpern, B. S., Walbridge, S., Selkoe, K. A., *et al.* (2008). A global map of human impact on marine ecosystems. *Science*, **319**, 948–52.

Hays, G. C., Richardson, A. J., and Robinson, C. (2005). Climate change and marine plankton. *Trends in Ecology and Evolution*, **20**, 337–44.

Healey, M. C., Thomson, R. E., and Morris, J. F. T. (1990). Distribution of commercial troll fishing vessels off southwest Vancouver Island in relation to fishing success and oceanic water properties and circulation. *Canadian Journal of Fisheries and Aquatic Sciences*, **47**, 1846–64.

Hilborn, R., Orensanz, J. M. L., and Parma, A. M. (2005). Institutions, incentives and the future of fisheries. *Philosophical Transactions of the Royal Society Series B*, **360**, 47–57.

Hobday, A. J. (2010). Ensemble analysis of the future distribution of large pelagic fishes in Australia. *Progress in Oceanography*, **86**, 291–301.

Hobday, A. J. and Hartmann, K. (2006). Near real-time spatial management based on habitat predictions for a longline bycatch species. *Fisheries Management and Ecology*, **13**, 365–80.

Hobday, A. J., Smith, A. D. M., Webb, H., *et al.* (2007). *Ecological Risk Assessment for the Effects of Fishing: Methodology*. Report R04/1072. Canberra, ACT:. Australian Fisheries Management Authority. Available at www.afma.gov.au/ environment/eco_based/eras/eras.htm.

Hobday, A., Arrisabalaga, H., Fragoso, N., *et al.* (2009a). Applications of electronic tagging to understanding marine animals – Preface. In *Tagging and Tracking of Marine Animals with Electronic Devices II, Reviews: Methods and Technologies in Fish Biology and Fisheries*, eds. J. Nielsen, J. R. Sibert, A. J. Hobday, *et al.* Dordrecht, the Netherlands: Springer, pp. v–xvi.

Hobday, A. J., Flint, N., Stone, T., and Gunn, J. S. (2009b). Electronic tagging data supporting flexible spatial management in an Australian longline fishery. In *Tagging and Tracking of Marine Animals with Electronic Devices II, Reviews: Methods and Technologies in Fish Biology and Fisheries*, eds. J. Nielsen, J. R. Sibert, A. J. Hobday, *et al.* Dordrecht, the Netherlands, Springer, pp. 381–403.

Howell, E. A., Kobayashi, D. R., Parker, D. M., Balazs, G. H., and Polovina, J. J. (2008). TurtleWatch: a tool to aid in the bycatch reduction of loggerhead turtles *Caretta caretta* in the Hawaii-based pelagic longline fishery. *Endangered Species Research*, **5**, 267–78.

Hyrenbach, K. D., Forney, K. A., and Dayton, P. K. (2000). Marine Protected Areas and ocean basin management. *Aquatic Conservation: Marine and Freshwater Ecosystems*, **10**, 437–58.

Hyrenbach, K. D., Keiper, C. A., Allen, S. G., Ainley, D. G., and Anderson, D. J. (2005). Use of marine sanctuaries by far-ranging predators: commuting flights to the California Current System by breeding Hawaiian albatrosses. *Fisheries Oceanography*, **15**, 95–103.

Kaplan, D. M., Chassot, E., Gruss, A. and Fonteneau, A. (2010). Pelagic MPAs: the devil is in the details. *Trends in Ecology and Evolution*, **25**, 62–3.

Lombard, A. T., Reyers, B., Schonegevel, L. Y., *et al.* (2007). Conserving pattern and process in the Southern Ocean: designing a Marine Protected Area for the Prince Edward Islands. *Antarctic Science*, **19**, 39–54.

Louzao, M., Hyrenbach, K. D., Arcos, J. M., *et al.* (2006). Oceanographic habitat of an endangered Mediterranean procellariiform: implications for marine protected areas. *Ecological Applications*, **16**, 1683–95.

Lubchenco, J., Palumbi, S. R., Gaines, S. D., and Adelman, S. (2003). Plugging a hold in the oceans: the emerging science of marine reserves. *Ecological Applications*, **13**, S3–S7.

Luschi, P., Hays, G. C., and Papi, F. (2003). A review of long-distance movements by marine turtles, and the possible role of ocean currents. *Oikos*, **103**, 293–302.

Lyons, J. E., Runge, M. C., Laskowski, H. P., and Kendall, W. L. (2008). Monitoring in the context of structured decision-making and adaptive management. *Journal of Wildlife Management*, **72**, 1683–92.

Martell, S. J. D., Essington, T. E., Lessard, B., *et al.* (2005). Interactions of productivity, predation risk, and fishing effort in the efficacy of marine protected areas for the central Pacific. *Canadian Journal of Fisheries and Aquatic Sciences*, **62**, 1320–36.

Martin, T. G., Chadès, I., Arcese, P., *et al* (2007). Optimal conservation of migratory species. *PLoS One*, **2**, e751.

Martinez, E., Antoine, D., D'Ortenzio, F., and Gentili, B. (2009). Climate-driven basin-scale decadal oscillations of oceanic phytoplankton. *Science*, **326**, 1253–6.

Nichols, J. D. and Williams, B. K. (2006). Monitoring for conservation. *Trends in Ecology and Evolution*, **12**, 668–73.

Nieblas, A. E., Sloyan, B. M., Hobday, A. J., Coleman, R., and Richardson, A. J. (2009). Variability of biological production in low wind-forced regional upwelling systems: a case study off southeastern Australia. *Limnology and Oceanography*, **54**, 1548–58.

NOAA (2000). *Regulatory Amendment 1 to the Atlantic Tunas, Swordfish, and Sharks Fishery Management Plan: Reduction of Bycatch, Bycatch Mortality, and Incidental Catch in the Atlantic Pelagic Longline Fishery*. Silver Spring, MD: National Marine Fisheries Service, National Oceanic and Atmospheric Administration.

Notarbartolo di Sciara, G., Agardy, T., Hyrenbach, K. D., Scovazzi, T., and Van Klavern, P. (2008). The Pelagos Sanctuary for Mediterranean marine mammals. *Aquatic Conservation: Marine and Freshwater Ecosystems*, **18**, 367–91.

Nye, J. A., Link, J. S., Hare, J. A., and Overholtz, W. J. (2009). Changing spatial distribution of fish stocks in relation to climate and population size on the Northeast United States continental shelf. *Marine Ecology Progress Series*, **393**, 111–29.

Oliver, M. J. and Irwin, A. J. (2008). Objective global ocean biogeographic provinces. *Geophysical Research Letters*, **35**, L15601, doi:10.1029/2008GL034238.

Orr, J. C., Fabry, V. J., Aumont, O., *et al.* (2005). Anthropogenic ocean acidification over the twenty-first century and its impact on calcifying organisms. *Nature*, **437**, 681–6.

Palacios, D. M., Bograd, S. J., Foley, D. G., and Schwing, F. B. (2006). Oceanographic characteristics of biological hot spots in the North Pacific: a remote sensing perspective. *Deep-Sea Research II*, **53**, 250–69.

Parmesan, C. and Yohe, G. (2003). A globally coherent fingerprint of climate change impacts across natural systems. *Nature*, **421**, 37–42.

Parnell, P. E., Dayton, P. K., Lennert-Cody, C. E., Rasmussen, L. L., and Leichter, J. J. (2006). Marine reserve design: optimal size, habitats, species affinities, diversity, and ocean microclimate. *Ecological Applications*, **16**, 945–62.

Pauly, D., Christensen, V., Guénette, S., *et al.* (2002). Towards sustainability in world fisheries. *Nature*, **418**, 689–95.

Perry, A. L., Low, P. J., Ellis, J. R., and Reynolds, J. D. (2005). Climate change and distribution shifts in marine fishes. *Science*, **308**, 1912–15.

Piatt, J. F., Wetzel, J., Bell, K., *et al.* (2006). Predictable hotspots and foraging habitat of the endangered short-tailed albatross (*Phoebastria albatrus*) in the North Pacific: implications for conservation. *Deep-Sea Research II*, **53**, 387–98.

Poloczanska, E. S., Babcock, R. C., Butler, A., *et al.* (2007). Climate change and Australian marine life. *Oceanography and Marine Biology Annual Review*, **45**, 409–80.

Possingham, H. P., Wilson, K. A., Andelman, S. J., and Vynne, C. H. (2006). Protected areas: goals, limitations, and design. In *Principles of Conservation Biology*, 3rd edn, eds. M. J. Groom, G. K. Meefe, and C. R. Carroll. Sunderland, MA: Sinauer Associates, pp. 509–33.

Pressey, R. L., Cabeza, M., Watts, M. E., Cowling, R. M., and Wilson, K. A. (2007). Conservation planning in a changing world. *Trends in Ecology and Evolution* **22**, 583–92.

Richardson, A. J. and Schoeman, D. S. (2004). Climate impact on plankton ecosystems in the Northeast Atlantic. *Science*, **305**, 1609–12.

Richardson, A. J., Bakun, A., Hays, G. C., and Gibbons, M. J. (2009). The jellyfish joyride: causes, consequences and management responses to a more gelatinous future. *Trends in Ecology and Evolution*, **24**, 312–22.

Rosenzweig, C., Karoly, D., Vicarelli, M., *et al.* (2008). Attributing physical and biological impacts to anthropogenic climate change. *Nature*, **453**, 353–8.

Sale, P. F., Cowen, R. K., Danilowicz, B. S., *et al.* (2005). Critical science gaps impede use of no-take fishery reserves. *Trends in Ecology and Evolution*, **20**, 74–80.

Shillinger, G. L., Palacios, D. M., Bailey, H., *et al.* (2008). Persistent leatherback turtle migrations present opportunities for conservation. *PloS Biology*, **6**, e171.

Sibert, J. R., Lutcavage, M. E., Nielsen, A., Brill, R. W., and Wilson, S. G. (2006). Interannual variation in large-scale movement of Atlantic bluefin tuna (*Thunnus thynnus*) determined from pop-up satellite archival tags. *Canadian Journal of Fisheries and Aquatic Sciences*, **63**, 2154–66.

Sims, D. W., Genner, M. J., Southward, A. J., and Hawkins, S. J. (2001). Timing of squid migration reflects North Atlantic climate variability. *Proceedings of the Royal Society Series B*, **268**, 2607–11.

Pauly, D. and Watson, R. (2003). Counting the last fish. *Scientific American*, **289**, 42–7.

Riebesell, U., Zondervan, I., Rost, B., *et al.* (2000). Reduced calcification of marine plankton in response to increased atmospheric CO_2. *Nature*, **407**, 364–7.

Sumaila, U. R., Zeller, D., Watson, R., Alder, J., and Pauly, D. (2007). Potential costs and benefits of marine reserves in the high seas. *Marine Ecology Progress Series*, **345**, 305–10.

Sydeman, W. J., Brodeur, R. D., Grimes, C. B., Bychkov, A. S., and McKinnell, S. (2006). Editorial: Marine habitat "hotspots" and their use by migratory species and top predators in the North Pacific Ocean: introduction. *Deep-Sea Research II*, **53**, 247–9.

Waluda, C. M., Yamashiro, C., and Rodhouse, P. G. (2006). Influence of the ENSO cycle on the light-fishery for *Dosidicus gigas* in the Peru Current: an analysis of remotely sensed data. *Fisheries Research* **79**, 56–63.

Ward, P. and Myers, R. A. (2005). Shifts in open-ocean fish communities coinciding with the commencement of commercial fishing. *Ecology*, **86**, 835–47.

Weimerskirch, H. (2007). Are seabirds foraging for unpredictable resources? *Deep-Sea Research II*, **54**, 211–23.

Weimerskirch, H., Åkesson, S., and Pinaud, D. (2006). Postnatal dispersal of wandering albatrosses *Diomedea exulans*: implications for the conservation of the species. *Journal of Avian Biology*, **37**, 23–8.

Wood, L. J., Fish, L., Laughren, J., and Pauly, D. (2008). Assessing progress towards global marine protection targets: shortfalls in information and action. *Oryx*, **42**, 340–51.

Young, J. W., Bradford, R. W., Lamb, T. D., *et al.* (2001). Yellowfin tuna (*Thunnus albacares*) aggregations along the shelf break off south-eastern Australia: links between inshore and offshore processes. *Marine and Freshwater Research*, **52**, 463–74.

Index